Broadening the Horizon of TBLT

Task-Based Language Teaching:
Issues, Research and Practice (TBLT)
ISSN 1877-346X

Task-Based Language Teaching (TBLT) is an educational framework for the theory and practice of teaching second or foreign languages. The TBLT book series is devoted to the dissemination of TBLT issues and practices, and to fostering improved understanding and communication across the various lines of TBLT work.

For an overview of all books published in this series, please see
benjamins.com/catalog/tblt

Editors

Marta González-Lloret
University of Hawai'i at Manoa

John M. Norris
ETS Japan

Andrea Révész
University College London

Volume 17

Broadening the Horizon of TBLT. Plenary addresses from the second decade of the International Conference on Task-Based Language Teaching
Edited by Martin East

Broadening the Horizon of TBLT

Plenary addresses from the second decade
of the International Conference
on Task-Based Language Teaching

Edited by

Martin East
The University of Auckland

John Benjamins Publishing Company
Amsterdam / Philadelphia

The paper used in this publication meets the minimum requirements of the American National Standard for Information Sciences – Permanence of Paper for Printed Library Materials, ANSI z39.48-1984.

DOI 10.1075/tblt.17

Cataloging-in-Publication Data available from Library of Congress:
LCCN 2025005789 (PRINT) / 2025005790 (E-BOOK)

ISBN 978 90 272 2104 9 (HB)
ISBN 978 90 272 4483 3 (E-BOOK)

© 2025 – John Benjamins B.V.
No part of this book may be reproduced in any form, by print, photoprint, microfilm, or any other means, without written permission from the publisher.

John Benjamins Publishing Company · https://benjamins.com

Table of contents

Series editors' preface   VII

SECTION 1. **Introduction**
CHAPTER 1. Broadening the horizon of task-based language teaching: Where
has the most recent decade brought us?   2
    Martin East

SECTION 2. **Practical issues for task-based courses and curricula**
CHAPTER 2. Task design: A history of resilience and a space for innovation   22
    Roger Gilabert

CHAPTER 3. How real is real? Can task-based language courses properly
prepare students for reality?   41
    Kris Van den Branden

CHAPTER 4. The coursebook in TBLT: Lost cause or launching pad?   60
    Jonathan Newton

SECTION 3. **Task implementation in distinct instructional contexts**
CHAPTER 5. Task-based language learning among children in an EFL context:
Research and challenges   82
    María del Pilar García Mayo

CHAPTER 6. "It takes a village": Developing and maintaining sustainable
TBLT curricula   101
    YouJin Kim

SECTION 4. **Task-based language assessment**
CHAPTER 7. Aligning classroom tasks with can-do descriptors helps
TBLT programs be chock-full of proficiency indicators   124
    Paula Winke

CHAPTER 8. From CAF to CAFFA: Measuring linguistic performance
and functional adequacy in task-based language teaching   147
    Folkert Kuiken & Ineke Vedder

SECTION 5. Theories informing task-based language teaching

CHAPTER 9. Reflecting on task-based language teaching from an Instructed SLA perspective 164
Nina Spada

CHAPTER 10. How a processability perspective frames the potential of tasks in instructed second language acquisition 183
Anke Lenzing

CHAPTER 11. Exploring task-based cognitive processes: Methodological advances and challenges 212
Andrea Révész

SECTION 6. Ethnographic studies into TBLT as researched pedagogy

CHAPTER 12. Tasks for diverse learners in diverse contexts: A case study of Australian Aboriginal vocational students 236
Rhonda Oliver

CHAPTER 13. The teacher variable in TBLT: Broadening the horizon through teacher education and support 255
Martin East

List of contributors 273

Index 277

Series editors' preface

Published in 2015 and edited by Martin Bygate, Volume 8 in this book series was entitled *Domains and directions in the development of TBLT: A decade of plenaries from the international conference*. That book featured eleven chapters that originally had been presented as plenary addresses at the initial five biennial convenings of the International Conference on Task-Based Language Teaching between 2005 and 2013, thereby capturing many of the primary themes and topics in TBLT research and practice of the early 2000s. It is very fitting — and reflective of the sustained if not expanded global interest in TBLT — that now in 2025 a second volume of plenaries selected from the intervening decade of conferences should appear. In *Broadening the horizon of TBLT: Plenary addresses from the second decade of the International Conference on Task-Based Language Teaching*, editor Martin East (another Martin!) has brought together twelve chapters based on plenaries that were delivered between 2015 and 2023. We are particularly enthusiastic about publishing this new volume, not least because — much in the spirit of the TBLT conference itself — it reflects a truly diverse collection of new authors covering critical topics in the ongoing development of task-based theory, research, and practice. In fact, there is only a single author (Kris Van den Branden) with chapters featuring in both plenary volumes, underscoring the notion that this collection of work does, indeed, broaden the horizons of TBLT by representing distinct voices from across the domain and around the world.

In this volume, Martin East has also meaningfully organized the chapters into sections that reflect a variety of critical work streams in TBLT efforts of the past decade. Following his insightful semi-autobiographical recounting in Chapter 1 of the development of TBLT theory and research in tandem with the international conference, and the corresponding international association, East sets out five areas of endeavour, including: (a) the practical design of task-based curricula and courses; (b) the implementation of TBLT in specific language teaching and learning settings; (c) task-based language assessment; (d) theorizing TBLT and associated research paradigms; and (e) in-depth ethnographic investigations of TBLT as a researched pedagogy. Each of these sections features several chapters by leading experts who explore and exemplify core issues, associated research approaches and findings, and implications for practice. Not to be missed in these chapters, by comparison with the 2015 volume, is an important shift in emphasis. Much of the discussion in the first decade of plenaries focused on staking out the territory, clarifying the 'what' of TBLT, its theoretical antecedents and premises, and its proposals for practice. In this new volume, there is a decidedly 'how-to' orientation in the presentations, focusing much more closely on the details and realities of task-based ideas as they are put into practice. As plenary addresses tend to reflect the overall orientation of conference themes and contemporary discussions, we find this shifting emphasis inspiring and perhaps indicative of the maturation of the TBLT domain.

It is also important that we acknowledge the close and sustained relationship between this book series and the international TBLT conference series, a relationship that we believe has proven particularly fruitful. Indeed, the idea for a book series devoted to TBLT came quickly on the heels of the initial conferences, when the original conveners of the first three events (Kris Van den Branden, John Norris, Martin Bygate) approached Kees Vaes at John Benjamins with the proposal. The book series was in many ways intended as an outlet for expanding the impact of the cutting-edge work being presented at the conferences, and it is no coincidence that the authors and editors of volumes in the series have all presented at the conference, many of them as invited plenarists. The first book in the series, a collection of foundational publications on TBLT, appeared in 2009, in conjunction with the Lancaster, UK conference. A few years later, following the 2011 conference in Auckland, NZ, Martin East authored Volume 3, an extended exploration of the critically important teacher perspective on TBLT in the context of New Zealand schools and language education. Martin East would, of course, go on to become the first elected president of the newly formed International Association for TBLT in 2017, serving as president for five years and playing a pivotal role in sustaining the conference series and guiding it to new locations around the globe.

It is a pleasure now to see another important scholarly outcome of this relationship between the international conference series, the TBLT association, and this book series. We congratulate Martin East and the contributing authors on bringing this project to fruition, and we look forward to another decade of conferences and plenaries, along with associated advances in TBLT.

John Norris
Marta González-Lloret
Andrea Révész

SECTION 1

Introduction

CHAPTER 1

Broadening the horizon of task-based language teaching
Where has the most recent decade brought us?

Martin East
The University of Auckland

Since 2005 the biennial International Conferences on Task-based Language Teaching (TBLT) have provided an important catalyst for theorists, researchers, and practitioners to discuss the latest research findings and developments and to consider the vital interface between research and practice. A first volume of plenaries (Bygate, 2015) included addresses delivered at the TBLT conferences between 2005 and 2013. This chapter introduces the second volume which presents a range of plenaries given between 2015 and 2023. It is divided into two parts. Part I presents a historically-situated summary of some of the wider trends that have influenced the emergence and development of TBLT, ending with a brief exploration of several themes that have further broadened the horizon of TBLT, in particular in the most recent decade. Part II interweaves an overview of the past two decades of conferences with my own unfolding story as a TBLT-oriented researcher and teacher educator to illustrate how the conference series has been a significant part of my own journey, culminating in my role as editor of this second collection. I thereby give an account of how my experiences fit together with the broadening TBLT endeavour. I conclude by presenting the themes explored by the range of plenarists whose presentations have been included in this volume.

Keywords: task-based language teaching, communicative language teaching, task-based curricula, TBLT implementation, TBLT conferences

Introduction

The International Conferences on Task-based Language Teaching (TBLT), first launched in 2005 in Leuven, Belgium, and occurring every two years after that, have provided an important catalyst for theorists, researchers, and practitioners

https://doi.org/10.1075/tblt.17.01eas
© 2025 John Benjamins Publishing Company

to meet together. They have created a forum to discuss and mull over the latest research findings and developments, and to consider the vital interface between research and actual classroom practice — something that is particularly pertinent to TBLT as a "researched pedagogy" (Samuda et al., 2018). The first volume of plenaries (Bygate, 2015) included representative addresses delivered at the TBLT conferences between 2005 and 2013. This second volume presents a range of plenaries delivered between 2015 and 2023.

The decade that almost exactly parallels the one represented in this volume (the decade starting in 2013) was labelled by Jia and Bava Harji (2023) as a "fast-growing" phase in the task-based literature. Their analysis of publication trends revealed that, compared to the previous few decades, this phase evidenced a strong increase in both interest in and publications across a range of task-based areas, including TBLT. In East (2025), I utilised Jia and Bava Harji's observations as a springboard to review some of the issues for TBLT that appeared to have been rising to greater prominence in the task-based literature since 2013 and, as a consequence, have continued to broaden the horizon of TBLT.[1] Although these years do not exactly coincide with the decade that is the focus of the present volume, the overlap is close enough to infer that this period has been particularly significant for TBLT and that some of the issues I identified in East (2025) will become increasingly visible in our conference series.

This introductory chapter is divided into two parts. In Part I, I provide a historically-located summary of wider trends that have influenced the emergence and development of TBLT, ending with a brief exploration of what I identified in East (2025) as several themes apparent in the most recent decade. In Part II, I interweave an overview of the past two decades of TBLT conferences with my own unfolding story as a TBLT-oriented researcher and teacher educator to illustrate how the conference series has been a significant part of my own journey, leading to my role as editor of the second collection of plenaries. Taken in conjunction with my plenary write-up in this volume (Chapter 13), I give an account of how my own experiences fit together with the broadening TBLT endeavour. I conclude Part II by presenting the themes explored by the range of plenarists in the most recent decade whose presentations have been included in this volume.

---

1. The phrase "broadening the horizon" as used here and for the title of this collection of plenaries reflects both the title of my own keynote at the 9th International Conference in Innsbruck, Austria, and the title of the conference itself — "Widening the horizon of task-based language teaching."

Part I.   The impetus for the emergence and development of TBLT

As I outline later in this chapter, numerous issues for the ongoing implementation of TBLT are raised in the chapters presented in this volume. In what follows, I provide an historical overview of some of the wider influences that created the momentum for TBLT's rise and development.

1960s and 1970s

The educational theories, approaches, and research that have come to influence TBLT go back many decades (Bygate, 2016). Arguably the most important historical antecedent of TBLT was the development of Communicative Language Teaching or CLT. Benson and Voller (1997) provided what I have long regarded as a clearly expressed articulation of the what and why of CLT's beginnings. I quote from them, as I have done elsewhere (East, 2021a, 2022), at some length:

> From time to time, a new concept enters the field of language education as an alternative method or approach, but rapidly grows in significance to the point where it comes fundamentally to condition thinking throughout the field. Such was the case with Communicative Language Teaching ... which began life in the late 1960s as an alternative to 'structural' and 'grammar-translation' models of teaching, but rapidly became an axiom of language teaching methodology. The question ceased to be, 'Should we be teaching languages communicatively?', and became, 'How do we teach languages communicatively?'. As part of this paradigm shift, other concepts (authenticity, learner-centredness, negotiation, etc.) began to cluster around a 'communicative' core.   (p.10)

The growing importance of CLT reflected an increasing recognition that language learning was shifting away from being a largely academic pursuit, with a focus on grammar teaching, translation, and studying literature in the target language, and towards the more pragmatic and utilitarian goals of "learners who were learning languages because they needed to *use* them in an ever-shrinking world" (Benson & Voller, 1997, p.11).

As far as CLT was concerned, the different factors at play contributed to the appearance of a wholly or chiefly experiential form which negated any place or necessity for grammar teaching, largely on the basis of Krashen's (1977a, 1977b) distinction between acquisition and learning — so-called strong CLT. However, despite the positive messages apparent in Benson and Voller's (1997) articulation of the beginnings of CLT and a growing emphasis on learner-centred classrooms, as well as, in some circles, a radical ("teacher-free") interpretation of what CLT should be, shifting the status quo was easier said than done. With many teachers caught in the middle of the philosophical transition from structuralist to communicative approaches, CLT in practice often ended up looking little different to the behaviourist-informed, teacher-led procedures that were such crucial elements of grammar-translation and audio-lingualism — so-called weak CLT. By the 1980s, weak CLT had become "more or less standard practice" (Howatt, 1984, p.279). If the communicative agenda was to embrace the ideals expressed by Benson and Voller more fully and in a workable way, a new direction was needed.

The 1980s and beyond

Long (2015b) characterised the extreme ends of the two polarisations of CLT (weak and strong) as "excessively interventionist, on the one hand, and irresponsibly, wholly non-interventionist, on the other" (p.20). The notion of TBLT began to surface during the early 1980s as a counterbalancer to some of the limitations of teacher-dominant weak CLT — in large part influenced by broader educational debates about the elements that constituted effective pedagogy. It also began to develop as a corrective to the wholly experiential (zero grammar) approach of strong CLT that might seem to countenance a standpoint of "anything-goes-as-long-as-you-get-the-message-across" (Savignon, 1983, p.1).

Certainly the *sociocultural*-interactionist stance underpinned by constructivism — that learners learn best through scaffolded interactional opportunities — was one important influence on TBLT's development. However, there was also a good deal going on in the sphere of theorising second language acquisition (SLA) that began to exert considerable impact. In particular, the appearance of a *cognitive*-interactionist perspective as a development to the notion of Krashen's input hypothesis (Krashen, 1977a, 1977b) was inspired by Long's (1981) articulation of the roles of both input *and* interaction in driving forward SLA. This became a significant stimulus for the theories that began to inform TBLT research. Long (e.g., 2015a) saw expansions in both educational thinking and SLA as important influences on the impetus for and development of TBLT, even though his own work and theorising were more cognitively-oriented.

Quite independently to the theorising that led to the proposition of the interaction hypothesis and the cognitive-interactionist stance, Prabhu's (1982) classroom-level work, which also reflected aspects of Krashen's hypothesising, proposed three representative task types — information gap, reasoning gap, and opinion gap. Prabhu's proposals illustrate an important first step in putting TBLT ideas into operation and thereby initiating the vital *practice* dimension of TBLT. In a chapter published a few years later, Long (1985) presented what has become an archetypal umbrella description of what tasks are — "the hundred and one things that people *do* in everyday life at work, at play, and in between" (p.89, my emphasis) — thereby pointing to the crucial focus on meaning-making in authentic contexts. In turn, target tasks in the real world (identifying which of those 101 things may be useful for a particular set of language learners) could be broken down into pedagogic tasks for the classroom through which learner-learner interactions (and, as a consequence, SLA) would occur.

Just as Benson and Voller (1997) neatly articulated the driving forces leading to the emergence of CLT, Norris et al. (2009) succinctly encapsulated the essential drivers for TBLT, and their summary is also worth quoting at length:

> From educational philosophy came important roles for holism, experiential learning, and learner-centered pedagogy; from research into second language acquisition, key insights into the benefits of learner interaction, feedback, and focus-on-form; from cognitive psycholinguistics, possible mechanisms for guiding learner attention, noticing, and awareness of language form-function-meaning relationships; and from socio-cultural learning theories the interactive roles of the social and linguistic environment in providing learning opportunities and scaffolding learners into them. (p.15)

Building on the above diverse spheres of influence since its beginnings in the early 1980s, TBLT has been gaining momentum across the globe in all three areas of theory, research, and practice as a "potentially very powerful language pedagogy" (Van den Branden et al., 2009, p.1). In particular, TBLT challenges aspects of the sage on stage weak CLT model, not by negating any space for teacher intervention (as in the case of the strongest forms of CLT) but by casting the role of the teacher in a different light — very much a present guide, even if often on the side (see, e.g., Van den Branden, 2009, 2016).

The 1990s to 2010s: Decades of growth and expansion

Jia and Bava Harji's (2023) systematic analysis of bibliographic records to detect and determine emerging trends and themes with regard to task-based teaching and learning across a range of curriculum areas (i.e., not just restricted to language teaching and learning) identified, in addition to the fast-growing phase of the most recent decade, an initial phase (Phase 1: 1991–2004) and a growing phase (Phase 2: 2005–2012).

With regard to TBLT, it is apparent that TBLT's initial locus of interest (and one that continues to remain dominant in the literature) was the teaching of English as an Additional Language (EAL). Very early studies into TBLT were principally situated in the English as Second Language (ESL) context. In this context, it was generally the case that learners with a wide range of language backgrounds were learning in an "immersion" environment and would potentially have access to first language (L1) speakers outside the classroom. In situations such as this, the approach advocated in TBLT was arguably beneficial because the multilingual nature of the classroom necessitated in-class use of English for communicative purposes, and the external (English-speaking) environment demanded interaction with L1 speakers in a variety of authentic contexts — or negotiating real-world tasks to meet real-world needs. Thus, pedagogic tasks in classrooms were logical preparatory vehicles for undertaking target tasks in the real world. With English (the target language) as often the only language shared in common with all participants, it made sense for there to be a strong (or exclusive) focus on using English, and for up-front teacher instruction to be less dominant.

A broadening of the TBLT agenda beyond ESL is illustrated in a collection of studies edited by Shehadeh and Coombe (2012) that focused attention on the realm of English as Foreign Language (EFL). From their perspective, this widening in emphasis began to push the boundaries of TBLT research, allowing new research findings to become apparent. There was also a broadening of scope in the task-based literature beyond EAL to language learning across a *range* of additional languages (e.g., Doughty & Long, 2003; East, 2012; Hill & Tschudi, 2011; Leaver & Willis, 2004; Van den Branden et al., 2007).

In contrast to immersion (second language) environments, teaching and learning in instructed (foreign language) contexts, where learners may often share the same L1 and access to target language L1 speakers may be limited, point to different classroom dynamics and practices. These include, on the one hand, the need to ensure adequate interactional opportunities to use the target language in class (for which tasks would be valuable) and, on the other hand, the possible need to explain more about how the target language functions (thereby potentially bringing teachers into a more prominent instructional role). The common L1 shared by many of the learners adds another dynamic and raises questions around what is and what is not legitimate L1 use in the L2 classroom.

The most recent decade: Further broadening the horizon of TBLT

On the back of a clear expansion of emphasis beyond ESL to EFL and other languages, in East (2025) I identified four themes that I argued have received greater attention in the most recent decade (i.e., since 2013). My identification of these issues was intended to be neither exclusive nor exhaustive, but, rather, illustrative of themes becoming more prevalent in recent years.

Enlarging on the increased emphasis on languages other than English, two key themes to rise to greater visibility have been less commonly taught languages (e.g., Heidrich Uebel & Van Gorp, 2023) and indigenous languages (e.g., East, 2020; Ko, 2017; Riestenberg & Cruz Manzano, 2019; Riestenberg & Sherris, 2018;

Sherris et al., 2013). Although the two themes could be conflated under the larger heading of languages other than English, in East (2025) I argued for their distinctiveness on this basis: less commonly taught languages represent those that may be commonly spoken but are comparatively less observable in teaching contexts, and indigenous languages are those that are less frequently taught but are moreover potentially at risk because they are also less regularly spoken. In the indigenous context in particular, Riestenberg and Sherris (2018) noted, "many of the methods for teaching second languages (L2) currently promoted in the field of applied linguistics have rarely been applied" (p. 435), thereby making this context particularly emergent and one that would benefit from a greater task-oriented research focus.

In turn, issues that have begun to receive greater attention in the most recent decade include technology — in particular, use of interactive computer software, the internet, and mobile devices — and translanguaging, which refers to "the process whereby language users draw on linguistic resources both in and beyond the L2, including aspects of their L1, to keep communication going when interacting with others" (East, 2025, p. 77). This greater visibility should not be taken to suggest that interest in both issues has not been apparent in work taking place before the most recent decade. Use of technology has become increasingly ubiquitous over several decades and interest in investigating the effectiveness of technology-mediated tasks has in fact been prevalent among TBLT researchers for many years (see, e.g., González-Lloret & Ortega, 2014; Lai & Li, 2011). Also, interest in L1 use as a scaffolding mechanism in L2 classrooms, including TBLT-oriented classrooms, has been subject to relatively early investigation (e.g., Anton & DiCamilla, 1998; Brooks & Donato, 1994; Swain & Lapkin, 2000). Arguments in favour of L1 use have emphasised the cognitive support that enables learners to work at a higher level than might be the case if learners were limited to just using the target language (Alegría de la Colina & García Mayo, 2009; Swain & Lapkin, 2000). Translanguaging represents a broader repertoire of communicative skills and strategies to enhance meaning negotiation than just the use of L1 but is itself not a new phenomenon since it represents what bi- or multilinguals have often done in communicative interactions (Bui & Tai, 2022).

When it comes to the most recent decade, however, Smith and Gonzáles-Lloret (2021) referred to technology-mediated TBLT as "an emerging field" (p. 518), and Jia and Bava Harji (2023) identified technology as a significant theme to rise to greater visibility. An informative recent overview of central research findings can be found in González-Lloret and Ziegler (2022). Also, translanguaging has been identified in the most recent decade as "an emerging concept" in the applied linguistics literature (Nagashima & Lawrence, 2022, p. 736) and a "new linguistic reality" (García & Li, 2014, p. 29). As such, Seals et al. (2020) claimed that, since a "translanguaging paradigm shift" is becoming more apparent, "this is a time for the well-established TBLT to work with and alongside it" (p. 276).

As I noted in East (2025), translanguaging is arguably the most controversial issue for TBLT to arise in recent times because it challenges the traditional orthodoxy of target language exclusivity or use of one language at a time that has "long dominated the TBLT field" (Bui & Tai, 2022, p. 8). Controversy is also found in the fact that translanguaging implies fluidity of boundaries between "named" languages whereas language revitalisation and reclamation are often predicated on maintaining a language's distinctiveness. As with indigenous languages, the debates around translanguaging in TBLT are particularly emergent and would benefit from a greater task-oriented research focus (see East & Wang, 2024, in this regard).

Part II.   The TBLT conferences

Having, in Part I, reviewed what TBLT is and aims to achieve as well as some of the themes apparent in the literature over the last few decades and gaining more visibility in the most recent decade, I turn to the international biennial TBLT conferences that have become a significant part of ongoing and broadening knowledge dissemination and understanding. In Part II, I include how aspects of my own professional journey have intersected with the conference series.

The first decade of conferences

In his introduction to the volume that presented a representative sample of plenary addresses from the first decade of the international TBLT conferences, Bygate (2015) remarked that the significant ramifications for so many stakeholders of what he referred to as the "TBLT project" were recognised in the launch of the conference series. This series was the brainchild of Martin Bygate, John Norris, and Kris Van den Branden. They also established (in 2006) the International Consortium on Task-Based Language Teaching (ICTBLT), a key mission of which was to oversee the implementation of the series of conferences that dominated the first decade. The first five conferences took place in diverse locations across the world — Leuven, Belgium (2005), Hawai'i, US (2007), Lancaster, UK (2009), Auckland, New Zealand (2011) and Banff, Canada (2013) — thereby signalling the worldwide interest that TBLT was generating.

Bygate (2015) highlighted the unique dimensions that set TBLT apart from other approaches to language pedagogy. He underscored the construct of task as the core component of the TBLT endeavour. He explained that, as a result — and seen in the broader context of the theories that inform TBLT as outlined in Part I – TBLT places demands on a whole range of stakeholders to adjust, sometimes significantly, their understanding and use of other approaches and learning activities. These stakeholders include the learners themselves and their teachers, but also incorporate materials and curriculum writers and administrators. There are also implications for language assessment and the creation and use of tests (for which adjustments in understanding and expectation may be required) as well as for teacher education and professional development. Bygate concluded that the implications were substantial, in theory at least, but perhaps more manifestly in practice – a theme he revisited several years later (Bygate, 2020). In essence, TBLT may have the support of theorists and researchers, but it remains, at the level of the classroom, a "contested endeavour" (East, 2021b, p. 552).

The first decade of conferences coincided with a significant time of professional and academic transition for me as I moved into a role as a language teacher educator at the University of Auckland, New Zealand. As I explore in more detail in Chapter 13, the challenges for TBLT that Bygate (2015) outlined were very real as I sought to navigate TBLT ideas with my own students who often came to the teacher education programme from backgrounds influenced by teacher-led weak CLT. The expectations placed on me as a teacher educator to promote a learner-centred and experiential curriculum alongside the challenges for TBLT raised by teachers in classrooms as they came up against more entrenched traditional practices advanced my initial interest in what TBLT means for teachers at the chalkface (East, 2012), an interest that has informed a continuing research agenda.

The 2011 conference, held in Auckland, was my inauguration into a conference series wholly dedicated to TBLT and I welcomed the opportunity to be involved in several ways. One standout memory for me was facilitating a panel discussion on TBLT with Martin Bygate (Bygate & East, 2011) where we could engage with audience questions about TBLT and tasks in classrooms. Billed, at least informally, as a session with "the two Martins," I felt a little hesitant to be leading a discussion with someone who had been such a significant player in the worldwide TBLT community for quite some time. I need not have been concerned. My co-facilitator (Martin B.) was gracious and supportive, and I (Martin E.) appreciated the opportunity to get to know him better as we planned how the discussion might go over a meeting at a local coffee house. I recall we faced some curly questions (or they seemed so to me at least), but we managed to navigate our way through. I have been committed to attending as many of the TBLT conferences as I could since that time.

The second decade of conferences

The 10th anniversary conference in 2015 returned the venue to its inaugural home of Leuven, and this was seen as a celebration of the persistent and growing interest that TBLT seemed to be generating. Bygate's (2015) volume marked this anniversary. The next decade of conferences continued the practice of selecting locations across the globe — Leuven, Belgium (2015), Barcelona, Spain (2017), Ottawa, Canada (2019), Innsbruck, Austria (2022)[2] and Khon Kaen, Thailand (2023).

The second Leuven conference was of significance for the wider TBLT community. In place of the original Consortium, 2015 saw the launch of the International Association for Task-Based Language Teaching (IATBLT), with a charter for the IATBLT drawn up by Martin, John, and Kris. Its beginnings were explained to the conference delegates by Kris who was conference chair at that time and became inaugural President of the new Association. The whole original Executive Board was appointed rather than elected — a necessary first step to set in motion what would eventually become a fully elected representative body.

The launch of the IATBLT was of particular significance for me. I valued the invitation to become a member of the inaugural Executive Board, and it was a further privilege to progress to the presidency of the Association at the 2017 conference. Having served as President of the New Zealand Association of Language Teachers (NZALT) since 2012, a role that included a level of oversight for our own biennial national conferences, stepping up to the presidency of the IATBLT represented a translation of my locally-based service on behalf of teachers of languages to the international sphere. I held the President role for five years, finishing my term at the 2022 conference. My time on the IATBLT Executive Board has meant that, in one way or another, I have played a part in the conferences that make up the second decade. (The 2023 conference was the only one I have been unable to attend in this most recent decade due to other work commitments, but I took part in the selection of this site and the plenarists, and undertook initial liaison with the conference organisers.)

Perusal of the conference programmes for the TBLT conferences between 2015 and 2023 reveals that the themes in the literature I identified in East (2025) have been in evidence, although this has not yet translated to large-scale representation in conference presentations (with the possible exception of technology). Essentially, at least some of the themes I acknowledged, whilst clearly taking on greater importance, remain somewhat nascent and arguably on the outer edges to what still appears to be the core of TBLT's research/practice agenda — the realm of

---

2. It was originally planned for the Innsbruck conference to take place in 2021, but the Covid pandemic put paid to many plans across the world.

EAL. However, less commonly taught languages have been represented. In some cases, this has included more mainstream international languages which the presenters have chosen to label as "less commonly taught" (which, in comparison with EAL, they no doubt are). This has included Japanese and Korean. In other cases, the languages of focus have included genuinely less commonly taught languages, but languages that are still spoken by a significant number of people, such as Afrikaans, Swahili, or Hebrew. The inclusion of Swahili and Hebrew also signals representation, albeit very small at this stage, of presentations devoted to indigenous languages such as endangered native American Zapotec and Salish.

One theme that is considerably under-represented in the TBLT agenda as evidenced by conference presentations to date is translanguaging. A search for the keyword "translanguaging" across the conference programmes between 2015 and 2023 indicates only three occasions when it seemed presenters directly addressed this theme — although one of these occasions was a colloquium, thereby providing several presenters with space to explore the phenomenon (Van Gorp & Jordens, 2015). The relative lack of attention paid to translanguaging is also reflected in my own comments in East (2025) about the controversial nature of translanguaging vis à vis TBLT. Nonetheless, as Seals et al. (2020) expressed it, "actively making and maintaining space for translanguaging in TBLT will both enrich TBLT's research agenda and extend the impact of TBLT beyond its typical second/foreign language education sphere of influence" (p. 276), thereby further broadening the horizon of TBLT research and practice. It would be exciting to see more papers addressing this as well as the other emergent themes in future TBLT conferences.

In the final part of this introductory chapter, I turn to the plenaries that have contributed to the conferences in the most recent decade.

The plenary addresses in this volume

Plenary speeches represent both a unique opportunity to inspire others and a unique genre. This is reflected in the chapters published in this collection. Several chapters present more personal narratives where the focus is on what TBLT has meant to the individual in question. This does not detract from the academic rigour exemplified in the extensive references that authors draw on. It does, however, enable readers to connect with the authors at a more personal level and to gain some insights into the individual stories that contribute to the overall picture of TBLT theorising, research, and practice across the globe. Following Bygate (2015), the chapters in this volume are not presented chronologically in terms of year of presentation. Rather, they have been grouped together under five broad themes. These are outlined below.

Practical issues for task-based courses and curricula

As a reflection of TBLT's orientation as a researched pedagogy, the first three chapters (Gilabert; Van den Branden; Newton) address practical considerations when developing task-based courses and curricula. The chapter by Gilabert makes the claim that needs analysis may help ensure greater task relevance for learners, but Gilabert acknowledges that, in many classroom scenarios, the kinds of tasks learners engage in are prescribed in a top-down way. In this regard, he asserts that task and syllabus design must incorporate the perspectives of teachers and teaching communities. Van den Branden builds on this issue, but asserts that, even when classroom tasks have been created on the basis of needs analysis, pedagogic tasks that make up task-based language courses may not adequately prepare students for the target tasks they find they need to undertake. In other words, given that what goes on in language classrooms can only ever be a simulation of the world beyond the classroom, how authentic, meaningful, and relevant are pedagogic tasks for learners' real lives? Van den Branden concludes by questioning the level of task authenticity that can be achieved through using coursebooks, even though he acknowledges the reliance teachers often place on these. This makes their use often questioned by TBLT enthusiasts. Newton's contribution tackles this issue head-on. Drawing on case studies of coursebook use in Thailand, China, and Vietnam, Newton considers both the benefits and limitations of coursebooks from a TBLT perspective and explores how tasks can be operationalised even when coursebooks form the basis of a course.

Task implementation in distinct instructional contexts

I stressed earlier that TBLT research has expanded substantially from its original ESL base into a range of foreign language contexts. Two chapters (García Mayo; Kim) build on some of the planning issues presented in the first chapters in this volume and explore the practical implementation of tasks in distinct domains. García Mayo investigated task-based language learning among young EFL learners when performing collaborative tasks in mainstream and content and language integrated learning (CLIL) classrooms. Situated within both cognitive- and sociocultural interactionist perspectives, findings demonstrate that young learners successfully collaborated to negotiate meaning and focus on form as well as experiencing enhanced motivation towards the tasks. The chapter by Kim provides a useful addition to García Mayo's contribution by looking at curriculum development projects in a range of languages and contexts. Her review of studies brings out the benefits and challenges of different curriculum implementation models. Kim concludes that establishing sustainable TBLT curricula requires not only institutional support but also collaboration among a range of stakeholders with different expertise. Her review and the findings presented by García Mayo show that it is possible to draw on TBLT principles and adapt tasks effectively to vastly different learner audiences and needs.

Task-based language assessment

Two chapters (Winke; Kuiken & Vedder) shift attention beyond what might happen pedagogically in the classroom to task-based language assessment or TBLA. Both chapters draw on data in several languages other than English, with findings generalisable across languages. Winke argues that TBLT programmes need to articulate a match between increasingly more complex, challenging, diverse, and culturally rich tasks and the ways in which performances on those tasks will be measured. Her chapter usefully builds a bridge between TBLT and TBLA by relating tasks to so-called Can-do statements. These statements, which articulate what learners can do with aspects of language at different stages of learning, can be used as a basis to determine and measure the learning that is going on as learners undertake tasks. As Winke rightly points out, any task can be used for assessment purposes. She suggests that all tasks can be used as indicators of communicative proficiency and can therefore, from an assessment perspective, be truly formative. Kuiken and Vedder expand on the notion of measuring communicative proficiency. They start from the premise that the more mainstream way of operationalising and measuring facets of proficiency elicited by language use tasks has been carried out in relation to complexity, accuracy, and fluency (CAF). They maintain, however, that these kinds of measurement data are incomplete and should be supplemented by measures of the effectiveness and appropriacy of L2 performances, or so-called functional adequacy (FA). They go on to discuss a rating scale for FA that can be used for the assessment of oral and written performance (see, e.g., Kuiken & Vedder, 2022) and look at the measure in relation to the (sub)facets of CAF.

Theorising and researching TBLT

Three chapters (Spada; Lenzing; Révész) take a step back from practical issues regarding the implementation of task-based teaching and assessment. Spada explores the interface between TBLT and Instructed SLA or ISLA, recognising the commonalities between the two with regard to theory, research, and practice. She notes, as Bygate (2015) and others have done, the construct of task as the distinguishing characteristic of TBLT and TBLA whereas ISLA is broader in the range of instructional activities and assessment practices it draws on. The chapter goes on to provide a research-informed overview of form-focused instruction and corrective feedback and the differences in how outcomes are measured in TBLT and ISLA. Lenzing's chapter is also framed within ISLA and examines the relevance of a processability theory (PT) perspective on the potential of tasks in the instructed context. Drawing on speech samples of learners at a range of proficiency levels who completed the same task at different points in their language development, Lenzing argues that PT might enhance our understanding of how both the common and individual features of L2 development can be seen in learners' speech. Révész suggests that TBLT researchers need to put greater effort into examining the cognitive processes in which L2 learners engage when completing a task. The chapter presents various methods to investigate these processes, noting that a combination of methods is likely to lead to more valid understanding and mediate the limitations of each individual method. Recommendations are offered to inform future cognitively-oriented TBLT research.

Ethnographic studies into TBLT as researched pedagogy

The final two chapters (Oliver; East) bring us back to the central notion of TBLT as researched pedagogy. Furthermore, they take a longitudinal ethnographic perspective in two southern hemisphere contexts. Oliver outlines research work she has undertaken over a 14-year period among Aboriginal high school students and their teachers from remote locations in Western Australia. The students in question were studying in a vocational boarding school quite a way from where they lived, and English was a second language or dialect for them. Findings from classroom observations and interviews demonstrate the importance of needs analysis when it comes to contextually appropriate and culturally suitable task selection. In my own chapter, I explore a variable that I maintain is crucial to the successful implementation (or otherwise) of TBLT — the teachers themselves. Taking something of an autoethnographic approach, I draw on both my own early experiences as a language learner and language teacher and, more particularly, my more recent experiences as a language teacher educator to reflect on how teachers receive and respond to TBLT ideas and how they can be supported with implementing these ideas.

Conclusion

I hope you will find the chapters that make up this volume thought-provoking in the various ways they address the ongoing opportunities for and challenges of the TBLT project. In his introduction to the first collection of plenaries, Bygate (2015) wrote that, above all other considerations, the volume brought together "a set of distinctive and substantial position papers, offering a richness and engaging with a breadth of issues and discussion unusual in a single collection of papers" (xxiii). These words are just as apposite for the collection of chapters that have made their way into this second volume.

I end this introductory chapter with some words shared by Mike Long, a loyal supporter of TBLT and our conferences who, sadly, passed away in February 2021 after a battle with illness. In the updated write-up to his own plenary address given at the first TBLT conference, Long described TBLT is "a work in progress" and "certainly no panacea" (Long, 2015b, p.20). As Long explained, some problems with implementing TBLT are very apparent; others will no doubt emerge as we progress a teaching-informed research agenda. Long went on to laud the efforts to confront the problems being made by "very talented researchers ... in several countries" (p.20). The TBLT conferences present a significant opportunity to hear from a whole range of these very talented researchers as we share a vast array of colloquia, papers, and workshops with each other. This volume enables the focus to be on the plenarists who have contributed their expertise in a range of spheres.

In their preface to the first volume of plenaries, the series editors wrote of their genuine hope that a similar collection would appear at the time of the 20th anniversary of the international conferences. As someone who has been centrally involved with aspects of our conferences over the past decade, I recognised the importance of bringing together the insights and wisdom that had been shared over the past ten years by those invited to give our plenary addresses and the need to publish a second volume of plenaries. (It is entirely coincidental, but also provokes a sense of continuity for me, that the baton should have passed on to me, as one of the "two Martins," to ensure that we have a second volume.) Just as the 10th anniversary 2015 conference was a cause for celebration and coincided with the release of Bygate's (2015) volume, the 2025 conference in Groningen, the Netherlands, provides the opportunity to celebrate our 20th anniversary, to acknowledge the release of this second volume of plenaries from the 2015 to 2023 conferences, and to launch the third decade.

Acknowledgements

I would like to thank the plenarists whose chapters appear here for not only providing written accounts of their plenary addresses but also acting as peer reviewers for their colleagues' submissions. I am also very grateful to the series editors, Marta González-Lloret, John Norris, and Andrea Révész, for their thoughtful comments and editorial suggestions on the final manuscript. I also acknowledge Cambridge University Press for permission to reproduce the plenary given by Nina Spada and John Benjamins Publishing Company for permission to reproduce the plenary given by Andrea Révész.

References

Alegría de la Colina, A., & García Mayo, M. P. (2009). Oral interaction in task-based EFL learning: The use of the L1 as a cognitive tool. *International Review of Applied Linguistics in Language Teaching, 47*(3/4), 325–345.

Anton, M., & DiCamilla, F. (1998). Socio-cognitive functions of L1 collaborative interaction in the L2 classroom. *The Modern Language Journal, 83*(2), 233–247.

Benson, P., & Voller, P. (Eds.). (1997). *Autonomy and independence in language learning.* Longman.

Brooks, F. B., & Donato, R. (1994). Vygotskyan approaches to understanding foreign language learner discourse during communicative tasks. *Hispania, 77*(2), 262–274.

Bui, G., & Tai, K. W. (2022). Revisiting functional adequacy and task-based language teaching in the GBA: Insights from translanguaging. *Asian-Pacific Journal of Second and Foreign Language Education, 7*(Article 40), 1–14.

Bygate, M. (Ed.). (2015). *Domains and directions in the development of TBLT. A decade of plenaries from the international conference.* John Benjamins.

Bygate, M. (2016). Sources, developments and directions of task-based language teaching. *The Language Learning Journal, 44*(4), 381–400.

Bygate, M. (2020). Some directions for the possible survival of TBLT as a real world project. *Language Teaching, 53*(3), 275–288.

Bygate, M., & East, M. (2011, November 18–20). *Tasks in classrooms* [Facilitated panel discussion]. 4th International Conference on Task-Based Language Teaching: Crossing Boundaries, Auckland, New Zealand.

Doughty, C., & Long, M. H. (2003). Optimal psycholinguistic environments for distance foreign language learning. *Language Learning & Technology, 23*, 35–73.

East, M. (2012). *Task-based language teaching from the teachers' perspective: Insights from New Zealand.* John Benjamins.

East, M. (2020). Task-based language teaching as a tool for the revitalisation of te reo Māori: One beginning teacher's perspective. *The Language Learning Journal, 48*(3), 272–284.

East, M. (2021a). *Foundational principles of task-based language teaching.* Routledge.

East, M. (2021b). What do beginning teachers make of task-based language teaching? A comparative re-production of East (2014). *Language Teaching, 54*(4), 552–566.

East, M. (2022). *Mediating innovation through language teacher education.* Cambridge University Press.

East, M. (2025). Taking communication to task once more — A further decade on. *The Language Learning Journal, 53*(1), 71–83.

East, M., & Wang, D. (2024). Advancing the communicative language teaching agenda: What place for translanguaging in task-based language teaching? *The Language Learning Journal*, 1–13.

doi García, O., & Li, W. (2014). *Translanguaging: Language, bilingualism and education*. Palgrave Macmillan.

doi González-Lloret, M., & Ortega, L. (Eds.). (2014). *Technology-mediated TBLT: Researching technology and tasks*. John Benjamins.

doi González-Lloret, M., & Ziegler, N. (2022). Technology-mediated task-based language teaching. In M. J. Ahmadian & M. H. Long (Eds.), *The Cambridge handbook of task-based language teaching* (pp. 326–345). Cambridge University Press.

Heidrich Uebel, E., & Van Gorp, K. (2023, March 18–21). *What makes a task a task? Expert, teacher, and student perspectives* [Conference presenation]. AAAL 2023 Conference: Collaborating and Mentoring in Applied Linguistics, Portland, OR.

doi Hill, Y. Z., & Tschudi, S. L. (2011). Exploring task-based curriculum development in a blended learning conversational Chinese program. *International Journal of Virtual and Personal Learning Environments, 2*(1), 19–36. https://www.learntechlib.org/p/187095/.

Howatt, A. P. R. (1984). *A history of English language teaching*. Oxford University Press.

doi Jia, S., & Bava Harji, M. (2023). Themes, knowledge evolution, and emerging trends in task-based teaching and learning: A scientometric analysis in CiteSpace. *Education and Information Technologies, 28*, 9783–9802.

Ko, E. (2017, April 19–21). *A task-based approach to curriculum and material development to support Crow language revitalization* [Conference Presentation]. First International Conference on Revitalization of Indigenous and Minoritized Languages, Barcelona, Spain.

Krashen, S. (1977a). The Monitor Model for adult second language performance. In M. Burt, H. Dulay, & M. Finocchiaro (Eds.), *Viewpoints on English as a second language* (pp. 152–161). Regents.

Krashen, S. (1977b). Some issues relating to the Monitor Model. In H. D. Brown, C. Jorio, & R. Crymes (Eds.), *Teaching and learning English as a second language: On TESOL '77*. TESOL.

doi Kuiken, F., & Vedder, I. (2022). Measurement of functional adequacy in different learning contexts: Rationale, key issues, and future perspectives. *TASK, 2*(1), 8–32.

doi Lai, C., & Li, G. (2011). Technology and task-based language teaching: A critical review. *CALICO Journal, 28*(2), 498–521.

Leaver, B. L., & Willis, J. (Eds.). (2004). *Task-based instruction in foreign language education: Practices and programs*. Georgetown University Press.

doi Long, M. H. (1981). Input, interaction, and second language acquisition. *Annals of the New York Academy of Sciences, 379*(1), 259–278.

Long, M. H. (1985). A role for instruction in second language acquisition: Task-based language teaching. In K. Hylstenstam & M. Pienemann (Eds.), *Modelling and assessing second language acquisition* (pp. 77–99). Multilingual Matters.

Long, M. H. (2015a). *Second language acquisition and task-based language teaching*. Wiley-Blackwell.

doi Long, M. H. (2015b). TBLT: Building the road as we travel. In M. Bygate (Ed.), *Domains and directions in the development of TBLT: A decade of plenaries from the international conference* (pp. 1–26). John Benjamins.

doi Nagashima, Y., & Lawrence, L. (2022). To translanguage or not to translanguage: Ideology, practice, and intersectional identities. *Applied Linguistics Review, 13*(5), 735–754.

Norris, J. M., Bygate, M., & Van den Branden, K. (2009). Introducing task-based language teaching. In K. Van den Branden, M. Bygate, & J. Norris (Eds.), *Task-based language teaching: A reader* (pp. 15–19). John Benjamins.

Prabhu, N. S. (1982). *The Communicational Teaching Project, South India*. The British Council.

Riestenberg, K., & Cruz Manzano, R. (2019). Teaching task-based writing in Zapotec in Oaxaca, Mexico. In A. Sherris & J. Kreeft Peyton (Eds.), *Teaching writing to children in indigenous languages: Instructional practices from global contexts* (pp. 126–142). Routledge.

Riestenberg, K., & Sherris, A. (2018). Task-based teaching of indigenous languages: Investment and methodological principles in Macuiltianguis Zapotec and Salish Qlispe revitalization. *Canadian Modern Language Review, 74*(3), 434–459.

Samuda, V., Van den Branden, K., & Bygate, M. (Eds.). (2018). *TBLT as a researched pedagogy*. John Benjamins.

Savignon, S. (1983). *Communicative competence*. Addison-Wesley.

Seals, C. A., Newton, J., Ash, M., & Nguyen, T. B. T. (2020). Translanguaging and TBLT: Crossovers and challenges. In Z. Tian, L. Aghai, P. Sayer, & J. Schissel (Eds.), *Envisioning TESOL through a translanguaging lens — Global perspectives* (pp. 275–292). Springer.

Shehadeh, A., & Coombe, C. A. (Eds.). (2012). *Task-based language teaching in foreign language contexts: Research and implementation*. John Benjamins.

Sherris, A., Pete, T., Thompson, L. E., & Haynes, E. F. (2013). Task-based language teaching practices that support Salish language revitalization. In M. C. Jones & S. Ogilvie (Eds.), *Keeping languages alive: Documentation, pedagogy and revitalization* (pp. 155–166). Cambridge University Press.

Smith, B., & Gonzáles-Lloret, M. (2021). Technology-mediated task-based language teaching: A research agenda. *Language Teaching, 54*(4), 518–534.

Swain, M., & Lapkin, S. (2000). Task-based second language learning: The uses of the first language. *Language Teaching Research, 4*(3), 251–274.

Van den Branden, K. (2009). Mediating between predetermined order and chaos: The role of the teacher in task-based language education. *International Journal of Applied Linguistics, 19*(3), 264–285.

Van den Branden, K. (2016). The role of teachers in task-based language education. *Annual Review of Applied Linguistics, 36*, 164–181.

Van den Branden, K., Bygate, M., & Norris, J. M. (2009). Task-based language teaching: Introducing the reader. In K. Van den Branden, M. Bygate, & J. Norris (Eds.), *Task-based language teaching: A reader* (pp. 1–13). John Benjamins.

Van den Branden, K., Van Gorp, K., & Verhelst, M. (Eds.). (2007). *Tasks in action: Task-based language education from a classroom-based perspective*. Cambridge Scholars.

Van Gorp, K., & Jordens, K. (2015, September 16–18). *Tasks and translanguaging: Real meaning-making practices?* [Colloquium]. 6th International Conference on Task-Based Language Teaching: Tasks for Real, Leuven, Belgium. http://www.tblt.org/conferences/2015/colloquia/

SECTION 2

Practical issues for task-based courses and curricula

CHAPTER 2

Task design

A history of resilience and a space for innovation[*]

Roger Gilabert
The University of Barcelona

Task design is serious business for teachers and syllabus designers around the world. Despite the proliferation of TBLT programmes, concerns have been raised about a disconnect existing between research findings and decision-making by teachers. This chapter firstly presents an exploration of top-down sources for teachers wanting to engage in task design, such as the vast task-based research literature, in order to provide historical context for issues with task design. Secondly, the chapter explores needs analysis as a practice that may offer a partial solution to the emergent issues, drawing on the author's own direct experiences. Thirdly, it is suggested that task and syllabus design need to open up to principles outside TBLT that provide considerable room for bottom-up design by incorporating teachers and teacher communities into the design process. An inspection of other fields that may inform task-based design, such as human-machine interaction design or learning design, is followed by a reflection on how principles and practices from neighbouring fields may generate innovation and new avenues for task-based design as we move further into the 21st century.

Keywords: task design, needs analysis, history of task design, learning design, automation of task design, taskGen

Introduction

Task design has been at the heart of the TBLT agenda for the last 40 years. While researchers, language policy makers, teachers, teacher educators, and syllabus designers have also been interested in areas like task-based needs analysis (Long, 2005) or task-based assessment (Norris, 2016), the most immediate need generating interest in tasks has been their pedagogic design. It seems this has become the number one goal of teachers and syllabus designers worldwide. Task design is

---

[*] Revised version of a plenary given to the 10th International TBLT Conference, Khon Kaen, Thailand, 2023.

https://doi.org/10.1075/tblt.17.02gil
© 2025 John Benjamins Publishing Company

a compelling and fascinating, and yet challenging, human endeavour. It was the theme of my plenary at the 10th international conference on TBLT in Khon Kaen, Thailand, and is the focus of this chapter. In this chapter, I will go through some of the key concepts in the area of task design that have been advanced in relation to how language educators have faced the challenges and processes of designing tasks for second or foreign language (L2) learning.

I will undertake my exploration of task design from my own perspective as a task designer. Hopefully, my experience with task design will help those with an interest in TBLT to reflect on how we, as a research and teaching community, may go about designing our tasks in order to generate impactful, effective, and motivating tasks that promote L2 use and development. Although the chapter is framed from my own perspective, I will also make reference to the literature in our field and other contexts where TBLT has been adopted as an educational initiative by various governments around the world.

One issue that potentially unites many of us who have a stake in the task-based agenda is that, at some point or another in our careers, for different reasons and in diverse contexts, we have been faced with the challenge of designing a task — whether for teaching the L2, for research purposes, or for testing. This raises the question of what task design requires in order for the tasks to be effective for language learning. In essence, task design entails becoming acquainted with a vast literature, receiving some kind of teacher education or professional development input (often self-directed), time, institutional support, a lot of risk-tasking, and decision-making. Task design and syllabus design are critical issues for teachers and syllabus designers around the world. Proof of this is the proliferation over the last 40 years of task-based language programmes designed to provide teacher education and professional development in all aspects of TBLT, as well as the incorporation of TBLT in national education policy in many countries worldwide (e.g. Thailand, China). However, concerns have been raised about a disconnect between research findings and decision-making by teachers and syllabus designers, who are often left to their own devices during design. This requires considerable work and resilience from them.

In this chapter, I will first provide an overview of what have been mostly top-down sources of information for teachers wanting to engage in task design, such as a vast task-based research literature in the context of my own experiences of task design. As I present an overview of the literature, I will keep coming back to task design for pedagogic purposes. Secondly, I will provide some insights from needs analysis (NA) that may aid both micro- and macro-level decision-making during task and syllabus design. Thirdly, I will claim that both task and syllabus design need to open up to principles outside TBLT, and I will address how we may deal with task design as we move further into the 21st century.

An overview of task and syllabus design

Setting up a fully task-based language programme

To provide context for the review of literature that I present here, I interweave my own experiences as a task and syllabus designer with developments presented in the literature in order to illustrate the different dimensions that are required in task and syllabus design.

In the late 1990s, and right after the completion of my PhD courses and as I started working on my PhD thesis, I was tasked, with two other colleagues, with the construction of a new language programme. The Blanquerna Department of Communication Studies (Ramon Llull University in Barcelona, Spain), where I took up my first major tertiary-level teaching job before embarking on my thesis, had just started up and, as is sometimes the case, it was anticipated that from the apparent chaos of a messy but energetic beginning, interesting things would emerge. In this programme, quite exceptionally, we had complete institutional support and freedom to take as many risks as we wanted, and we chose to throw away the textbook and adopt a fully-fledged TBLT approach. This was consistent with the European Union's multilingual and second and foreign language directives, as well as with local educational authorities' emphasis on teaching through competencies and not through discrete grammar points. This was, however, an exception in our context which was still dominated by the textbook industry and textbook use and where heavily grammar-oriented lessons were the norm.

It may be assumed that all we had at the time was only top-down sources of information for the creation of a programme. This was not quite the case. The existing literature was certainly helpful, but ours was a collective effort that drew on NA involving many stakeholders — programme designers, teachers, students, professional communicators, and university leaders — who engaged in regular joint meetings for design and re-design as well as a lot of trial-and-error over the two initial years of the programme.

However, our starting point was of course a review of the TBLT literature. What we had at the time, in the late 1990s, were mostly top-down sources of information for teachers wanting to engage in task design such as a manageable number of studies in the task-based research literature, incipient specific task-based programmes around the world, and an acknowledgment of the reality that general teacher education initiatives at the time were minimally task-based.

From the mid-1980s to the mid-1990s (i.e., the literature that was available to us as we began our programme), the theoretical work emerging from scholars like Mike Long, Graham Crookes, and Susan Gass had a major impact on research into the interactive features of tasks. The literature available to us at the time we initiated our programme back in the late 1990s was rich, but still manageable in terms of the number of studies that had been published. From a theoretical point of view while designing our programme, we had access to general theories such as the Interaction Hypothesis (Long, 1985; Gass, 1997) and the Output Hypothesis (Swain, 1993), and two specific task-based theories with targeted and well-defined research agendas, such as the Cognition Hypothesis (Robinson, 2001) and the then emerging Trade-off Hypothesis (Foster & Skehan, 1996; Skehan & Foster, 1997; Skehan, 2009), in relation to task performance.

From an operational perspective, the work of Pica et al. (1993) showed us how we may distribute information among participants (the split versus shared design variable), or how information may flow among task users (the one-way versus two-way/multiple way distinction), what participant roles and their goals in the task may be (convergent versus divergent), or whether tasks could have a single or many solutions (open versus closed tasks). At the time, the main concerns of researchers and theorists in the field were with how those design decisions would affect interactional patterns among learners, working on the assumption that interaction had benefits for language learning. These design variables are still of utmost importance today since they determine information distribution, information flow and management, and interaction opportunities for learners.

Developments in the TBLT literature

At the time we were establishing our new programme, issues had begun to emerge with regard to two particular research agendas (interactive and cognitive), such as the lack of generalisability of studies, the emergence of isolated studies, or the lack of replication. Since the time of the establishment of the programme, and indeed over the last four decades, TBLT as a field for research and pedagogy has seen an enormous growth and sophistication in the use of quantitative, qualitative, and mixed methods research, as well as development and divergence in theoretical underpinnings. Through researching tasks, we have also learned a lot about pedagogic task design features, such as interactive and cognitive features.

Studies into interaction and development continued throughout the 1990s and then into the 2000s and the association between interaction and learning became well established (see Mackey & Goo, 1997, for one of the first meta-analyses on interaction). The pedagogic unit around which this body of research revolved was not always a task as we understand it in TBLT, but it was often the case that the research focused on tasks as the TBLT literature would understand them.

Soon after the advent of the interactive agenda, the cognitive agenda in TBLT came in like a storm. The work of Robinson (1995, 2001, 2003) and Skehan (Skehan & Foster, 1997) largely operated as reference points for task-based researchers around the world who were trying to conduct research within the

TBLT field in the 2000s and part of the 2010s (i.e., after we had begun to establish our programme). Frameworks included task variables such as the number of elements, reasoning demands, pre-task planning time, and task repetition. Skehan's trade-off model (2009) was consolidated and Robinson's model looking at complexity, interaction, and learner factors generated a growing number of studies. The socio-cultural, socio-cognitive, and constructivist agendas of TBLT also moved to greater prominence (see, e.g., East, 2012) as well as new approaches like Dynamic Systems Theories (see, e.g., Thelen & Smith, 2007).

By this time, we had learned a considerable amount about task design in the process of pursuing the goals of the above research agendas and theoretical frameworks. We had learned to consider how many elements participants may need to deal with during task performance (i.e., how much reasoning is involved), how much perspective-taking the task entails (see Jackson & Suethanapornkul, 2013, for a meta-analysis on task complexity factors), and how this may affect learners' performance. We had also learned, from emerging planning time studies, how tweaking planning time at different phases of the task may impact performance (see Ortega, 1999, for an early discussion of this that informed our own work), and whether we might wish to include a single task, or whether multi-tasking is involved.

Prior knowledge through content, task type, or exact task repetition (Bygate, 2001) has also been heavily investigated in research in the last few decades. Studies into these cognitive agendas were primarily interested in measuring the effects of task design on complexity, accuracy, and fluency in task performance. Later on in this agenda, researchers such as Révész (Révész, 2009; Révész et al., 2015) would stress the need to focus not just on performance and outcome measures but also on the intermediary, underlying cognitive mechanisms involved in task complexity manipulations, such as their impact on conceptualisation and formulation, or on attention and memory. The interest in TBLT and technology was there from very early in the field and was consolidated, in the last decade, with the work of researchers such as González-Lloret (e.g., González-Lloret & Ortega, 2014) and Ziegler (e.g., Ziegler & González-Lloret, 2022). Surprisingly, research into task-based pragmatics appeared considerably later in the task-based agenda. While the first few studies on TBLT and pragmatics emerged in the early 2010s, the consolidation of the strand on task-based pragmatics did not come until later (Taguchi & Kim, 2016, 2018). Finally, the focus on task-based writing and the issue of oral and written modes were only advanced in the second half of the 2010s (Byrnes & Manchón, 2014; Gilabert et al., 2016; Vasylets et al., 2017).

It is clear, then, that we now have a good deal of information available to us, emerging from both theorising and empirical studies. Despite having access to all that source material on task-based theory and design, this type of knowledge alone does not say anything about the actual teaching and learning needs of particular stakeholders in particular contexts. In the context of our own programme, for example, there was still the need to obtain information about the type of tasks our students would be able to perform outside class in the realm of communication (such as advertising, public relations, journalism, and audiovisual communication). It was here that the work of Long (e.g., 2005) on NA was crucial to our understanding of what our programme would require.

From needs analysis to task design

At an early point in our language programme development, we needed to combine the kind of top-down knowledge coming from the literature with actual information about the needs of our learners. With three teacher-researchers and a minimal budget of a few hundred euro, we identified the stakeholders involved in the sector of communication (e.g., advertising agencies, newspapers, news websites, press offices) and we conducted a NA over a period of three months by using multiple sources and multiple methods. The goal of our NA was to identify the most frequent tasks communication experts need to perform and obtain detailed information about performance conditions (see Gilabert, 2005, for a NA focusing on journalists in Catalonia, Spain). Information coming from face-to-face interviews, observations, and surveys was triangulated, and several sources, such as domain experts (journalists using the L2 in their jobs) or company representatives, participated in the study. Speech and written samples were collected and analysed. The three of us, in the double role of researchers and teachers, participated in data collection and analysis, which took most of a whole four-month term. NA provided us with the following insights:

- Very precise task descriptions — we obtained information about the context of each task: their goals, steps, expected outcomes; their physical space; tasks' linguistic demands, participants, and interaction; tasks' cognitive demands, communication, and technology, among several other aspects; their interconnectedness.
- The language associated with each task — since in TBLT the use of language is heavily contingent and contextualised in accordance with the goals of the particular task at hand.
- Information about the cognitive complexity of each task — the reasoning demands and the number of elements the tasks imposed on task users; whether they were undertaken in the here-and-now/there-and-then; whether they were performed under time pressure, among many other aspects.
- Information about performance standards and what constituted a successfully or poorly performed task.
- The general functioning of the discourse community of journalists.

However, as Malicka et al. (2019) have pointed out for NA in general, at the end of our own NA several empirical issues remained unresolved: (1) how the information obtained in the NA would transfer to actual task and syllabus design; (2) how the information about the variables contributing to the task's intrinsic complexity and domain experts' perceptions of difficulty could be used to manipulate such features in instructionally sound ways during pedagogic task design; and (3) how task information could be used for sequencing and grading pedagogic tasks, one of the unresolved conundrums in TBLT.

As illustrated in Table 1, information about real-life tasks obtained through NA provided information about the configuration of task structures and the number of participants involved in a task (e.g., one speaker and a whole audience, two colleagues working over the phone, a small team making a joint decision or designing a project), how information flowed among participants, their roles, and what was a well-performed or poorly-performed task. These impacted pedagogic decisions about whether to design monologic or dialogic tasks, and whether to break down complexity by creating a number of sub-tasks in preparation for a final complex task.

Table 1. From NA to task design

Type of task	Under what conditions does communication happen?	What language is associated with the task?
Real-life target task	– number and role of participants – information flow – psychosocial profiles – performance standards	– communication channel – linguistic features – technical vocabulary – discourse features
Pedagogic task version	– monologic/dialogic – assigning profiles to participants – degree of complexity – integration of technology	– vocabulary items – multi-word units – grammatical features – pragmatic moves – phonetic contrasts

For example, when designing tasks to prepare learners for e-mail writing in a professional context, criteria contributing to complexity came from task descriptions in NA, but the design was also adjusted on the basis of existing task performance models such as Skehan's or Robinson's respective hypotheses. In Table 2, the criteria emerging from NA as well as from what we learned after the first implementation of the course led us to include criteria such as:

– the familiarity and status of the people writing (e.g., two colleagues as opposed to a boss and an employee);

Chapter 2. Task design **29**

- the causal reasoning involved in interpreting each message (e.g., was the point of each message easy to interpret or did it push learners to work out several possible interpretations?);
- the level of deciphering people's intentions in each message (i.e., ranging from straightforward and transparent to opaque and indirect);
- the number of elements the responder had to handle simultaneously (e.g., the number and quality of requests in each message);
- the frequency of the words and expressions in the input (i.e., ranging from familiar and highly frequent words to unfamiliar low frequency words).

Table 2. Example of criteria used for sequencing e-mail writing tasks in a programme

Condition	Simple	Less simple	Complex	More complex
± familiarity or ± equal status	Familiarity with interlocutors/ Same status (colleagues)	Less familiarity/ high status (e.g., boss)	Unfamiliar/high status (unknown person in an institution)	Very unfamiliar/ very high status (a personality)
± causal reasoning	Low reasoning demands (simple info transfer and independent instructions (e.g., ask for and offer info)	Moderately low reasoning demands (info transfer, minor reasoning and independent instructions) (e.g., ask for something in an unfavourable situation)	High reasoning demands (complex reasoning and interconnected instructions) (e.g., in an unfavourable situation, try to persuade by providing convincing reasons)	Very high reasoning demands (highly complex reasoning and interconnected instructions) (e.g., try to justify a major mistake and persuade interlocutor to still help you)
± intentional reasoning	Explicit message (e.g., straightforward)	Less explicit message (e.g., some irony)	Implicit message (e.g., irony and an implicit threat)	Very implicit message (e.g., a hard to figure out intention)
± elements	Very few instructions	Few instructions	Many instructions	A lot of instructions
± frequency of input	Frequent/known input (e.g., thanks for)	Less frequent or known input	Infrequent/ unknown input	Very infrequent/ unknown input

Task and syllabus design beyond needs analysis

Despite the fact that we could use theory and task-based models as well as the information from NA for the design of tasks to inform our first draft of the programme, which took another four-month term, syllabus design was far from being completed. A first implementation of the course was needed in order to get feedback from teachers and students about how well task designs and task sequences in the syllabus were working. Critical voices in the field (e.g., Van den Branden, 2009) would later suggest that tasks are not blueprints for action and presented evidence from a number of studies carried out in authentic classrooms that teachers and students reinterpret the tasks they are offered by syllabus designers in ways that suit their own goals, perceived needs, interaction styles, and personal preferences. They often change their designs, deviate from suggested procedures, and go about task implementation in their own idiosyncratic ways.

The teacher and learner adaptations of tasks in real classrooms are exactly what happened in our programme. During our first implementation in the first term of the second year, teachers reinterpreted our task designs and adapted some of the task goals as well as the task structures (pre-tasks, tasks, post-tasks) we had designed for them. They detected gaps in the language issues and form focus to be covered through tasks, and they provided useful information on learners' perceptions of the interest, difficulty, and usefulness that tasks generated. Adjustments were made after the first iteration of the course tasks, which helped the tasks work more precisely and smoothly the second time. Once again, feedback from teachers and learners was collected for the second iteration, which already consolidated some of the tasks and gave teachers and learners opportunities to come to their own understanding about the effectiveness of the tasks. Through this process we learned that task design is also about task re-design, revisiting task designs and task sequences, and applying minor changes and adaptations, modifying NA for changes in the field and the community, and integrating stakeholder views in task design. Each of these elements was (and is) crucial. I am pleased to report that now, 25 years later, the programme is still running.

Task and syllabus design in the 21st century

In this final section, I will explore what new designers and teachers are currently facing and what task and syllabus design may look like as we move further into the 21st century. The TBLT research and pedagogic agendas have yielded powerful lessons about how to design tasks and syllabi that will contribute to learners' L2 performance and development to maximum effect. However, I believe that task and syllabus design need to open up to principles outside TBLT that provide considerable room for bottom-up design involving teachers and teacher communities. In the remainder of this section, I will discuss other fields that may inform task-based design, such as *human-machine interaction design* and *learning design*. I will then reflect on how principles and practices coming out of those neighbouring fields may generate new spaces for innovation and new avenues for task-based design in the 21st century.

Task design in the 21st century

When new teachers and syllabus designers are faced with the complex and sophisticated job of designing tasks for L2 use and development, they will need to become acquainted with and equip themselves with a theoretical, empirical, and design toolkit that will help them to make informed decisions about task and syllabus design. A range of features needs to be considered in task design (see Table 3). The design toolkit will include:

- theories informing task and syllabus design, including indirect theories such as the Interaction Hypothesis and Output Hypothesis, and direct theories such as the Cognition Hypothesis and Limited Capacity Model;
- interactive features determining information flow and information distribution during task performance: split versus shared, one-way versus two-way/multiple-way tasks, open versus closed, convergent versus divergent;
- cognitive features contributing to the simplicity or complexity of each task, including the number of elements, the amount of reasoning, the familiarity with the task or topic, or time available for planning the task;
- knowledge about focus on form, including the what (i.e., dimensions and features of language), when (e.g., preemptively, during task performance, or post-actively in the form of delayed feedback), and how (through input enhancement techniques, corrective oral feedback by means of recasts, among others) in the context of language lessons that are mainly driven by meaning;
- knowledge about the effect of manipulating pragmatic features during task design and their effect on interlanguage pragmatics;
- being acquainted with the intercultural dimension of tasks;
- information about how to integrate individual differences and accommodate special needs in task design.

Taking into account the range of task features to be considered, as illustrated in Table 3, task design can become an overwhelming endeavour. Even if teachers take part in teacher education or professional development programmes and have

Table 3. Task features to be considered during task design

Task design features				
Interactive variables	Cognitive variables	Input features	Individual difference features	Other
Split v. shared	± no. of elements	Input enhancement	Dyslexia	Pragmatic moves
Convergent v. divergent	± reasoning demands	Input flooding	Refugee perspective	Phonetic dimension
One-way v. two-way	± perspective-taking	Input elaboration		Intercultural dimension
Open v. closed	± planning time			
	± prior knowledge/ task repetition			

opportunities to test out their designs, task design is often a solitary experience where teachers are left to their own resources. In a recent NA for the creation of a task design tool (Castellví et al., 2024), teachers reported often working individually during task design, with some instances of joint task design in small groups of teachers. They saw a disconnect between theories of task design and actual practical decision-making. They were faced with what they perceived to be a vast and scattered literature that does not always translate well from research into practice. They also reported lacking time and resources for task design, and they suggested that task design requires a considerable investment of time, planning, and effort that typically get lost once the task is taught. In sum, task design requires considerable expertise and resilience from teachers.

The above conditions may render task design difficult and even discouraging. This reality led us in our research teams at the University of Barcelona to create a task design tool that would tackle all of those problems while facilitating task design. We put together a group of researchers that included experts in second language acquisition (SLA), alongside experts in task design, computational linguistics, language teaching, computer programming, and web design, to develop a tool for assisting with L2 task design.

Based on the principles of TBLT, models, and frameworks (e.g., Long, 2015), we have recently developed the task design tool taskGen,[1] a semi-automated, flexible, and adaptive web-based tool designed to assist L2 task designers in creating tasks for L2 learning. The tool guides teachers in the design of communicative tasks, including their associated pre-tasks and post-tasks (see Castellví et al., 2024, for a full description), and it integrates all knowledge about task design and focus of form that we have accrued over the last four decades.

---

1. https://taskgen.eu

In order to create the tool, we needed to open up our task-based design approach to include theories, constructs, concepts, and practices coming from fields such as Natural Language Processing (NLP), human-machine interaction, or learning design.

Natural Language Processing (NLP)

As a subfield of artificial intelligence (AI), we learned from NLP that programming can enable computers to understand, interpret, and generate human language, with important consequences for focus on form during task-based design. In the taskGen project, the focus of the NLP module is specifically directed towards automating the processing of written texts, as typically used in pre-tasks, student prompts in tasks, or post-tasks. NLP aids teachers in swiftly identifying and extracting pertinent linguistic information (words, collocations, verb tenses, among other dimensions and features) so that they can easily apply focus on form techniques automatically, such as input enhancement (through colour and font size highlighting). As used in taskGen, the "analyse" functionality automatically analyses a piece of written text inserted by the teacher and identifies linguistic traits in the text at different linguistic levels (i.e., morphology, syntax, and pragmatics). This automatic analysis is performed thanks to existing tools, such as the Stanza NLP package (Qi et al., 2020), a neural pipeline with several processors for tokenisation, lemmatisation, PoS-tagging, and dependency parsing, as well as other resources which have been especially developed for the taskGen project (e.g., pragmatic formulae dictionary).

While the linguistic features associated with each task can be obtained through careful analysis after NA or by observing learners' linguistic gaps and needs during task implementation, I believe that NLP can systematically help teachers with text analysis (e.g., finding pragmatic expressions in a dialogue from a TV series) during task design. NLP is going to be an inevitable feature of task design in the near future, as in the case of taskGen, by which teachers can explore the linguistic characteristics of text that will help them with focus on form decisions during task design. Focusing on the language associated with each task and each text will certainly impact how learners pay attention to and process language during task performance.

Human-machine interaction

Interaction design focuses on the relationship of humans and products (although see Schleidgen et al., 2023, for a broader discussion of "interaction"), with our main interest being on the relationship between teachers and our task design website. Of particular interest to us is the interaction between teachers and designers and the space (our website) for task design, the motion, the optionality and flow, as well as sound and atmosphere created by our web tool. Typically, interaction design requires designers to "empathise" with their end users, which is what teachers and syllabus designers can do through NA, since the more they know about the needs of their community of learners, the better job they can do with their designs. For each task, it is necessary to determine the needs to be solved, ideate or generate the solution, create a prototype, and test the prototype with users and stakeholders. In our context, knowledge about interaction design can apply to both our creation of the taskGen tool and to teachers creating their own tasks. Interaction design has been part of our tool development which began with the identification of teachers' needs (Arnold, 2023, 2024). We generated ideas for a website that would meet those teachers' needs and solved each of the identified problems, and we created a prototype that we are currently testing with hundreds of users worldwide. I also believe a lot of the ideas coming from interaction design can be transferred to supporting teachers in task design through teacher education, where teachers learn about and empathise with the communities they are to serve before ideating and creating their tasks. Task prototypes need to be created and tested and re-tested, tweaked, and adjusted to better serve the needs of the learners and to lead them to successful L2 performance and development.

Learning designer software

As we learned from Van Driel and Berry (2012; cited in Laurillard et al. 2018), knowledge development is "a complex process that is highly specific to the context, situation, and person" (p. 1044). Teaching can turn into a design science "to keep improving its practice, in a principled way, building on the work of others" (Laurillard, 2012, p. 1045). An excellent instantiation of this knowledge development is the software programme Learning Designer. Developed at University College London by Laurillard and her team (Laurillard, 2012; Laurillard et al., 2018), the Learning Designer supports the process of sharing "instructional products" by developing the teacher-as-designer, in this case by scaffolding teachers' development and representation of learning designs that can be shared online and adapted by other teachers. The creation of a community of teachers is central to the idea of such a designer.

Inspired by the work of Laurillard (2012) and Laurillard et al., (2018), in taskGen we have incorporated two important functionalities:

- the "cloning" function which serves the purpose of creating a copy of the task design in order to create slightly different versions of the designed task that will adapt to the different levels, preferences or needs of the different learners within each group of students;

– the "sharing" function which allows teachers to share their designs with other teachers and get feedback from their adaptations and implementations.

In line with Laurillard, taskGen leans towards the idea of creating a sense of community and shared knowledge among teachers. At least from the cognitive-interactionist strand of TBLT, the idea of community building was more assumed rather than directly tackled by the research agendas. The incorporation of a learning design perspective can only enrich debates within the TBLT community and therefore help teachers with their task and syllabus design.

Conclusion

In this chapter I have provided a short historical overview of the TBLT field in general, and task and syllabus design in particular, in the last four decades, and have used this to inform and illustrate my direct experiences as a teacher-designer involved in programme development. A number of conclusions can be drawn from the ideas presented in this chapter.

First, it is undeniable that task and syllabus design have attracted the attention of many policy makers as well as teachers and syllabus designers all over the world. Evidence of this is seen in the exponential growth of task-based programmes as well as task-based teacher education and development courses around the world: in Europe (e.g., the University of Groningen, the University of Barcelona, Universitat Oberta de Catalunya, University College London); in the US (Norquest College, Indiana University, Georgia State University, Florida International University, Georgetown University, among others), and Oceania (The University of Auckland and Victoria University of Wellington in New Zealand, and Curtin University in Australia), and more and more in Africa (South Africa, Swaziland, Kenya) and Latin America (Ecuador, Colombia, Chile, among others). TBLT courses are not limited to university settings: they also feature in private language schools and entities, teacher cooperatives (Serveis Linguistics Barcelona) or collaboration projects for the introduction of TBLT in schools (Swaziland). TBLT is also becoming part of national language policies in many countries around the world for the teaching of foreign languages (China, Thailand, Indonesia). As a consequence of this proliferation of TBLT as an approach to L2 learning, and in order for TBLT initiatives to thrive, facilitating and systematising task design is an important priority. This, in turn, should generate further research that will influence pedagogy in the form of sustained feedback between these two core dimensions of the TBLT endeavour (research and practice).

Second, throughout this chapter I have aimed to emphasise the multi-faceted nature of task design. For task and syllabus design to be meaningful and successful, a combination of sources needs to be drawn on by teaching communities, and task design must include the voices, knowledge, and experience of its ultimate stakeholders for it to be effective and improve language use and language learning. That is, information and knowledge coming from the vast and rich literature available to teachers and task designers needs to be combined with information emerging from stakeholders such as domain experts, teachers themselves, and learners and their communities. Only the combination of top-down and bottom-up approaches to task design can guarantee sound and meaningful designs.

Third, while the literature can provide teachers and syllabus designers with a few fundamental constructs and concepts, as well as with empirical evidence about how task design may affect language use and language development, the use of NA within communities needs to be promoted (Gilabert & Malicka, forthcoming) for it to inform design decisions that will have important consequences for task implementation and language use and learning. I would say at this point that NA can take many shapes and forms, and it can therefore be applied by institutions with considerable resources (governments, universities) but also by communities with more limited resources. As this chapter has demonstrated with regard to interaction design and the Learning Designer, end users and stakeholders (teachers, learners) should be involved in the process of task design, and the information obtained through NA can be fed back to the ideation, prototyping, and implementation of task design.

Fourth, opening up the area of task and syllabus design to new perspectives has been extremely useful and productive in the development of the taskGen design tool in our group. The privileged combination in our mixed team of knowledge coming from SLA, task and syllabus design, needs analysis, focus on form, natural language processing, interaction design, and learning design has made it possible to create a tool that teachers can use for the design of tasks, for cloning tasks to achieve the integration of diversity in classrooms, and for teachers to share their task designs with other users of the tool as well as co-construct tasks with other members of the community. Technology can provide the kinds of innovation that relate to the very basic features of task design: its recursive nature where tasks need to be designed and redesigned until they become effective; its adaptability and personalisation of teaching and learning; and its dynamic nature that combines knowledge and information sources coming from multiple perspectives.

In addition to the enormous advances we have seen in the field in the last four decades, exciting challenges lay ahead of us. At a time when AI, and its most well-known instantiation ChatGPT, may be seen as a quick and easy solution to most teachers' problems, we need to claim the importance of engaging in intelligent human design. AI has certainly become a fascination among teachers and designers all over the world. Although rapidly changing, significant limitations affect AI because it draws mainly on summaries, abstracts, and public access documents (as mentioned by one of the reviewers). At least for now, ChatGPT does not contain the rich and meaningful type of knowledge that teachers and syllabus designers can generate on the basis of the literature, NA analysis, and the involvement of teachers and students in their community through interaction design and learning design. As suggested by a reviewer of this chapter, what ChatGPT does not have is the imagination to create new content, even if it appears to do so by mashing existing content. There is therefore considerable room for human intelligence to thrive in task and syllabus design in ways that will continue to attract many teachers and designers across the globe.

Funding

The studies and project included in this chapter were made possible by Grant PID2020-119009RB-I00 funded by the Ministerio de Ciencia, Innovación y Universidades of the Spanish government, and the National Research Agency (AEI) 10.13039/501100011033. I am also grateful for the support of the Catalan government to our research group by means of Grant 2021SGR0303. Thanks to the members of the GRAL research group (https://ubgral.wordpress.com/) for their relentless support and resources, and to Aleksandra Malicka for her feedback on the first draft of this chapter.

Acknowledgements

Special thanks to the people of the Blanquerna Communication Studies Department at Universitat Ramon Llull who made the language programme possible. For tool access please contact us at taskgenproject@gmail.com.

References

Arnold, G. (2023). Teacher perceptions on task design & technological integration in lesson planning for the EFL/ESL classroom [Unpublished masters' thesis]. Universitat de Barcelona.

Arnold, G. (2024, January 23–24). *Teacher perceptions on task design & technological integration in lesson planning for the EFL/ESL classroom* [Conference presentation]. UPCEL 2024: Language Beyond Boundaries, Madrid, Spain.

Bygate, M. (2001). Effects of task repetition on the structure and control of oral language. In M. Bygate, P. Skehan, P., & M. Swain (Eds.), *Researching pedagogic tasks. Second language learning, teaching, and testing* (pp. 23–48). Routledge.

Byrnes, H., & Manchón, R.M. (2014). Task-based language learning: Insights from and for L2 writing – an introduction. In H. Byrnes & R. Manchón (Eds.), *Task-based language learning – Insights from and for L2 writing* (pp. 1–23). John Benjamins.

Castellví, J., Gilabert, R., & Comelles Pujadas, E. (2024). Automating task design: Bridging the gap between second language research and L2 instruction. *Tecnologías para la Investigación en Segundas Lenguas, 3*, 1–21.

East, M. (2012). Addressing the intercultural via task-based language teaching: Possibility or problem? *Language and Intercultural Communication, 12*(1), 56–73.

Foster, P., & Skehan, P. (1996). The influence of planning and task type on second language performance. *Studies in Second Language Acquisition, 18*(3), 299–323.

Gass, S.M. (1997). *Input, interaction, and the second language learner*. Lawrence Erlbaum Associates.

Gilabert, R. (2005). Evaluating the use of multiple sources and methods in needs analysis: A case study of journalists in the autonomous community of Catalonia (Spain). In M. Long (Ed.), *Second language needs analysis* (pp. 182–199). Cambridge University Press.

Gilabert, R., Manchón, R.M., & Vasylets, O. (2016). Mode in theoretical and empirical TBLT research: Advancing research agendas. *Annual Review of Applied Linguistics, 36*, 117–135.

Gilabert, R. & Malicka, A. (forthcoming). *From task-based needs analysis to task and syllabus design: Insights from across educational contexts*. John Benjamins.

González-Lloret, M., & Ortega, L. (2014). *Technology-mediated TBLT: Researching technology and tasks*. John Benjamins.

Jackson, D., & Suethanapornkul, S. (2013). The cognition hypothesis: A synthesis and meta-analysis of research on second language task complexity. *Language Learning, 63*(2), 330–367.

Laurillard, D., Kennedy, E., Charlton, P., Wild, J., & Dimakopoulos, D. (2018). Using technology to develop teachers as designers of TEL: Evaluating the learning designer. *British Journal of Educational Technology, 49*(6), 1044–1058.

Laurillard, D. (2012). *Teaching as a design science: Building pedagogical patterns for learning and technology*. Routledge.

Long, M.H. (1985). A role for instruction in second language acquisition: Task-based language teaching. In K. Hyltenstam & M. Pienemann (Eds.), *Modelling and assessing second language acquisition* (pp. 77–79). Multilingual Matters.

Long, M.H. (2005). *Second language needs analysis*. Cambridge University Press.

Long, M.H. (2015). *Second language acquisition and task-based language teaching*. Wiley-Blackwell.

Mackey, A. & Goo, J. (2007). Interaction research in SLA: A meta-analysis and research synthesis. In A. Mackey (Ed.), *Conversational interaction in second language acquisition: A series of empirical studies* (pp. 407–453). Oxford University Press.

Malicka, A., Gilabert, R., & Norris, J.M. (2019). From needs analysis to task design: Insights from an English for Specific Purposes context. *Language Teaching Research*, 23(1), 78–106.

Norris, J.M. (2016). Current uses for task-based language assessment. *Annual Review of Applied Linguistics*, 36, 230–244.

Ortega, L. (1999). Planning and focus on form in L2 oral performance. *Studies in Second Language Acquisition*, 21(1), 109–148.

Pica, T., Kanagy, R., & Falodun, J. (1993). Choosing and using communication tasks for second language instruction. In G. Crookes & S. Gass (Eds.), *Tasks and language learning. Integrating theory and practice* (pp. 9–34.) Multilingual Matters.

Qi, P., Zhang, Y., Zhang, Y., Bolton, J., & Manning, C. (2020). Stanza: A Python natural language processing toolkit for many human languages. *Proceedings of the 58th Annual Meeting of the Association for Computational Linguistics: System Demonstrations*, 101–108.

Révész, A. (2009). Task complexity, focus on form, and second language development. *Studies in Second Language Acquisition*, 31(3), 437–470.

Révész, A., Michel, M., & Gilabert, R. (2015). Measuring cognitive task demands using dual-task methodology, subjective self-rating, and expert judgments. *Studies in Second Language Acquisition*, 38(4), 703–737.

Robinson, P. (1995). Task complexity and second language narrative discourse. *Language Learning*, 45(1), 99–140.

Robinson, P. (2001). Task complexity, cognitive resources, and syllabus design: A triadic framework for examining task influences on SLA. In P. Robinson (Ed.). *Cognition and second language instruction* (pp. 287–318). Cambridge University Press.

Robinson, P. (2003). The cognition hypothesis, task design and adult task-based language learning. *Second Language Studies*, 21(2), 45–107.

Schleidgen, S., Friedrich, O., Gerlek, S. et al. (2023). The concept of "interaction" in debates on human–machine interaction. *Humanities and Sciences Communications*, 10, 551, 1–13.

Skehan, P. (2009). Modelling second language performance: Integrating complexity, accuracy, fluency, and lexis, *Applied Linguistics*, 30(4), 510–532.

Skehan, P. & Foster, P. (1997). Task type and task processing conditions as influences on foreign language performance. *Language Teaching Research*, 1(3), 185–211.

Swain, M. (1993). The output hypothesis: Just speaking and writing aren't enough. *Canadian Modern Language Review*, 50(1), 158–164.

Taguchi, N., & Kim, Y. (2016). Collaborative dialogue in learning pragmatics: Pragmatic-related episodes as an opportunity for learning request-making. *Applied Linguistics*, 37, 416–437.

Taguchi, N., & Kim, Y. (2018). Task-based approaches to teaching and assessing pragmatics: An overview. In N. Taguchi & Y. Kim (Eds.), *Task-based approaches to teaching and assessing pragmatics* (pp. 1–26). John Benjamins.

Thelen, E., & Smith, L.B. (2007). Dynamic systems theories. In W. Damon & R.M. Lerner (Eds.), *Handbook of child psychology, Volume I: Theoretical models of human development* (pp. 258–312).

Van den Branden, K. (2009). Mediating between predetermined order and chaos: The role of the teacher in task-based language education. *International Journal of Applied Linguistics*, 19(3), 264–285.

Vasylets, O.; Gilabert, R. & Manchón, R. (2017). The effects of mode and task complexity on second language production. *Language Learning, 67*(2), 394–430.

Ziegler, N. & González-Lloret, M. (2022). Introduction. *The Routledge handbook of second language acquisition and technology* (pp. 1–5). Routledge.

CHAPTER 3

How real is real?[*]
Can task-based language courses properly prepare students for reality?

Kris Van den Branden
University of Leuven

This chapter addresses the link between activity in the task-based classroom and target language use outside the classroom. It starts from the observation that needs analyses, constituting an essential part of task-based curriculum design, serve to identify the target language tasks that additional language learners are expected to perform in "real life," more particularly in relevant situations that require the comprehension of input or production of output in the target language. To prepare students for the latter, task-based language teaching builds on a series of gradually more complex pedagogic tasks. But how "real" are those, and how real do they need to be? In which ways are links between pedagogical tasks and outside-school language use established to foster students' competences to use the target language for real-life purposes and to participate in interactions outside the classroom? To answer these questions, I will explore the notion of task authenticity in this chapter. Deconstructing that notion into different layers of authenticity will allow me to describe different ways in which links between task-based classroom activity and real-life language use can be established. The different types of links will be illustrated with examples taken from authentic (no pun intended) classrooms.

Keywords: real-world tasks, pedagogic tasks, needs analysis, curriculum design, target language use domains, authenticity

Introduction

Establishing a link with reality — and with language use outside the classroom — can safely be called an inherent key feature of task-based language teaching

---

[*] Revised version of a plenary given to the 6th International TBLT Conference, Leuven, Belgium, 2015.

https://doi.org/10.1075/tblt.17.03van
Available under the CC BY-NC 4.0 license. © 2025 John Benjamins Publishing Company

(TBLT). That link becomes particularly manifest in the design stage of devising a task-based curriculum, more particularly in needs analysis. Drawing on a variety of methods and sources, needs analyses attempt to document in detail the kinds of tasks that students need to be able to perform in real life and the kind of language use that is involved in completing these tasks. The results of a needs analysis directly inform the task-based curriculum, in the sense that, in the classroom, students are expected to gradually develop the language competences to perform the target tasks.

It could be argued, however, that needs analyses typically feature at the input or preparatory stage of the actual language course: they are carried out and reported before any student has entered a classroom. At the same time, needs analyses have an obvious link with the expected output of a task-based language course. But what happens in between? To what extent does there need to be a link between outside-school reality and classroom activity throughout the course? Is that link necessary to ensure that course output (in terms of students' language development) coincides with the output that is aimed at by the teacher? In other words, do all activities that students engage in while in the classroom need to involve some link with real-life language use?

In his seminal articles on TBLT, Long (1985) described classroom activities in a task-based classroom as being shaped by "pedagogical tasks." If sequenced cleverly, those pedagogical tasks could constitute a series of gradual approximations to target task performance. That, however, might suggest that there might be good reasons why, in the early stages of any task-based language course, reality should be stripped from the classroom task for pedagogical purposes (hence, "pedagogical task"), for instance not to make things too complex for the learner. However, if that is the case, what guarantee is there that students will ultimately develop the kind of language competences that will allow them to perform target tasks in authentic situations? At which stage, and in which guises, should reality and target language use be integrated into classroom tasks?

The question of authenticity goes right to the heart of TBLT. As a research-based pedagogy, it was born out of a fundamental discontent with the observation that students in structure-based courses built up substantial explicit knowledge of the language, yet were often found to lack the competence to apply that knowledge effectively to perform communicative tasks. Thus, the question becomes how to avoid students attending a task-based course facing the same kind of transfer problem that we have been told students in structure-based courses have suffered from. The easy answer seems to be: by having students perform communicative tasks in which they have to exchange meaningful messages. However, even in a task-based course, students find themselves in a tightly secluded environment (the classroom), which, as Meddings and Thornbury (2017) pointed out, can turn out to be a very artificial environment that makes true conversation (i.e., the way people interact outside the classroom) virtually impossible. Moreover, even in task-based syllabi, language input can be stilted or restricted in terms of registers and styles, and, as a result, not reflect the way target language users outside the classroom talk and sound.

In this chapter, I will explore the link between task-based work in the classroom and language use in the target language domain. The main question this chapter will address can be formulated as follows: if the goal of the task-based language course is for students to develop the competences to perform authentic tasks in real life, to what extent should what students actually do in task-based classrooms be related to what they are expected to do with the target language in real life? In other words, to what extent should teachers or students attempt to introduce real life in the task-based classroom?

Before I start answering the key question of the authenticity-classroom task interface, a note on the term "real life." Many of the needs analyses that have been documented in the TBLT field focus on work-related domains (see, e.g., Gilabert, this volume). For instance, a task-based language course preparing second language learners of the official language of a particular country for a nursing job will typically be based on a needs analysis that describes the kinds of tasks that nurses will have to perform on the job and the kinds of language use that task completion in the context requires; in the task-based classroom, second language learners are prepared to perform those tasks. In that case, one could argue that there is a clear and conscious — both temporal and physical — barrier between the language course and task performance on the authentic job floor. "Real life" is the job; "learning for real life" happens in the classroom. In some cases, however, the classroom, or rather a future classroom, can be "real life." That is an insight that tends to be overlooked in the literature. For instance, in the academic strands of higher secondary education or in second language courses offered to students who study abroad, students will typically develop the language competences that they will need in the higher education they want to enrol in: for example, they will learn to write summaries or read academic articles for comprehension in order to learn new content. Clearly, those are the kinds of tasks that they will be expected to perform in the target language in higher education far more than in other domains of their life during the years that they are enrolled as a university student. Real life is the educational domain. It is the next classroom, so to speak.

In respect of real life as the educational domain, I find it somewhat awkward to read that needs analyses are of no use for students in compulsory education; those students seem to be portrayed as creatures without linguistic needs. They surely are not. For example, a needs analysis describing the needs of adolescent newcomers entering Flanders (age range 12–18 years) made it clear that their

Dutch language learning needs could be situated in four domains: (a) they need to acquire Dutch in order to use it to learn new content across the curriculum; in other words, they need to become linguistically ready to be successful students in Flemish secondary education; (b) they need to acquire Dutch in order to integrate into their school environment and make new friends; (c) they also need to integrate into social networks outside school (e.g., leisure-time activities); and (d) they have to acquire Dutch to participate in Flemish society (e.g. shopping, taking their parents to the doctor, brokering for their parents or siblings, communicating with community services), as most of their family members have a relatively lower Dutch language proficiency. Some of the tasks they are expected to perform are clearly related to life outside school, while others are directly related to the kinds of language tasks students in secondary education typically need to perform across the curriculum. Building on the needs analysis, task-based syllabi were developed to support the teachers of newcomer classes.

Authenticity in the task-based classroom

Authenticity is a useful term to explore the link between classroom activity and language use in the target domain. Tasks can be said to be authentic if they are closely linked to the tasks that people typically perform, or are expected to perform, in relevant target language domains. Authenticity is, however, a multidimensional concept; as such, it may be helpful to disentangle the different dimensions it comprises to establish the link between classroom activity and real life in more detail. In particular, I will distinguish between several types of authenticity:

1. *Contextual authenticity*: This refers to the extent to which the physical or virtual context in which the students find themselves is similar to the context in which target language users typically perform tasks. Instances of contexts are a classroom, a street, the entrance hall of a railway station, a kitchen, a restaurant, a shop, the virtual environment generated in an online game.
2. *Situational authenticity*: This refers to the extent to which the situations in which the students find themselves are similar to the situations in which target language users typically perform tasks. The concept "situation" refers to the conditions under which the task needs to be performed. These could be, for instance, temporal conditions like time pressure, social conditions like the relationship between interlocutors, output-related conditions like how much is at stake, or acoustic conditions such as how much background noise there is.

3. *Goal-related authenticity*: This refers to the extent to which the goals that the students have in mind while performing tasks are similar to the goals that target language users typically have in mind when performing similar tasks in real life. In this respect, it should be noted that one of the key defining characteristics of a task is its goal-orientedness.

4. *Interactional authenticity*: This refers to the extent to which the kinds of interactions in which students participate, and the interactional roles they are asked to adopt, are similar to the interactions and roles in which target language users typically engage.

5. *Content-related authenticity*: This refers to the extent to which the topics and content that are discussed are similar to the content and topics that are typically discussed by target language users in relevant situations.

6. *Linguistic authenticity*: This refers to the extent to which the linguistic elements (words, phrases, sounds, and so on) to which language learners are exposed, or which they are asked to use, are similar to the ones that target language users typically use or are exposed to in the classroom.

Taken together, the above different layers can be said to constitute the authenticity of the tasks that the students are asked to perform. The target tasks that are described in needs analyses can be said to be authentic in all respects (linguistically, content-wise, interactionally speaking, in terms of goals, situations, and contexts), at least if the needs analysis is properly done. Conversely, the grammar exercise in Example (1) below, which focuses on the verb tenses of conditional clauses, can be said to show very low levels of task authenticity, and that statement actually applies to all above-mentioned dimensions of authenticity. This is not to say that the activity is useless. Reducing authenticity may actually be the very goal and essence of the exercise: it is claimed to allow learners to (a) tightly focus on one specific grammatical aspect of the target language, and (b) consolidate their explicit knowledge related to that grammar rule. It builds on the premise that building up explicit knowledge about the grammar rules of the target language and automatising that knowledge through focused practice will help additional language learners to perform authentic tasks in a later stage by applying what they learned explicitly.

Example 1. Grammar exercise focusing on the conditional

Fill in the correct tense of the verb:

❏ *If I ... (to be) rich, I would buy a nice car.*
❏ *If I had known she was in hospital, I ... (to send) her a message.*
❏ *If I .... (get) there in time, I will be very happy.*
Etc.

The available empirical research strongly suggests that the impact of explicit grammar instruction (and, for the same matter, explicit vocabulary instruction) on students' communicative competence increases to the extent that it is skillfully integrated into, rather than isolated from, the performance of meaningful tasks (e.g., Benati & Schwieter, 2019; Cobb, 2010; Webb, 2019). Among other reasons, this has to do with the fact that what students are asked to do in Example (1) is, cognitively speaking, something fundamentally different from what they are asked to do when trying to produce a meaningful message in which specific instances of grammar knowledge are appropriately and correctly applied, and reaching a particular goal by doing so.

At the other end of the authenticity continuum, additional language learners acquire the target language outside a classroom (i.e., in relevant target language domains) without receiving any formal instruction. They are immersed in the language learning environment and in the performance of meaningful tasks which serve different goals than the mere learning of the language. For instance, at the age of 11 (just before they enter secondary education), children growing up in Flanders (the Dutch-speaking part of Belgium) have acquired, on average, a vocabulary in English of 3000 words (Peters et al., 2019). At that age, they have not received a single hour of formal English as Foreign Language (EFL) education, which starts at the age of 12. These children acquired all those words by playing English-medium digital and online games, watching programmes on television and online, listening to the lyrics of the pop songs they love, and singing them aloud. In other words, these young learners' early acquisition of EFL is the byproduct of behaviour that appears to be primarily driven by a desire to play games, get better at them, and to do so together with others; to enjoy music; to watch and enjoy movies, series, soaps, television shows, and video clips; to inform themselves and gain knowledge on topics they find of personal interest; to bond with valued others, both locally and internationally. Satisfying those kinds of desires happens to be mediated through the use of an additional language, which in many cases happens to be English today.

However powerful the type of implicit language learning through the performance of authentic tasks may be for certain groups of learners, research shows convincingly that classroom instruction does speed up the language learning process and may actually be crucial in terms of extending the students' linguistic repertoire and raising their accuracy levels (Lightbown & Spada, 2013). The question becomes where, in terms of authenticity, the task-based language classroom (which can be identified as an attempt to integrate focus on form skillfully into the performance of meaningful tasks) can be situated in the continuum ranging from the lowly authentic environment of the structure-based classroom to the highly authentic environment of relevant situations in which the target language is used for real-life purposes. Even in task-based classrooms, teachers may actually have good reasons to, temporally at least, reduce the level of authenticity of the language tasks that their students are invited to perform in the classroom, in ways such as these:

- *Dealing with complexity:* Authentic target tasks, such as those performed in real life, may be too complex for students to perform right away; teachers may prefer to build scaffolds and manipulate some of the authenticity dimensions in order to make the task manageable for the students.
- *Motivational power:* In some cases, teachers may want to make classroom tasks more appealing, exciting, or motivating than the actual target tasks, and thereby add some ingredients to the tasks in order to engage their learners (e.g., an element of competition, a fun factor, a topic suggested by the students).
- *Organisational reasons:* For teachers, it may simply not be feasible to have all students perform target tasks and interactionally support them while doing so in full authentic conditions, for instance because there are too many students in the classroom at the same time.
- *Curricular goals:* Teachers and syllabus designers may have goals in mind that deviate from the goals target language users in real life have in mind. Some teachers may want their students to produce highly accurate output from the beginner level onwards, for instance. In that particular example, it is striking that those teachers are actually *raising* the complexity of output-based tasks by reducing authenticity.

The following question arises: if (1) stripping reality from classroom activity (for instance, by isolating language features in form-focused exercises) is not considered ideal, and (2) completely immersing the language learning process in authentic task performance may have its limitations as well, how "authentic" should classroom tasks be? In the next section, I will describe a number of examples of actual classroom tasks to illustrate how the teachers who introduced them in their classrooms tried to ensure that there was a sufficient link with real life in order to avoid unproductive isolation of the classroom content from target language use outside the classroom, yet at the same time make sure that the lesson content was "learnable" for the students and "teachable" for the teacher.

The authenticity of pedagogic tasks

Example (2) was designed to be performed by adult learners who learn Dutch in order to integrate into Flemish (Dutch-speaking) society in Flanders. One of those students' most prominent learning goals is to use the target language to socialise and strike up informal conversations with Dutch-speaking neighbours, colleagues, or fellow-parents at the school where their children are enrolled.

Example 2. Describing pictures in order to solve a crime

Adult learners of Dutch at low-intermediate level work together in groups of four. They have each been given a unique series of six pictures describing what a suspect was doing on the night a certain crime was committed. The newcomers take turns at describing the actions depicted in their pictures. The listeners are allowed to ask questions. If each group member describes their pictures in full detail, the group will be able to determine who committed the crime.

First, this is a task, and not a form-focused exercise. Tasks have been defined as the kinds of things that people do in order to achieve a goal and which involve the comprehension and/or production of meaningful messages (Van den Branden et al., 2009). In Example (2), the students have to exchange meaningful messages and collaborate in order to solve the given puzzle (i.e., who committed the crime?). It scores relatively low, however, in terms of contextual, situational, and content-related authenticity: solving crimes does not rank high among the students' real-life language learning needs. Nevertheless, there is some limited degree of situational authenticity: the students could be imagined performing the very same task in a very similar situation when they would be playing a similar game in their leisure time. That being said, most additional language teachers will recognise this as the typical kind of pedagogical task in which students have to cooperate around problems that they will not encounter in their life outside school on a daily basis and use language to do so. The task does score higher in terms of interactional and linguistic authenticity. To start with the latter, the designers have made sure that the pictures contain actions that are very commonly performed by people in all sorts of situations: walking from one place to another, shaking hands, taking a picture, dropping an object, running away, etc.

To prompt the students to also verbally refer to the time at which the actions were performed, a small clock (indicating an exact time) is inserted in the left-hand corner of each picture. As a result, the kinds of lexis (words, multi-word combinations, idioms) the students are pushed to produce strongly resemble the lexis involved in target task performance during informal conversations in outside-school life, particularly the kinds of informal conversations in which people are talking about their own and other people's actions. In fact, talking and gossiping about what other people have done is quite typical for the kinds of informal conversations that the students would like to engage in in real life. Interactional authenticity can equally be claimed to be relatively high if students seize the opportunity to negotiate meaning, ask their interlocutors for clarification when needed, check their listeners' comprehension, and attempt to interrupt their interlocutor in a respectful way. In addition, the task also gives the teacher ample opportunity to focus on form (whether vocabulary, pronunciation, grammar, or pragmatic aspects of informal conversations), either before, during, or after task performance.

Pedagogic tasks like the information gap task in Example (2) can be said to differ from target tasks in that certain layers of authenticity are deliberately reduced while others are maintained. This reduction in layers of authenticity is typically done to lower task complexity and avoid cognitive overload. This allows the learner to focus on the layers that are maintained. Because contextual and situational authenticity are deliberately lowered, the stakes are also lower. There are no immediate (negative) consequences to be expected by the students if the task is not performed to criterion, and time pressure may be reduced on purpose; in addition, scaffolding and teacher support are raised, as a result of which anxiety levels are likely to be further reduced. At the same time, the "solve the crime" challenge and the format of the information gap task are deliberately adopted by the task developer to motivate students to actively engage in the performance of the task, both as listeners and as speakers.

It should be noted, however, that reducing contextual and situational authenticity does not *automatically* imply that task difficulty is reduced. In some cases, the task may actually become less difficult if task performance is fully embedded within an authentic, rich context. Tourists at the beginner stages of learning a foreign language know very well that, when abroad, authentic contexts can be a true blessing when they try to perform target language tasks related to shopping, placing orders in restaurants and bars, or using public transport. Here-and-now contexts can be strongly supportive for the learner to make target language vocabulary comprehensible and learnable; likewise, the context may offer strong support (for instance, in the shape of chunks and lexis that are physically embedded in the here-and-now-context in signs, notices, information boards, and the like) for the performance of speaking tasks at the beginner level.

Gradually approximating reality

Example (3) describes a successful needs-based Spanish language course for students at the US Border Patrol Academy (BPA) (González-Lloret & Nielson, 2015). US Border Patrol requires all of its agents-in-training to complete a rigorous Spanish language programme. These agents use Spanish on a daily basis in high-stakes and high-stress situations. The agents are expected to participate in complex interactions with individuals who do not speak English at all. Amongst others, they have to assist injured people, communicate with immigrants who have been abandoned by smugglers, calm detained families, explain legal rights and immigration procedures, reunite parents with children, and resolve conflicts with minimal risk and damage.

Example 3. A task-based Spanish course for US Border Patrol

- Because of many students' discontent with the grammar-based course they were offered, the BPA sought to replace it with a task-based course. A needs analysis was carried out to identify the job tasks agents might be required to perform in Spanish. Each of the target tasks that were identified established the goal of a week-long module of instruction, incorporating a sequence of increasingly complex pedagogic tasks.
- In the task-based course, each module begins with simple pedagogic tasks during which students watch and listen to genuine video and audio recordings of experienced agents doing their jobs in Spanish. Afterwards, students engage in output activities with minimal production as they work toward completing role plays of the target tasks with native speakers. The course activities are interactive and engaging, with hours of relevant, real-world video footage broken into manageable segments and used in game-like exercises and group activities that encourage teamwork and cooperation. The students are systematically given formative feedback during the course.

The description above nicely illustrates how the designers of the course manipulate the different layers of authenticity to create a sequence of increasingly complex pedagogic tasks that gradually approximate task performance in real work floor conditions. Contextual authenticity is strongly reduced in that all activities take place in a classroom and not in the stressful, high-stakes environment of real life. In a first stage, a fair degree of situational, content-related, and linguistic authenticity is maintained in that audio and video recordings of experienced agents performing the target tasks are shown. In this way, a strong link with language use and language use conditions in the target domain is established. Nonetheless, interactional authenticity is purposefully reduced in that the students do not have to produce appropriate output to participate in the interactions at this stage. Rather, in this initial stage, they are invited to merely observe how the agents use the target language. To the extent that the recordings reflect agents' real-life language use with authentic interlocutors, the degree of linguistic authenticity can be claimed to be very high and the modelling in the video can provide rich and relevant input the students can learn from. To an equal extent, content-related authenticity is held high.

In the next stages, interactional authenticity is raised, in that the students are being asked to participate actively in role plays and game-like activities. However, interactional authenticity is gradually developed, in that students first participate in output activities that require minimal output, with video footage being broken down into manageable segments. Only in a later stage is interactional authenticity built up in that students are asked to do role plays with native speakers. Even though at this stage, goal-related, contentwise, interactional, and linguistic authenticity can be claimed to be high, contextual authenticity is still reduced to allow the students to develop target language skills in a low-stress environment that offers more interactional support and feedback than the authentic, high-stakes context. On the whole, Example (3) illustrates that authenticity can be regarded as one of the factors that contribute to task complexity, and that teachers can purposefully decrease or increase certain dimensions of authenticity to gradually raise task complexity so that it slowly but surely matches genuine authenticity conditions.

High authenticity, high support

Example (4) was taken from a second language course in Dutch for lowly-educated adults at low-intermediate level in Flanders. The students are asked to prepare and organise a joint field trip to the nearby city of Antwerp (a destination they have chosen themselves).

Example 4. Planning a field trip

- To plan and organise their joint field trip to the city of Antwerp, the students are divided into groups of four. One group is made responsible for making all transport arrangements: they have to check tariffs and timetables of both train services, fill out an authentic form to arrange seat arrangements in the train (so that they can sit together), and order the tickets online. Another group has to get in touch with a museum the students want to visit to ask whether there are any guides available who have experience with second language learners and to check whether all rooms in the museum are accessible for wheelchairs. Another group has to find and make reservations in a bar where the students are allowed to eat their own lunch. A fourth group has to contact the tourist information office to find out more about two other activities the group is interested in.

> – Throughout all stages of task performance (pre-task planning, task performance, and post-task reflection), the teacher strongly supports the students. For instance, the teacher provides feedback on the students' first drafts of the email messages they must send, brainstorms with a group on how they can manage a particular phone call and reflects on their actual performance after they made the call, and provides a short instruction on using search machines in web browsers after she noticed many students were struggling with obtaining relevant information.

Quite a number of tasks that are carried out by the students in Example (4) show high levels of authenticity. The students have to communicate (in written or oral communication) with target language users outside the classroom and perform authentic tasks in order to achieve authentic goals. This caters for high levels of linguistic, interactional, content-related, and goal-related authenticity. Situational and contextual authenticity are deliberately reduced by the teacher, in that the students do not have to perform the tasks independently but can lean on the support of both their fellow group members and their teacher. In other words, contextual, situational, and interactional authenticity are partly brought down by enriching the support structure in the classroom context. In that way, Example (4) displays, so to speak, the task-based variant of the mentor-trainee model in which learning takes place in semi-authentic conditions involving a high degree of scaffolding. Gradually, the scaffolds should be removed, so that situational, contextual, and interactional authenticity levels can be raised even further.

With judicious teachers, the removal of the scaffolds will happen to the extent that the students show that they have built up the (linguistic and other) competences required to perform the full-blown authentic tasks independently. For the teacher, this model hinges on careful balancing: maintaining a sufficient degree of authenticity so that the transfer problem is less likely to pose itself, while at the same time maintaining a sufficient degree of support so that students can cope with the task and maintain their language learning motivation and confidence. As for motivation, Van den Branden (2022) presented an integrated, research-based model of additional language learning motivation that emphasises that additional language students will be motivated to engage in classroom activity to the extent that they (a) find (utility, intrinsic, or social) value in the activity they are invited to participate in; (b) believe they can be successful; and (c) retain a certain degree of autonomy. Example (4) presents itself as a potentially highly motivating task: students are likely to experience a high degree of utility value, because they get to perform tasks with a high degree of authenticity and real-world relevance, have a heightened opportunity for success because of the interactional support offered to them, and still retain a fair degree of autonomy in that they get to make decisions and choices together.

Example (4) also vividly illustrates that modern technology in the 21st century has turned into a key factor for determining, and manipulating, task authenticity in the language classroom. That applies to additional language learners worldwide. Not only are a growing number of target tasks carried out with the use of modern technology, but also the technology provides teachers with ample opportunities to establish relevant and strongly motivational links between life in the classroom and life outside. As for the latter, modern technology can aid teachers to expose their students to rich, elaborate, high-quality, authentic input, including input produced by native speakers. It allows them to introduce authentic texts of various genres illustrating various registers and varieties of the target language, such as they are used in real life by different groups and communities, and thereby familiarise the students with authentic target language use. In this way, linguistic and content-wise authenticity can be substantially enhanced in the classroom.

In addition, modern technology presents students with a wide range of opportunities to produce target language output for authentic goals, for instance through mobile phone applications, social media, correspondence classes, skype, e-mail, and wikis. It also allows students to engage in authentic (spoken and written) interaction with native speakers, pen pals, and other students outside their own classroom. Moreover, modern technology offers a great range of support options (including visual support, multimodal input, captions, subtitling, and online dictionaries) to enhance the comprehension of target language input and the production of target language output. In other words, it can be integrated in a "high authenticity — high-support" classroom context. This is not to say that modern technology has advantages only: the digital authentic input can simply be too complex for the learners to learn from, or the feedback may be too superficial or not tailored to the students' needs, to give only two examples. The available research strongly suggests that the integration of modern technology in the language classroom will positively impact students' language development if it is consistent with principles of effective instruction and is informed by research into the effectiveness of language education (González-Lloret, 2017; Ziegler, 2016). To the extent that the latter is the case, modern technology and TBLT can be powerful allies.

Learning in the wild

Example (5) was drawn from a beginner course addressing lowly-educated adult learners of Dutch as a second language in Flanders. One of the most crucial language learning needs that the students in this class share is that they want to learn Dutch to become more independent when dealing with public services and when they go shopping.

Example 5. Shopping for the teacher

- On a Thursday morning, Teacher S. puts her course book aside and tells the students that they will go outside to run her errands together. She tells them they will be given written street directions that will lead them to a number of shops: they will first have to go to the bank to withdraw some cash (using the teacher's credit card), next to the baker's to buy bread and sweets, and then on to the pharmacy to buy cheap but efficient medicine for headaches. On their way, they also have to pop into a local tourist office to try and find out more about the statue that stands in front of the school building. Finally, they have to post a birthday card the teacher is sending to her mum.
- After the teacher has made that announcement, she first asks the students to leave the classroom and walk with her through the school building. Because she is fully aware that the students are just halfway through their beginner course, she decides to freshen up their prior knowledge on giving and comprehending street directions in Dutch: in the school building, she gives individual students simple oral directions that resemble street directions (e.g., "walk on and stop at the first door on your left"), while the other students are asked to observe and help the student who has to carry out the instructions, if necessary. All students get a chance to practise, which results in a lot of recycling of relevant vocabulary and multi-word units.
- Next, the group returns to the classroom: the teacher asks one student who comes to school on foot to give her address. The teacher uses Google Street View to project the student's apartment on the digital whiteboard and then asks the student to describe the route she takes to walk from her home to school. The teacher follows the given route on Google Street View and recasts the student's instructions, so that all students receive rich linguistic input and visual support to aid comprehension.
- Next, the students go shopping in the real world: the teacher is right by their side all the time. She supports them while trying to comprehend the written street directions they were given by negotiating for meaning. She also practises the dialogues the students are supposed to have with the shopkeepers before they enter the shop and encourages students to ask for additional information at the tourist office.
- Afterwards, the teacher returns to the classroom to reflect on the real-life tasks the students performed and the language that was used. She discusses all conversations the students had, focuses on a number of relevant and useful expressions and words, and invites the students to make explicit what they have learned.

In Example (5), lowly-educated beginner learners of Dutch learn from performing target tasks in authentic conditions. Task authenticity, including contextual authenticity, is purposefully raised high by the teacher. In an interview, she makes clear that, first and foremost, she believes that this will motivate her students in that they will find a lot of utility value and relevance in the tasks they perform and the conditions under which they are asked to perform these. What they do linguistically is directly related to what they are asked to do with language in real life. However, to make the learning in the authentic context be truly productive, the authentic task performance is enclosed by highly supportive activities. For instance, before the students enter the pharmacy and do their shopping, they practise the conversation they will be likely to have while standing outside the door of the shop; and afterwards, right after the students who bought the medicine leave the shop, all students reflect together on how it went, with the teacher drawing students' attention to some of the words and expressions the pharmacist used.

Before the students enter the streets and start following the authentic street directions, the teacher practises the comprehension of highly frequent directions within the safe environment of the school premises, with fellow students and the teacher giving feedback and lending support when some students fail to understand. All the supportive activities surrounding the authentic task performances raise the likelihood that students will learn more from them: they have a strong awareness-raising dimension and may also raise the potential that students will notice certain linguistic forms and aspects of authentic conversation. At the same time, they have strong motivational power, in that they heighten the probability that students retain an expectancy of success, and therefore are more likely to tackle the target tasks in an engaged manner.

Eskildsen and Theodorsdottir (2015) have argued that through promoting language learning "in the wild" (i.e., with high levels of authenticity for all dimensions, including contextual authenticity), students are given opportunities to acquire competences related to the interactional and intercultural dimensions of additional language acquisition. Just because in real life there may be more at stake, both for themselves and for their interlocutors, than in a classroom, students may actually be prompted to devote more attention to those interpersonal and intercultural dimensions of interaction. According to Wagner (2015), in real-life social encounters, meaning is not a feature that lives in the linguistic form, but only comes about through the intersubjective exchange of actions and interpretations between co-participants. In the language classroom, words and expressions are often defined in terms that suggest they have a fixed meaning, while in real life the meaning of messages can be strongly dependent on the context, co-participants' meaning intentions and interpretations, and the dynamics of the ongoing interaction. This means that additional language learners need to learn how people in real life interpret, and react to, certain messages, and what linguistic forms mean and do in particular situations. As a result, through learning language in the wild, students can:

> ... figure out how the language works by experiencing how the locals treat what others are saying and doing. They can study the consequences of their own action in their co-participants' responses. They can experience how their utterances are handled by other participants and the sense that is given to them.
>
> (Wagner, 2015, p. 88)

This, then, also brings us back to Medding and Thornbury's (2017) views on the power of true conversation in the classroom. Even though their "unplugged Dogme" approach may have its limitations in terms of covering the curriculum at higher-intermediate and more advanced levels of target language proficiency, they are right in pointing out that teachers can quite easily create the conditions for more authentic conversation to become an inherent part of classroom activity. In my own classroom observations as a teacher trainer, I have seen so many times how the mere re-arrangement of the furniture in the classroom, with the teacher shoving the desks against the wall and inviting the students to sit together in a big circle (so that everyone can face each other) makes a big difference in terms of promoting the kinds of natural conversations that people have outside the classroom. That is, conversations that are not overly dominated by the teacher in terms of topic nomination, turn-taking, and focus on accuracy.

Particularly when the group is invited to share personal experiences and views on topics that truly matter in the real world, the situational, linguistic, content-related, goal-related, and interactional authenticity dimensions of classroom interaction are raised substantially. Casual, informal conversations tend to be underestimated in language classrooms: they tend to be seen as mere introductions in the pre-task stage, before the real work is done, or the kind of thing that can be done when there are five minutes left at the end of the lesson. That view, I believe, should be revised. Particularly for language learners who need to develop the proficiency to talk about a variety of topics in informal conversations, the power of true informal conversation (with the teacher participating as a conversational partner and a more proficient interlocutor at the same time) needs to be restored.

Authenticity and textbooks

Many additional language teachers around the world rely on commercial textbooks to organise their classroom instruction. Although commercial textbooks can offer teachers a lot of pedagogical comfort and constitute a major source of inspiration for classroom activity, it can be inferred from the above that textbooks have certain limitations with regard to authenticity and in terms of building bridges between pedagogical activity and real-life language use. For one, commercial textbooks tend to be written for a broad, diverse audience, as a result of which content-related authenticity may be far from optimal. Very often, topics of so-called general interest are introduced, which may be insufficiently related to both the personal interests and the language learning needs of specific groups of learners. Secondly, some textbooks may use texts as a primary source to illustrate the use of particular forms (grammar rules, lexis) that will be explicitly taught and practised in the next stage: in some cases, flooding of target forms is bound to damage the linguistic authenticity of the input.

Moreover, in textbooks there is little room to showcase local and informal registers, and, because the texts were selected at least a couple of years before students are exposed to them, they may not reflect current language use in real life and may, in the worst case, be outdated. For all those reasons, teachers who aim at gradually approximating classroom activity to the performance of target language tasks by raising authenticity levels should complement the use of a commercial textbook with other types of input (digital or not) that reflect current-day language use outside the classroom, issues of topical interest, and content that is directly related to their students' language learning needs. Obviously, the internet, and current-day media in general, offer a wealth of input sources in this regard. In addition, teachers should consider closing the textbook from time to time, and even closing the doors of the classroom behind them, in order to enter the real world (or the real virtual world, for the same matter) to allow their students to perform tasks with a higher degree of content-related, contextual, goal-oriented, and situational authenticity.

Conclusion: A new kind of symbiosis

For a long time, the rationale of TBLT seems to have focused on the tension between meaning and form. In earlier publications (see, e.g., Van den Branden, 2022), I have argued in favour of a symbiosis between explicit and implicit language teaching:

> So, ultimately, high-quality language teaching is not a matter of choosing between a focus on meaning and a focus on form. Rather, it is about finding clever ways to *integrate* them and so raise the effectiveness and efficiency of the time teachers and students spend together in a classroom. (p. 51)

I have been far from the only one to undertake the kind of integration between meaning and form that I spoke of in Van den Branden (2022). In this chapter, clearly following from the ground covered in the previous sections, I want to add a second kind of symbiosis: the clever integration of classroom life with life outside the classroom, more particularly the language use demonstrated by target language users in the target language use situations determining the curriculum. Task-based language classrooms should be about blending life inside school with life outside school. They should: infuse language learning oriented classroom activity with features and dimensions of authenticity to raise the possibility that what students do in the classroom is motivating, interesting, and relevant to their real-life language learning needs; heighten the likelihood that cognitive bridges are built between behaviour in the classroom and behaviour outside the classroom, and therefore minimise the transfer problem; raise students' motivation in that they find more social, intrinsic, and utility value in the activities undertaken under the supervision of their teachers. In this chapter, I have aimed to demonstrate that there are plenty of ways in which teachers can manipulate authenticity levels in the classroom by adapting the settings of the various dimensions that constitute authenticity.

References

Benati, A., & Schwieter, J. (2019). Pedagogical interventions to L2 grammar instruction. In J. Schwieter & A. Benati (Eds.). *The Cambridge handbook of language learning* (pp. 477–499). Cambridge University Press.

Cobb, M. (2010). Meta-analysis of the effectiveness of task-based interaction in form-focussed instruction of adult learners in foreign and second language teaching [Unpublished doctoral dissertation]. University of San Francisco, CA.

Eskildsen, S., & Theodorsdottir, G. (2015). Constructing L2 learning spaces: Ways to achieve learning inside and outside the classroom. *Applied Linguistics, 38,* 143–164.

González-Lloret, M. (2017). Technology for task-based language teaching. In C. Chapelle & S. Sauro (Eds.), *The handbook of technology and second language teaching and learning* (1st ed., pp. 234–247). John Wiley & Sons.

González-Lloret, M., & Nielson, K. B. (2015). Evaluating TBLT: The case of a task-based Spanish program. *Language Teaching Research, 19*(5), 525–549.

Lightbown, P., & Spada, N. (2013). *How languages are learned* (4th ed.) Oxford University Press.

Long, M. H. (1985). A role for instruction in second language acquisition: Task-based language teaching. In K. Hyltenstam & M. Pienemann (Eds.), *Modelling and assessing second language acquisition* (pp. 77–79). Multilingual Matters.

Meddings, L., & Thornbury, S. (2017). *Teaching unplugged. Dogme in English language teaching.* Delta Publishing.

Peters, E., Noreillie, A., Heylen, K., Bulté, B., & Desmet, P. (2019). The impact of instruction and out-of-school exposure to foreign language input on learners' vocabulary knowledge in two languages. *Language Learning, 69*, 747–82.

Van den Branden, K. (2022). *How to teach an additional language: To task or not to task?* John Benjamins.

Van den Branden, K., Bygate, M., & Norris, J. M. (2009). *Task-based language teaching: A reader.* John Benjamins.

Wagner, J. (2015). Designing for language learning in the wild. Creating social infrastructures for second language learning. In T. Cadierno & S. Eskildsen (Eds.), *Usage-based perspectives on second language learning* (pp. 75–101). De Gruyter Mouton.

Webb, S. (2019). *The Routledge handbook of vocabulary studies.* Routledge.

Ziegler, N. (2016). Taking technology to task: Technology-mediated TBLT, performance, and production. *Annual Review of Applied Linguistics, 36*, 136–163.

CHAPTER 4

The coursebook in TBLT[*]
Lost cause or launching pad?

Jonathan Newton
Victoria University of Wellington

Coursebooks are the mainstay of language classrooms around the world but
are often dismissed in the TBLT community for perpetuating synthetic
syllabi and for an undue focus on the language code. In this chapter, I
review the case against and for coursebooks and argue for a more
contextualised understanding of the limitations and affordances of
coursebooks from a TBLT perspective, drawing on case studies of
coursebook use in Thailand, China, and Vietnam. National language
curricula in these contexts stipulate tasks and therefore provide an
opportunity to investigate how tasks are being realised in mandated
coursebooks and in classroom teaching based on these coursebooks. I
conclude by offering a response to the question posed in the title of this
chapter.

Keywords: coursebooks, textbooks, TBLT, task-based language teaching,
teacher agency, mentoring

Introduction

For at least the last decade, TBLT research has broadened its reach to focus on
the practice of TBLT in diverse contexts (Lambert & Oliver, 2020; Newton, 2022;
Thomas & Reinders, 2015). This does not suggest that research on the practice of
language teaching with tasks is new — far from it. Earlier work by Bygate et al.
(2001), Van den Branden (2006), Samuda (2001) and many others has, for some
decades, drawn attention to the final "T" in TBLT.

Even within the body of TBLT research that has focused on teachers, teaching, and real-world classrooms, little attention has been given to the question of

---

[*] Revised version of a plenary given to the 10th International TBLT Conference, Khon Kaen,
Thailand, 2023.

https://doi.org/10.1075/tblt.17.04new
© 2025 John Benjamins Publishing Company

how TBLT can find relevance in contexts where coursebooks hold sway. If, as is often claimed, TBLT in practice is still poorly understood, this is nowhere truer than in the fraught relationship between tasks and coursebooks. This is hardly surprising given the antipathy towards coursebooks in the field (Jordan & Long, 2022). However, as I will argue in this chapter, a blanket dismissal of coursebooks is not necessarily helpful for moving TBLT forward. TBLT can dismiss coursebooks, but in doing so, TBLT becomes largely irrelevant to a large part of the teaching profession for whom coursebooks are the mainstay of practice. This is especially true of compulsory sector education in public schools and, notably, in Asia where much of my research and that of my co-researchers has been focused.

My position is that for TBLT to take hold, in particular in Asian contexts, the field must engage productively with coursebooks. Even if, in principle, we acknowledge the limitations of coursebooks from a TBLT perspective, research that articulates more substantively and evidentially the intersections and divergences between TBLT and coursebooks is needed. I believe that TBLT has much to gain from engaging with coursebooks, especially for the purpose of bringing practitioners on side and empowering their work. (As a side note, it would be great to see more dialogue between the TBLT community and the teams of professional coursebook writers employed by commercial publishers.)

In exploring coursebooks from a TBLT perspective in this chapter, I will draw on research by five PhD students whom I have supervised over the past 10 years or so. As displayed in Table 1, these students taught and conducted their research in a range of educational sectors focused on English as a Foreign Language (EFL), from primary schools to universities, and from rural to urban settings in Southeast Asia or China. A common theme across the five studies is the challenge of finding room for TBLT in classrooms where coursebooks are a mandated and inescapable focus of instruction. Their research has been (or will be) published in other places, but in this chapter, I seek to treat it as a body of work from which to synthesise implications for making better sense of the relationship between TBLT and coursebooks.

Table 1. The five studies discussed in this chapter

Researcher	Context	Textbook
Paweena Jaruteerapan	A pre-service English Language Teaching teacher course at a Thai university and practicum classes at local schools	Evans & Dooley (2015) *Access 2.* Express Publishing.
Hao Thi Thanh Dao	EFL classes for non-majors at a university in the North of Vietnam	Cunningham & Moor (2007). *New Cutting edge intermediate* (2nd ed.). Longman.

Table 1. *(continued)*

Researcher	Context	Textbook
Bao Trang Thi Nguyen	EFL classes at a high performing high school in a major city in Vietnam	Hoang et al. (2007). *English 12:* Education Publishing House.
Trang Le Diem Bui	EFL classes at selected urban, semi-rural and rural primary school in the Mekong Delta	Hoang et al. (2015). *Tieng Anh 3,4,5 (English 3, 4, 5)* (3rd ed.). Education Publishing House.
Jing Yixuan	ELF classes at a rural secondary school in a remote province in the Northwest of China	Nunan (2005). *Go for it!* (2nd ed). Heinle ELT.

In the five studies reported here, we were interested in the question of what we, as teachers, teacher educators, and researchers who advocate for TBLT, can do to support teachers who teach from coursebooks. Our agenda addressed a range of related questions, including the following:

1. To what extent does a coursebook align with TBLT?
2. How do teachers translate task alignments in coursebooks into practice? (e.g., by de-tasking or re-tasking coursebook activities)
3. What factors explain the coursebook implementation decisions that teachers make?
4. How effective are task-based coursebooks (an oxymoron to some, perhaps) as a de facto form of teacher professional development and learning for TBLT?
5. What role do such coursebooks play in facilitating or inhibiting "diffusion of innovation" (i.e., TBLT) (Long, 2015)?
6. What can we, as a community of teachers, teacher educators, and researchers who advocate for TBLT, do to support teachers who teach from coursebooks?
7. What impact do different kinds of teacher learning and mentoring have on the capacity and willingness of teachers to *taskify* their coursebooks, and with what impact on sustainable practice and student learning?

In this chapter, I lay out the case that has been made against coursebooks within the TBLT community and provide support for their use with evidence from the five studies listed in Table 1. I then offer an alternative perspective on this case, where I seek to reconcile the relationship between TBLT and coursebooks, again drawing on findings from the five studies. I conclude by answering the question posed in the title of this chapter.

Materials evaluation

Materials evaluation in English language teaching provides a useful starting point for understanding coursebooks (Breen et al., 1979; Harwood, 2010; Tomlinson, 2011; Tomlinson & Masuhara, 2013). While it is not possible in this chapter to do justice to this rich seam of scholarship, nevertheless the findings from three recent coursebook evaluations offer insights to set the scene for the remainder of the chapter. (For a recent overview of the field of materials evaluation, see Mishan, 2022.)

The first of the three studies, Butler et al. (2018), is the only one to approach coursebook evaluation from a task-based perspective. Butler et al. analysed the range of activities in government approved coursebooks for primary school English language learners in China and South Korea, two contexts where TBLT was referenced in policy. They found that non-tasks, including activities that focused on grammar and accuracy, predominated in all the books, and, where tasks were present, they were often embedded within a Presentation — Practice — Production (PPP) activity sequence.

The second of the three coursebook evaluation studies, Tórrez and Lund (2021), came to similar conclusions in their analysis of a series of coursebooks for the teaching of English in Grades 7 to 9 in public secondary schools in Nicaragua. Although their analysis was not directly informed by TBLT, they found that "few activities go beyond the focus on language practice and encourage the learners to use the language for real world purposes" (p. 73) and that task-based activities were completely absent from the Grade 9 coursebook, which was effectively organised around linguistic units (mainly vocabulary and grammar).

In the largest and most recent of the coursebook evaluations under consideration here, Gregson (2023) surveyed seven coursebook series for young learners at the lower primary level, all written for a global market. While Gregson concluded from this analysis that coursebooks for young learners have "come quite some distance" (p. 267), she noted a continued emphasis on a teacher-centred approach, and a heavy focus on grammar and controlled practice, with a concomitant lack of personalisation and freer practice. Gregson concluded that further development of such coursebooks to make them more learner-centred could involve "taking on a task- or project-based approach or placing the learner more firmly in the driving seat in activity- or play-based learning" (p. 265).

Even in the above limited review, we see a pattern of coursebooks not aligning at all well with TBLT, and reflecting a view where language is seen as a set of linguistic units and their grammatical relationships, which will be no surprise to many readers. Mishan's (2022) conclusion from his review of the current state of global English Language Teaching (ELT) coursebooks echoes the findings presented above. That is, "findings from the fields of applied linguistics and SLA [second language acquisition], which should have fed into language learning approaches and hence language coursebooks, have been slow to do so in any systematic or significant way" (p.1). These findings are likely to be grist to the mill for those in the TBLT community who have been the most veracious critics of coursebooks. Thus, I turn now to their criticisms.

The case against coursebooks

From a TBLT perspective, coursebooks are problematic for two main reasons: they are insensitive to the needs of particular groups of learners in specific contexts, and they are predicated on a synthetic syllabus.

The first argument against coursebooks, that they adopt a one-size-fits-all approach, is directly at odds with Long's (2009) position that TBLT, by definition, derives from needs analysis and thus will always be local and situated. It is, however, necessary to say a few words about Long's view of TBLT and to contrast it with a broader view adopted by Ellis (2017). Long has consistently argued that "true" TBLT will always be derived from an analysis of the needs and target tasks that a specific group of learners need to perform in the language they are learning. A TBLT curriculum will therefore consist of pedagogic tasks that progressively approximate the full complexity of target tasks (Long, 2015). Ellis (2017), on the other hand, argues that this version of TBLT is unrealistic in many contexts, especially because the process of identifying needs and target tasks is difficult, if not impossible, where the target language is not widely used in society and where the learners are not studying the language for any specific purpose, such as in relation to common vocational goals. Primary school EFL classes in, say, China, are just one of many examples of such contexts. On this basis, Ellis argued for a broader conceptualisation of TBLT which encompasses what he referred to as task-supported language teaching (TSLT), an approach that allows for a hybrid syllabus in which "specific linguistic forms are first taught explicitly and then practised under 'real operating conditions' using tasks" (p.514).

In engaging with coursebooks from a task-based perspective, I see no option but to allow for a more flexible version of TBLT such as that proposed by Ellis (2017). Indeed, the reality in several contexts reported in this chapter is of coursebooks delivering a grammar-based syllabus, with support from some task-like activities.

Returning to the one-size-fits-all issue, the following comment by an EFL teacher at a secondary school in Vietnam, as reported in Nguyen et al. (2018), captures the problem of generic coursebook content not related to learner needs (or interests — see Ellis, 2017):

> This [coursebook] task is constraining, dry and boring ... so I must design tasks that engage them, so that they are motivated to talk. Students like tasks that allow them to think for themselves, as they are very creative, you know. If they can speak freely, they will be more engaged and speak more with interesting ideas.
>
> (p. 62)

Other teachers at the same school made similar comments on the coursebook, noting that students made little effort to engage in coursebook tasks that they did not see as relevant to their lives and context.

The second main criticism of coursebooks from a TBLT perspective is that they perpetuate synthetic syllabi and thus over-emphasise the study of language as an object. As Jordan and Long (2022) point out:

> coursebook writers take the target language as the object of instruction and they divide it up into bits of one kind or another — words, collocations, grammar rules, sentence patterns, notions, and functions, for example — which are presented and practiced in a sequence. The criteria for sequencing can be things like valency, criticality, frequency, or saliency, but the most common criterion is 'level of difficulty', which, as always, is intuitively defined by the writers themselves.
>
> (p. 123)

Jordan and Long (2022) put *New Headway Intermediate* in the dock as a main offender. As they argued, this series adopts a synthetic, grammar-based syllabus using a Situational Approach and PPP sequencing of lesson content. Teacher led activities predominate and most classroom time is devoted to explicit teaching and learning.

The five studies that this chapter draws on offer evidence to support the claim that coursebooks perpetuate a synthetic grammar-based curriculum. This juncture is therefore an appropriate point to introduce four of the studies in more detail. The first, Bui and Newton (2021), was situated in primary schools in the Mekong Delta Vietnam. It investigated the practices and perceptions of seven EFL teachers from a mix of urban, rural, and semi-rural schools concerning the PPP approach to speaking lessons in their coursebook. In our findings, the seven teachers were evenly divided on whether the PPP approach in the coursebook was useful (with one teacher remaining fairly neutral in her opinions), but all of them were keen to explore a more task-based alternative. The comments of the teachers who were dissatisfied with PPP were especially insightful, as in the following comment from teacher Hoa:

> I think the steps are so fixed. It's like we arrange and assign things for students. We show them this is what they should say. Then students just have to follow the structural patterns we have taught them. ... I think this cannot enhance students' ability to use English language. It is like we force them to do what we want them to do, speak what we want them to speak. (Bui & Newton, 2021, p. 264)

Hoa's comment articulates insightfully, from a practitioner's perspective, the case against a synthetic syllabus argued by Jordan and Long (2022).

The following three studies focused not just on what teachers said about their teaching but on their classroom practice. Jaruteerapan (2019) explored the emerging understandings and practices of TBLT by Thai EFL student teachers. As part of this study, she investigated evidence of TBLT in the teaching practice and cognition of three student teachers in their Year 5 teaching practicum. These student teachers had learnt about TBLT in a four-week module which was part of a Year 4 teaching methods course in their teacher education programme. In the practicum, the three teachers were all based at the same high school and used the coursebook *Access 2* (Evans & Dooley, 2015), which was modelled on PPP principles. Their supervising teachers encouraged them to be creative and selective in the way they designed lessons based on the coursebook. Data were collected over three months from the second month of the practicum onwards and included observation of lesson planning sessions and classroom teaching, alongside stimulated recall interviews.

The data showed that all three teachers implemented teacher-centred, forms-focused lessons. They rarely used interactive activities and did so only for lexico-grammar practice. They made little reference to tasks when lesson planning, and de-tasked even the limited tasks in the coursebook. In other words, they emphasised — in fact overemphasised — the synthetic syllabus inherent in the coursebook by selecting coursebook activities that focused on language forms, and they taught these explicitly. Later in the chapter I will outline what happened when the teachers were supported to adopt a more task-based approach. At this point, it was clear that learning about TBLT in their teacher education course work had no observable impact on their teaching practice.

While Jaruteerapan's findings could be attributed, at least in part, to the inexperience of her participating teachers, this is not the case in the next two studies, both of which involved experienced EFL teachers. Dao and Newton (2021) evaluated the communicativeness and task-likeness of activities in the coursebook *New Cutting Edge, Elementary* (Cunningham & Moor, 2005) and then contrasted these findings with classroom observation data on the way three Vietnamese EFL teachers at a Vietnamese university taught from the coursebook. The three teachers had between five- and nine-years' teaching experience, and they were observed and recorded teaching three 90-minute lessons each. While the selected coursebook was designed on PPP principles, an analysis of each activity in sample units showed that a high proportion of them met three or four of the features of tasks and could therefore be considered tasks or "task-like." However, since form-focused activities typically preceded the tasks, as is typical of PPP, these tasks reflected a task-supported rather than task-based approach.

Dao and Newton (2021) found that the teachers in the observed lessons consistently reduced the communicativeness and task-likeness of the coursebook activities, for example by replacing interactive groupwork or pairwork activities with teacher-centred, explicit grammar explanation and drill practice. In explaining their pedagogic decision-making they frequently referred to the need to teach and drill language forms before students could use them. As teacher Minh said (translated from Vietnamese), "[t]o do the tasks, first of all, the students should be taught relevant language then they will do the tasks to practise such language and to remember it more" (Dao & Newton, 2021, p.118). Interestingly, all three teachers expressed dissatisfaction with their teaching.

While the Dao and Newton (2021) study was situated in a major university in Hanoi, the study I move to next is a study in contrasts, being situated in a rural high school in the poorest province in China. In this study (Jing et al., 2022), we reported on the first phase of a two-month field study which examined the teaching of English in a typical rural secondary school in the Northwest of China. Data were collected on the EFL lessons taught by ten 7th-grade teachers through lesson observations, conversations with the teachers and administrative staff, and in-depth reflective fieldnotes. Despite the English language curriculum explicitly encouraging the use of TBLT, the prescribed coursebook, *Go for it!* (Nunan, 2005), contained few activities that would be considered tasks using the four criteria proposed by Ellis and Shintani (2014)r, namely, a primary focus on meaning, a gap, learners using their own resources, and a communicative outcome. Consequently, the observed lessons reflected either a grammar-translation methodology or PPP, although typically with the third P, the communicative production stage, missing. As we noted:

> even the simple coursebook task of matching phrases with pictures was turned into a teacher-directed exercise to practice those phrases. ... The teachers ... consistently turned communication activities into drills or individual pen-work.
>
> (Jing et al., 2022, p.263)

In summary, pulling together the findings from the above four studies, we see support for the two arguments against coursebooks that were presented earlier. Teachers in these studies recognised and experienced frustration with the limitations of the one-size-fits-all nature of coursebooks (Bui & Newton, 2021; Nguyen et al., 2018) while also consistently strengthening the synthetic syllabi inherent in their coursebooks (Dao & Newton, 2021; Jaruteerapan, 2018; Jing et al., 2022).

However, the more traditional or PPP-oriented practices observed are not the end of the story. I now present the case *for* coursebooks, or at least for the TBLT community to engage more directly with coursebooks. In doing so, I return to the five studies and show what happened when these teachers were given opportunities to learn about TBLT and received mentoring to put it into practice with their coursebooks. The findings I discuss offer a more complex and perhaps more promising picture of the potential for TBLT in a coursebook dominated classroom.

The case for coursebooks

In making a case for coursebooks from a TBLT perspective, my argument is, in the first instance, pragmatic rather than theoretical. As already sketched out in the introduction to this chapter, whatever our scholarly distaste for them, coursebooks will not be disappearing anytime soon. For many thousands of teachers, and for millions of students, coursebooks continue to be the inescapable realisation of the curriculum and the mandated resource that teachers are required to use to implement that curriculum. Given this reality, if we are too quick to dismiss coursebooks for the sake of theory, we automatically become irrelevant to perhaps most of the ELT teaching profession, especially in Global South contexts, notably in many parts of Southeast and central Asia, where my experience lies. This is particularly the case in poorly resourced contexts such as rural schools in remote areas, where a coursebook (along with whatever ancillary resources, digital or otherwise, that it comes with) may be the only resource available to teachers, and one that makes the difference between being able to teach or not.

A second and rather obvious point is that coursebooks come in all shapes and sizes and are continuing to evolve (a point also made by Gregson, 2023). Jordan and Long's (2022) polemic against coursebooks seems predicated on a relatively narrow sample of coursebooks designed for the global market. It is true that a good number of coursebooks such as *Cutting Edge* (Cunningham & Moor, 2007) refer to tasks in their promotional materials, but deliver a synthetic syllabus. However, others such as *On Task* (Harris & Leeming, 2018) are avowedly task-based in conception and design. In fact, we can go back as far as 1989 and the *Collins COBUILD English course* (Willis & Willis, 1989) to find a textbook series that was dedicated to teaching through tasks. (See Moser, 2023, for an interesting discussion of the task-based principles that informed the design of this series.) Furthermore, in contexts where coursebooks are written to national curriculum specifications, and where, as is increasingly the case, these specifications require a focus on communicative skills and tasks, such as in Vietnam and China, our analysis shows that coursebooks, by virtue of being focused on meaningful skills and mandated to include tasks, increasingly align with TBLT, or at least with an Ellis (2017) view of TBLT. The use of bespoke coursebooks designed for a national curriculum is standard practice for public schools throughout many parts of the world, and certainly across Asia. Thus, these coursebooks do a lot of the heavy lifting of language teaching. This reason alone makes a compelling case for strengthening the influence of TBLT in the design of such coursebooks and in the training and support for teachers who will teach from these books.

Options for strengthening TBLT in existing curricula bring us back to the question of just what version of TBLT is in play. With generic coursebooks, I see little choice but to adopt a version of TBLT in which pedagogic tasks rather than needs analysis and target tasks constitute the essence of task-based teaching.

Taking into account an emphasis on pedagogic tasks, in Cao and Newton (2021) we used Ellis and Shintani's (2014) four features as criterial in a coding scheme to quantify the alignment of secondary school coursebooks with TBLT. To do so, we analysed all the activities in six sample units from the Grades 10, 11, and 12 coursebooks (two units from each) in the *Tieng Anh* series for the Vietnamese Upper Secondary School English curriculum. Each unit contained around five lessons, and each lesson contained four to seven distinct activities, resulting in a data set of 234 activities. If all four features were present, an activity was coded as a task; if three features were present, it was coded as task-like; if only two or fewer task features were present, it was coded as a non-task. East (2021, p. 91) speaks of tasks as being not absolute (one activity is a task, but another is not a task), but relative, that is, as more or less task-like when evaluated against theoretical definitions of the task construct. Accordingly, our analysis revealed that 21% of activities were tasks, 33% were task-like, and the remaining 46% of activities were non-tasks.

While, on the face of it, the small proportion of tasks we identified might not seem particularly promising, three points are worth making. First, the tasks embedded in the lessons were typically much more substantial than the non-tasks and would therefore take up a greater proportion of class time. For example, a task in Unit 1 (Family life) of the Grade 12 coursebook required learners to work in groups and discuss whether they agreed with a series of statements about roles of parents in the family and then discuss roles in their own families, culminating in a report to the class. In contrast, a much shorter non-task in the same unit required learners to read a short description of the present continuous tense and then read a series of six sentences (e.g., "I'm afraid you can't talk to him now. He (*take out*) the rubbish.") and use the correct form of the verbs in brackets to complete the sentences.

Second, in Vietnam, coursebooks developed in line with the primary and secondary curricula must be project-based, with each unit culminating in a lesson-long project, or, in our terms, a task. For example, a Grade 10 project in a coursebook unit on pollution required learners to work in groups to identify a local source of pollution, describe its causes and effects, find pictures to illustrate it, and propose practical solutions. Learners would then organise this information into a report, which they would present to the class. At the lower primary levels, these projects tend to involve visual representation such as to draw one's family and tell a classmate about the drawing (Grade 3), or to draw a weather icon for tomorrow's weather and talk about it (Grade 5). Coursebooks such as these, which emphasise meaningful skills practice and communication, offer a short bridge to TBLT. We see a similar trend in China, where the Shanghai Center for Research in English Language Education (SCRELE) has developed a primary school EFL coursebook series in which a central component of each unit is a project (Shu & Zhu, in press).

Returning to the analysis of the Vietnamese secondary school coursebooks, a third point of alignment with TBLT in our analysis was the sizeable proportion of activities that we coded as task-like (33%). In many cases, such activities require relatively modest changes to be turned into tasks. For example, one activity we coded as task-like required learners to list all the household chores that are mentioned in a conversation they had just listened to and then add more chores to the list. We coded this activity as task-like because, while it is meaning-focused, contains a gap, and requires learners to draw on their own resources, a communicative outcome is underspecified. (Although even without a specified communicative outcome, this activity is likely to generate communicative behaviours, and on this basis, this fourth task feature might be seen to be weakly present.) The question becomes how a teacher might taskify this activity, without too much additional effort or planning. One simple option would be to create a game-like outcome by giving the learners a specified time to write as many additional chores as they could in the time available, and then, in pairs or groups, to combine their lists to obtain a total number of different chores. The pair or group with the most chores on their list wins. Alternatively, once they have finished their lists, learners might be asked to decide on their favourite and least favourite chore and then share their choices in groups or as a whole class to find similarities and differences.

To sum up, I have sought to make the case for greater attention to coursebooks in the TBLT community on the basis, first, that coursebooks are a reality in the professional lives of many teachers, and, second, that coursebooks come in many different forms, including coursebooks that align much more closely with TBLT than those selected for criticism by Jordan and Long (2022). In support of this latter point I drew on an analysis of a coursebook series, *Tieng Anh*, designed for EFL classes at Vietnamese high schools.

However, as the classroom-based studies presented above show, even the presence of tasks in coursebooks does not get us very far if teachers are not aware of what a task is or resist the move to TBLT. Carless (2003) reached a similar conclusion from his research on the failed attempt to introduce TBLT in secondary schools in Hong Kong over 20 years ago. In the remainder of this chapter, I discuss in more detail the role of teacher agency in the implementation of coursebooks and the impact of mentoring to support task-informed implementation of coursebooks.

Coursebooks, teacher agency, and mentoring

According to Long (2015), one of the "obvious areas in need of serious research effort" is "detailed classroom studies of the ways teachers and students perform classroom lessons" (p. 371). This is exactly what the five studies at the heart of this chapter set out to do. I have provided evidence from these studies of teachers following and indeed strengthening the synthetic syllabus and teacher-centredness of their coursebooks. This is, however, only part of the story. Alongside these instances of compliance, in two of the studies (Bui & Newton, 2021; Nguyen et al., 2018) we also found evidence of teacher creativity and resistance.

Bui and Newton (2021) was introduced earlier in the chapter where we noted the mixed views of seven Grade 3 and 4 Vietnamese primary school teachers concerning the PPP lessons in their coursebook. The study also included classroom observations over a three-month period in which the teachers were seen to frequently add interactive activities to the presentation phase of PPP lessons and to adapt the production activities to make them more communicative. In one case, teacher Nga moved the communicative activity from the third production phase to the start of the lesson. This is what she said about doing this:

> I decided to reverse the steps if lessons were easy. I had students do the difficult part first [the production phase] and moved quickly through the other two parts. Then I provided them with the rules or something they need in the end. ... For example, as you can see in activity 3, I asked them to look at the pictures and encouraged them to say about the pictures. The aim was to see what had been known to them. Their performance helped me decide whether they were able to cover the lesson of the day. If it was enough, I got them to practice right after that.
>
> (Bui & Newton, 2021, p. 110)

Nga's perspective demonstrates the teacher working as task designer in the way the lesson was implemented, illustrating what Samuda (2015) referred to as the task as "dynamic workplan." Similarly, in Nguyen et al. (2018), the teachers in a Vietnamese high school enacted agency by frequently replacing coursebook tasks with tasks they designed that were more personalised and situationally authentic to the lives of their learners. As one of the teachers commented:

> I often adapt text tasks or use my own tasks. I tend not to use tasks that are not practical, not real world. What I pay particular attention to is the real-world application of the task into students' future life. ... Practical tasks engage students more than 'far away' tasks. (Nguyen et al., 2018, p. 64)

In the above instances, we see teacher agency at work as teachers demonstrate the ability to make informed pedagogic decisions based on their sensitivity to learner needs, even within the confines of teaching from a mandated coursebook. As Connolly (2022) argued, "I might not be able to choose the coursebook I use, but I can control how I use it" (p. 286). To this point, I have presented the cases for and against coursebooks from a TBLT perspective. My position is that while the theoretical case against coursebooks from a TBLT perspective is strong, it fails to account for both diversity and evolution of coursebooks and is tone deaf to the reality of the lives of many teachers. The solution is not (or not only) to fight against coursebooks, but to find ways to strengthen them both as a source of tasks and through the expertise that teachers apply to their engagement with the books. Whether teachers approach their coursebook as a script to follow closely or as a resource to selectively draw on in the way espoused by Connolly will doubtless be influenced by a complex array of contextual and individual factors (Priestly et al., 2015). The next question we sought to answer in the five studies was the extent to which awareness-raising about TBLT and in situ mentoring could mediate the way the teachers understood and implemented their coursebooks. To answer this question, I return to three of the studies introduced earlier in the chapter — Jaruteerapan (2019), Dao and Newton (2021), and Jing (in press).

To recap, Jaruteerapan's (2019) research involved three student teachers teaching in a Year 5 practicum after having learnt about TBLT in Year 4 of their teacher education programme. Jaruteerapan undertook a second cycle of data collection in which the three teachers took part in collaborative lesson planning along with her in which she reminded them of the principles of TBLT and explored with them ways to apply TBLT to their coursebook-based lessons. She then observed their subsequent lesson planning and teaching. While the teachers varied in their struggles to implement tasks along different developmental trajectories, they all grew in their confidence and ability to implement interactive tasks and were frequently moving explicit focus on form to the post-task phase of their lessons. In final interviews, all three teachers reported a deeper understanding of learner-centred, interactive teaching, and learning by doing. Although two of them noted the value of the three-stage task framework — pre-task, during task, post-task (Willis, 1996) — none of them mentioned the defining features of tasks, which had been the focus of their earlier collaborative lesson planning with the researcher. In conclusion, while the three teachers were all some way off from task-based teaching, this study showed how TBLT helped them to develop more learner-centred, interactive approaches and to shift from a primary focus on teaching forms explicitly to engaging more communicatively with the target language focused on in each lesson. Finding out how teachers design tasks is necessary for understanding task design options and seeing whether and how these may be informed by TBLT principles and findings. Both qualitative and quantitative studies in this area are urgently needed.

Dao and Newton (2021) was a study situated in EFL classes at a Vietnamese university. We earlier reported how the three case study teachers all consistently avoided teaching with the tasks in their coursebook, preferring to either turn them into teacher-fronted activities or skip over them and focus instead on the lexico-grammar exercises in the coursebook. These teachers were not satisfied with the way they were teaching and willingly took part in a second, participatory action research phase of the study in which the researcher (Dao, 2022) worked collaboratively with the teachers to understand the principles of TBLT and then apply these principles in a series of action research cycles. In these cycles, they planned lessons together from the coursebook, reflected together on their experience of implementing the lessons, identified priorities for improvement, and continued to plan for the next lessons. Data from lesson planning sessions, classroom observations, and interviews showed a dramatic shift in the extent to which the lessons taught by all three teachers in this second phase increasingly aligned with TBLT. One of the notable shifts in the way the teachers taught from the coursebook after engaging with TBLT was in foregrounding the communicative tasks in the coursebook lessons and spending less time on the lexico-grammatical exercises. In this way, we see their identities moving from teacher as knowledge provider to teacher as mediator of learning (Van den Branden, 2016). A comment from Huong, one of the teachers, captures this shift:

> I think I will use tasks frequently in my future lessons because it is interesting. Last time, I did not use this approach because I did not have a good understanding of it, and I always thought that communicative activities were not really necessary and suitable for my low-proficiency students. However, after six task-based lessons, I realised that the students could do the tasks and the important thing is they appeared more engaged and active in the lessons. So, this is the motivation for me to frequently use tasks in my future lessons. (Dao, 2022, pp. 145–146)

While we have no evidence of a sustained shift towards teaching with tasks by these teachers beyond the duration of the research, Huong's comments reveal a promising combination of raised awareness and understanding about TBLT, positive experiences, and visible evidence of improved student engagement (see also Erlam & Tolosa, 2022, in this regard).

Jing (2024) reports a similarly positive outcome from her experience of mentoring EFL teachers in a rural Chinese secondary school. Jing found that the teachers were teaching in a very traditional way when she began her research there, using methods akin to grammar-translation and audio-lingualism. However, the teachers were receptive to change, and through Jing's mentoring were able to shift their teaching to deliver lessons that, while not necessarily task-based, reflected principles of TBLT. For example, prior to mentoring, one of the teachers, Yan, implemented a coursebook activity in which learners were meant to work in pairs and ask and answer questions about a series of pictures. Instead, the teacher had pairs of students come to the front of the class and perform the activity as a carefully teacher-controlled drill while the rest of the class remained passive onlookers. After mentoring, her lessons became much more interactive and reflected principles of task-based learning, a point illustrated in a reading lesson the teacher taught (with Jing's support). In the coursebook, the reading lesson contained two short passages recounting visits to a museum by two children, followed by a set of comprehension questions. To make this lesson more task-like, the teacher (Yan) worked with Jing to turn it into a test-the-teacher task in which the learners worked in groups to come up with a set of questions to ask the teacher about the two reading passages. The groups then took turns to ask their questions and the group who asked the most questions was given the status of the star group of the day. According to Jing, learners were animated and engaged in the lesson and successfully generated a wide range of questions. Notably, they were reluctant to finish the lesson when the bell rang and some groups had yet to ask their questions. While the effect of novelty is at work here, this lesson illustrates how Jing and Yan were able to successfully taskify the design and implementation of a coursebook lesson in the kind of context (large classes in a rural school) which is often perceived to be ill-suited to TBLT.

In the above three studies, teachers were either teaching as best they knew how in the circumstances or felt constrained to teach in a traditional way by the circumstances (e.g., a tightly prescribed curriculum, large classes, and examinations focused on language knowledge). In either case, in the absence of knowledge about TBLT, there was little evidence of teachers making use of the task affordances, as limited as they may be, in their coursebooks. Nonetheless, the teachers seemed aware of deficiencies in the way they were teaching and were receptive to learning how to draw on TBLT to improve their teaching. In these circumstances, mentoring made a difference and was quite transformative, at least in the short term. In reaching this conclusion, I am reminded of an insight into changing teachers' beliefs offered by Fullan (2020):

> Earlier I discussed how one might change a teacher's beliefs about whether their students could learn. I showed that such beliefs would not be shaken by research evidence, or moral exhortation, but rather, through having new experiences in relatively nonthreatening circumstances with help from a leader or peer whereby the students responded differently (i.e., they started learning). (p. 56)

Despite the promise held out by Fullan (2020), in each of the studies I have presented mentoring was intense and individualised and therefore not easily scalable. If these findings are to be relevant to the real world, mentoring must be delivered in a way that is scalable. The approach to a teacher education ecosystem described in Zhu et al. (2024) is one possible way forward. Task design requires considerable guidance and effort when people have been teaching from the paradigm imposed by coursebooks.

Conclusion

Despite growing awareness of TBLT in language teaching and the widespread availability of models of task-based classroom-ready materials such as the TBLT Language Learning Task Bank,[1] little research or scholarship has investigated the extent to which commercially published coursebooks align with or offer affordances for TBLT. The research presented here has aimed to address this gap. The studies sought to identify where coursebooks align and misalign with TBLT, and (where they misalign) what teachers can do to strengthen alignment with TBLT, and how mentoring can contribute to this project.

In conclusion, I recap the three main threads concerning TBLT and coursebooks that this chapter has explored. First, I outlined the theoretically-based reasons for discounting the value of coursebooks, especially from the perspective of Long's (2015) view of TBLT which privileges needs analysis and in which tasks that are derived from needs analysis (i.e., pedagogic versions of target tasks) constitute both the curriculum and the means of delivering the curriculum. The five studies presented in this chapter provided evidence in support of this critique of coursebooks. The teachers, who taught in a range of different teaching contexts in Asia, consistently emphasised the synthetic syllabus in their coursebooks and

---

1. https://tblt.indiana.edu/index.html

accordingly ignored or de-tasked tasks and task-like activities to the extent that these were present in the coursebooks.

Second, while recognising the adherence to more traditional practices as reflected in the coursebooks, I argued that TBLT must engage more constructively with coursebooks, since they are a reality in the lives of many language teachers. I also made the case that a blanket dismissal of coursebooks fails to do justice to the variety of coursebooks and the way they are evolving, notably, in many cases, in closer alignment with TBLT, as seen in greater emphasis on communicative skills, twenty-first century skills, tasks and projects, and a de-emphasis on a grammatical syllabus. These shifts offer scope for TBLT to be more relevant to coursebook-based teaching.

In the third thread in this chapter, I discussed the respective roles of teacher agency and mentoring as factors that offer to bridge the gap between coursebooks and TBLT. Drawing from two of the five studies that underpin this chapter, I first presented evidence of teachers in Vietnamese primary and secondary schools who were making principled decisions to adapt their coursebooks in ways that drew them much closer to the principles of TBLT. Next, I drew on the other three studies where no such trends were evident but where mentoring to support a shift towards teaching with tasks had a profound and positive impact, increasing learner-centredness, interactivity, and opportunities for meaningful language use in the classroom practice of these teachers.

Where does this leave us with respect to the question posed in the title of this chapter — the coursebook in task-based language teaching: Lost cause or launching pad? My position is that neither of these options quite captures the body of complex and sometimes contradictory evidence presented in this chapter. This evidence points not only to situations where coursebooks reinforce ways of teaching that are diametrically opposed to TBLT, but also to situations where, with appropriate support, teachers can use coursebooks in ways that are much closer to TBLT than the coursebook designers may have intended.

However, perhaps the question can be more helpfully reframed as *tasks* in *coursebook*-based language teaching: Lost cause or launching pad? In this case, the studies presented in this chapter provide abundant evidence of tasks functioning as a launching pad, that is, as a powerful cognitive tool for applying evidence-based principles from SLA to coursebook-based teaching. One reason for this is that, across the textbooks used in these studies, there were many examples of task-like activities that involved using language communicatively, even if the placement of these activities in a lesson sequence often implied a role of practising target forms. This suggests that a valuable skill for teachers to develop is learning how to efficiently taskify such activities. This in turn requires well-informed, motivated teachers who are prepared to treat the coursebook as a resource, not a script. Textbooks are here to stay, and taskifying them seems a necessary step towards (hopefully) more task-based, student-centred syllabi that will allow for TBLT principles to thrive. Here, I am reminded of Jing's (2024) advice to the EFL teachers at a rural high school in her study: "*Use* the coursebook, don't *teach* the coursebook" (p. 49).

To conclude, for TBLT to engage fruitfully with coursebooks requires a community of teachers, teacher educators, materials designers, and researchers to advocate for task-informed coursebook design; to conduct research relevant to many of the thousands of language teachers who teach with coursebooks; to investigate the potential of task-informed coursebooks to play a role in "diffusion of innovation" (Long, 2015); to address coursebook-based teaching from a TBLT perspective in mentoring, teacher education, and teacher learning; and to advocate for TBLT in the language policy and national/institutional language curricula that shape coursebook design. Ultimately, TBLT is legitimised among practitioners to the extent that it provides credible, practical, workable opportunities for them to help learners to develop their language proficiency in ways that best serve their needs (and wants). I am confident that the research I have drawn on in this chapter by Paweena Jaruteerapan, Hao Thi Thanh Dao, Bao Trang Thi Nguyen, Trang Le Diem Bui, and Jing Yixuan goes some way towards this aspiration.

References

Breen, M. P., Candlin, C., & Waters, A. (1979). Communicative materials design: Some basic principles. *RELC Journal, 10*(2), 1–13.

Bui, T. L. D., & Newton, J. (2021). PPP in action: Insights from primary EFL lessons in Vietnam. *Language Teaching for Young Learners, 3*(1), 93–116.

Butler, Y. G., Kang, K. I., Kim, H., & Liu, Y. (2018). 'Tasks' appearing in primary school textbooks. *ELT Journal, 72*(3), 285–295.

Bygate, M., Skehan, P., & Swain, M. (Eds.). (2001). *Researching pedagogic tasks: Second language learning, teaching and testing*. Routledge.

Cao, P., & Newton, J. (2021, October 22–24). *Using the textbook series Tieng Anh, 10, 11, 12 more effectively: Tips from task-based teaching* [Conference presentation]. VietTESOL International Convention, Nha Trang City, Vietnam.

Carless, D. R. (2003). Factors in the implementation of task-based teaching in primary schools. *System, 31*(4), 485–500.

Connolly, D. (2022). Practitioners respond to Freda Mishan's 'The Global ELT coursebook: A case of Cinderella's slipper?' *Language Teaching, 55*(2), 284–287.

Cunningham, S., & Moor, P. (2007). *New cutting edge intermediate* (2nd ed.). Longman.

Dao, H., & Newton, J. (2021). TBLT perspectives on teaching from an EFL textbook at a Vietnam university. *Canadian Journal of Applied Linguistics, 24*(2), 99–126. https://journals.lib.unb.ca/index.php/CJAL/article/view/31371.

Dao, H. T. T. (2022). Perspectives from task-based language teaching on EFL textbook use: A participatory action research study at a Vietnamese university [Unpublished doctoral dissertation]. Victoria University of Wellington, New Zealand.

East, M. (2021). *Foundational principles of task-based language teaching*. Routledge.

Ellis, R. (2017). Position paper: Moving task-based language teaching forward. *Language Teaching, 50*(4), 507–526.

Ellis, R., & Shintani, N. (2014). *Exploring language pedagogy through second language acquisition research*. Routledge.

Erlam, R., & Tolosa, C. (2022). *Pedagogical realities of implementing task-based language teaching*. John Benjamins.

Evans, J., & Dooley, V. (2015). *Access 2*. Express Publishing.

Fullan, M. (2020). *Leading in a culture of change* (2nd ed.). Jossey-Bass.

Gregson, K. (2023). Tracking trends in coursebooks for young learners. *ELT Journal, 77*(2), 245–273.

Harris, P., & Leeming, J. (2018). *On task* (Vol. 2). Abax ELT Publishing.

Harwood, N. (Ed.). (2010). *English language teaching materials: Theory and practice*. Cambridge University Press.

Hoang, V. V., Hoang, T. X. H., Vu, T. L., Dao, N. L., Do, T. M., & Nguyen, Q. T. (2007). *English 12: Teacher's book*. Education Publishing House.

Hoang, V. V., Nguyen, T. Q., Phan, H., Do, H. N. T., Dao, L. N., & Truong, M. N. T. (2015). *Tieng Anh 3, 4, 5 (English 3, 4, 5)* (3rd ed.). Education Publishing House.

Jaruteerapan, P. (2020). The emerging understandings and practices of task-based language teaching (TBLT) by Thai EFL student teachers [Unpublished doctoral dissertation]. Victoria University of Wellington, New Zealand.

Jing, Y. (2024). *An ethnographically informed case study of school-based EFL teacher professional development for TBLT in rural China*. Palgrave Macmillan.

Jing, Y., Newton, J., & Jing, Z. (2022). A case study of curriculum aspirations and classroom realities for TBLT in a remote rural secondary school in Northwestern China. *TASK, 2*(2), 248–268.

Jordan, G., & Long, M. H. (2022). *English language teaching now and how it could be*. Cambridge Scholars.

Lambert, C. P., & Oliver, R. (Eds.). (2020). *Using tasks in second language teaching: Practice in diverse contexts*. Multilingual Matters.

Long, M. H. (2009). Methodological principles for language teaching. In M. H. Long & C. Doughty (Eds.), *The handbook of language teaching* (pp. 373–394). Wiley-Blackwell.

Long, M. H. (2015). *Second language acquisition and task-based language teaching*. John Wiley & Sons.

Mishan, F. (2022). The global ELT coursebook: A case of Cinderella's slipper? *Language Teaching, 55*(4), 490–505.

Moser, J. (2023). Back to the future for task-based learning with Jane and Dave Willis's Collins COBUILD English Course. *PanSIG Journal 2023*, 23–29. https://pansig.org/pansig-publications

Newton, J. (2022). The adoption of TBLT in diverse contexts: Challenges and opportunities. In M. J. Ahmadian & M. H. Long (Eds.), *The Cambridge handbook of task-based language teaching* (pp. 649–670). Cambridge University Press.

Nguyen, B. T. T., Newton, J., & Crabbe, D. (2018). Teacher transformation of oral textbook tasks in Vietnamese EFL high school classrooms. In V. Samuda, K. Van den Branden, & M. Bygate (Eds.), *TBLT as a researched pedagogy* (pp. 52–70). John Benjamins.

Nunan, D. (2005). *Go for it!* (2nd ed). Thomson Heinle.

Priestley, M. R., Biesta, G., & Robinson, S. (2015). *Teacher agency: An ecological approach.* Bloomsbury.

Samuda, V. (2001). Guiding relationships between form and meaning during task performance: The role of the teacher. In M. Bygate, P. Skehan, & M. Swain (Eds.), *Researching pedagogic tasks: Second language learning, teaching and testing* (pp. 119–140). Routledge.

Samuda, V. (2015). Tasks, design, and the architecture of pedagogical spaces. In M. Bygate (Ed.), *Domains and directions in the development of TBLT: A decade of plenaries from the international conference* (pp. 271–302). John Benjamins.

Shu, D., & Zhu, Y. (2024). *Primary school English.* Shanghai Education Press.

Thomas, M., & Reinders, H. (Eds.). (2015). *Contemporary task-based language teaching in Asia.* Bloomsbury.

Tomlinson, B. (2011). *Materials development in language teaching.* Cambridge University Press.

Tomlinson, B., & Masuhara, H. (2013). Adult coursebooks. *ELT Journal, 67*(2), 233–249.

Tórrez, N. M., & Lund, R. E. (2021). Textbook analysis: The case of the first Nicaraguan ELT series. *ELT Journal, 75*(1), 67–76.

Van den Branden, K. (2006). *Task-based language education: From theory to practice.* Cambridge University Press.

Van den Branden, K. (2016). The role of teachers in task-based language education. *Annual Review of Applied Linguistics, 36*, 164–181.

Willis, J. (1996). *A framework for task-based learning.* Longman.

Willis, J., & Willis, D. (1989). *Collins COBUILD English course.* Collins ELT.

Zhu, Y., Peng, B., Shu, D., & Newton, J. (2024). Implementing CLIL innovation in a collaborative teacher education ecosystem. *TESOL Quarterly*, 1–27.

SECTION 3

Task implementation in distinct instructional contexts

CHAPTER 5

Task-based language learning among children in an EFL context[*]
Research and challenges

María del Pilar García Mayo
University of the Basque Country

Task-based language teaching (TBLT) research has expanded substantially in foreign language contexts. However, most studies until relatively recently have been carried out with young adults in university settings, despite the fact that, among young children, exposure to a foreign language (mainly English) is on the increase worldwide. This chapter focuses on current research with children learning English as a Foreign Language (EFL) while they perform collaborative tasks in mainstream and content and language integrated learning (CLIL) contexts. The studies, carried out within interactionist and socio-cultural frameworks, are first steps in charting the territory with regard to young EFL learners and will hopefully lead to improved task-based language programs for such learners. Our findings show that children successfully negotiate to make language meaningful, show mainly collaborative patterns, focus on form, and feel motivated towards the tasks. Moreover, the findings reveal how some implementation variables (learner setup, task repetition, task modality) impact the children's output and task performance. The chapter concludes by highlighting challenges and future research directions.

Keywords: young learners, EFL, task-based language learning, task performance, content and language integrated learning

Introduction

This chapter is based on the plenary talk I was invited to deliver at the 7th International Conference on Task-Based Language Teaching (TBLT) that took place

---

[*] Revised version of a plenary given to the 7th International TBLT Conference, Barcelona, Spain, 2017.

https://doi.org/10.1075/tblt.17.05gar
© 2025 John Benjamins Publishing Company

in Barcelona (Spain) in April 2017. I am writing it seven years after that event and I cannot but realise how much work has been done on the topic of TBLT in child foreign language (FL) learning, mostly English as a Foreign Language (EFL), in those intervening years.

As is well known, a FL context is one in which the target language is taught and learned in a setting in which it is not the official language of the community. In Shehadeh's (2012) words, a FL language context is one in which the focus is on "[t]he teaching of the language other than the native language in the student's own country and as a school subject only" (p. 4). These settings, as opposed to second language contexts, are generally characterised by very few hours of exposure to the target language and limited access to it outside the classroom (although the situation is rapidly changing with, for example, the use of the internet and access to games in the target language — see Butler et al., 2014). FL contexts have received TBLT researchers' attention in the past two decades in different parts of the world (Belgium, Chile, Japan, New Zealand, Spain, and Thailand, for example — see Shehadeh, 2021, for specific references) but, until relatively recently, most studies have had adult and/or adolescent learners as participants.

However, over the past three decades, and as clearly explained in Enever (2018), there has been a worldwide trend to introduce FLs at earlier ages in school contexts. If we consider Europe, the 2017 Eurydice Report (European Commission/EACEA/Eurydice, 2017) stated that in most countries compulsory FL learning starts before the children are 8 years old, that is, at the beginning of primary education. In a recent edition (2023),[1] the report states that in 11 educational systems 90% of students learn English from the beginning of primary education. In Spain, where most of the studies reported on below have been carried out, children start their exposure to instruction in EFL at the age of 6 in most autonomous communities, although some begin this instruction at age 3 (see Guadalmillas & Alcaraz Mármolo, 2017, for details). Children in FL contexts are, therefore, a very important population whose language learning process needs to be documented, because evidence about what they can achieve with very few hours of weekly exposure is highly relevant to make appropriate and research-based decisions about educational provision in order to maximise their learning opportunities.

Undoubtedly, one of the reasons leading to an emphasis on early exposure to instructed FL learning is the well-known "the younger, the better" argument, which was carried over from immersion settings to FL contexts featuring very different conditions (García Mayo & García Lecumberri, 2003). However, research

---

1. Accessible from https://eurydice.eacea.ec.europa.eu/publications/key-data-teaching-languages -school-europe-2023-edition

has shown that age cannot be considered the most important factor affecting FL learning but, rather, the amount and quality of the input the learners are exposed to (Dixon et al., 2012; Muñoz, 2011). Of course, another powerful argument is that knowledge of a FL increases future career and job opportunities, and parents press governments to offer high-quality early FL education (Carmel, 2022).

Clearly, there are advantages of an early introduction to instructed FL learning. As Nikolov (1999) has pointed out, children may develop positive attitudes toward other languages and cultures and language-awareness strategies. However, as some authors (e.g., Oliver et al., 2017) have highlighted, research on child instructed second language (L2) acquisition has developed at a slower pace than research on adult L2 acquisition, mainly because of the potentially time-consuming nature of doing research with children. García Mayo (2021a) also reflects on her experience of over two decades of data collection and emphasises ethical issues (informed consent) and methodological issues such as access to schools, choice of data collection venue, child attrition, and task design, among others. Even so, the growth of research in the area of child FL learning has expanded at a fast pace, which has led to the founding of the Early Language Learning Research Association (ELLRA)[2] — an international association which seeks to advance and disseminate research into early language learning by children in formal educational contexts. Moreover, several monographs and edited books/journal issues have been published recently (García Mayo, 2017; García Mayo, 2021b; García Mayo & Gutierrez Mangado, 2020; Lázaro-Ibarrola, 2023; Pinter, 2023). One major publisher (Multilingual Matters) has a series devoted to early language learning in school contexts, edited by Enever and Pinter, and another (John Benjamins) launched the journal *Language Teaching for Young Learners* in 2019.

The main aim of the present chapter is to provide a brief overview of the work done mainly in the Spanish EFL setting with primary school children (age range 6–12) interacting while performing different communicative tasks, both in mainstream EFL and in CLIL settings. While sticking to the topic of my IATBLT 2017 plenary talk, the contents in the chapter have been updated and expanded. The children in the studies belong to the middle-school childhood stage (Philp et al., 2008), at which stage they have an already developed first language (L1), they do not mind disagreeing with their partners, and they have become quite logical in their thinking. The data have been analysed from a cognitive-interactionist (Long, 1996) and a sociocultural (Vygotsky, 1978) perspective. Our findings throughout these years have shown that children successfully negotiate to make language meaningful, display mainly collaborative

---

2. https://ellra.org

patterns, focus on formal aspects of the target language, and feel motivated towards the tasks. Moreover, the findings reveal how some implementation variables (form-focused instruction, learner setup, task repetition, task modality) impact the children's output and task performance. The chapter concludes by highlighting challenges and future research directions.

Children negotiating for meaning

According to Long (1996), learners' engagement in conversational interaction facilitates the L2 acquisition process because they are exposed to input, produce output, negotiate for meaning and form, and receive feedback on their output. For Long, although interaction cannot completely explain the whole process of L2 learning, it is a necessary condition for learners to acquire L2 communicative competence. Numerous studies have shown that incidental learning is facilitated through the negotiation of meaning, defined by Pica (1994) as:

> ... the modification and restructuring of interaction that occurs when learners and their interlocutors anticipate, perceive or experience difficulties in message comprehensibility. As they negotiate, they work linguistically to achieve the needed comprehensibility, whether repeating a message verbatim, adjusting its syntax, changing its words, or modifying its form and meaning in a host of other ways. (p. 494)

Long (1983) operationalised the main conversational adjustments that interlocutors use during negotiation of meaning as confirmation checks, clarification requests, and comprehension checks.

Pinter (2007) was probably the first study that analysed the benefits of young learner-learner interaction in an EFL setting with one pair of 10-year-old Hungarian children while they completed a spot-the-difference task. She reported instances of peer assistance and of learners' attention to each other's utterances. Building on Pinter's early study, child interaction research carried out in the Spanish EFL setting is characterised by a much larger sample size, control of the children's proficiency level by means of standardised tests, and teacher-researcher collaboration. Thus, García Mayo and Lázaro Ibarrola (2015) examined the oral interaction of 80 children (ages 8–9 and 10–11, 40 in each group) enrolled in EFL and CLIL programs while they performed a picture-placement task. The researchers showed that both groups negotiated for meaning with age- and proficiency-matched peers. When matched for age, CLIL learners produced twice the amount of conversational adjustments as compared to EFL learners and made less use of their L1. When matched for context, the younger learners negotiated more while the older learners relied on their L1 more frequently. Interestingly, Azkarai and Imaz Aguirre (2016) carried out a follow-up study with the same learners one year later (a longitudinal design not very common with this type of participants and this context). They reported that, once again, the younger learners in both settings (EFL and CLIL) negotiated more, but, regarding context, CLIL children were less likely to use conversational adjustments. The study highlighted the need for longitudinal research in school settings.

A longitudinal research design was used by García Mayo and Imaz Aguirre (2017). In their study, 26 EFL and 28 CLIL children carried out a picture-placement and a guessing game task, and the findings provided support for the general tendencies referred to above while also adding that there was a decrease in the use of negotiation of meaning among both groups of learners over time. However, in another study with a similar population — young EFL 9–10 and 11–12 years old learners — Pladevall-Ballester and Vraciu (2020) did not find differences in meaning strategies generated by means of a spot-the-difference peer interaction task undertaken twice, which could be due to the fact that the children in their study completed a different type of task.

An interesting recent study on negotiation of meaning undertaken by Lázaro-Ibarrola and Azpilicueta-Martínez (2022) compared the amount and types of negotiation of meaning strategies of child-child ($n=20$) and adult-adult ($n=14$) pairs with a similar proficiency level (A1 on the Common European Framework of Reference for Languages, 2020), all performing the same communicative oral task with proficiency and age-matched peers. Their findings showed that children produced as many negotiation of meaning moves as adults and both age groups primarily used their moves to prevent misunderstandings.

Overall, then, the studies on negotiation of meaning by child EFL learners indicate that, like adults and English as a Second Language (ESL) children (Oliver, 2002), EFL children are able to interact and negotiate with their peers in spite of their low exposure to the language and their relatively low proficiency level.

Effects of task repetition as an implementation variable

As mentioned above, research in TBLT from a cognitive-interactionist perspective has focused, on the one hand, on how tasks influence negotiation of meaning strategies among learners and, on the other hand, on the impact of task conditions on language processing (Bygate, 2016). Among the latter, task repetition (TR) has received substantial attention in the past decades (Bygate, 2018). The main claim in the L2 literature is that giving learners the opportunity to repeat a task offers them the possibility of focusing their attention on meaning the first time the task is performed and on focus-on-form processes upon TR. Thus, TR has been claimed to be a favourable context for learning (Bygate, 2016). It is also linked to learners' attentional processes, usually analysed in terms of Levelt's (1989) speech production model: when learners perform a task, they need time to conceptualise their message, but if they are given the chance to repeat it, they might devote more attentional resources to formulation and articulation stages.

Empirical research carried out with adult participants has shown the benefits of TR regarding several aspects of their performance such as enhanced accuracy, fluency, and lexical repertoire, although the findings have not been clear-cut (see Bygate, 2006, vs. Ahmadian & Tavakoli, 2010). In comparison, few studies have involved children, and, much less, EFL children, as participants. Pinter's pioneering (2007) research with a pair of 10-year-old Hungarian boys showed that, by repeating the task, the children's confidence increased and they made less use of their L1. Most studies with EFL children have focused on the impact of TR on complexity, accuracy, and fluency (CAF) measures of learner performance – Shintani (2012) with Japanese L1 learners ($n = 15$, age: 6); Kim and Tracy-Ventura (2013) with Korean L1 learners ($n = 36$, mean age: 13.42); Sample and Michel (2014) with Cantonese L1 learners ($n = 6$, mean age: 9.5). All studies have reported mixed findings.

In what follows, I will briefly highlight research with Spanish EFL children which studied the impact of TR on negotiation of meaning strategies, pair dynamics, CAF, attention to form, L1 use, and writing quality. García Mayo and Imaz Aguirre (2016) analysed the interaction of 60 dyads of third- and fourth-year primary EFL learners (8–9, 9–10 years old, respectively) while they performed communicative tasks. They assessed whether TR had an impact not only on negotiation of meaning strategies but also on pair dynamics. Learners' interactional styles had already been studied in the pioneering work by Storch (2002), who established how each type of the four she identified (collaborative, dominant/dominant, dominant/passive, and expert/novice) affected L2 learning. In García Mayo and Imaz (2016), the children had a beginner proficiency level in English and completed different tasks in dyads at two testing times: at Time 1, all participants completed a spot-the-difference task. At Time 2, 21 dyads repeated exactly the same task, 16 dyads completed a similar task with a different content (procedural repetition group), and the final 23 dyads completed a guessing game. The video-recorded oral production was transcribed and codified for negotiation of meaning strategies (namely, clarification requests, confirmation and comprehension checks, self- and other-repetition, L1 use) and pair dynamics. The findings showed that, overall, there were no statistically significant differences between production at Time 1 and Time 2 regarding the use of negotiation of meaning strategies. Regarding pair dynamics, procedural TR seemed to have a positive effect on collaborative patterns. Age was an important variable in the sense that the younger children fitted in the collaborative pattern, whereas fourth-year children fitted in the passive-parallel pattern identified by Butler and Zeng (2015) for Chinese EFL learners of the same age (see also Pladevall-Ballester, 2021, for more information on pair dynamics among child EFL learners).

Sample and Michel (2014) were the first to examine CAF measures in the oral interaction of six Chinese EFL children. They reported that, by the third time the task was repeated, the children were able to focus their attention on CAF simultaneously. It is important to note, however, that the database of their study was very small. Lázaro-Ibarrola and Hidalgo (2017) explored the effects of procedural TR on the oral interactions of 20 young EFL learners (age 11) who had to repeat a task three times. Their negotiation strategies and general performance (CAF) were analysed. Findings showed that, in the third repetition, the amount of confirmation checks and repetitions decreased significantly, while accuracy mildly improved. Neither complexity nor fluency were affected by TR. The sample population in García Mayo et al. (2018) was much larger than in the previous two studies. They analysed the oral interaction of 120 children, 60 with a mean age of 8 and 60 with a mean age of 9, who completed a spot-the difference task at two different times and under two conditions, namely, same TR and procedural TR. The researchers reported that procedural TR had a positive influence on fluency and accuracy at Time 2. In addition, there was an age effect, specifically, the 8-year-old learners were more fluent, whereas the 9-year-old learners were more accurate, thus illustrating trade-off effects (Skehan, 2009).

As for learners paying more attention to formal aspects of language upon TR, Hawkes (2012) was probably the first study that considered the issue with an EFL group. In his study, recordings were made of three second-year classes (aged 13–14 years), with 10 to 16 Japanese EFL learners in each class, performing three oral tasks both before and after a form-focus stage. The findings showed that there were indications that more attention was being placed on form upon TR, such as an increase in the number of form- and pronunciation-focused corrections. Moreover, in the repeated performance, the participants did not ignore the target language and tried to use it.

To the best of my knowledge, the first study that considered the impact of TR on EFL children's attention to formal aspects of language was Hidalgo and García Mayo (2021). They analysed the impact of TR on 40 EFL children's (age 11–12) attention to form, operationalised as language-related episodes (LREs). LREs have been defined as "any part of a dialogue in which students talk about the language they are producing, question their language use, or correct themselves or others" (Swain & Lapkin, 1998, p. 326). The children repeated a collaborative writing task three times on a weekly basis with the same partner; half of the group worked with exact TR (ETR), where the participants repeated exactly the same task, and the other half with procedural TR (PTR), where the participants repeated task type but with different content. Contrary to most previous research, most LREs were form-focused and resolved the issue in a target-like manner in both groups. The results also revealed a statistically significant decrease in the number of LREs at Time 3 in the ETR group, whereas the LREs in the PTR group remained stable. The findings of the study raised important implications of these TR types when working with children and supported previous research stating that TR promotes learners' attention to form. Nevertheless, PTR seems to be more effective in maintaining learners' attention to language (operationalised as LREs), whereas ETR seems to free up more attentional resources, thus reducing the need for LREs during subsequent task performances. The findings also showed that children seemed to mainly focus on formal aspects (producing more form-focused LREs), and that they were able to correctly resolve most of these episodes, regardless of the TR type.

Once again, Pinter (2007) was the first study that considered the impact of TR on L1 use. Her findings from the interaction of a pair of Hungarian children pointed to a decrease in the use of their shared language upon TR. Azkarai and García Mayo (2017) explored the extent to which TR (ETR and PTR) had an impact on EFL children's L1 use and the functions it served. In their study, 42 9–10 year-old EFL children worked in pairs while they completed a spot-the-difference task twice. The findings showed that the children did not make excessive use of their shared L1; rather, they fell back on it mainly when they appealed for help or when they used borrowings, thus preventing communication breakdowns. They also used their L1 with a metacognitive function, that is, to plan and organise the task so that it moved along without abrupt interruptions. Furthermore, repeating a task, whether in an ETR or a PTR condition, decreased L1 use and seemed to increase the children's engagement, especially of those in the ETR group.

Pladevall-Ballester and Vraciu (2017) also looked into the L1 patterns in the oral production of 74 primary school learners (some EFL, some CLIL) over a period of two academic years. Production data were elicited from a non-collaborative pushed output narrative task. At the beginning of data collection, the children were 9–10 years old, and at the end they were aged 11–12. The findings of the study indicated that there was a significant decrease in the use of the L1 in the oral output of both EFL and CLIL children, who produced longer narratives with more L2 words. The children resorted to their L1 as a compensatory strategy during L2 production irrespective of the type of instruction.

Finally, TR has also been considered when analysing the written output from collaborative writing tasks. Lázaro-Ibarrola and Hidalgo (2021) considered the effects of collaborative writing (vs. individual writing) and of PTR (vs. ETR) in the writings of 59 Spanish EFL learners (aged 11). Unlike findings reported with adult learners (Storch, 2013), the children's drafts displayed no differences that could be attributed to collaboration but some improvements were due to TR, with children in the ETR group obtaining overall better holistic grades.

Needless to say, much more research on TR and its effects on different constructs needs to be carried out. Findings from this strand would be welcomed by primary school teachers because repetition in terms of deliberate practice is clearly linked to the education of young learners (see Lázaro-Ibarrola, 2023, p. 112). Teachers would appreciate having information about the type of repetition that is most useful to trigger changes in their learners' interlanguage.

Other implementation variables: Task-modality and learner set-up

Research on L2 interaction among adults in ESL contexts has shown that different tasks offer different language learning opportunities, mostly operationalised as LREs. Thus, Adams (2006) argued that task modality is a variable that should be considered since tasks including a written component lead learners to draw attention to formal aspects of the language whereas tasks including only an oral component draw learners' attention mainly to meaning. Similar findings were reported with adults in an EFL setting in García Mayo and Azkarai (2016), in which the researchers studied the impact of task modality on the LREs and the level of engagement (Storch, 2008) of 44 Spanish-Basque participants who completed four communicative tasks. The findings pointed to a significant impact of task modality on the incidence, nature, and outcome of LREs but a minor impact on learners' level of engagement. Research with adults has also shown the importance of another variable, namely, learner set-up.

Mozaffari (2017) compared how pair formation method affected the quantity and quality of LREs and patterns of interaction by a group of 40 intermediate Iranian female EFL learners who were randomly assigned to student-selected and teacher-assigned pairing conditions and were asked to write a composition collaboratively in the classroom. The findings showed that student-selected pairs engaged in more off-talk episodes — that is, they were less task-oriented than teacher assigned ones, and there was a greater focus on language use in the teacher-assigned pairs, although both pairing conditions featured a collaborative interactional pattern.

The study by García Mayo and Imaz Aguirre (2019) was the first to be carried out on the topic of task-modality and learner set-up with young EFL learners. They examined the interaction of 32 dyads of 11–12-year-old Spanish EFL learners with an elementary proficiency level while they completed an oral task and an oral + written task. Learners were divided into proficiency-paired, teacher-selected, and self-selected groups, whose interaction was video recorded, transcribed, and analysed for interactional patterns and frequency, nature, and outcome of LREs. The findings revealed that children were mostly collaborative in both modalities and that they generated more LREs in the oral + written task. The qualitative analysis showed that they pooled their linguistic resources together in order to correctly solve at least half of the LREs produced. In a follow-up study with the same database, Imaz Aguirre and García Mayo (2020) showed that researcher-assigned dyads produced more LREs and used more L2 turns in interaction.

More recently, Martínez Adrián et al. (2021) examined the incidence, nature, resolution, and incorporation of LREs in two tasks that differed in the modality of the final outcome but offered equal opportunities to revise and edit the final product. Previous studies had not controlled for either the different levels of accuracy that both task modalities demand, as a consequence of their on-line and off-line nature, or the opportunity for revising the output equally in both modalities. Martínez Adrián et al. compiled the findings from various studies conducted with the same cohorts of 5th and 6th grade Spanish primary school EFL learners (10–12-year olds). The authors reported that the tasks incorporating a written component led to a significantly higher number of LREs, which were more form-focused and correctly resolved. Moreover, the oral + writing task promoted more incorporated LREs, which had been resolved in a target-like way, in the final product.

Clearly, more research that considers task-modality and learner set-up is needed. It will again be useful for practitioners to know that incorporating a written component in a meaningful task will draw their learners' attention to formal aspects of the language they are learning.

Collaborative writing in child EFL contexts

A strand of research with child EFL learners that is gaining importance is that of collaborative writing. Collaborative learning in general has played an important role in the L2 classroom since the times of communicative language teaching (García Mayo, 2021c). Sociocultural theory places great emphasis on learners' co-construction of knowledge, which is socially created via interaction with others and then internalised. Storch (2016, p.389) mentions that Swain (2000) reconceptualised her Output Hypothesis to reflect the fact that language production, whether spoken or written, was both a communicative and a cognitive activity. Swain highlighted the dialogue generated by learners while completing communicative tasks and referred to that dialogue as collaborative. She also referred to the process in which learners verbalise their thinking as languaging (Swain, 2006). During collaborative tasks learners may consciously reflect on their own language use and produce LREs.

As I have illustrated above, there are tasks that lead to oral production and tasks that also incorporate a final written product (i.e., a task modality distinction). Although writing in an L2 is hard for young learners, it is clearly worthwhile as writing has been claimed to be a learning tool in research with adults (Manchón, 2011). Furthermore, it affords several other advantages for children, such as providing a picture of learning in progress and promoting creativity (Lázaro-Ibarrola, 2023). Among the most popular collaborative writing tasks is the dictogloss (Wajnryb, 1990), a task in which learners consciously reflect on the form of the language they produce while at the same time re-constructing meaning. The final product in the dictogloss is a text that can be written individually or collaboratively.

The efficacy of collaborative writing tasks has been claimed to be moderated by proficiency, as low proficiency learners tend to focus more on meaning than on form (Leeser, 2004). However, there is evidence that children can identify and resolve some grammatical issues during communicative exchanges, especially in collaboration (Collins & White, 2019). That said, little work has been carried out with low proficiency learners, particularly EFL children. Calzada and García Mayo (2021) analysed the oral production of 31 dyads of L1 Spanish young EFL learners (aged 11–12) while completing a collaborative dictogloss task in which the embedded target form was the 3rd person singular morpheme -s. The instances in which the children deliberated about language were coded as LREs according to their focus and resolution. The researchers also quantified the resolved deliberations incorporated into the collaborative written output. The findings showed that the children focused significantly more on form than on meaning but also focused significantly more on other grammatical forms than on the target -s. Regarding resolution, there were significantly more correctly resolved LREs than incorrectly resolved or unresolved ones. Finally, resolved LREs were mostly incorporated in the writing, regardless of their focus. The findings also indicated that young EFL learners with a very basic command of the language managed to hold a considerable amount of discussion about grammar.

Another important line of research with child EFL learners is that of the provision of written corrective feedback (WCF) in collaborative writing, mainly with the use of model texts implemented via multi-stage writing tasks. Until relatively recently, most studies have elicited data from adult and adolescent learners (García Mayo & Loidi Labandibar, 2017) and only a handful have been conducted with child EFL learners. Due to space constraints, I will briefly refer to this line of research here, but see Lázaro-Ibarrola (2023), Chapter 3, for a more thorough treatment of the topic. Coyle and Roca de Larios (2014) studied the effect of error correction and models on the noticing and revisions of 46 Spanish EFL children (aged 11–12). Their findings showed that the group that received both error correction and models had the highest scores in accuracy and fluency. Coyle et al. (2018) examined the role of models in collaborative writing and feedback cycles. The participants were 16 Spanish 10–11-year-old children divided into a group that received instruction over a period of six weeks and a group that did not. The researchers analysed the process of writing and identified the trajectories the children followed across tasks, showing that those trajectories impacted differentially on their L2 development. Moreover, the group that received instruction with models used more beneficial trajectories than the group that did not. Unlike other studies, Coyle et al. (2018) added a longitudinal component, but the database was small, and no statistical analysis could be carried out, which makes extrapolation of findings difficult.

Luquin (2022) examined the short- and long-term effects of collaborative writing and model texts on L2 learning by young EFL learners. The participants were sixty 11- to 12-year-old Spanish EFL children forming a total of 30 pairs from three classes randomly assigned to a control group (CG), a treatment group (TG), and a long-term treatment group (LTG). The groups were engaged in two four-stage collaborative writing cycles of three weeks, each separated by four months. The four-stage task involved: (a) noticing of linguistic problems while writing a picture-based story (Stage 1); (b) comparison of their texts with a native-speaker model (Stage 2) followed by self-correction of the students' own texts; (c) rewriting of their original output (Stage 3); and (d) delayed post-test (Stage 4). The CG did not receive the models, but self-corrected their own texts; the TG was only exposed to the feedback on two occasions (one per cycle) and the LTG benefitted from this technique during the two writing cycles and the period in between. Results showed that the use of model texts brought about an increase in the number of LREs generated and a greater attention to lexical and content aspects. Nevertheless, after prolonged exposure, the models helped the children diversify their linguistic concerns. This was reflected in their drafts, as many of the aspects noticed were fully or partially incorporated. In the short term, the models led the children to reduce the number of basic clauses and increase the grammatical complexity of their texts. In the long term, the children were able to produce more clauses, show greater lexical diversity in their texts, make fewer mistakes, and improve coherence and cohesion.

Conclusion and lines for further research

The main aim of the present chapter has been to provide a brief overview of research on tasks carried out with primary school EFL children. What different studies have shown is that, even in the EFL low-input setting: (i) EFL/CLIL primary school children successfully negotiate for meaning when completing communicative tasks; that is, they make themselves understood by using conversational adjustments similar to those used by ESL children and ESL/EFL adults; (ii) they negotiate more the younger they are; (iii) procedural task repetition increases collaborative patterns and the learners' attention to form and decreases L1 use; (iv) oral + written tasks draw children's attention to form; (v) learner set-up impacts the production of LREs and L2 use; (vi) children can identify and solve grammatical issues; and (vii) exposure to written models throughout time leads to more accurate writing.

As to where to go next, there are still many research lines in need of further work. For example, there is a broad consensus that pedagogical intervention is facilitative and may even be indispensable in some contexts such as FL contexts (Nassaji, 2017). Considering how important it is for L2 learners to pay attention to formal aspects of the language they are learning, we need appropriate instructional procedures to draw children's attention to form in order to promote effective grammar pedagogy for young learners such as TR and pre-task form-focused instruction (García Mayo, 2025; Calzada & García Mayo, 2023) or pre-task planning (García Mayo & Luquin, 2023), or metalinguistic explanations (Delgado-Garza & García Mayo, 2024). The role of metacognitive instruction (making children aware of their own learning) should also be explored (Sato & Dussuel-Lam, 2021).

Research on individual differences in child EFL interaction also deserves close attention. Some work has been carried out on attitudes toward collaborative writing (Calzada & García Mayo, 2020) as well as on motivation (Kopinska & Azkarai, 2020; Pladevall-Ballester, 2018) and on children's communication strategies (Martínez Adrián et al., 2019). Other topics, such as willingness to communicate and interaction mindset, are beginning to be explored (Azkarai & Calzada, 2024). Considering the increasing importance of digital environments even at the primary school level, studies such as Criado et al. (2022), examining the impact of model texts on child EFL learners' fluency in digital writing, are a welcome line of research, as well as the study of the impact of online/digital gaming in the children's language learning experience (Pinter et al., 2024).

Last but not least, researchers should not forget that only if there is a smooth teacher-research collaboration will findings in this area of research advance (García Mayo, 2021a; Paran, 2017). In that sense, it is of paramount importance to document how teachers actually use tasks and the challenges they face when trying to include them in their teaching (Erlam & Tolosa, 2022). Following Pinter's (2023) work on the topic, researchers should also consider engaging children in research, listening to their ideas, and carrying out more research with children instead of just research on children.

Funding

My research was supported by the Ministerio de Ciencia e Innovación (grant number PID2020-113630GB-I00) and the Basque Government (grant number: IT1426-22). The help of these funding agencies is hereby gratefully acknowledged.

Acknowledgements

I would like to thank the schools that have collaborated with the research team throughout the years. Without their help none of this work would have ever been possible.

References

Adams, R. (2006). L2 tasks and orientation to form: A role for modality? *ITL- International Journal of Applied Linguistics, 152*, 7–34.

Ahmadian, M.J., & Tavakoli, M. (2010). The effects of simultaneous use of careful on-line planning and task repetition on accuracy, complexity and fluency in EFL learners' oral production. *Language Teaching Research, 15*(1), 35–59.

Azkarai, A., & Calzada, A. (2024). A multi-faceted view of engagement with language: A study with young EFL learners working on a collaborative writing task. *Classroom Discourse.*

Azkarai, A., & García Mayo, M.P. (2017). Task repetition effects on L1 use in EFL child task-based interaction. *Language Teaching Research, 21*(4), 480–495.

Azkarai, A., & Imaz Aguirre, A. (2016). Negotiation of meaning strategies in child EFL mainstream and CLIL settings. *TESOL Quarterly, 50*(4), 844–870.

Butler, Y.G., & W. Zeng. (2015). Young foreign language learners' interactional development in task-based paired assessment in their first and foreign languages: A case of English learners in China. *Education 3–13, 44*(3), 292–321.

Butler, Y.G., Someya, Y., & Fukuhara, E. (2014). Online games for young learners' foreign language learning. *ELT Journal, 68*(3), 265–275.

Bygate, M. (2006). Areas of research that influence L2 speaking instruction. In E. Usó-Juan, & A. Martínez-Flor (Eds.), *Current trends in the development and teaching of the four language skills* (pp. 159–186). De Gruyter.

Bygate, M. (2016). Sources, developments and directions of task-based language teaching. *The Language Learning Journal, 44*(4), 381–400.

Bygate, M. (Ed.) (2018). *Learning language through task repetition.* John Benjamins.

Calzada, A., & García Mayo, M. P. (2020). Child EFL learners' attitudes towards a collaborative writing task: An exploratory study. *Language Teaching for Young Learners, 2*(1), 52–72.

Calzada, A., & García Mayo, M. P. (2021). Child learners' reflections about EFL grammar in a collaborative writing task: When form is not at odds with communication. *Language Awareness, 30*(1), 1–16.

Calzada, A., & García Mayo, M. P. (2023). Do task repetition and pre-task focus on form instruction impact collaborative writing performance? Evidence from young learners. In M. Li & M. Zhang (Eds.), *L2 collaborative writing in diverse learning contexts* (pp. 78–106). John Benjamins.

Carmel, R. (2022). Parents' discourse on English for young learners. *Language Teaching Research, 26*(1), 141–159.

Collins, L., & White, J. (2019). Observing language-related episodes in intact classrooms. Context matters! In R. M. DeKeyser & G. Prieto Botana (Eds.), *Doing SLA research with implications for the classroom. Reconciling methodological demands and pedagogical applicability* (pp. 127–154). John Benjamins.

Council of Europe. (2020). *Common European framework of reference for languages: Learning, teaching, assessment — Companion volume.* Council of Europe Publishing, Strasbourg. www.coe.int/lang-cefr

Coyle, Y., & Roca de Larios, J. (2014). Exploring the role played by error correction and models on children's reported noticing and output production in a L2 writing task. *Studies in Second Language Acquisition, 36*(3), 451–485.

Coyle, Y., Cánovas Guirao, J., & Roca de Larios, J. (2018). Identifying the trajectories of young EFL learners across multi-stage writing and feedback processing tasks with model texts. *Journal of Second Language Writing, 42,* 25–43.

Criado, R., Garcés-Manzanera, A., & Plonsky, L. (2022). Models as written corrective feedback: Effects on young L2 learners' fluency in digital writing from product and process perspectives. *Studies in Second Language Learning and Teaching, 12*(4), 697–719.

Delgado-Garza, P., & García Mayo, M. P. (2024). Can we train young EFL learners to 'notice the gap'? Exploring the relationship between metalinguistic awareness, grammar learning and the use of metalinguistic explanations in a dictogloss task. *International Review of Applied Linguistics.*

Dixon, L. Q., Jing Zhao [...] & Snow, C. (2012). What we know about second language acquisition: A synthesis from four perspectives. *Review of Educational Research, 82*(1), 5–60.

Enever, J. (2018). *Policy and politics in global primary English.* Oxford University Press.

Erlam, R. & Tolosa, C. (2022). *Pedagogical realities of implementing task-based language teaching.* John Benjamins.

European Commission/EACEA/Eurydice. (2017). Key data on teaching language at school in Europe- 2017 edition. Eurydice Report. Publications Office of the European Union.

García Mayo, M. P. (Ed.). (2017). *Learning foreign languages in primary school: Research insights.* Multilingual Matters.

García Mayo, M. P. (2021a). "Are you coming back? It was fun". *Turning ethical and methodological challenges into opportunities in task-based research with children.* In A. Pinter & K. Kuchah (Eds.), *Ethical and methodological issues in researching young language learning in school contexts* (pp. 68–83). Multilingual Matters.

Chapter 5. Task-based language learning among children in an EFL context **97**

García Mayo, M. P. (Ed.). (2021b). Research on EFL learning by young children in Spain. *Language Teaching for Young Learners* (special issue), *3*(2).

García Mayo, M. P. (Ed.). (2021c). *Working collaboratively in second/foreign language learning.* De Gruyter.

García Mayo, M. P. (Ed.). (2025). *Investigating attention to form and individual differences: Research with EFL children.* Springer.

García Mayo, M. P., & Azkarai, A. (2016). EFL task-based interaction: Does task modality impact on language related episodes? In M. Sato & S. Ballinger (Eds.), *Peer interaction and second language learning: Pedagogical potential and research agenda* (pp. 242–266). John Benjamins.

García Mayo, M. P., & García Lecumberri, M. L. (Eds.). (2003). *Age and the acquisition of English as a foreign language.* Multilingual Matters.

García Mayo, M. P., & Gutierrez Mangado, M. J. (Eds.) (2020). English language learning in primary schools: Variables at play. *Studies in Second Language Learning and Teaching* (special issue), *10*(3).

García Mayo, M. P., & Imaz Aguirre, A. (2016). Task repetition and its impact on EFL children's negotiation of meaning strategies and pair dynamics. An exploratory study. *The Language Learning Journal, 44*(4), 451–466.

García Mayo, M. P., & Imaz Aguirre, A. (2017). Child EFL interaction; age, instructional setting and development. In J. Enever & E. Lindgren (Eds.), *Early language learning. Complexity and mixed methods* (pp. 249–268). Multilingual Matters.

García Mayo, M. P., & Imaz Aguirre, A. (2019). Task modality and pair formation method: Their impact on patterns of interaction and attention to form among EFL primary school children. *System, 80*, 165–175.

García Mayo, M. P., & Lázaro Ibarrola, A. (2015). Do children negotiate for meaning in task-based interaction? Evidence from CLIL and EFL settings. *System, 54*, 40–54.

García Mayo, M. P., & Loidi Labandibar, U. (2017). The use of models as written corrective feedback in English as a foreign language (EFL) writing. *Annual Review of Applied Linguistics, 37*, 110–127.

García Mayo, M. P., & Luquin, M. (2023). Does repeated pre-task planning have an impact on form-focused LREs? Evidence from EFL children. *Language Teaching for Young Learners, 5*(2), 149–169.

García Mayo, M. P., Imaz Aguirre, A., & Azkarai, A. (2018). Task repetition effects on CAF in EFL child task-based interaction. In M. J. Ahmadian & M. P. García Mayo (Eds.), *Recent perspectives on task-based language learning and teaching* (pp. 9–28). De Gruyter.

Guadalmillas Gómez, M. V., & Alcaraz Mármol, G. (2017). Bilingual legislation. Analyzing the legal framework for primary education in Spain. *Multiárea: Revista de Didcáctica, 9*, 82–103.

Hawkes, M. L. (2012). Using task repetition to direct learner attention and focus on form. *ELT Journal, 66*(3), 327–336.

Hidalgo, M. A., & García Mayo, M. P. (2021). The influence of task repetition type on young EFL learners' attention to form. *Language Teaching Research, 25*(4), 565–586.

Imaz Aguirre, A. & García Mayo, M. P. (2020). The impact of agency in pair formation on the degree of participation in young learners' collaborative dialogue. In C. Lambert & R. Oliver (Eds.), *Using tasks in diverse contexts* (pp. 306–323). Multilingual Matters.

Kim, Y.K., & Tracy-Ventura, N. (2013). The role of task repetition in L2 performance development: What needs to be repeated during task-based interaction? *System*, *41*(3), 829–840.

Kopinska, M., & Azkarai, A. (2020). Exploring young EFL learners' motivation: Individual vs. pair work on dictogloss tasks. *Studies in Second Language Learning and Teaching*, *10*(3), 607–630.

Lázaro-Ibarrola, A. (2023). *Child L2 writers. A room of their own*. John Benjamins.

Lázaro-Ibarrola, A., & Azpilicueta-Martínez, R. (2022). Negotiation of meaning in child-child vs. adult-adult interactions: Evidence from low proficiency EFL learners. *International Review of Applied Linguistics*, *60*(2), 463–489.

Lázaro-Ibarrola, A., & Hidalgo, M.A. (2017). Procedural repetition in task-based interaction among young EFL learners: Does it make a difference? *International Journal of Applied Linguistics*, *168*(2), 183–202.

Lázaro-Ibarrola, A., & Hidalgo, M.A. (2021). Give me a second chance: Task repetition and collaborative writing with child EFL learners. *Language Teaching for Young Learners*, *3*(2), 275–299.

Leeser, M. (2004). Learner proficiency and focus on form during collaborative dialogue. *Language Teaching Research*, *8*(1), 55–81.

Levelt, W.J.M. (1989). *Speaking: From intention to articulation*. The MIT Press.

Long, M.H. (1983). Native speaker/nonnative speaker conversation and the negotiation of comprehensible input. *Applied Linguistics*, *4*(2), 126–141.

Long, M.H. (1996). The role of the linguistic environment in second language acquisition. In W. Ritchie & T. Bathia (Eds.), *Handbook of second language acquisition* (pp. 413–468). Academic Press.

Luquin, M. (2022). Collaborative writing and feedback: A longitudinal study of the potential of models in primary EFL students' writing performance (Unpublished doctoral dissertation). Universidad del País Vasco (UPV/EHU).

Manchón, R. (Ed.) (2011). *Learning-to-write and writing-to-learn in an additional language*. John Benjamins.

Martínez Adrián, M., Gallardo-del-Puerto, F., & Basterrechea, M. (2019). On self-reported use of communication strategies by CLIL learners in primary education. *Language Teaching Research*, *23*(1), 39–57.

Martínez Adrián, M., Gutierrez Mangado, M.J., Gallardo-del-Puerto, F., & Basterrechea, M. (2021). Language-related episodes by young CLIL learners: A review of task modality effects. *Language Teaching for Young Learners*, *3*(2), 213–245.

Mozaffari, S.H. (2017). Comparing student-selected and teacher-assigned pairs on collaborative writing. *Language Teaching Research*, *21*(4), 496–516.

Muñoz, C. (2011). Input and long-term effects of starting age in foreign language learning. *International Review of Applied Linguistics*, *49*(2), 113–133.

Nassaji, H. (2017). Grammar acquisition. In S. Loewen & M. Sato (Eds.), *The Routledge handbook of instructed second language acquisition* (pp. 205–223). Routledge.

Nikolov, M. (1999). "Why do you learn English?" "Because the teacher is short". A study of Hungarian children's foreign language learning motivation. *Language Teaching Research*, *3*(1), 33–65.

Oliver, R. (2002). The patterns of negotiation for meaning in child interaction. *The Modern Language Journal*, *86*(1), 97–111.

Oliver, R., Nguyen, B., & Sato, M. (2017). Child ISLA. In S. Loewen & M. Sato (Eds.), *The Routledge handbook of instructed second language acquisition* (pp. 468–487). Routledge.

Paran, A. (2017). "Only connect": Researchers and teachers in dialogue. *ELT Journal*, *71*(4), 499–508.

Philp, J., Oliver, R., & Mackey, A. (Eds.). (2008). *Second language acquisition and the younger learner. Child's play.* John Benjamins.

Pica, T. (1994). Research on negotiation: What does it reveal about second language learning conditions, processes and outcomes? *Language Learning*, *44*(3), 493–527.

Pinter, A. (2007). Some benefits of peer-peer interaction: 10-year-old children practicing with a communication task. *Language Teaching Research*, *11*(2), 189–207.

Pinter, A. (2023). *Engaging children in applied linguistics research.* Cambridge University Press.

Pinter, A., Butler, Y. G., Sherwin, E., Tabali, P., Mathew, R., & Peng, X. (2024). *Language learning 'in the wild'. Children playing online games in English.* British Council.

Pladevall-Ballester, E. (2018). A longitudinal study of primary school EFL learning motivation in CLIL and non-CLIL settings. *Language Teaching Research*, *23*(6), 765–86.

Pladevall-Ballester, E. (2021). Pair dynamics and language-related episodes in child EFL task-based peer interaction. *Language Teaching for Young Learners*, *3*(2), 189–213.

Pladevall-Ballester, E., & Vraciu, A. (2017). Exploring early EFL: L1 use in oral narratives by CLIL and non-CLIL primary school learners. In M. P. García Mayo (Ed.), *Learning foreign languages in primary school: Research insights* (pp. 124–148). Multilingual Matters.

Pladevall-Ballester, E., & Vraciu, A. (2020). EFL child peer interaction: Measuring the effect of time, proficiency pairing and language of interaction. *Studies in Second Language Learning and Teaching*, *10*(3): 449–472.

Sample, E., & Michel, M. (2014). An exploratory study into trade-off effects of complexity, accuracy and fluency in young learners' oral task repetition. *TESL Canada Journal*, *31*(8), 23–46.

Sato, M., & Dussuel Lam, C. (2021). Metacognitive instruction with young learners: A case of willingness to communicate, L2 use, and metacognition of oral communication. *Language Teaching Research*, *25*(6), 899–921.

Shehadeh, A. (2012). Introduction: Broadening the perspective of task-based language teaching scholarship: The contribution of research in foreign language contexts. In A. Shehadeh & C. A. Coombe (Eds.), *Task-based language teaching in foreign language contexts* (pp. 1–20). John Benjamins.

Shehadeh, A. (2021). Foreword: New frontiers in task-based language teaching research. In M. J. Ahmadian & M. P. García Mayo (Eds.), *Recent perspectives on task-based language learning and teaching* (pp. vii–xxi). De Gruyter.

Shintani, N. (2012). Repeating input-based tasks with young beginner learners. *RELC Journal*, *43*(1), 39–51.

Skehan, P. (2009). Modelling second language performance: Integrating complexity, accuracy, fluency, and lexis. *Applied Linguistics*, *30*(4), 510–532.

Storch, N. (2002). Patterns of interaction in ESL pair work. *Language Learning*, *52*(3), 119–158.

Storch, N. (2008). Metatalk in pair work activity: Level of engagement and implications for language development. *Language Awareness*, *17*(2), 95–114.

Storch, N. (2013). *Collaborative writing in L2 classrooms*. Multilingual Matters.

Storch, N. (2016). Collaborative writing. In R. M. Manchón & P. K. Matsuda (Eds.), *Handbook of second and foreign language writing* (pp. 387–407). De Gruyter.

Swain, M. (2000). The Output Hypothesis and beyond. Mediating acquisition through collaborative dialogue. In J. Lantolf (Ed.), *Sociocultural theory and second language learning* (pp. 97–114). Oxford University Press.

Swain, M. (2006). Languaging, agency and collaboration in advanced language proficiency. In H. Byrnes (Ed.), *Advanced language learning: The contribution of Halliday and Vygotsky* (pp. 95–108). Continuum.

Swain, M., & Lapkin, S. (1998). Interaction and second language learning: Two adolescent French immersion students working together. *The Modern Language Journal*, *82*(3), 320–337.

Vygotsky, L. S. (1978). *Mind in society: The development of higher psychological processes*. Harvard University Press.

Wajnryb, R. (1990). *Grammar dictation*. Oxford University Press.

CHAPTER 6

"It takes a village"[*]
Developing and maintaining sustainable TBLT curricula

YouJin Kim
Georgia State University

Over the last three decades, the field of task-based language teaching (TBLT) has expanded significantly in terms of research topics, research methods, and practical applications to language teaching (Ahmadian & Long, 2022). For instance, by adapting several aspects of second language acquisition (SLA) research methods, an increasing amount of research has examined various task design and implementation features as well as task-based language performance and development (Ellis et al., 2020). However, several "real issues" in TBLT still remain (Long, 2016), including research-informed TBLT curriculum development, task-based assessment, researcher-practitioner collaborations, and in-service teacher education. In this chapter, I focus on one of the issues in TBLT that goes beyond individual task design and addresses concerns regarding course and program curricular development. I first review the research trends in TBLT curricula design and introduce four TBLT curricular design collaboration models. I argue that in order to implement and systematize TBLT curricula in language programs, a collaborative endeavor involving a collection of stakeholders is needed — that is, it takes a village to establish sustainable TBLT curricula.

Keywords: TBLT curricular design, curriculum development, curriculum sustainability, researcher-practitioner collaborations, collaboration models

---

[*] Revised version of a plenary given to the 10th International TBLT Conference, Khon Kaen, Thailand, 2023.

https://doi.org/10.1075/tblt.17.06kim
© 2025 John Benjamins Publishing Company

Introduction

Over the last three decades, there have been noticeable developments in the research domain of task-based language teaching (TBLT) in terms of research methods and the range of empirically researched topics (see Ahmadian & Long, 2022). One of the most widely researched areas pertains to task design and implementation variables such as task complexity, task characteristics, task planning, and task repetition (see Kim, 2015, for a review). This area of research has raised our awareness of key factors that should be considered in the instructed second language (L2) learning process, such as task sequencing. However, task-based learning research that focuses on these variables (e.g., task complexity, task characteristics, task planning) does not provide information about how or why TBLT language education programs are established. Therefore, empirical findings from task-based language learning research should not be interpreted as having direct implications for the creation of TBLT-based educational programs.

Similarly, Long (2016) discusses what he labels as both nonissues and real issues for TBLT and its implementation across educational contexts. He argues that nonissues are aspects of TBLT that have been perceived as being problematic but have been empirically researched, with findings indicating that they are not as problematic in practice (e.g., TBLT neglects grammar and vocabulary; task-focused peer-peer interaction is restricted and often ungrammatical; evidence for successful long-term classroom implementation of TBLT is lacking; the role of the teacher is downgraded in TBLT). Conversely, real issues for TBLT that require further exploration are, for example, aspects related to determining task complexity that would inform task sequencing decisions, task-based assessment, the transferability of task-based abilities, and teacher training initiatives for TBLT. Due in part to the vibrant research agenda in the field so far, we now have empirical evidence of the benefits of tasks in language learning. For instance, Bryfonski and McKay's (2019) meta-analysis, which included 52 studies focusing on the effectiveness of TBLT on L2 learning, reported positive and strong effects of TBLT on such learning.

In this chapter, I put forward a further real issue: the lack of documentation on the collaborative efforts between stakeholders in the development and implementation of sustainable TBLT curricula. I begin with a review of four collaborative models for developing and implementing TBLT curricula based on previously reported research and provide guidance to encourage the development and maintenance of sustainable TBLT curricula.

Research reporting TBLT curricular development

To survey the extent to which TBLT curricular development has been reported, I first conducted a systematic review of recent research studies that report on TBLT curricular development and, second, targeted stakeholders in the TBLT endeavor, specifically the members of curriculum design teams. The questions that guided this investigation were:

1. What are the characteristics of previous TBLT curricular development research in terms of regions, target languages, and instructional contexts?
2. Who are the key stakeholders involved in TBLT curricular development in previous TBLT research?

To answer these questions, research articles investigating TBLT curricular development published between 2000 and 2022 were collected. To ensure the inclusion of all potential research studies conducted in this area, the following data sources were used: two databases (Google Scholar, Linguistics and Language Behavior Abstracts), studies included in previous meta-analyses (Boers & Faez, 2023; Bryfonski & McKay, 2019), and dissertations/theses. The keywords used for the research article and dissertations/theses search were various combinations of the following words: TBLT, TSLT (Task-Supported Language Teaching), task-based, task-supported, curriculum, program, needs analysis, course development, and implementation. The exclusion criteria included studies that (1) examined task-level or lesson-level effects on learning; (2) compared TBLT with another pedagogical approach without further information on how the TBLT course was developed; and (3) investigated teacher training in TBLT without describing TBLT curricular development. In total, 44 studies were included in the analysis. Figure 1 displays the publication trends by year. No obvious pattern emerges from this analysis.

In addition to the year of publication, it was considered important to explore the contexts of this research. Figure 2 shows the location of the projects by continent. The results indicate that North America and Asia are the most common contexts for TBLT curricular development research. Countries represented in North America include the United States (e.g., Lai & Lin, 2015) and Canada (e.g., Campbell et al., 2014), while those in Asia include China (e.g., Baralt et al., 2022), India (e.g., Lochana & Deb, 2006), Japan (e.g., Lambert, 2022), Korea (e.g., Kim et al., 2017), and Thailand (e.g., McDonough & Chaikitmongkol, 2007). Based on the findings of this analysis, it is apparent that TBLT curricular development has not yet been documented in South America, at least as evidenced in published research.

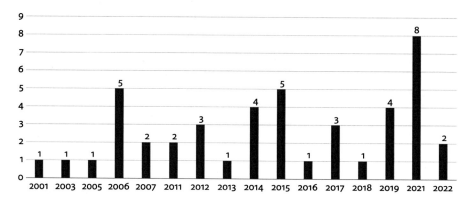

Figure 1. Publication trends of TBLT curricular research by year

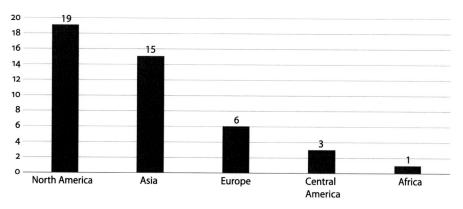

Figure 2. TBLT curricular development research by geographic region ($k=44$)

In terms of the target languages investigated, Figure 3 demonstrates that English (e.g., Lambert, 2022) is clearly the dominant target language in previous TBLT curricular research, followed by Spanish (e.g., Morris, 2017) and Chinese (e.g., Lai et al., 2011). Figure 4 reports the instructional contexts investigated in previous TBLT curricular development research projects. The findings show that university (e.g., Zhang, 2019) and K-12 (e.g., Gurzynski-Weiss et al., 2022) are two of the most frequently researched instructional contexts.

As stated earlier, the second question I was interested in targeted the stakeholders, specifically the members of the curriculum design teams. As shown in Figure 5, the most common option involved only the researcher and the teacher, which could be further divided into researcher as teacher ($k=10$) or researcher and teacher collaboration ($k=7$). For instance, Zhang (2019) used a wiki-enhanced TBLT approach implemented at the syllabus level to support lower-intermediate learners of Chinese as a Foreign Language in the US and explored

Chapter 6. "It takes a village" 105

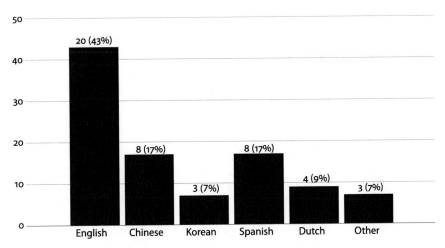

Figure 3. Target languages investigated in TBLT curricular research
Note: The total number of target languages is 46, as one study involved three target languages. The "Other" category includes one instance each for French, German, and Japanese.

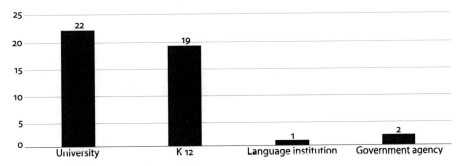

Figure 4. Instructional contexts of TBLT curricular research ($k=44$)

how wikis were adopted to motivate learners' interactions. During the development of a TBLT syllabus, the researcher-teacher created a task-based syllabus and went through four critical stages: (1) the designing phase; (2) the developing phase; (3) the implementing phase; and (4) the evaluating phase. Another category includes the researcher collaborating with the teachers. For example, in the development of a task-based Spanish course for a governmental agency in the US by González-Lloret and Nielson (2015), a course design team carefully created real-world tasks based on a needs analysis. In this project, the design team included language teachers who, in addition to implementing tasks in their classrooms, also contributed to developing assessment tools and conducting a final program evaluation.

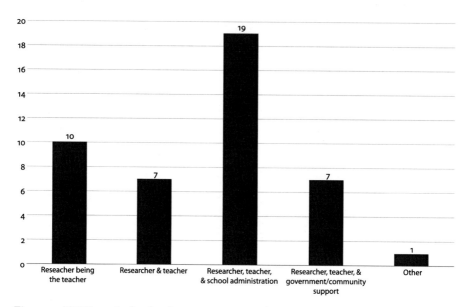

Figure 5. TBLT curricular development team members
Note: The "other" category includes studies that either did not report or inadequately specified the stakeholders involved in TBLT curriculum development.

In addition to researchers and teachers, school administrators were also involved in the development of TBLT curricula ($k=19$). For example, Tinker-Sachs (2007) discusses the development of task-based curricula for school-aged children (grades 4–6) learning English in Hong Kong. The researchers collaborated with both teachers and school administrators. Specifically, they worked with the school administrators to grant permission for at least four to five teachers to participate in action research for the development of task-based curricula. They also obtained the administrators' permission to allocate one English period for the project lessons. Several workshops were also conducted with teachers during the project to support their understanding of the development of tasks. In another study, Lambert (2022) reports on a case where the researcher was asked to coordinate an oral English strand at a university in southern Japan. A collaboration between one researcher and two experienced English as a Foreign Language (EFL) teachers led to the development of a new TBLT program. In this context, financial support was provided by the university, which enabled the team to conduct a thorough task-based needs analysis. Additionally, funding ensured continuous meetings between all members, which helped build a consensus on the goals and objectives of the new program to meet students' needs in oral English.

The final category included researcher, teacher, and government/community support, which created synergistic effects in developing TBLT curricula ($k=7$).

One example is the federally funded three-year project on a task-based approach to teaching Korean as a Foreign Language at the University of Hawaii's National Foreign Language Resource Center by Chaudron et al. (2005). Consisting of the design, implementation, and evaluation of the TBLT program, the project involved not only researcher-teacher collaborations, but also financial support from the US Department of Education under the Language Resource Centers program. McAllister et al. (2012) provides another example of task-based curricula developed as a collaborative effort by researchers and teachers that was also supported at the government level. Financial support was awarded by the regional authority known as *Région des Pays de la Loire*. Their large-scale research project for developing and implementing a task-based program for first-year Business English undergraduate university students in France consisted of a team of ten researchers and teachers.

Considering the two posed research questions, interesting trends emerged, which also highlight areas requiring greater consideration. The review of previous research focusing on TBLT curricular development showed that such projects favored English instructional contexts (47%), mainly in North America and Asia (77%), and both university and K-12 contexts were equally targeted. In terms of the stakeholders included in the curricular development teams, researcher-teacher collaboration or the researcher performing as the teacher option were the two most common arrangements. School administrators were also involved in the development of TBLT curricula, albeit infrequently. There have also been recent TBLT curricular development projects that have not been publicly documented but could offer useful insights in practice. In the next section, I review four models that I have observed or have been directly involved with and discuss in depth the strengths of each model and the challenges involved with such models.

Cases of different collaborative models for TBLT program implementation

As has been noted, it would seem that developing new TBLT curricula requires engagement from many stakeholders. In other words, it takes a village to establish sustainable TBLT curricula. However, collaborations can take many shapes and sizes, each with their unique strengths and challenges. Below, I share four collaboration models incorporating different stakeholders:

– Collaborative Model #1: Teacher as a single village member with a TBLT expert's guidance.
– Collaborative Model #2: Institution as policy implementer of TBLT but with a lack of resources for curricular updates.

- Collaborative Model #3: Ambassadors as continuous TBLT implementers with institutional support.
- Collaborative Model #4: Multiple village members as TBLT actualizers with institutional support.

Teacher as a single village member with a TBLT expert's guidance

This model refers to a case where teachers take on the major responsibility of creating a curriculum, often with a TBLT expert's guidance. In these cases, teachers typically become very interested in TBLT curricula after finishing formal TBLT training during graduate studies. For instance, in the study reported by Kim et al. (2017), I was the instructor of the mandatory English courses at a Korean university. At that time, I was relatively new to TBLT, and I became interested in exploring whether implementing TBLT was feasible in a Korean EFL context. Under the guidance of Kim McDonough, a TBLT expert, I designed a TBLT syllabus. The study demonstrates how the TBLT syllabus was created based on Korean university students' needs and reports students' evolving perceptions of TBLT over the course of the semester. Kim et al. (2017) report that students' perceptions of TBLT changed over time and various factors, such as task repetition, task content, and novelty effects affected how learners felt about TBLT. For instance, when the task content was related to students' lives, students seemed to show more interest in completing the task. Additionally, after going through several phase shifts while repeating a similar procedure of tasks, the focus participant, Miran (pseudonym), seemed to show that her view of TBLT became more positive.

A similar example was presented by Van Gorp et al. (2022) as a colloquium at the International Association for Task-Based Language Teaching conference in Innsbruck, Austria. Jiayi (pseudonym), an MA student in the US, took a TBLT course and developed a TBLT curriculum for a Chinese university setting upon returning to China. The motivation behind this initiative was to examine whether TBLT was a feasible approach in an Asian EFL context, particularly one where language classrooms are often quite large and place significant emphasis on grammatical and written accuracy. The aim was to create task-based English classes for Business English majors at a Chinese university. Following TBLT curriculum development practices, she completed the following five steps: (1) needs analysis; (2) target task identification and selection in domains; (3) task-based learning objective formulations; (4) target task analysis; and (5) task sequencing. For this year-long program, a research-informed TBLT curriculum design was put forward; namely, several data types were collected throughout the design and implementation of the curriculum. The first research project focused on learner motivation and interest in task performance measured via various surveys over time. The results showed that students' ratings of their interest in tasks and the usefulness of tasks were significantly higher towards the end of the semester. Also, students felt that TBLT helped to improve their speaking skills. The second research project carried out over the year compared TBLT and non-TBLT curricula on language development. It was shown that the group that participated in TBLT outperformed traditional instruction on language learning. The third research project examined a novice TBLT teacher's experience. The results suggest that concrete, detailed, specific, and actionable guidance is required for effective implementation. In this model, because of the teacher's enthusiasm about TBLT and her familiarity with the foundations of TBLT, she was able to design the TBLT curriculum with support from her mentor in her MA program.

In both cases above, the teachers had complete autonomy in the design of their courses, working in a silo without consulting with the program directors. Instead, they sought guidance from their former supervisors (i.e., TBLT experts) and were in a position to establish the TBLT curricula. However, there are several limitations to this model. Most importantly, this model was not sustainable, and although the teachers were able to implement their respective TBLT curricula, once they stopped teaching the course, the curriculum was also discontinued. Since the projects did not involve policy makers, the curricular developments were not institutionalized and were short-lived. This is a common collaboration model, especially for novice TBLT teachers who are enthusiastic about trying out TBLT in instructional contexts wherein mandatory curricula are not in place and a program director's approval is not necessary in curricular reform.

Institution as policy implementer of TBLT but with a lack of resources for curricular updates

The second model — institution as policy implementer of TBLT but with a lack of resources for curricular updates — reflects the initiation of curricular development and updates at the institutional level. More specifically, the institutional requests that a department make important revisions, drawing on expertise from curriculum committee members. An example of this kind of project is introduced in McDonough and Chaikitmongkol (2007) as well as McDonough (2015), which has been widely acknowledged as a good example of TBLT curriculum development in Asia and program evaluations in general. In this project, McDonough was the TBLT expert. In response to the upper administrator's request for curricula change for the fundamental English classes at Chiang Mai University in Thailand, a curriculum committee for creating a task-based English curriculum was created. It consisted of the TBLT expert alongside the university English teachers and department leaders. Collaboratively, they developed an English curriculum that was implemented over a six-year period, from 2004 to 2009 (McDonough, 2015). The project was successful in some ways (e.g., increasing students' independence and the relevance to the learners' real world academic needs), but some challenges were also identified (McDonough, 2015): teachers' concerns regarding students' language development, particularly grammar; class size being too large; a lack of language input; and the use of the same task materials over time. After the six-year period, the program became somewhat outdated. As a result, the curriculum was discontinued because of a lack of resources for updating it. This case highlights the importance of long-term commitment by upper-level policy makers in supporting TBLT development projects, particularly for on-going program evaluation and updating curricula.

Ambassadors as continuous TBLT implementers with institutional support

In the third model TBLT experts work with program directors and teachers to collaboratively create the curriculum with institutional support, often facilitated by the government. In this model, the role of ambassadors who receive formal TBLT training and become experienced instructors in the program is key to successful implementation. Two successful examples of TBLT projects that follow this model are described in Baralt et al. (2021) and Gurzynski-Weiss et al. (2024). Florida International University (FIU) in the US and Qingdao University (QU) in China created an undergraduate-level task-based dual degree Spanish-Language Program in Qingdao, China. This collaboration took more than 10 years to develop between the two universities with these shared goals: "(1) cultivating multilingual, globally aware citizens, (2) strengthening the educational relationship between China, the United States, and Latin America, and (3) developing a top-tier Spanish-language teacher-training program" (Baralt et al., 2021, p. 135). Based on a very thorough needs analysis, the task-based Spanish dual degree program was established, and the curricular development team, which consisted of a TBLT expert, permanent TBLT ambassadors, and Spanish teachers in China, also had strong support from upper administrators (e.g., department chair, vice provost). The TBLT ambassadors included two teachers who completed training in TBLT: one who oversaw the program permanently in China and another who was sent to China each year. Baralt et al. (2021) reported some challenges with establishing task-based dual degree programs. For instance, it was observed that two years of a more traditional four-year program curriculum informed by the Ministry of Education's basic Spanish textbooks, and the final two years, which follow a TBLT curriculum, resulted in both teachers and students not feeling prepared for the shift to the new task-based curriculum. To solve this problem, the research team took a gradual approach to TBLT implementation, while mentoring teachers, addressing their concerns, and helping students to understand the core tenets of TBLT.

The second challenge is associated with the ideology that "native speaker status is better" (Wang, 2019; as cited in Baralt et al., 2021, p.137) — specifically, that first language (L1) speakers of the target language are more equipped and qualified to teach the target language than L2 speakers. This ideology results in teachers doubting their proficiency level or not believing in themselves, which leads to minimal exposure to and use of Spanish in China. It also fosters a feeling of a tiered system of native and nonnative teachers in the same department, which negatively impacts team-based work in implementing TBLT. To address this concern, the research team explicitly acknowledged this ideology in their workshops and teacher training, emphasizing the strengths that nonnative speaker teachers of Spanish have.

Finally, creating authentic contexts for Spanish use outside the classroom was challenging, as there was a lack of communication needs in Spanish in Qingdao for both teachers and students. The curriculum development team made extra efforts to address this concern, such as creating various Spanish programs throughout the Qingdao community and linking these programs to students' task-based assessments. Overall, the FIU-QU Spanish dual language program represents a successful model of developing sustainable TBLT curricula that has lasted over 10 years based on well-designed, ongoing needs analyses and program evaluations.

Another successful TBLT curriculum project that followed the third collaboration model is reported in Gurzynski-Weiss et al. (2024). The goal of the program was to create an exposure-track Spanish program in an elementary school in a rural area in the US, promoting early bilingual education to boost communicative competence and enjoyment in learning Spanish. The curriculum development team consisted of a TBLT expert, two graduate students who were trained by the TBLT expert as part of their graduate studies, and one local teacher. The school district provided financial support for this initiative. Based on the detailed needs analysis results, they created a TBLT curriculum and trained a local teacher to become familiar with TBLT, who then became the TBLT ambassador. Over the course of one academic year, the research team and the teacher collaboratively established a task-based additional language program in the elementary school. Through a systematic program evaluation with data triangulation (students' task performance data; teacher immediate post-lesson quick checks; teacher/researcher weekly discussions; end-of-year teacher/researcher meetings; student immediate post-task enjoyment measures), they continuously modified the curriculum. According to Gurzynski-Weiss et al. (2024), the teacher, students, and administration are looking to continue the program, and there is additional interest at other schools in adopting the curriculum. The teacher who was in the curriculum development team is now a TBLT ambassador who can share her experiences with other novice teachers and can be a leader who promotes TBLT in exposure-track L2 programs in elementary school contexts.

Both the FIU-QU dual degree and the Spanish exposure-program projects represent ideal collaborative endeavors, with TBLT ambassadors playing a key role in the sustainability of the programs. Furthermore, both curriculum development projects inspire more practice-based collaborations, highlighting the important roles of TBLT ambassadors and upper administration support in working towards the sustainability of TBLT programs.

Multiple village members as TBLT actualizers with institutional support

The last collaboration model of multiple village members as TBLT actualizers with institutional support demonstrates how village members with different views of TBLT work together to create a localized TBLT curriculum, and how practice-based research throughout the curriculum development process can inform curriculum design (Kim et al., 2021). What makes this collaboration model unique is that not every curriculum development member may be keen on pursuing TBLT in their instruction; however, following the administrator's (e.g., the program director's) decision to implement TBLT, teachers are sometimes involved with the curricular reform, albeit with some reservations. The sample TBLT curriculum project was carried out in a Korean language program at a private university in the US, and the curriculum is still sustained. Initially, I, as the TBLT expert, approached the Korean language program director to suggest conducting a small-scale task-oriented SLA research project in Korean classes. At that time, the program director was interested in revising the second semester of the Korean language class. After observing students' progress in developing their Korean language skills while carrying out tasks for one unit, he and I agreed to expand the project to the curriculum level. The curriculum team consisted of one TBLT expert, one program director, two novice Korean language teachers in the US context, and one research assistant who had taken a TBLT course at the graduate level. The uniqueness of this project was the opportunity to work with two novice teachers who were initially not supportive of TBLT, which made it very challenging to collaboratively design and implement the curriculum (Kim et al., 2017).

The approach taken by the curriculum development team was to discuss concerns related to TBLT implementation in beginner-level Korean language classes during weekly meetings and to carry out research projects addressing questions raised by the teachers. By conducting practice-based research (Sato & Loewen, 2022), the team began collecting evidence of the role of TBLT in language development among beginner-level Korean students and answering pedagogical questions that arose during task implementation phases. For example, as TBLT is learner-centered, teachers who are used to teacher-centered instruction often worry about inaccurate language use during task performance and the role of teachers. In response to this concern, the curriculum team designed a study examining the role of synchronous written corrective feedback or SWCF (Kim et al., 2020). More specifically, two popular feedback types, direct and indirect SWCF, were compared in terms of students' learning of Korean grammar and their perceptions of receiving feedback while performing tasks. The findings suggested that although direct SWCF led to higher accuracy of task outcomes, there was no significant difference between the two feedback types in the subsequent learning of grammar. The curriculum adopted indirect SWCF as it requires less time for teachers to offer feedback in class and encourages learners to process feedback while performing tasks. Additionally, when designing the curriculum, the extent to which different aspects of tasks could be repeated was another concern faced by the team. Consequently, the curriculum development team conducted a research project examining the role of task repetition (Kim et al., 2020, 2022).

Overall, during the course of curriculum design and implementation, a series of practice-based research studies was conducted, and the following decisions were made based on these studies: (1) the adoption of procedural repetition to help students become familiar with the procedure of each task type; (2) the use of various task modalities such as collaborative writing, speaking, and integrated tasks; (3) the consideration of task complexity when sequencing tasks, while making sure that the content and vocabulary requirements of subsequent tasks are not too challenging; (4) the utilization of indirect SWCF, which is time-efficient and offers students opportunities for negotiation of meaning; (5) the sequencing of tasks from pedagogic tasks to real-world tasks, and the use of the latter as task-based assessment tools; and (6) beginning with English input only and gradually increasing Korean input or using mixed input.

The curriculum development process took more than four years, and tasks were modified according to ongoing program evaluations focusing on students' language learning outcomes, student perceptions of various aspects of the curriculum (e.g., task repetition, teacher feedback provision), and teacher and director perceptions of the new curriculum. Similarly to Baralt et al. (2021), the team took a gradual approach to incorporating tasks in their course syllabi, following a task-supported curriculum. During the first round of the curriculum implementation phase, the TBLT expert created the initial tasks with the support of the research assistant. However, after the first year of implementation, teachers began to draft new tasks, and gradually took charge of modifying tasks to meet the learning needs of the students and program goals. The program team highlighted the importance of localized TBLT approaches to curriculum design. As teachers and the director believed in the importance of offering grammar and vocabulary lessons prior to task performance, the syllabus was designed based on a task-supported curriculum, keeping the original textbook as the main instructional material. All tasks were designed as focused tasks and were sequenced from pedagogic tasks to real-world tasks, considering contextual factors while avoiding a "one size fits all approach" to implementing TBLT (McDonough, 2015).

Working with stakeholders who do not share a similar vision of TBLT is not uncommon. This collaboration model comes with unique challenges that should be addressed to ensure its longevity. It is crucial to focus on the stakeholders' common goal, which is to promote student language learning. Another important consideration that can contribute to the success of this type of collaboration is acknowledging the rich and diverse types of professional knowledge and expertise among the members of the curriculum design team. More specifically, the classroom-based teachers are the experts in language program administration and the pedagogy of specific target languages, such as Korean, not the TBLT experts. Thus, it is critical to respect and draw on the program directors' as well as the experienced teachers' expertise.

Developing and implementing a TBLT curriculum also requires time and energy, and it is important that the curriculum team members respect each other's professional duties, responsibilities, and philosophies about teaching and learning. More specifically, if large-scale curriculum development projects fail to offer additional incentives (e.g., course release, monetary compensation) and are mere add-on duties, teachers may not be eager to be involved in the collaboration. Additionally, as the curriculum development process can be lengthy and time-consuming, setting up tangible collaborative professional development outcomes could encourage team members to participate in such large-scale projects. In the collaborative TBLT curriculum project conducted among different stakeholders previously described, the members were engaged in various professional tasks, including presenting project progress reports at local/international conferences, writing research articles, and publishing task materials. Creating opportunities for the team members to share their knowledge and expertise with a larger audience can reinforce the value of the projects, while allowing them to feel accomplished (Kim et al., 2020, 2021).

Innovation in education: Suggestions for developing sustainable TBLT curricula

Innovation refers to "an attempt to bring about educational improvement by doing something which is perceived by implementers as new or different" (Carless, 2013, p.1). Drawing on this definition, implementing TBLT curricula in a new context can be considered a type of innovation in education. However, as Van den Branden (2022) notes, "the implementation of TBLT has been shown to give rise to diverse tensions, worries, and doubts" (p.234). Fullan and Park (1981) proposed three phases in educational innovation: initiation, implementation, and institutionalization. Building on this work, I add a fourth dimension, *systematization*, to develop TBLT curricula in a sustainable way across contexts, in order to reduce potential negative outcomes related to innovation in education. Figure 6 illustrates the four phases of implementing sustainable TBLT and shows a list of various potential stakeholders as well as their roles in each phase. Four groups of stakeholders are introduced: policy maker, TBLT expert/researcher, [novice] teachers, and students. However, it is possible that there is an overlap between the roles of program director and TBLT expert, or between teachers and policy maker, as the program director's role can vary depending on the director's expertise.

As shown in Figure 6, implementers need to be informed and persuaded of the needs and benefits of a TBLT-based curriculum during the *initiation* phase [Phase 1]. Critically, all four stakeholders (i.e., policy maker/program director, TBLT expert/researcher, [novice] teachers, students) need to be involved, and their voices and opinions need to be taken into consideration throughout this important first stage. The second phase, *implementation*, enables implementers to start using and experimenting with TBLT in the classroom. In tandem, the third phase, *institutionalization*, entails support from the program and the institution, and the innovation becomes fully incorporated into everyday classes. Finally, to make TBLT implementation sustainable for an extended period of time, the fourth phase, *systematization*, is necessary. This dimension captures the idea that TBLT should be a regular part of the curriculum, which in turn should go through periodic program evaluations and necessary revisions. Furthermore, upper administrators/policy makers would need to provide additional resources during this time. Also, as shown in Figure 6, ongoing practice-based research conducted by TBLT experts/researchers and teachers could inform decisions made throughout the entire process.

For educational innovation to become sustainable, we should also consider scaling educational research. Scaling educational research focuses on maximizing the magnitude, variety, and sustainability of impact. Scaling educational research innovation, therefore, increases the likelihood that innovation will have a positive

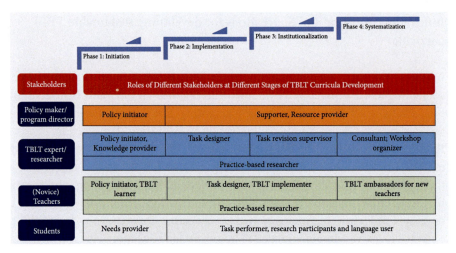

Figure 6. Role of stakeholders during different phases in implementing sustainable TBLT
Note: Adapted from Fullan & Park (1981), as cited in Van den Branden (2022)

impact on society. When designing TBLT curricula, various ways of scaling the project should be prioritized. With this goal in mind, I make the following five recommendations for designing sustainable TBLT curricula: (1) ensure policy makers' involvement; (2) break down the walls among various stakeholders; (3) make resources available for all stakeholders through community efforts; (4) prioritize teamwork with TBLT ambassadors over time; and (5) rely on TBLT ambassadors for the sustainability of the curriculum.

Ensure policy makers' involvement

To promote scaling educational research innovation, ensuring policy makers' involvement in TBLT implementation is critical. Indeed, aligning national standard curricula with TBLT, along with educational policymakers' support, would ensure systematic program evaluations and curriculum revisions. Implementing sustainable TBLT requires funding to offer necessary training for teachers for materials design and to support school administrators. The engagement of policy makers would greatly facilitate securing funding. As a result, one can expect to maximize the magnitude and sustainability of the impact of innovation in education — that is, implementing TBLT.

Break down the walls among various stakeholders

It is very important to facilitate dialogue about educational innovation with all stakeholders, especially with teachers who implement the curriculum (Sato et al., 2021; Van den Branden, 2022). There has been a surge of TBLT research motivated by SLA theories, but implementation cannot be sustainable if experts work in silos and are limited to testing hypotheses motivated by theoretical frameworks. Task-based SLA research helps us become aware of task and learner factors that could potentially affect the language learning process, but it does not directly inform how TBLT-oriented language programs operate. Sato and Loewen (2022) called for more dialogue between researchers and teachers in education research to promote the quality of language teaching; TBLT is not an exception to this endeavor.

Make resources available for all stakeholders through community efforts

Over the last decade, there have been noticeable efforts to make TBLT resources available. For instance, the Language Learning Task Bank, initiated by Laura Gurzynski-Weiss, offers a site for educators and researchers to share their tasks.[1] Additionally, developing special interest groups for TBLT in language teaching/learning associations is a great way to make TBLT initiatives visible. Finally, TBLT experts offer accessible workshops to teachers and program directors. The Georgetown Startalk program for teacher training on task use is a good example of such initiatives.[2]

Prioritize teamwork with TBLT ambassadors over time

While all team members may share similar views on the value of TBLT, getting everyone on board is an important foundational work that needs to be accomplished during the TBLT implementation project. As Borg (2015) states, teachers should not be considered "mechanical implementers of external prescriptions" as they are "active, thinking decision-makers" (p.8) who impact what happens in the classroom. The major stakeholders (i.e., upper-level policy makers, program directors, teachers, TBLT experts, students) need to play their unique roles while collaborating with other stakeholders. For instance, program directors and experienced teachers need to offer ongoing TBLT teacher training to novice teachers, who then subsequently become TBLT ambassadors. Using TBLT approaches in teacher training (see Bryfonski, 2022) would be ideal, as teachers will have

---

1. https://tblt.indiana.edu
2. see https://startalk.georgetown.edu for more information.

first-hand experience. Creating practice-based research opportunities for teachers that draw on their experiences and knowledge would be important, and TBLT experts could facilitate such a process. Furthermore, students' understanding of the value of TBLT in their language learning also needs to be promoted. With students' belief in the benefits of TBLT for their own language learning, the benefits of TBLT could be enhanced. Overall, ensuring that all stakeholders share similar views on the value of TBLT should be prioritized to establish a sustainable TBLT curriculum.

Relying on TBLT ambassadors for sustainability of curriculum

As illustrated in Baralt et al. (2022), the role of TBLT ambassadors in the program is critical to the establishment of sustainable TBLT curricula. As previously discussed, TBLT ambassadors are usually experienced teachers or program directors with a wealth of knowledge about the curriculum and the local context. As such, they are well positioned to offer workshops or to co-teach with teachers who are new to TBLT. Such a hands-on and collaborative training process would contribute to the longevity of the curriculum. Furthermore, TBLT ambassadors' ongoing professional development interventions would help more experienced teachers gain up-to-date knowledge about TBLT. Finally, TBLT curricula need to be evaluated periodically, as discussed above ("systematization" in innovation in education), and appropriate modifications need to be made as learners' emerging needs may change based on societal/contextual changes. As Norris and Davis (2022) note, the formative orientation of TBLT program evaluation "may be of the most value for educators seeking a way of embarking systematically on a TBLT innovation" (p. 543). Ambassadors, working with teachers and participating more directly in research-based initiatives, are in an ideal position to carry out program evaluations and offer the necessary modifications.

Suggested model for developing and implementing sustainable TBLT curricula

As I have been arguing throughout this chapter, it takes a village to establish sustainable TBLT curricula. Collaboration among villagers with different expertise, along with institutional support, are the most critical components of curricular development. Figure 7 illustrates a model that I propose for developing and implementing sustainable TBLT curricula. I suggest that the five recommendations presented in the previous section be incorporated into the process. When developing new TBLT curricula (the left side of Figure 7), the contributions of five stakeholders (i.e., TBLT experts, upper administrators/policy makers, teachers, students, program directors) are equally important in different ways (see Figure 6 for their roles).

As the TBLT curricula go through the systematization process, TBLT experts' involvement becomes less required, and the teachers' role as TBLT ambassadors grows (the right side of Figure 7). Teachers who have received TBLT training may become autonomous TBLT ambassadors capable of modifying the original curricula and associated tasks to meet the evolving needs of the students and the program. Teachers who are either novice or experienced remain an important part of this process as they will most likely be the main task designers and frontline task implementors. Furthermore, upper administrators' ongoing support remains one of the main fundamental resources without which long-term systematization may not be possible.

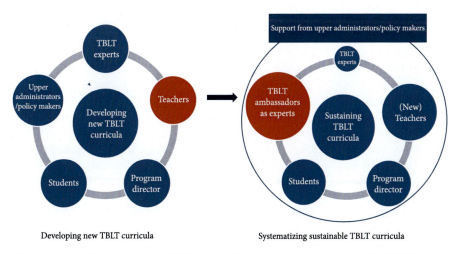

Figure 7. From developing new TBLT curricula to systematizing sustainable TBLT curricula

Conclusion

I began this chapter by highlighting a lack of documentation on detailed steps for a longitudinal approach to sustainable TBLT curricular development as one of the real issues in the field of TBLT. Among the articles that report such processes, results have shown that the teacher-researcher collaboration model was very common, sometimes with upper administrators' involvement. However, previous research did not highlight the different roles of stakeholders and how each could contribute to TBLT curricular development. I reviewed four different collaboration models that I have observed or been a part of, and discussed the strengths and challenges associated with each model. I conclude that it takes a village to design and maintain sustainable TBLT curricula that are effective for language education, and this design and maintenance require many stakeholders' persistent efforts. I argue that villagers' ongoing collaboration and the contributions of TBLT ambassadors need to be prioritized during this process.

Acknowledgements

I am grateful to Yoon Namkung who assisted with the systematic review study presented in this chapter. Special thanks go to Nicole Tracy-Ventura, Melissa Baralt, Caroline Payant, and Nicole De Los Reyes who shared invaluable comments throughout various stages of this project. I would also like to thank Martin East and an anonymous reviewer for offering very helpful feedback.

References

* indicates the studies that were included in the research synthetic review.

Ahmadian, M. J., & Long, M. H. (Eds.). (2022). *The Cambridge handbook of task-based language teaching*. Cambridge University Press.

*Baralt, M., Fei, W., Bu, Z., Chen, H., Gómez, J.M., & Luan, X. (2022). The implementation of a task-based Spanish-language program in Qingdao, China: A case study. In M.J. Ahmadian & M.H. Long (Eds.), *The Cambridge handbook of task-based language teaching* (pp. 135–150). Cambridge University Press.

Boers, F., & Faez, F. (2023). Meta-analysis to estimate the relative effectiveness of TBLT programs: Are we there yet? *Language Teaching Research*.

Borg, S. (2015). *Teacher cognition and language education: Research and practice*. Bloomsbury Academic.

*Bryfonski, L. (2022). Connecting teacher training to TBLT implementation: A case study of pre-service teachers in Honduran bilingual schools. In M.J. Ahmadian & M.H. Long (Eds.), *The Cambridge handbook of task-based language teaching* (pp. 463–477). Cambridge University Press.

Bryfonski, L., & McKay, T.H. (2019). TBLT implementation and evaluation: A meta-analysis. *Language Teaching Research, 23*(5), 603–632.

*Campbell, C., MacPherson, S., & Sawkins, T. (2014). Preparing students for education, work, and community: Activity theory in task-based curriculum design. *TESL Canada Journal, 31*(8), 68–92.

Carless, D. (2013). Innovation in language teaching and learning. In C.A. Chapelle (Ed.), *The encyclopedia of applied linguistics*, 1–4. Blackwell.

*Chaudron, C., Doughty, C. J., Kim, Y., Kong, D., Lee, J., Lee, Y., Long, M. H., Rivers, R., & Urano, K. (2005). A task-based needs analysis of a tertiary Korean as a foreign language program. In M. Long (Ed.), *Second language needs analysis* (pp. 225–261). Cambridge University Press.

Ellis, R., Skehan, P., Li, S., Shintani, N., & Lambert, C. (2020). *Task-based language teaching: Theory and practice.* Cambridge University Press.

Fullan, M., & Park, P. B. (1981). *Curriculum implementation: A resource booklet.* Ontario Ministry of Education.

*González-Lloret, M., & Nielson, K. B. (2015). Evaluating TBLT: The case of a task-based Spanish program. *Language Teaching Research, 19*(5), 525–549.

*Gurzynski-Weiss, L., Giacomino, L., & Jarrett, D. (2022). Examining high-school learners' experience of task motivation and difficulty in a two-week Spanish immersion camp. In M. J. Ahmadian & M. H. Long (Eds.), *The Cambridge handbook of task-based language teaching* (pp. 566–584). Cambridge University Press.

Gurzynski-Weiss, L., Wray, M., Coulter-Kern, M., & Bernardo, J. (2024). Task-based elementary Spanish in rural Indiana: A practice-based collaboration. *Studies in Second Language Learning and Teaching, 14*(1), 121–147.

Kim, Y. (2015). The role of tasks as vehicles for learning in classroom interaction. In N. Markee (Ed.), *Handbook of classroom discourse and interaction* (pp. 163–181). Wiley-Blackwell.

Kim, Y., Choi, B., Kang, S., Kim, B., & Yun, H. (2020). Comparing the effects of direct and indirect synchronous written corrective feedback: Learning outcomes and students' perceptions. *Foreign Language Annals, 53*(1), 176–199.

Kim, Y., Choi, B., Kang, S., Yun, H., & Kim, B. (2017, April 19–21). *TBLT might not work with low-level foreign language learners taught by novice teachers: Overcoming the challenges for the better* [Conference presentation]. 4th International Conference on Task-Based Language Teaching: Tasks in Context, Barcelona, Spain.

Kim, Y., Choi, B., Yun, H., Kim, B., & Choi, S. (2022). Task repetition, synchronous written corrective feedback and the learning of Korean: A classroom-based study. *Language Teaching Research. 26,* 1106–1132.

Kim, Y., Choi, B., Yun, H., Kim, B., & Kang, S. (2021). *Learning Korean through tasks: High beginner to low intermediate.* Kong & Park Publishing.

*Kim, Y., Jung, Y., & Tracy-Ventura, N. (2017). Implementation of a localized task-based course in an EFL context: A study of students' evolving perceptions. *TESOL Quarterly, 51*(3), 632–660.

Kim, Y., Kang, S., Yun, H., Kim, B., & Choi, B. (2020). The role of task repetition in a Korean as a foreign language classroom: Writing quality, attention to form, and learning of Korean grammar. *Foreign Language Annals, 53*(1), 827–849.

*Lai, C., & Lin, X. (2015). Strategy training in a task-based language classroom. *The Language Learning Journal, 43*(1), 20–40.

*Lai, C., Zhao, Y., & Wang, J. (2011). Task-based language teaching in online ab initio foreign language classrooms. *The Modern Language Journal, 95*(1), 81–103.

*Lambert, C. (2022). Task-based language teaching in a Japanese university: From needs analysis to evaluation. In M. J. Ahmadian & M. H. Long (Eds.), *The Cambridge handbook of task-based language teaching* (pp. 121–134). Cambridge University Press.

*Lochana, M., & Deb, G. (2006). Task based teaching: Learning English without tears. *Asian EFL Journal, 8*(3), 140–164.

Long, M. H. (2016). In defense of tasks and TBLT: Nonissues and real issues. *Annual Review of Applied Linguistics, 36*, 5–33.

*McAllister, J., Narcy-Combes, M. F., & Starkey-Perret, R. (2012). Language teachers' perceptions of a task-based learning programme in a French University. In A. Shehadeh & C. A. Coombe (Eds.), *Task-based language teaching in foreign language contexts: Research and implementation* (pp. 313–342). John Benjamins.

McDonough, K. (2015). Perceived benefits and challenges with the use of collaborative tasks in EFL contexts. In M. Bygate (Ed.), *Domains and directions in the development of TBLT* (pp. 225–246). John Benjamins.

*McDonough, K., & Chaikitmongkol, W. (2007). Teachers' and learners' reactions to a task-based EFL course in Thailand. *TESOL Quarterly, 41*(1), 107–132.

*Morris, K. J. (2017). Learning by doing: The affordances of task-based pragmatics instruction for beginning L2 Spanish learners studying abroad [Unpublished doctoral dissertation]. University of California Davis, US.

Norris, J., & Davis, J. (2022). Evaluating task-based language programs. In M. J. Ahmadian & M. H. Long (Eds.), *The Cambridge handbook of task-based language teaching* (pp. 529–548). Cambridge University Press.

Sato, M., & Loewen, S. (2022). The research–practice dialogue in second language learning and teaching: Past, present, and future. *The Modern Language Journal, 106*(3), 509–527.

Sato, M., Loewen, S., & Pastushenkov, D. (2021). 'Who is my research for?': Researcher perceptions of the research–practice relationship. *Applied Linguistics, 43*(4), 625–652.

*Tinker-Sachs, G. (2007). The challenges of adopting and adapting task-based cooperative teaching and learning in an EFL context. In K. Van den Branden, K. Van Gorp, & M. Verhelst (Eds.), *Tasks in action: Task-based language education from a classroom-based perspective* (pp. 235–264). Cambridge Scholars.

Van den Branden, K. (2022). *How to teach an additional language: To task or not to task?* John Benjamins.

Van Gorp, K., Coss, M., Tuzcu, A., & Guan, X. (2022, August 29–31). *TBLT in a Chinese university: Course development, implementation, reflections, and results* [Colloquium]. 9th International Conference on Task-Based Language Teaching: Broadening the Horizon of TBLT, Innsbruck, Austria.

Wang, F. (2019). *The status of Spanish language teachers in China* [Paper presentation]. Qingdao University.

*Zhang, S. (2019). The effectiveness of a wiki-enhanced TBLT approach implemented at the syllabus level in the teaching of Chinese as a foreign language. *Chinese as a Second Language Research, 8*(2), 197–225.

SECTION 4

Task-based language assessment

CHAPTER 7

Aligning classroom tasks with can-do descriptors helps TBLT programs be chock-full of proficiency indicators[*]

Paula Winke
Michigan State University

In this chapter, I discuss how teachers can create sets or series of Can-do based statements to define their task-based curriculum. Teachers can also use the Can-do statements to have students self-assess their language proficiency and their task-based gains before and after learning, especially if the Can-do statements are associated, through teacher expert judgement, to proficiency levels on a national or international standardized scale of language proficiency. I suggest that the string or network of Can-do statements that outline a task-based curriculum and that are used for student self-evaluation may help researchers and teachers better understand language development pathways. That is, Can-do statements can be used as descriptors of task-based curricular goals, articulating the essence of the key communicative tasks that are learning targets for the classroom; they can also act as reflections of published language frameworks. The chapter showcases sets of Can-do statements created by teachers across several languages (Russian, Chinese, and Hindi) that were based on the local curriculum in those language teachers' programs.

Keywords: Can-do descriptors, Can-do statements, proficiency, tasks, language assessment, language testing, task-based language assessment, TBLA

Introduction

In essence, task-based language teaching (TBLT) is about enhancing and developing language users' performance on communicative tasks — their ability to

---

[*] Revised version of a plenary given to the 8th International TBLT Conference, Ottawa, Canada, 2019.

https://doi.org/10.1075/tblt.17.07win
© 2025 John Benjamins Publishing Company

respond to and complete the tasks with which they are presented. This chapter builds a link between TBLT and language assessment. It is about concrete, classroom-based and performance-based Can-do statements and their use and value in determining and measuring the learning that is going on in communicative and task-based classrooms. The chapter is based on the plenary address that I was invited to give at the 8th International Conference on TBLT, held in Ottawa, Canada, in 2019.

I began my plenary by highlighting, albeit briefly, the pioneering work of a female scientist. As I explained there, if you are looking for an academic hero, and you work in language assessment like I do, I highly recommend the astronomer Dr. Vera Rubin. Figure 1 is a picture of Dr. Rubin at the Ohio Telescope in Flagstaff, Arizona, in the USA. Another fantastic image of Dr. Rubin from the 1970s appeared in her obituary in the New York Times on December 27, 2016 (Overbye, 2016). I encourage you to read her obituary and ponder the pictures of her. In the photos, she can be seen working with a telescope, analyzing data from space. Dr. Rubin was 88 when she passed away in 2016. Her life work was to look for patterns in data. She was an observationist.

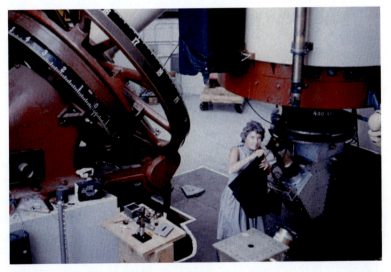

Figure 1. Dr. Vera Rubin at the 183-centimeter (72-inch) Ohio Telescope in Flagstaff. (Copyright: Carnegie Science. Reprinted with permission from Carnegie Science.)

During her life's work, and by studying patterns of gravitational pull in the universe, Dr. Rubin kept seeing that, where something should be, there was in fact nothing. This nothing, she plotted, must weigh quite a lot, at least by her calculations. But people told her that her calculations must be wrong. Her calculations did not fit the theories held at that time. Fortunately, Dr. Rubin was extremely diligent and was not one to be deterred. She was very used to thinking outside the box. As a woman scientist at a time when few women were recognized as such, and even fewer were promoted as such, she had to fight to get access to telescopes. She wanted to gather data on the distributions of mass in spiral galaxies, which she could measure by mapping how fast the galaxies rotated (American Museum of Natural History, n.d.). She eventually did obtain access. However, as the New York Times (Overbye, 2016) described, when she arrived at one of the buildings to do her research work, there was no women's restroom. So, Dr. Rubin taped an outline of a woman on one of the bathroom doors, making it a ladies' room. I think some of these experiences of making herself fit, where she did not fit at first, helped her understand that not everything needs to fit at first. Rather, systems can change. Expectations can change. How one views the world can change. Theories can (and probably must) change as we learn new things or start to see things in a different light. It is okay if things do not align with the standards. The standards can change too.

At the start of this chapter I ask you, the reader, to remember what can be learned from Dr. Rubin's work — that it is okay if things do not align because the universe is bigger than our world of data. Data simply provide a window into the world, and as more data are collected, the more of the world we can see. Our tasks as second language scientists are to observe and to fit the second language acquisition (SLA) theories to what we accurately see. Non-conforming data or patterns that deviate from the norm are to be inspected closely. Outlying data or patterns will challenge the theories. And rightfully so. (Dr. Rubin, by the way, discovered dark matter, which challenges Einstein's theory of relativity — I will refer back to Dr. Rubin at the end of the chapter.)

For the purposes of this chapter, I think of concrete, classroom-based and performance-based Can-do statements as little stars in the universe of language learning that we can collect, write down, and study. Standardized tests are out of the hands of teachers, and scores from them can be frustrating to teachers and learners alike who may feel that the content of the tests does not reflect the learning that has occurred. As a supplement, or as an ancillary measure of development, I describe in this chapter how using Can-do based self-assessments is a way to capture additional evidence of learning: one that can track learning no matter how small, and no matter in which direction (vertical or horizontal) it grows. In other words, Can-do based statements can be an additional microscope and way to observe learning. Moreover, as I will explain below, they are innocuous for learners to respond to, and rather inexpensive to design in terms of teacher effort and assessment construction resources. Thus, they should be an easy addition to any classroom and give valuable information at a low cost. Also, they should reflect and align with any classroom's TBLT goals and ethos.

As described by Bygate et al. (2022), tasks are "the pedagogical thread and reference point for teaching" (p. 28). Listing a course's most salient tasks as Can-do statements for purposes of self-assessment, and then administering the self-assessment both at the start and the end of the course to practically and efficiently sample students' perceived task-based gains, can help teachers understand whether individual key tasks were perceived as useful by the students, and whether, after task performance and instruction, the students perceived that they could do the tasks. Bygate et al. explained that teachers need to ensure that students focus on form and meaning while engaging in tasks because form and meaning build on and contribute to each other. The checks on form and meaning growth within students can be observed and recorded by teachers who evaluate concrete task performance. At the same time, Bygate et al. stressed that teachers need to check that tasks are at the center of learning.

In this chapter, I explain that self-assessments with Can-do statements can be one way to check that tasks are at the center of learning. The self-assessments can reinforce in students' minds that "classroom tasks constitute the main focus of instruction" (Shehadeh, 2018, p. 1). The repeated administration of the self-assessments, and the follow-up discussions on the results from them, can additionally reinforce in students the notion that their opinions and views on the tasks used in their classrooms are valued and that they matter — one hallmark of TBLT. That is, TBLT is based on students' needs; furthermore, TBLT involves a democratic learning process wherein learning relies on classroom citizens' active participation and shared values and goals in advancing their communication skills.

What are Can-do statements?

Can-do statements are positively written, short, concrete, and clear statements about what a person can do in the target language at a given level of proficiency or at a certain point in time in a person's learning trajectory. Early but highly influential examples of Can-do statements were those produced by the Council of Europe (2001). The aim of presenting the Can-do statements as the heart of an international language framework, known as the Common European Framework of Reference (CEFR) for language learning, teaching, and assessment, was to provide an interface between these three elements (learning, teaching, assessment) that could be applied across a broad range of languages. That is:

> The Common European Framework provides a common basis for the elaboration of language syllabuses, curriculum guidelines, examinations, textbooks, etc. across Europe. It describes in a comprehensive way what language learners have to learn to do in order to use a language for communication and what knowledge and skills they have to develop so as to be able to act effectively. The description also covers the cultural context in which language is set. The Framework also defines levels of proficiency which allow learners' progress to be measured at each stage of learning and on a life-long basis.   (Council of Europe, 2001, p. 1)

The CEFR presents holistic statements at six different levels of language proficiency (A1, A2, B1, B2, C1, C2), where A1 and A2 represent the performances that might be expected of a basic user of a language, whereas C1 and C2 represent performances of a proficient user. The CEFR has a global scale. This scale has been further divided into scales for different dimensions of proficiency (e.g., reading, spoken interaction). A range of information is available so that language users (including teachers and learners) can self-assess their proficiency level. The scales have also informed the design of a range of textbooks and are useful for teachers when it comes to designing their own tasks for pedagogical and assessment purposes. As a consequence of data derived from a large-scale international project, an updated and extended version is available (Council of Europe, 2020).

Can-do statements are designed to promote independence, agency, and motivation in language learners who read them and who consider their own proficiency and language abilities while they read them. Teachers have reported that they agree with this, and find Can-do statements help students "become aware of their potential and recognize their limitations" (Faez et al., 2011, p. 10). One of the goals of task-based language assessment (TBLA) is for the assessments to function "as a means for clearly stating the learning outcomes valued by the program" (Norris & East, 2022, p. 514). A good-sized list of Can-do-based statements, which represent a course's learning objectives, can serve as an explicit list of learning outcomes valued by the program. Students' reflections on these statements are important for understanding if the outcomes were achieved, and if the values were shared by the students.

Normally, Can-do statements for classroom purposes or for language learners themselves are responded to by language learners on a Likert-scale. For example, a language learner may read a Can-do statement, and then consider how well they can do what is described in the statement on a scale of one to four, one to five, or one to six (the size of the scale is up to the teacher or researcher), with the highest number on the Likert-scale representing mastery of the task being described, and the lowest number representing inability or very little ability (at that time) to perform or do the task, with the notion that skills to complete the task well are to be developed and learned in the future. As described by Tigchelaar et al. (2017),

Can-do statements "use specific, understandable language that describes functional skills rather than linguistic jargon (e.g., "I can describe a childhood experience") and they divide complex language features into short, simple descriptions (e.g., "I can describe a place I have visited")" (p. 585).

The inner core (or operationalization) of each Can-do statement is found in the lesson plan and materials that the teacher uses to teach and enact the task described by the Can-do statement. However, the Can-do statements, if written by the teachers as they reflect on their teaching and their students' learning, can be even more informative for understanding language learning, and certainly would be more informative than an analysis of textbook materials and syllabi alone, because materials and textbooks for classrooms are used within *lived experiences* in the language classroom. Textbook tasks and activities may be "insufficiently relevant and appealing to the actual learners who use them" (Tomlinson, 2023, p. 4), and in practice teachers supplement or adjust their teaching to match the needs of the students who are learning.

Matching needs to students such that tasks that are included in the curriculum are needs-based (Long, 2015) is a further hallmark of TBLT (alongside, as previously stated, the notion that students' viewpoints on the tasks used in their classroom are valued). On a day-to-day basis, or on a very local and temporal level, teachers adjust their tasks to meet the needs of their students who are in the classroom, right in front of them, asking questions and stating their needs. Can-do statements, written as a result of reflection on what was taught in the classroom, and with special emphasis placed on the tasks that were *successful* in the classroom (i.e., focusing on what appeared to be well learned by the students), can be a road map to proficiency. At the end of the journey, based on various selected criteria, one can evaluate whether that road was okay, good, or great.

For example, if, after two weeks of teaching, a teacher can positively see in their students that each one can say, "Yes, for certain, I as a learner can confidently state that 'I can respond to a classmate who asks me how I am feeling,'" then we know for certain about one thing regarding language learning in that classroom: that outcome of self-evaluated confidence in task performance ability on the one Can-do statement is one data point per student — that is, one piece of information related to a level of performance on the task in question (responding to a request for information about how I am feeling). Strings or sets — or even networks — of Can-do statements would be able to tell us even more about learning at the individual and group level in the classroom. For example, a teacher may ask students *before* the two weeks of teaching if they could respond to a classmate who asks how they are feeling, and most might reply "not yet" or only "with much help" at that time. *After* two weeks of learning, the teacher may ask the same question again, and at that second time (post-learning the task) the students might indicate "yes," they can do that task well. The teacher would have two linear data points (one string) indicating learning per student. This chapter is about teachers laying those strings or networks out to capture data about learning. This chapter is therefore also about teachers taking ownership of tracking their students' learning.

How teachers can use can-do statements: An example

Within language classrooms, teachers can design self-assessments made up of Can-do statements to help gauge how students are feeling about their learning, to promote language learning awareness among the students, to share knowledge about proficiency development with their students, and to obtain documentation on students' self-perceptions of their proficiency growth. In sum, Can-do based self-assessments can be used for language learning, that is, as formative assessment (Butler, 2016, 2022) because the statements can foreshadow for students what they will learn in the future (e.g., when Can-do based self-assessments are given as a pre-test by the teacher), and they can be used to evaluate the student-perceived effectiveness of instruction and the students' reflections on their own learning if they are given to students post-learning (i.e., as a post-test).

Can-do statements can also be considered as part of TBLA in that TBLA "involves evaluating the degree to which language learners can use their L2 to accomplish given tasks" (Weaver, 2012, p. 287). However, in the case of Can-do-based self-assessments, it is not a person external to the students (such as a teacher, a professional rater, or a peer) who is doing the evaluating; the students themselves are the evaluators, reflecting on their performance, which positions Can-do based self-assessments as an "alternative" TBLA assessment method, one that is indirect and to be used to complement or add to direct assessments of task-based performance.

For example, one classroom teacher — Dr. Rajiv Ranjan, who is the author of the textbook that students at Michigan State University use for learning Hindi — *Basic Hindi* (Ranjan, 2021), an Open Source textbook offered through the University library[1] — provides four examples of Can-do statements designed specifically for his beginning Hindi language learning students, and in conjunction with what the teacher teaches in class:

- Example 1: I can respond to a classmate who asks me how I am feeling.
- Example 2: I can introduce myself to new teachers at a school orientation.
- Example 3: I can ask a friend questions about their family.

---

1. https://openbooks.lib.msu.edu/basichindi

- Example 4: I can tell a new student about interesting things that are in my hometown.

A basic assumption in the above four Can-do statements is that the learner is a student learning the language in a classroom-based setting. A second assumption is that the learner can read English: it is up to the teacher to decide if Can-do statements should be in the learner's home language, should be in the target language, or both. Overall, the general aim is for learners to be able to reflect on their proficiency in relation to the statement without the ability to read the statement being a barrier to responding.

A third assumption is that these statements are actualized by tasks that are taught and operationalized in the classroom. Teachers can ask students to consider such statements and then respond to them using a response format or scale of their choosing. Indeed, teachers can choose from a large variety of response-option types for their students to use to indicate their level of ability to perform a given task. For example, Brown et al. (2014) used a 5-point Likert-scale to gather self-perceived task-performance abilities. The response scale they designed for their B1/B2-level learners was based on how well a student could perform a task with or without preparation:

1. Can not do this even with extensive preparation.
2. Unsure as to whether I can do this.
3. Can do this with extensive preparation.
4. Can do this with minimal preparation.
5. Can do this without any preparation. (p.269)

Other options abound. For example, teachers can use 1 to 3 point Likert-scales, or even a check-box of whether or not it is believed the students can do the task, which would be a 2-point, dichotomous scale (checked=1, no check=0). Alternatively, a Likert-scale for self-assessment could be 1 to 10. It is up to the teacher. An important maxim for teachers to follow is that the ascending response (e.g., 1 to 5) should align with ascent in the level of ability. That is, the lowest number should indicate the lowest ability level, while the highest number should represent the highest ability level. Research has shown that normally respondents do not need the middle points to be explained within a Likert-scale. If a teacher tries that option, only the two poles (the far ends) of the scale are described. Popular online survey response programs, often used by teachers, such as Google Forms and Microsoft Office Forms, have Likert-scales as response option types, but these, by default, have pole-only descriptors available.

As another concrete scale example, Dr. Ranjan used approximately the same Likert-scale for his Can-do-based items as Tigchelaar et al. (2017), which is represented as follows:

1. I cannot do this yet.
2. I can do this with much help.
3. I can do this with some help.
4. I can do this well by myself.

The exact number of Likert-scale responses does not matter too much, especially within lower-stakes self-assessments. Teachers can start with what they think their students will understand. Young learners can be presented with fewer or less complex options to better align with their cognitive development levels (e.g., 1. I can't do this yet; 2. I can almost do this; 3. I can do this!) or can be presented with emojis instead of written/textual descriptors (see İlhan et al., 2022, for examples). As described by İlhan et al., a scale's option-wording, or its representation by different types or numbers of emojis, may slightly affect how students respond to the scale. However, teachers should trust their instincts in designing scales. Subsequently, they can try out their assessments and make adjustments if needed based on student feedback.

Research shows that students improve over time when they must repeatedly self-assess (Ma & Winke, 2019). Part of students' increased reliability and consistency in self-assessment may stem from becoming better at the process of self-reflection or from becoming more familiar with the Likert-scale and how to interpret it. Alternatively, it may evolve from coming to better understand proficiency development and students' personal trajectory within it through the process of self-assessment and discussion on that self-evaluation. An excellent practice would be for teachers, when discussing the results of self-assessments with their students, to ask their students for their feedback on the scale being used, so that the scale can be refined or changed to better align with students' interpretation abilities and needs.

Can-do statements as descriptors of curricular goals

In sum, the four Can-do statements from Dr. Ranjan in Examples 1 through 4 are, in this case, for classroom purposes. In general, the Can-do statements are for the students to read and use to ponder or imagine their future learning (when the statements are used as a pre-test) or to reflect on and evaluate their past learning (when used as a post-test). In this sense, Can-do statements can be considered as boiled-down, lay-person descriptors of some of the major curricular goals that a teacher may have for a language classroom or for a given language learner. For classroom purposes, therefore, the Can-do statements should be tied to the curriculum, so that the pondering at the pre-test, or reflection at the post-test, is real.

When a teacher drafts or writes out Can-do statements, they are listing out the essence of the key communicative tasks that are learning targets for the classroom (i.e., the dimensions or constructs that will inform task design), and the statements correspond with the class's overall communicative goals. Like a fine wine, classroom-based Can-do statements will get better over time. Each time teachers teach the course, they can review their Can-do statements and reflect on whether these need to be adapted or changed. They can also consider whether their tasks and materials, and the way they teach, need to change to better address the important Can-do statements. The Can-do statements thus can become part of the classroom learning loop, in which students are shown what the teacher will teach before learning, teachers receive feedback on whether students can do the tasks at any self-perceived level before teaching and learning, and students self-evaluate how the learning went for them post instruction, with the teacher receiving the information from the students at each stage as part of a diagnostic (of learning, of teaching, of the effectiveness of the curricular tasks) obtained through student responses to the Can-do statements. In the case of Dr. Ranjan, his students learn and undertake tasks that reflect Example 1 through 4 predominately when he teaches from his textbook's Chapter 2, Section 2.2, on greetings and introductions, and Chapter 4, on describing places. It is during the coverage of those parts of the textbook that Dr. Ranjan has the students act out the tasks communicated in Examples 1 to 4.

Can-do statements as reflections of language frameworks

It is important to note that each Can-do statement can be labeled or marked by the teacher who writes it as at a specific level on a proficiency scale. To do this, teachers must first decide which language framework they are using or working within to describe language proficiency. This is normally rather easy to do: teachers need only to choose to use the predominate language framework employed by their school, district, or language program.

In the United States, many or most language programs will use the ACTFL Proficiency Guidelines (2024) scale of proficiency, a scale that generally describes proficiency development for children to adults as Novice, Intermediate, Advanced, or Superior. Alternatively, they may use the 1 to 6 levels of proficiency of the World-Class Instructional Design and Assessment (WIDA, 2020) Consortium, which is for English-language learning children in US public schools, with the highest levels signaling English attainment on par with their same-aged, non-English learning peers. Meanwhile, in Europe, the United Kingdom, Canada, Australia, and New Zealand, many or most language programs will use the CEFR for languages (Council of Europe, 2020), with a scale of proficiency (applicable for children and adults), as previously stated, of A1, A2, B1, B2, C1, and C2, with C2 indicating the ability to communicate professionally in the language with fluency, confidence, and linguistic sophistication. Canadians teaching English or French to immigrants or refugees in Canada will use the Canadian Language Benchmarks (CLB) scale of proficiency that goes from 1 to 12, with 12 generally meaning being able to use the language for advanced professional employment purposes, which is generally on par with C2 on the CEFR scale, or Superior on the ACTFL scale (see Centre for Canadian Language Benchmarks, 2012). Teachers in China teaching English may use China's Standards of English (CSE) Language Ability (National Education Examinations Authority, Ministry of Education, People's Republic of China, 2018), a 1 to 9 scale designed for K-16 learners of English, with 9 roughly equivalent to C2 on the CEFR scale. Teachers of North American military or government personnel will most likely use the Interagency Language Roundtable (ILR, n.d.) scale of 1 to 5, which was designed by the US government to describe adult military and government workers' language proficiency in military or government settings, with 5 being the highest level of ability.

Once teachers pick the scale, the teachers can look at the Can-do statements they wrote for their students, and label them one-by-one as corresponding to which level on the scale the statements are. This is generally an estimate and is thus being assigned through the teacher's "expert judgement." If several teachers are crafting the Can-do statements together, they can then assign the proficiency-scale level through multiple "expert judgements" and through peer review of the item or through socialization: that is, they can together come to a consensus on the level estimate for each Can-do statement using the combined efforts of their collective expert judgements and democratic negotiations. After assignment of a proficiency scale level for each item, teachers may then have an "item bank" of Can-do statements that looks like what is presented in Table 1. Dr. Ranjan, for example, is also able to tie each specific Can-do item to locations in his curriculum and textbook, wherein the task is presented. In sum, Can-do statements can be based on students' needs, embedded in the local curriculum, tied to a proficiency scale, and refined over time to home in on steps that an individual teacher takes to teach and foster communicative language ability.

Obtaining a list of Can-do statements for a teacher's classroom that are tied to a proficiency framework is powerful. By doing this, for example, with the ACTFL Proficiency scale levels as the anchors, ACTFL's proficiency guidelines are transformed by the teacher or the teachers into discrete, proficiency-level based, Can-

Table 1. Can-do item bank

Can-do item ID	Can-do statement	ACTFL level	"Basic Hindi" textbook location where students practice this task
1	I can respond to a classmate who asks me how I am feeling.	Novice low	2.2 & 2.3, Greetings, with supplement on feelings
2	I can introduce myself to new teachers at a school orientation.	Novice low	2.3 & 2.4, Formal conversations
3	I can ask a friend questions about their family.	Novice low	3.8, Family, Wh-questions, & 4.5, describing family
4	I can tell a new student about interesting things that are in my hometown.	Novice low	4.8, Describing places; "There" constructions, with supplement on describing "In my hometown..."

do descriptors that cover the curriculum. Or, in reverse, each classroom-based, Can-do statement (backed up by a classroom task that students can practice or perform in the classroom) can be placed on the ACTFL scale. Thus, an individual language classroom (e.g., Hindi 101 at Michigan State University) can be classified as teaching a number of tasks that are described as Can-do statements and that are identified on the ACTFL scale, rendering the class chock full of ACTFL-identified, Can-do descriptors. In essence, by creating Can-do statements with associated tasks for the classroom and tying them to a language framework, the teacher is transcribing the classroom's plan for communicative language proficiency development on top of the model of ACTFL's theory of language acquisition, as in Figure 2.

Figure 2. Plotting of a sample of a class's Can-do statements onto a selected (ACTFL, 2024) language proficiency scale. (The inverted pyramid model of the ACTFL Language Connects proficiency scale is from the ACTFL (2024) *Proficiency Guidelines*, page 11.[2] Reprinted with permission from ACTFL Language Connects.)

Teachers should note, however, that their classroom-based Can-do statements, and the tasks associated with the statements, should be plotted on the proficiency scale used by their program, district, or state. Figure 3 presents the same four Can-do statements, this time plotted on the CEFR scale instead of the ACTFL scale.

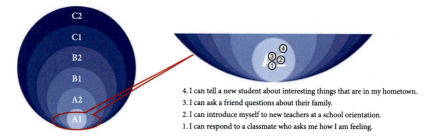

4. I can tell a new student about interesting things that are in my hometown.
3. I can ask a friend questions about their family.
2. I can introduce myself to new teachers at a school orientation.
1. I can respond to a classmate who asks me how I am feeling.

Figure 3. Plotting of the same sample (as in Figure 2) of a class's Can-do statements onto a second (CEFR, Council of Europe, 2020) language proficiency scale. (The concentric circles model of the CEFR proficiency scale is from the Council of Europe website[3] and is reprinted with permission from © Council of Europe.)

Can-do statements to explain language frameworks

At this juncture, it is important for me to explain that Can-do statements can be confusing to educators for a number of reasons. In what follows, I explain how language frameworks use Can-do statements to explain the framework to people using task-based terminology. First, almost all language frameworks use Can-do statements to explain the framework and its language proficiency scale to people. Thus, if language teachers, school and district supervisors, and educators look for examples of Can-do statements online, or look online to read more about them, they might find a plethora of Can-do statements, but, according to who wrote the Can-do statements, it may not be the case that those statements are qualified (or contextually valid or useful). It may not be clear for whom the Can-do statements were written. Also, it may be hard to tell for what exact purposes the available Can-do statements are designed. Different formats of Can-do statements are written by different groups of people for different audiences and purposes. Different sets of Can-do statements may have different sets of stakeholders. This means

---

2. Accessible from: https://www.actfl.org/uploads/files/general/Resources-Publications/ACTFL_Proficiency_Guidelines_2024.pdf

3. https://www.coe.int/en/web/common-european-framework-reference-languages/level-descriptions

that, if one finds Can-do statements online or in a book or pamphlet, one must ask these essential, following questions:

1. *Author:* Who is the author of these Can-do statements?
2. *Audience:* Who is intended by the author as readers of these Can-do statements?
3. *Purpose:* For what purpose did the author write these statements, and for what purpose would the audience members read these statements?
4. *Stakeholders:* After the audience members read the statements, cognitively process them, and use them (for the purposes intended by the author), who, beyond the author and audience (who are the *immediate* stakeholders), uses the information that results from this process, and for what purposes is that information used?

To explain better how statements may need to be evaluated and interpreted for specific contexts, consider the following Can-do statements, which were written by the Council of Europe as part of its Self-assessment grids (Table 2 – CEFR 3.3), which can be found online (see Council of Europe, n.d.a, for the link to the grids). This block of Can-do statements is intended to describe the entirety of the CEFR A1 level of speaking, within the domain of Spoken Interaction (in contrast to Spoken Production), and for English language learners:

> I can interact in a simple way provided the other person is prepared to repeat or rephrase things at a slower rate of speech and help me formulate what I'm trying to say. I can ask and answer simple questions in areas of immediate need or on very familiar topics.

There are a few things to note about this A1-level, English, Can-do block within the Council of Europe's self-assessment grids. First, it was not written by a classroom language teacher. Rather, it was written by professionals at or for the Council of Europe *for* teachers or curriculum designers who may be designing or identifying A1-level content for the instruction of communicative speaking tasks or skills to be taught in the language classroom. Thus, the purpose of this specific block of Can-do statements is to educate the public and other educators on what to expect in terms of communicative language ability from someone at the A1 level. The block can inform the curriculum designer about what to cover in the curriculum, but there are many possible tasks from which the designer could choose. The grid online in which this block is found spells out, in essence, language development along CEFR's scale in easy-to-comprehend, Can-do statements, but these statements are not tied to any one curriculum, nor to any one task or sets of tasks. The block has been translated into 32 languages used in the European Union, from Basque to Turkish. Thus the statements themselves are language agnostic, and are descriptive of communicative language abilities at the A1 level, but, again, do not prescribe any individual tasks or curriculum on any program that adheres to or follows the learning path and language development model outlined by the CEFR.

The block of online statements and the self-assessment grid itself, as written in CEFR's *Ideas for Implementation* (Council of Europe, n.d.b), are "a stimulus for reflection and subsequent innovation in language education" (para. 1). It is the job of the teacher or language educator, or the curriculum developer, to align their curriculum and assessment to them. This alignment, I explain below, may include an intermediary step of writing or expanding upon the general and language-agnostic Can-do statements written to explain the proficiency scale, as highlighted in Table 1, so that the Can-do statements read by students are comprehensible, envisionable, and useful to the students in a particular context. The responses from the results from the processing of the Can-do statements (and the results that appear) should be meaningful to the students, the teachers, and other stakeholders, which could include program supervisors, department heads, district leaders, parents, or funders who want to know more about the learning that takes place in the classroom. Teachers and curriculum developers work with a specific set of curricular materials that entail a certain set of articulated tasks wherein students practice performance and novel language forms. Transforming a language- and task-agnostic A1 level descriptor into discrete, comprehensible, Can-do statements tied to the curriculum is the job for teachers and curriculum designers, and they can usually do this by either looking at their current classroom-based materials and textbooks and describing what they teach, or by looking at the Al-level general descriptors and designing new A1-level tasks for their classroom to fill in any gaps in the curriculum that need to be filled to fully represent what an A1-level curriculum should entail.

For example, in Figure 4, the statements from the Council of Europe self-assessment grid for A1, Spoken Interaction for English, are plotted in the second column. The third column shows those statements articulated within and by the local Hindi curriculum by Dr. Ranjan at Michigan State University. Thus, on the left-hand side of the dotted line in Figure 4, the Can-do statements are general. A student reading such a statement on the left may have to embed the statement in their mind into a specific context of use. Much imagination may be needed to respond to the statements on the left-hand side of Figure 4 to estimate how well one can do such things. However, on the right-hand side of the dotted line in Figure 4, the statements have been contextualized and moved into more bite-sized statements that students can reflect on, hopefully more concretely and more quickly. These statements, on the right, and if designed by a classroom teacher, should be based on concrete tasks that the teacher presents as part of the local curriculum (as Dr. Ranjan did), thus binding or linking the local curriculum to the selected scale (in this case the CEFR scale) indicated in the first column.

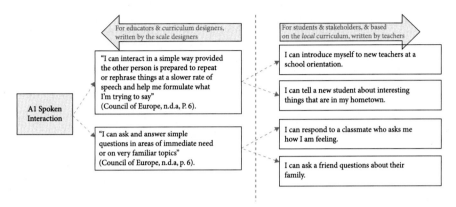

Figure 4. Example of aligning a Can-do, Self-assessment grid block from the Council of Europe (n.d.a, p. 6) to a local language program's curriculum. (The quoted statements for educators and curriculum designers also appear in the Council of Europe's CEFR English Self-Assessment Grid[4] and are additionally available in other European languages at the same site.)

The bi-directional progression from the label of a scale level of proficiency on one end (such as A1, Spoken Interaction) and classroom-based Can-do statements that students can use pre- and post-learning on the other end, can contain additional steps as well. For example, in Figure 5, the curriculum designer has embedded a unit's lesson on the A1 Spoken Interaction descriptor from the CEFR self-assessment grids. The textbook itself lists unit goals, which describe what the students will be able to do by the end of the unit. The Can-do statements are samples of performance derived from the unit goals and textbook and learning materials. The authors at each level may be different: the scale developers wrote the first two levels (scale level and general descriptors), while the textbook developer wrote the unit goals. The teacher, however, wrote the Can-do statements. The students in class only responded formally in writing to the Can-do statements. That is, the Can-do statements were the most easily digestible indicators of language learning and were the ones most easy for students to respond to on a Likert-scale pre- and post-learning.

---

4. https://www.coe.int/en/web/portfolio/self-assessment-grid

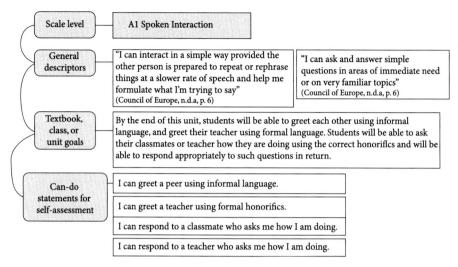

Figure 5. Example of multiple steps in moving from a standardized language proficiency scale level and its descriptors (A1 Spoken Interaction; Council of Europe, n.d.a, p. 6) to Can-do statements for self-assessment based on the local language program's curriculum

Notes on customizing Can-do statements to a particular language program

There is a bit of an epistemological debate on whether estimating proficiency on a standardized language scale, such as the ACTFL or CEFR scale, can be done if the items used to estimate the proficiency are based within the local curriculum. Theorists may posit that if the tasks used to measure what one can do in the language are from the curriculum, the assessment is an achievement test, and not a proficiency test. I believe a good way to think of it is as follows. Teachers are trying to measure gains achieved in their classrooms and based on their curriculum. When that is the goal at hand, it is imperative that the tasks used for measurement purposes represent what was taught in the classroom. Deviating far from the curriculum, especially at the lower levels of instruction, may end in a misalignment between what is taught and what is measured, and thus learning cannot be tracked, even if it has occurred.

In what follows, I showcase sets of Can-do statements created by teachers across several languages (Russian, Chinese, and Hindi) and based on the local curriculum in those language teachers' programs. All 12 Can-do statements in Table 2 are at the Novice low or mid or A1 level, but they differ slightly based on cultural necessities and importances in language learning that depend on the language being learned. The differences also stem from the linguistic attributes and features of the individual languages that need to be attended to for language development to advance most smoothly. There may be an infinite number of possible low-level language tasks that a teacher can teach at the Novice or A1 level, but the curriculum designer must select ones from within the range. This is recognized by general proficiency scale descriptors such as the Council of Europe self-assessment grids. Nonetheless, observationally, when you look with your microscope at what is being taught, you see differences in acquisitional paths. They are not linear, and they are a bit "jiggered," as one could say, meaning that they are not fully overlapping tasks, although they are all within the A1 or Novice levels of proficiency. Each set of four equally represents A1 or Novice proficiency. Each set of four is a good sample of A1 or Novice level tasks. Each set represents well what Al or Novice development looks like. Thus, the lists may challenge the notion that a random draw of four from the 12 would be a fair self-assessment of proficiency, if used for proficiency assessment measurement purposes. To truly measure the Russian, Chinese, or Hindi learners' learning at the A1 or Novice level within the classroom they experienced, it may be best to use the tasks they learned as the basis for measurement.

Table 2. Can-do statements aligned with the first few weeks of task-based instruction by teachers of Russian, Chinese, and Hindi

Russian, based on the textbook *Между нами* by deBenedette et al. (2015)		Chinese, based on the textbook *Elementary Chinese 1* by Zhou (2022)		Hindi, based on the textbook *Basic Hindi* by Ranjan (2021)	
1.	I can introduce myself to peers at a party.	1.	I can accept an invite to a meal from friends.	1.	I can respond to a classmate who asks me how I am feeling.
2.	I can tell my phone number to my peers at school.	2.	I can describe to a friend what kind of activities I like to do for fun.	2.	I can introduce myself to new teachers at a school orientation.
3.	I can tell a shop assistant what clothes I want to buy.	3.	I can place an order for beverages at a restaurant.	3.	I can ask a friend questions about their family.
4.	I can introduce family members to a friend while showing photos on my phone.	4.	I can introduce myself to new students in my classroom.	4.	I can tell a new student about interesting things that are in my hometown.

Using Can-do statements to measure classroom-based proficiency gains

Researchers have demonstrated that language gains on large, standardized proficiency scales, such as the ACTFL scale, are quicker to occur at the lower levels than at the upper levels of the scale. This can be seen in the inverted pyramid model of the ACTFL scale, and the concentric circles model of the CEFR scale, in Figures 2 and 3 respectively. In the models, there is more to learn at the upper levels of acquisition. This means that one might spend more time learning at the top to move up, vertically, from one level to the next. On average, learners in the USA gain only about one-third of an ACTFL sublevel (from Intermediate low to Intermediate mid, for example) per semester of college-level study — approximately 15 weeks (Isbell et al., 2019). Thus, using standardized tests to measure gains from instruction within an individual classroom may be difficult, because even though the learners are learning and acquiring skills across new task performances, a standardized test, which draws test items at random and may not be based on what the students have encountered as tasks in class, may not register vertical gains on the standardized scale. However, pre- and post-testing of Can-do statements based on the curriculum may show to learners and their teachers how much horizontal gain within a specific proficiency band has occurred.

Conclusion

Earlier in this chapter, I wrote about how there are many different standardized language proficiency scales and frameworks. Each standardized scale of proficiency, such as the ACTFL scale or the CEFR scale, is heavily influenced in design and constitution by the instructional, geographical, demographical, historical, and cultural contexts within which each scale is developed. The scales are developed for specific purposes, and for specific populations. They are time-bound as well, with all scales needing modifications and adjustments over time to keep up with the changes in the factors that influenced their birth.

For a language proficiency scale to have real currency, it must be understood and easily applied by those who want to adopt it. Modern scales all strive to have crosswalks to teachers, students, and the public at large. The crosswalks are oftentimes written as Can-do statements that describe or set the foundation for the selection of tasks. The Can-do statements, which Norris and East (2022) described as "what learners should be able to do with their language knowledge and skills" (p.510), emphasize that a curriculum has at its core goals to develop real-world, task-based communicative skills in learners. Curriculum developers must choose those tasks through textbook and materials design. Teachers have a strong hand in task design, of course, as they adapt classroom materials or supplement them for their own personal instruction in the language classroom (for examples, see the chapters in Section 2 of this volume). That instruction is influenced by the students in the classroom. Even when surveyed ahead of time, tasks designed for students can change on the day of instruction if students begin to ask questions that guide a task's trajectory and focus. Thus, an inventory of Can-do statements which is an inventory of tasks is a living document that teachers can change, especially in light of reflections on learning and teaching.

Can-do-based self-assessments designed for language classrooms and language programs can play an essential role in organizing the curriculum, instruction, and assessment around communicative tasks, which Norris and East (2022) noted as important primary work in task-based teaching and learning. Indeed, as they explained, self-assessments based on a class's main task goals can introduce regular *formative* task-based assessments into classrooms to provide a meaningful way for teachers and learners to move toward a common learning goal, establish transparent performance targets, and target feedback on key dimensions of language performance.

Can-do based statements that are inventories of tasks taught in the language classroom may be able to help teachers and researchers put a more powerful lens on theoretically shaky areas of language proficiency development theory. For example, there is a notion that there is more to learn at the upper levels of proficiency, which is also tied to the notion that language learning growth at the Novice or A-levels of language should be "fast." ACTFL's theory of language development in particular suggests that there is little to learn at the Novice level of language instruction. These theories are modeled, spatially, in the language proficiency scales shown in Figures 2 and 3 in this chapter. If early growth on the language proficiency scale is not fast for an individual or for a class or school of learners, people may believe that something is wrong either with the learner or learners, or with the instruction, or both. However, one can imagine a language class for 6-year-olds that holds instruction at the A level or Novice level for a long time, because A level or Novice level language is appropriate for the children's developmental stage: this does not mean the children are learning little or "less." Indeed, they could be learning a large quantity of language at the A1 level that college-aged learners at the A1 level never learn, because they do not spend enough time covering topics and language domains at that level. Even though language learning is described as "slow" at the upper levels of proficiency (because there is more to learn at the upper levels, as modeled in the scales), language learners can get frustrated after actively learning for long periods of time, yet still not obtain any measurable gains on standardized proficiency tests measuring the upper levels of development.

If development is measured on self-assessments of Can-do statements, and measured on standardized tests, both provide unique data on the trait being measured. One does not dismiss the other. It could be that the standardized test is not sensitive to the change or growth being experienced by the learner within a proficiency band. The standardized test may be measuring, to the best of its ability, vertical growth in task sophistication, while the Can-do statements can measure horizontal growth across task domains, capturing a learner's ability to perform a variety of new or additional tasks within a particular level of proficiency, that is *language and task-based depth* within a level.

A rather widely held belief is that if learners have, for example, a measured C2 level of language ability, they should be able to complete any level of language task below a C2 level. However, in practice, people can find that this is not always the case. For example, a diplomat may be able to discuss nuclear nonproliferation with generals and presidents but may struggle to discuss popular music venues with teenagers. Language knowledge is based on experience, and Can-do statements are inventories of experiences.

Teachers may find Can-do-based self-assessments to be useful in their classrooms and programs for many purposes. The self-assessment process for students can promote agency, self-regulation, and directedness in goal-orientation. Teachers can use the statements as a low-cost proficiency measure and as a snapshot of individual and classroom-level growth over time in a program. They could also be used as part of "a heightened emphasis on efficiency, for example to make quick decisions about placing learners into appropriate levels of an instructional program" (Norris & East, 2022, p. 508). As described by Norris and East, assessments such as cloze tests, elicited imitation, C-tests, and vocabulary-size tests are often used for student placement or proficiency-level identification purposes, but those kinds of tests do not focus on specific target tasks that learners need to be able to do. Can-do-based self-assessments do focus on target tasks that learners need to be able to do, and thus may serve the purposes for low-stakes placement or proficiency testing or could be used as a supplement alongside vocabulary-size tests and the like to better represent a program's task-oriented goals.

Coming back to Dr. Rubin, whom I introduced at the start of this chapter, Can-do statements may act as powerful telescopes on learning that shed light on what we do not know about language development. Thus, it is important for us to keep our minds open, and to observe language growth using a variety of tools. Keeping an open mind when observing was certainly a trait of Dr. Rubin. In other words, collect and use your Can-do based data to explore the universe of language learning. Use the feedback from the self-assessment to help you shape the future course of your teaching. By designing Can-do-based self-assessments that align with your TBLT goals, you, and we through you, just might learn something new.

References

ACTFL (2024). ACTFL proficiency guidelines. https://www.actfl.org/uploads/files/general/Resources-Publications/ACTFL_Proficiency_Guidelines_2024.pdf

American Museum of Natural History (n.d.). Vera Rubin and dark matter. [Excerpt from the volume *Cosmic horizons: Astronomy at the cutting edge*, by S. Soter & N. deGrasse Tyson (Eds.), 2000, New Press.] Cosmic Horizons Curriculum Collection. https://www.amnh.org/learn-teach/curriculum-collections/cosmic-horizons-book/vera-rubin-dark-matter

Brown, N.A., Dewey, D.P., & Cox, T.L. (2014). Assessing the validity of Can-do statements in retrospective (then-now) self-assessment. *Foreign Language Annals, 47*(2), 261–285.

Butler, Y.G. (2016). Self-assessment *of* and *for* young learners' foreign language learning. In M. Nikolov (Ed.), *Assessing young learners of English: Global and local perspectives* (pp. 291–315). Springer.

Butler, Y.G. (2022). Expanding the role of self-assessment: From assessing to learning English. In D. Valente & D. Xerri (Eds.), *Innovative practices in early English language education* (pp 191–210). Palgrave Macmillan.

Bygate, M., Samuda, V., & Van den Branden, K. (2022). A pedagogical rationale for task-based language teaching for the acquisition of real-world language use. In M.J. Ahmadian & M.H. Long (Eds.), *The Cambridge handbook of task-based language teaching* (pp. 27–52). Cambridge University Press.

Centre for Canadian Language Benchmarks. (2012). *Canadian Language Benchmarks: English as a second language for adults.* https://www.language.ca/product/pdf-e-01-clb-esl-for-adults-pdf/

Council of Europe. (2020). *Common European framework of reference for languages: learning, teaching, assessment: Companion volume.* https://www.coe.int/en/web/common-european-framework-reference-languages

Council of Europe. (2001). *Common European framework of reference for languages: Learning, teaching, assessment.* Cambridge University Press. https://rm.coe.int/1680459f97

Council of Europe. (n.d.a). *Common European framework of references for languages: Learning, teaching, assessment: Structured overview of all CEFR scales.* https://rm.coe.int/168045b15e

Council of Europe. (n.d.b). *Ideas for implementation.* https://www.coe.int/en/web/common-european-framework-reference-languages/ideas-for-implementation1

DeBenedette, L., Comer, W.J., Smyslova, A., & Perkins, J. (2015). *Между нами / Between you and me* [Online textbook]. https://www.mezhdunami.org/

Faez, F., Majhanovich, S., Taylor, S.K., Smith, M., & Crowley, K. (2011). The power of "Can Do" statements: Teachers' perceptions of CEFR- informed instruction in French as a second language classrooms in Ontario. *Canadian Journal of Applied Linguistics, 14*(2), 1–19. https://journals.lib.unb.ca/index.php/CJAL/article/view/19855/21653

İlhan, M., Taşdelen Teker, G., Güler, N., & Ergenekon, Ö. (2022). Effects of category labeling with emojis on Likert-type scales on the psychometric properties of measurements. *Journal of Psychoeducational Assessment, 40*(2), 221–237.

ILR (n.d.). *Interagency Language Round-table language skills descriptors — Speaking.* https://www.govtilr.org/Skills/ILRscale2.htm

Isbell, D. R., Winke, P., & Gass, S. M. (2019). Using the ACTFL OPIc to assess proficiency and monitor progress in a tertiary foreign languages program. *Language Testing, 36*(3), 439–465.

Long, M. H. (2015). *Second language acquisition and task-based language teaching.* Wiley-Blackwell.

Ma, W., & Winke, P. (2019). Self-assessment: How reliable is it in assessing oral proficiency over time? *Foreign Language Annals, 52*(1), 66–86.

National Education Examinations Authority, Ministry of Education, People's Republic of China. (2018). *China's Standards of English language ability.* https://cse.neea.edu.cn/res/ceedu/1811/6bdc26c323d188948fca8048833f151a.pdf

Norris, J. M., & East, M. (2022). Task-based language assessment. In M. J. Ahmadian & M. H. Long (Eds.), *The Cambridge handbook of task-based language teaching* (pp. 507–528). Cambridge University Press.

Overbye, D. (2016, December 27). Vera Rubin, 88, dies; Opened doors in astronomy, and for women. *New York Times.* https://www.nytimes.com/2016/12/27/science/vera-rubin-astronomist-who-made-the-case-for-dark-matter-dies-at-88.html

Ranjan, R. (2021). *Basic Hindi.* Michigan State University Libraries. https://openbooks.lib.msu.edu/basichindi/

Shehadeh, A. (2018). Task-based language assessment. In J. L. Liontas (Ed.), *The TESOL encyclopedia of English language teaching* (pp. 1–6). John Wiley & Sons.

Tigchelaar, M., Bowles, R. P., Winke, P., & Gass, S. (2017). Assessing the validity of ACTFL Can-do statements for spoken proficiency: A Rasch analysis. *Foreign Language Annals, 50*(3), 584–600.

Tomlinson, B. (2023). Materials evaluation. In B. Tominson (Ed.), *Developing materials for language teaching* (pp. 1–21). Bloomsbury Academic.

Weaver, C. (2012). Incorporating a formative assessment cycle into task-based language teaching in a university setting in Japan. In A. Shehadeh & C. A. Coombe (Eds.), *Task-based language teaching in foreign language contexts: Research and implementation* (pp. 287–312). John Benjamins.

WIDA. (2020). *WIDA English language development standards framework, 2020 edition: Kindergarten-grade 12.* Board of Regents of the University of Wisconsin System. https://wida.wisc.edu/sites/default/files/resource/WIDA-ELD-Standards-Framework-2020.pdf

Zhou, W. (2022). *Elementary Chinese 1.* Michigan State University Libraries. https://openbooks.lib.msu.edu/chs101/

CHAPTER 8

From CAF to CAFFA[*]
Measuring linguistic performance and functional adequacy in task-based language teaching

Folkert Kuiken & Ineke Vedder
University of Amsterdam

Linguistic performance elicited by language tasks has generally been operationalised and measured in terms of complexity, accuracy, and fluency (CAF). We argue, however, that the assessment of second language (L2) proficiency is impossible without considering the efficacy and appropriacy of L2 performance, so-called Functional Adequacy (FA). From the perspective of task-based language assessment, FA is conceived of as a multi-layered, goal-directed, task-related construct, in terms of successful task completion by the speaker/writer. In this chapter, we discuss the rating scale for FA with regard to the assessment of oral and written performance developed by Kuiken and Vedder (2017) which was tested out for different tasks and languages. We also indicate future directions for research on FA, particularly with respect to reliability and validity, FA in relation to (sub)components of CAF, use of the scale in classroom practice, and assessment of interactional tasks.

Keywords: CAFFA (Complexity, Accuracy, Fluency, Functional adequacy), rating scale, reliability, validity, classroom practice, interactional tasks, task-based language assessment, TBLA

Introduction

Linguistic performance elicited by language tasks has been generally assessed in terms of complexity, accuracy, and fluency, often abbreviated as CAF. An array of measures has been proposed to assess these three dimensions — for measures of grammatical and lexical complexity, see, for example, Bulté and Housen (2012);

---

[*] Revised version of a plenary given to the 8th International TBLT Conference, Ottawa, Canada, 2019.

https://doi.org/10.1075/tblt.17.08kui
© 2025 John Benjamins Publishing Company

for accuracy measures, for example, Wolfe-Quintero et al. (1998); for fluency measures, for example, Segalowitz (2010). In addition to these measures, supplementary measures have been proposed, like indices for morphological complexity (Pallotti & Brezina, 2019), phraseological complexity (Paquot, 2018, 2019), and propositional complexity (Vasylets et al., 2019). Next to the linguistic dimension of language performance on which much research has focused, it is crucial to consider its functional dimension, as has been argued in various studies (De Jong et al., 2012a, 2012b; Kuiken & Vedder, 2014, 2017, 2018; Pallotti, 2009; Révész et al., 2016). Our main claim in accordance with these studies is that language performance should not only be assessed by measures along the CAF-triad but also in terms of its functional adequacy (FA). In other words: CAF should be extended to CAFFA.

The above claim can be supported by two arguments. The first argument is two-fold. There is the assumption that the assessment of language performance is not possible without taking into consideration the efficacy and appropriacy of learners' performances (Kuiken & Vedder, 2014, 2017, 2018). If the primary goal of most language learning is to communicate successfully, second language (L2) performance needs to be evaluated with not only CAF indices but also measures of FA. This is in order, first, to capture a wider array of learning outcomes associated with the accomplishment of real-world tasks and, second, to meet the need to assess FA as a separate dimension from CAF (Pallotti, 2009). Although some studies have investigated the relationship between CAF and FA in L2 performance (see e.g., Herraiz Martínez, 2018; Herraiz Martínez & Alcón Soler, 2019; Nuzzo & Bove, 2020; Révész et al., 2016; Strobl & Baten, 2022), little is known about the specific linguistic features that contribute to the development of functionally adequate and appropriate speech, or about the relationship between CAF and FA.

The second argument is as follows: there may be asymmetries in proficiency between the linguistic and functional dimensions of learner performance. This can be illustrated by means of two examples: politicians and beginning second language learners. Journalists often ask politicians simple yes/no-questions, for example, are you planning to invest in nuclear energy, do you want to raise taxes or not, are you supporting measures against climate change? However, instead of answering by means of a straightforward "yes" or "no", their responses are often framed in long, laborious, complex sentences, pronounced accurately and fluently, therefore adequate from a linguistic point of view but not — at least for the listener — from a communicative perspective. The reverse may happen in the case of (beginning) second language learners. Take, for instance, Hassan, a 28-year-old Jordan Arabic speaking man, who was asked by his English neighbour how he would react if his neighbour's son had broken his window while playing football: "I say nothing because it's his son. I eh say, I say eh not. Or eh I ... eh, just eh ...

it's okay. It's small children. It's small children. I do nothing. For me I do nothing." Hassan is speaking in English as L2, with hesitations, using short, not always correct sentences, but he succeeds in getting his message across, so what he is saying may not be adequate from a linguistic point of view, but adequate from a functional perspective.

The two examples of politician and beginner L2 language user show how different language users perform a particular language task in a more or less successful way, either in terms of CAF or in terms of FA. In our daily lives we spend a lot of time carrying out similar and other language tasks. Thus, we conceptualise CAFFA from a task-based perspective, as Task-Based Language Assessment (TBLA) is primarily concerned with language use in social contexts and highlights the task as a vehicle for eliciting authentic, goal-directed, and meaning-focused L2 performance (Long, 2015, 2016). Just as complexity, accuracy, and fluency can be divided into several subcomponents, we conceive FA as a multi-layered construct that can be broken down into various dimensions. Before focusing on these subcomponents, we will define FA and its importance for TBLA more precisely. In the last two decades several researchers have interpreted FA in various ways (for an overview see Kuiken & Vedder, 2022). Considered within the framework of TBLA (e.g., Norris & East, 2022; Shehadeh, 2018), inspired by the conversational maxims of Grice (1975), and in line with De Jong et al. (2012a, b), we view FA as a task-related construct in terms of successful task completion.

TBLA has been defined by Norris (2016) as "the elicitation and evaluation of language use (across all modalities) for expressing and interpreting meaning, within a well-defined communicative context (and audience), for a clear purpose, toward a valued goal or outcome" (p.232). Norris and East (2022) expanded on this definition when they explained that "learners have to *use* their second language abilities to get things done" through the medium of communication tasks that "involve a goal or purpose of some kind, and that occur within a specific setting, situation, or context" (p.507, our emphasis). They went on to assert that to draw valid conclusions about what learners can do with language, TBLA "places a premium on *authenticity* of both the *nature* of language use that is elicited and the *situation* within which the task is performed" (p.507, our emphases). Taking the above definitions of TBLA into account, we argue that FA is an important sub-component of task performance that we need to measure. The main focus in our definition of FA is on the adequacy of L2 production in relation to a specific social context and target task, interlocutor, speech act, register, and task modality. In terms of the Gricean maxims, the adequacy of the message transmitted by the speaker or writer is judged by the receiver in terms of the quantity, relation, manner, and quality of the information (Kuiken & Vedder, 2017, 2018).

The FA rating scale

In order to construct an instrument by means of which FA can be assessed in a reliable and valid way, we have designed a rating scale, taking into account the following requirements:

1. deconstruction of relevant components of the construct;
2. independence of descriptors of FA from linguistic descriptors in terms of CAF
3. objective and countable scale descriptors;
4. applicability in various learning contexts (different types of learners, task types and modalities, expert and non-expert raters);
5. the possibility to use the scale for different source and target languages.

Designed as a six-point Likert scale, the FA rating scale comprises four dimensions: Task Requirements, Content, Comprehensibility, and Coherence & Cohesion. Inspired by the can-do statements and descriptors for oral and written production of the Common European Framework of Reference for languages, the CEFR (Council of Europe, 2001) scale descriptors have been formulated for each of the six levels of these four dimensions:

- *Task Requirements* focus on the extent to which the task is completed in accordance with the particular genre, task type, speech acts, and register required in the message transmitted by the speaker (or writer) to the listener (or reader), and the specific instructions and requirements of the task.
- *Content* takes into account the adequacy of the number of information units or concepts expressed in the (oral or written) text and their possible thematic elaboration in terms of main and secondary content elements.
- *Comprehensibility* refers to the extent to which the message expressed is comprehensible for the intended listener (or reader). Is the message immediately comprehensible or does the addressee need to reread or relisten to (certain fragments of) the message in order to understand what is meant?
- *Coherence & Cohesion* focus on the adequacy of the message of the speaker (or writer) in terms of the occurrence of coherent relationships (e.g., discourse markers, coherence breaks, number of repetitions) and cohesive ties (e.g., presence or absence of deictic elements, use of cohesive and anaphoric devices and strategies).

For the complete scale, including the descriptors of the four dimensions for all six levels, please refer to Appendix A.

The FA rating scale in research

In order to test the reliability and validity of the FA rating scale, four studies were conducted. The first two were pilot studies in which a preliminary version of the FA rating scale was used, based on two written decision-making tasks. Participants in the first study were L2 learners of Dutch ($n=34$), Italian ($n=42$) and Spanish ($n=27$), who were assessed by expert raters (Dutch: $n=4$; Italian and Spanish: $n=3$) (Kuiken et al., 2010). In the second study participants were also learners of Dutch as L2 ($n=32$) and Italian as L2 ($n=39$), as well as first language (native/L1) speakers of Dutch ($n=17$) and Italian ($n=18$), who were again evaluated by expert raters (Dutch $n=4$, Italian $n=3$) (Kuiken & Vedder, 2014). On the basis of the outcomes and a retrospective interview with the raters, a modified version of the scale was presented in Kuiken and Vedder (2017), based on the same written data from the 2014 study. Since expert raters, who are often used to non-native-like L2 performance, might — to some extent — be biased in judging FA, this time we asked non-expert raters to assess the data (Dutch $n=4$, Italian $n=4$). Subsequently, the scale was tested for oral speech using data from L2 learners of Dutch ($n=22$) and Italian ($n=26$), rated again by non-expert raters ($n=4$ for both Dutch and Italian) (Kuiken & Vedder, 2018). On the basis of these studies it was concluded that the FA rating scale was a reliable and valid tool. It should, however, be noted that in these four studies the scale was used exclusively for adult, highly educated L2 learners, who were subjected to one type of task.

In the last decade the scale has been used in several other studies with different learners and conducted in various learning contexts. An overview of fourteen of these studies (Kuiken & Vedder, 2022) demonstrated that the FA rating scale has been applied by both expert and non-expert raters for assessing the linguistic performance of diverse language learners (children, adolescents, adults, high- and low-educated L2 learners, L1 speakers), with several target languages (e.g., Dutch, English, German, Italian, Spanish) and source languages (e.g., Catalan, Chinese, Dutch, Hungarian, Italian, Japanese, Spanish), in a variety of oral and written tasks (advice, complaint, decision, description, instruction, motivation letter, narration, refusal, summary), and with different levels of proficiency (CEFR A2-C2). Also in these studies, the FA scale has proven to be a reliable, valid, and user-friendly tool, although raters reported finding it difficult to use the scale for both L1 and L2 learners in one and the same study. This may be due to the fact that descriptors were inspired by the CEFR (Council of Europe, 2001), which was designed for second language learners and not for native speakers.

Future directions

A number of key issues in need of further investigation, and pitfalls to be reconsidered in future studies, remain, such as the reliability and validity of the rating scale when adaptations to the FA scale are made. Other important topics concern the relationship between FA and (sub)components of CAF, the applicability of the FA scale in classroom practice, and the use of the FA scale for oral interactional tasks.

Reliability and validity

In some of the studies referred to in the previous section, adaptations were made to the dimensions of the FA rating scale. Strobl and Baten (2022) reduced the four dimensions of the rating scale to three by combining Task Requirements and Content into one dimension, which they labelled Content & Topic Development. Others have extended the scale. Herraiz Martínez (2018) and Herraiz Martínez and Alcón Soler (2019) observed that, for raters, it was sometimes difficult to assess Coherence & Cohesion: a text may be coherent without the use of anaphoric devices and connectives. They separated Coherence from Cohesion, resulting in a scale with five dimensions. The reason we merged them is that both in the assessment and teaching literature the two notions are often connected, although they are conceptually different. Pallotti (2017, 2022) left out Task Requirements but added the CEFR scale for Coherence & Cohesion. Still other researchers calculated a composite FA score, based on the average of the four subscales (Nuzzo & Bove, 2020, 2022).

It should, however, be pointed out that scale adaptations may not be unproblematic. As recommended by Loewen (2022), the reliability and validity of the FA scale need to be reconsidered each time adaptations to the test instrument are made. This is also the case when the scale is used in a different learning context, as the outcomes may be affected by type and number of participants, and the task type and learning context in which data collection takes place.

Rater training and standardisation of rating procedures may also lead to higher validity and reliability of the rating tool, as has been emphasised in several studies with respect to rating scales in general (Pill & Smart, 2020; Rezaei & Lovorn, 2010), as well as — more specifically — concerning the assessment of pragmatic skills and FA (González-Lloret, 2022; Kuiken & Vedder, 2014; Timpe-Laughlin, 2018). In order to familiarise raters with scale dimensions, levels, and descriptors, rater training and feedback during various stages of the rater process are therefore important.

With the FA rating scale we aimed to create a reliable and validated tool that can be employed for various task types. One of the dilemmas TBLA is confronted with, as noted by González-Lloret (2016, 2022), is that rating criteria should ideally be derived from the specific assessment task, the goal that needs to be reached by performing the task, and the interlocutors involved in fulfilling the task. A drawback of this approach is, obviously, that if evaluative criteria are relative to a particular task, inferences may not be made beyond the specific target task and test context (Bachman, 2002). A way to overcome this dilemma may be the development in TBLA of a set of so-called prototypical standardised tasks (e.g., describing a picture, making a decision, solving a [communication] problem). As has been suggested by Norris (2016), assessment of such prototypical tasks has proven to offer a meaningful basis for eliciting and generalising about learners' functional language proficiency, rather than mere knowledge of vocabulary and grammar rules. The launch of the TBLT Language Learning Task Bank[1] is an important step in that direction, due to its promotion of prototypical standardised tasks.

FA in relation to (sub)components of CAF

The association between FA and (sub)components of CAF, and the impact of proficiency level, task type, and modality, have been examined in only a few studies on FA conducted in different learning environments. This makes it difficult to compare the outcomes. Syntactic complexity seems to have little impact on FA, contrary to lexical diversity and accuracy, which appear to be related to FA (Kuiken et al., 2010; Révesz et al., 2016; Strobl & Baten, 2022). In oral tasks, fluency was found to be a strong predictor of FA: a lower number of false starts and silent pauses was associated with higher scores for FA (Ekiert et al., 2022). Nuzzo and Bove (2020) observed an association between FA and general levels of proficiency as measured by a C-test, although the correlation varied across task types. Révész et al. (2016) investigated to what degree task type and proficiency level influence the extent to which CAF measures predict FA. They found that the subordination ratio of speakers appeared to function as a predictor of FA. This, however, contradicts the findings of Kuiken et al. (2010), who did not identify subordination complexity as a significant predictor of FA. This different outcome may be due to a difference in task modality, as participants in the latter study were given a writing task. What this type of research shows is that, although FA and CAF appear — to some extent — to be associated, the two constructs measure different features of L2 competence. Further research on the association between

---

1. https://tblt.indiana.edu

specific (sub)components of both FA and CAF at different proficiency levels and the extent to which this relationship is impacted by task type and task modality is, therefore, necessary.

FA in classroom practice

Another issue for further exploration is the applicability of the FA scale in the language classroom. The user-friendliness of the scale for raters leads to the question of whether and how the scale can also be useful for classroom practice. For teachers, the FA scale can serve as a diagnostic instrument to establish the strengths and weaknesses of their learners. The rating scale allows them to give their students more focused feedback and may provide useful information in terms of teaching targets. For learners, the FA scale can be employed as a tool for peer feedback and self-assessment, helping them to gain more insight into their own and each others' abilities, not only for L2 but also for L1. One of the few studies in which the employment of the scale in language pedagogy has been explored is the study by Nuzzo and Bove (2022), who examined the potential application of the FA scale as a teaching tool for L1 academic writing instruction by native Italian university students. Positive effects were found for those participants who had been instructed to use the FA scale as a tool for self-assessment.

FA in interactional tasks

The main focus in research on oral performance has so far been on monologic rather than on interactional speech. This is also the case for the FA rating scale which was developed for the assessment of monologue tasks. Adequacy of interactional speech, as argued, among others, by González-Lloret (2022), Pallotti (2019), and Youn (2018, 2020), is affected by socio-pragmatic factors, cultural and situational variables, participant variables, and artefacts mediating the interaction (e.g., videochat, Whatsapp). As nearly all communication takes place in an interactional setting, one may wonder what this implies for the FA scale. A next step for research on FA is, therefore, to explore the applicability of the FA scale for interactional tasks.

In order to advance the research agenda on the applicability of the FA scale for interactional tasks, next to Task Requirements, Content, and Comprehensibility, we reformulated the Coherence & Cohesion dimension for oral interactional tasks in terms of the adequacy of speakers' engagement in situated communicative interaction. The reason why we chose to substitute Coherence & Cohesion with a new dimension, which we labelled Interaction, is that, in an interactional exchange, coherence is mainly realised by mutual alignment of conversational turns. Speakers ideally connect their contribution to what has just been said by the interlocutor. Moreover, utterances in interactional turns, comprising backchannels ("yes," "okay"), are generally shorter and contain a relatively lower number of cohesive and anaphoric devices compared to monologic turns.

The leading question underlying the substituton of the Coherence & Cohesion dimension with Interaction is: to what extent can the speaker take and keep the floor, contribute to the development of the interaction, and ask for and provide clarification? The scale descriptors of this new dimension were derived from the CEFR (Council of Europe, 2001). The six proficiency levels refer to the interlocutor's ability with regard to: (1) topic management; (2) taking/keeping the floor; (3) mutual co-operation; (4) asking for/providing clarification (see Appendix B for scale levels and descriptors of this dimension).

In order to establish the reliability, validity, and applicability of the FA scale for oral interactional tasks, the scale is now being piloted for different target and source languages. Interactional data have been elicited by means of an oral problem-solving task, with an information gap. The task requires pairs of participants to negotiate and to choose a holiday accommodation, on the basis of six descriptions of Bed and Breakfast establishments in various regions in Italy. The participants are 21 dyads of students of English L2, with Italian as their L1, and 28 dyads of students of Italian L2, in three different learning environments (study abroad students in Italy and L2 learners of Italian in Hungary and in Poland). At the time of writing this chapter, the oral data of the 47 dyads are currently being assessed, for each single participant, by two groups of raters. The aims are to investigate: (1) how judgments of raters on the Interaction dimension of the FA scale correspond; and (2) how their judgments on the four dimensions of the scale (Task Requirements, Content, Comprehensibility, Interaction) are associated.

Concluding remarks

In this chapter, we have claimed that when judging L2 proficiency, it is necessary — next to the assessment of the linguistic dimension (CAF) — to take into account the functional dimension of L2 performance (FA), extending CAF to CAFFA. To that end we proposed an FA rating scale for the assessment of monologic oral and written performance consisting of four scale dimensions (Task Requirements, Content, Comprehensibility, Coherence & Cohesion) and six proficiency levels. On the basis of four studies and various follow-up studies conducted by other researchers in a variety of contexts, for different learners and languages, we concluded that the scale has shown itself to be a reliable, valid instrument, and a user-friendly tool.

We pointed out that an important issue with regard to the reliability and validity of the rating scale concerns the modifications that were made in some of the studies in which the FA scale has been employed. As recommended by Loewen (2022), it is, however, necessary to be aware of the broader impact of each change to the FA rating scale: if scale dimensions are altered or new descriptors are added, cross-study comparisons are hindered and the reliability and validity of the rating scale need to be reconsidered.

We also emphasised the necessity of rater training and standardisation of rating procedures, since rater training has been found to increase both the reliability and validity of the test instrument. In order to increase the comparibility of studies on CAFFA, the development of prototypical standardised tasks, as undertaken by the TBLT Language Learning Task Bank, needs to be encouraged, as an important step for eliciting learner data and making inferences about a learner's linguistic and functional L2 proficiency beyond a specific task.

The relation between FA and (sub)components of CAF, which has only been investigated in a few studies, is another area that requires further research. The same is true for the influence of proficiency level, task type, and modality on FA. Concerning the last of these, it is not clear to what extent task modality affects assessment of FA. It is easy to imagine that Comprehensibility may be evaluated differently in written text than in oral speech, where raters may be influenced by pronunciation, intonation, rhythm, and pitch. Del Bono (2019, 2020) found that Coherence & Cohesion, for instance, turned out to be more difficult for raters to assess in speaking tasks than in written tasks.

Another issue that should be addressed in future research is the question of how the scale can fulfil a role in classroom practice, both for teachers as a diagnostic instrument and for students as a tool for peer feedback and self-assessment.

Finally, we indicated directions for extending the use of the FA scale to interactional tasks. To that aim, we have replaced Coherence & Cohesion by a new dimension labelled Interaction. Research to test the reliability, validity, and applicability of the FA scale for interactional tasks is currently being conducted, among dyads of participants of different L2s and L1s. The outcomes will demonstrate to what extent it is possible to use the adapted version of the FA rating scale for the assessment of oral interactional competence.

References

Bachman, L. F. (2002). Some reflections on task-based language performance assessment. *Language Testing, 19*(4), 453–476.

Bulté, B., & Housen, A. (2012). Defining and operationalising L2 complexity. In A. Housen, F. Kuiken, & I. Vedder (Eds.), *Dimensions of L2 performance and proficiency. Complexity, accuracy and fluency in SLA* (pp. 21–46). John Benjamins.

Council of Europe (2001). *Common European framework of reference for languages: Learning, teaching, assessment.* Cambridge University Press.

De Jong, N. H., Steinel, M. P., Florijn, A. F., Schoonen, R., & Hulstijn, J. H. (2012a). The effect of task complexity on functional adequacy, fluency and lexical diversity in speaking performances of native and non-native speakers. In A. Housen, F. Kuiken, & I. Vedder (Eds.), *Dimensions of L2 performance and proficiency. Complexity, accuracy and fluency in SLA* (pp. 121–142). John Benjamins.

De Jong, N. H., Steinel, M. P., Florijn, A. F., Schoonen, R., & Hulstijn, J. H. (2012b). Facets of speaking proficiency. *Studies in Second Language Acquisition, 34*(1), 5–34.

Del Bono, F. (2019). Aspetti pragmatici nella valutazione di testi scritti: Uno studio sull'adeguatezza funzionale in italiano L2. In E. Nuzzo & I. Vedder (Eds.), *Lingua in contesto. La prospettiva pragmatica. Studi AItLA 9* (pp. 231–244). Associazione Italiana di Linguistica Applicata (AitLA).

Del Bono, F. (2020). L'utilizzo delle scale dell'adeguatezza funzionale su testi narrativi in L2: Uno studio esplorativo sugli effetti del task design. In E. Nuzzo, E. Santoro, & I. Vedder (Eds.), *Valutazione e misurazione delle produzioni orali e scritte in italiano lingua seconda* (pp. 71–82). Franco Cesati Editore.

Ekiert, M., Révész, A., Torgersen, E., & Moss, E. (2022). The role of pausing in L2 oral task performance: Toward a complete construct of functional adequacy. *TASK 2*(1), 33–59.

González-Lloret, M. (2016). *A practical guide to integrating technology into task-based language teaching.* Georgetown University Press.

González-Lloret, M. (2022). The present and future of functional adequacy. *TASK* 2(1),146–158.

Grice, H. P. (1975). Logic and conversation. In P. Cole & J. L. Morgan (Eds.), *Speech acts* (pp. 41–58). Brill.

Herraiz Martínez, A. (2018). Functional adequacy: The influence of English-medium instruction, English proficiency, and previous language learning experiences [Unpublished doctoral dissertation]. Universitat Jaume I, Castellón de la Plana.

Herraiz Martínez, A., & Alcón Soler, E. (2019). Pragmatic outcomes in the English-medium instruction context. *Applied Pragmatics, 1*(1), 68–91.

Kuiken, F., & Vedder, I. (2014). Rating written performance: What do raters do and why? *Language Testing, 31*(3), 329–348.

Kuiken, F., & Vedder, I. (2017). Functional adequacy in L2 writing. Towards a new rating scale. *Language Testing, 34*(3), 321–336.

Kuiken, F., & Vedder, I. (2018). Assessing functional adequacy of L2 performance in a task-based approach. In N. Taguchi & Y-J. Kim (Eds.), *Task-based approaches to assessing pragmatics* (pp. 265–286). John Benjamins.

Kuiken, F., & Vedder, I. (2022). Measurement of functional adequacy in different learning contexts: Rationale, key issues, and future perspectives. *TASK 2*(1), 8–32.

Kuiken, F., Vedder, I., & Gilabert, R. (2010). Communicative adequacy and linguistic complexity in L2 writing. In I. Bartning, M. Martin, & I. Vedder (Eds.), *Communicative proficiency and linguistic development: Intersections between SLA and language testing research* (pp. 81–100). European Second Language Association.

Loewen, S. (2022). Functional adequacy, task-based language teaching and instructed second language acquisition: A commentary. *TASK 2*(1), 137–145.

Long, M.H. (2015). *Second language acquisition and task-based language teaching*. Wiley Blackwell.

Long, M.H. (2016). In defense of tasks and TBLT: Nonissues and real issues. *Annual Review of Applied Linguistics*, *36*, 5–33.

Norris, J.M. (2016). Current uses for task-based language assessment. *Annual Review of Applied Linguistics*, *36*, 23–244.

Norris, J.M., & East, M. (2022). Task-based language assessment. In M.J. Ahmadian & M.H. Long (Eds.), *The Cambridge handbook of task-based language teaching* (pp. 507–528). Cambridge University Press.

Nuzzo, E., & Bove, G. (2020). Assessing functional adequacy across tasks: A comparison of learners' and speakers' written texts. *E-JournALL*, *7*(2), 9–27.

Nuzzo, E., & Bove, G. (2022). Exploring the pedagogical use of the rating scale for functional adequacy in L1 writing instruction. *TASK* *2*(1), 115–136.

Pallotti, G. (2009). CAF: Defining, refining and differentiating constructs. *Applied Linguistics*, *30*(4), 590–601.

Pallotti, G. (2017). Applying the interlanguage approach to language teaching. *International Review of Applied Linguistics in Language Teaching*, *55*(4), 393–412.

Pallotti, G. (2019). Assessing tasks: The case of interactional difficulty. *Applied Linguistics* *40*(1), 176–197.

Pallotti, G. (2022). Holistic and analytic assessment of functional adequacy. *TASK* *2*(1), 85–114.

Pallotti, G., & Brezina, V. (2019). Morphological complexity in written L2 texts. *Second Language Research*, *35*(1), 99–119.

Paquot, M. (2018). Phraseological competence: A missing component in university entrance language tests? Insights from a study of EFL learners' use of statistical collocations. *Language Assessment Quarterly*, *15*(1), 29–43.

Paquot, M. (2019). The phraseological dimension in interlanguage complexity research. *Second Language Research*, *35*(1), 121–145.

Pill, J., & Smart, C. (2020). Rating: Behavior and training. In P. Winke & T. Brunfaut (Eds.), *The Routledge handbook of second language acquisition and language testing* (pp. 135–144). Routledge.

Révész, A., Ekiert, M., & Torgersen, E. (2016). The effects of complexity, accuracy and fluency on communicative adequacy in oral task performance. *Applied Linguistics*, *37*(6), 828–848.

Rezaei, A.R., & Lovorn, M. (2010). Reliability and validity of rubrics for assessment through writing. *Assessing Writing 15*, 18–39.

Segalowitz, N. (2010). *Cognitive basis of second language fluency*. Routledge.

Shehadeh, A. (2018). Task-based language assessment. In J.I. Liontas (Ed.), *The TESOL encyclopedia of English language teaching* (pp. 1–6). John Wiley & Sons.

Strobl, C., & Baten, K. (2022). Assessing writing development during study abroad: The role of task and measures of linguistic and communicative performance. *TASK* *2*(1), 60–84.

Timpe-Laughlin, V. (2018). Pragmatics in task-based language assessment. Opportunities and challenges. In N. Taguchi & Y-J. Kim (Eds.), *Task-based approaches to assessing pragmatics* (pp. 288–304). John Benjamins.

Vasylets, O., Gilabert, R., & Manchón, R.M. (2019). Differential contribution of oral and written modes to lexical, syntactic and propositional complexity in L2 performance in instructed contexts. *Instructed Second Language Acquisition*, *3*(2), 206–227.

Wolfe-Quintero, K., Inagaki, S., & Kim, H.-Y. (1998). *Second language development in writing: Measures of fluency, accuracy, and complexity*. University of Hawai'i Press.

Youn, S. J. (2018). Rater variability across examinees and rating criteria in paired speaking assessment. *Language Testing and Assessment, 7*(1), 32–60.

Youn, S. J. (2020). Interactional features of L2 pragmatic interaction in role-play speaking assessment. *TESOL Quarterly, 54*(1), 201–233.

Appendix A.   FA rating scale for functional adequacy (for writing)

Task Requirements: Have the task requirements been fulfilled successfully (e.g., genre, task type, speech acts, register, addressee)?

1	2	3	4	5	6
None of the requirements of the task have been fulfilled.	Some (less than half) of the requirements of the task have been fulfilled.	Approximately half of the requirements of the task have been fulfilled.	Most (more than half) of the requirements of the task have been fulfilled.	Almost all the requirements of the task have been fulfilled,	All the requirements of the task have been fulfilled.

Content: Is the number of ideas provided in the text adequate and are they consistent to each other?

1	2	3	4	5	6
The number of ideas is not at all adequate and the ideas lack consistency.	The number of ideas is scarcely adequate and the ideas are hardly consistent.	The number of ideas is somewhat adequate, even though they are not very consistent.	The number of ideas is adequate and they are sufficiently consistent.	The number of ideas is very adequate and they are very consistent with each other.	The number of ideas is extremely adequate and they appear very consistent with each other.

Comprehensibility: How much effort is required to understand text purpose anti ideas?

1	2	3	4	5	6
The text is not at all comprehensible. Purposes and ideas are unclearly stated and the efforts of the reader to understand the text are ineffective.	The text is scarcely comprehensible. Its purposes are not clearly stated and the reader struggles to understand the ideas of the writer. The reader has to guess most of the purposes and ideas.	The text is somewhat comprehensible and some sentences are hard to understand at a first reading. A second reading helps to clarify the purposes of the text and the ideas conveyed, but some doubts persist.	The text is comprehensible. Only a few sentences are unclear but are understood, without too much effort, after a second reading. Purposes and ideas are clearly stated.	The text is easily comprehensible and reads smoothly; comprehensibility is not an issue. Purposes and ideas are clearly stated.	The text is very easily comprehensible and highly readable; the purposes and ideas are clearly stated.

Appendix A. *(continued)*

Coherence & Cohesion: Is the text coherent and cohesive (e.g., use of strategies for coherence, cohesive devices)?

1	2	3	4	5	6
The text is not at all coherent. Unrelated progressions and coherence breaks are very common. The writer does not use any anaphoric devices. The text is not at all cohesive. Connectives are hardly ever used and ideas are unrelated.	The text is scarcely coherent. The writer often uses unrelated progressions; when coherence is achieved, it is often done through repetitions. Only a few anaphoric devices are used. There are some coherence breaks. The text is not very cohesive. Ideas are not well linked by connectives, which are rarely used.	The text is somewhat coherent. Unrelated progressions and/or repetitions are frequent. More than two sentences in a row can have the same subject (even when the subject is understood). Some anaphoric devices, are used. There can be a few coherence breaks. The text is somewhat cohesive. Some connectives are used, but they are mostly conjunctions.	The text is coherent. Unrelated progressions are somewhat rare, but the writer sometimes relies on repetitions to achieve coherence. A sufficient number of anaphoric devices is used. There may be some coherence breaks. The text is cohesive. The writer makes good use of connectives, sometimes not limiting this to conjunctions.	The text is very coherent: when the writer introduces a new topic, it is usually done by using connectives or connective phrases. Repetitions are very infrequent. Anaphoric devices are numerous. There are no coherence breaks. The text is very cohesive and ideas are well linked by adverbial and/or verbal connectives.	The writer ensures exceptional coherence by integrating new ideas into the text with connectives or connective phrases. Anaphoric devices are used regularly. There are few instances of unrelated progressions and no coherence breaks. The structure of the text is extremely cohesive, thanks to a skillful use of connectives (especially linking chunks, verbal constructions and adverbials), often used to describe relationships between ideas.

Chapter 8. From CAF to CAFFA   161

Appendix B.   FA rating scale for interactional adequacy

Interactional adequacy: To what extent can the speaker take and keep the floor, contribute to the development of the interaction and ask for and provide clarification?					
1	2	3	4	5	6
Not at all: the interaction doesn't take place or it is carried out only thanks to the contribution of the interlocutor.	Scarcely: the speaker participates minimally to the exchange; he/she needs a lot of help from the interlocutor to start, maintain or end the interaction; responses are given when asked by the interlocutor to do so; the utterances are scarcely connected to the interlocutor's contribution.	Somewhat: the speaker uses simple techniques to take and keep the floor and end the interaction with some help from the interlocutor; the utterances are partly connected to the interlocutor's contribution; he she asks for and gives clarification, by repeating the interlocutor and using keywords simple routines.	Sufficiently: the speaker takes and keeps the floor, he she maintains and ends the interaction, generally appropriately, with little help from the interlocutor; the utterances are sufficiently connected to the interlocutor's contribution: he she gives and asks for clarification and repetition, although not always appropriately.	Largely: the speaker takes and keeps the floor appropriately and autonomously, he/she contributes to the development of the interaction with follow up statements and inferences showing comprehension; he/she clarifies and confirms the utterances of the interlocutor.	Absolutely: the speaker adequately and effectively takes and keeps the floor and ends the interaction; he she can select suitable and appropriate phrases to invite the interlocutor to contribute or to gain time, and to ask for or to give detailed and relevant clarifications.

SECTION 5

Theories informing task-based language teaching

CHAPTER 9

Reflecting on task-based language teaching from an Instructed SLA perspective[*]

Nina Spada
University of Toronto

Task-based language teaching (TBLT) and instructed second language acquisition (ISLA) have much in common in terms of theory, research, and educational relevance. The distinguishing characteristic between the two is that TBLT adopts communicative tasks as the central unit for instruction and assessment, whereas ISLA comprises a broader range of instructional activities and assessment practices. In this presentation, I focus on two of the conference themes: Instruction and Outcomes. With respect to Instruction, I draw attention to the pedagogical timing of form-focused instruction (FFI) and corrective feedback. I discuss relevant studies within ISLA and TBLT and argue that TBLT is particularly well-suited to investigating questions about the timing of FFI. In discussing Outcomes, I consider differences in how outcomes are measured in TBLT (i.e., performance) and ISLA (i.e., development) and the different aspects of language examined within each, for example, accuracy, implicit/explicit knowledge in ISLA and complexity, accuracy, and fluency in TBLT. I discuss underlying similarities between fluency and implicit knowledge, how they are measured, and propose research to investigate the pedagogical timing of FFI in relation to fluency development. I conclude with a brief discussion of the need for a balance between theoretically and pedagogically motivated research within ISLA and TBLT.

Introduction

When I was invited to give a plenary at the International Conference on Task-Based Language Teaching (TBLT), I hesitated because my research has not been

---

[*] Revised version of a plenary given to the 8th International TBLT Conference, Ottawa, Canada, 2019. First published as Spada, N. (2022). Reflecting on task-based language teaching from an Instructed SLA perspective. *Language Teaching, 55*(1), 74–86. Reproduced with permission from Cambridge University Press.

https://doi.org/10.1075/tblt.17.09spa
© 2025 John Benjamins Publishing Company

carried out within TBLT theory, research, and practice. I expressed concerns to the conference organizers that as an "outsider" I do not bring TBLT credentials to the table and wondered whether the conference delegates would prefer to have a TBLT expert on this podium — someone with proprietary rights in the TBLT community. When I communicated my reservations, the conference organizers assured me not to worry ... that one of the reasons I had been invited was to provide an "outsider's perspective" on some of the issues facing TBLT. Admittedly, the perspective that I bring does not come from too far away. My research is situated within instructed second language acquisition (ISLA), a subfield of SLA that is concerned with second language (L2) acquisition in "classrooms, language laboratories, or other settings where language is intentionally taught and/or intentionally learned" (Spada & Lightbown, 2013, p.319).

Even though "instruction" is included in the ISLA acronym, there has been a tendency to focus more on learning than on teaching and the broader educational practices around L2 learning. This is related to the fact that most of ISLA research takes place in laboratory or quasi-laboratory settings. My own research has primarily taken place in intact classrooms with children, adolescent, and adult L2 learners and a good deal of it has focused on observing, describing, and characterizing language teaching in addition to investigating its contributions to L2 learning. Thus, I often feel more comfortable situating myself within the domain of classroom research in L2 learning and teaching. But for the purposes of this presentation, I will be using ISLA as the general reference point from which to examine ongoing and future work in TBLT.

TBLT and ISLA

Of course, there are strands of TBLT research that are also considered to be part of ISLA. This is because TBLT and ISLA have a shared history. Both have their roots in language education. Indeed, the origins of TBLT were to develop L2 curricula. Many TBLT and ISLA researchers started their careers as L2 teachers and were motivated to engage in research to improve teaching practices. They found a place to do this within the field of second language acquisition (SLA). Over the years, and as their work became more specialized, the two subfields of TBLT and ISLA emerged, with the focus on tasks in TBLT and instruction more broadly defined in ISLA.

Because of their common history, ISLA and TBLT share a similar path in terms of theoretical influences and empirical approaches and their evolution over time. Both emphasized psycholinguistic frameworks in the early years, and this has expanded to include sociolinguistic and sociocultural frameworks more recently.

An emphasis on laboratory and quasi-laboratory studies using quantitative methods has been typical of research in both domains although this is slowly shifting to more classroom-based studies using qualitative and mixed methodologies.

In preparation for this plenary presentation, I have been catching up on my reading in the TBLT literature with two of the themes for this year's conference to guide me: Instruction and Outcomes. With respect to the first theme, I will focus my discussion on type and timing of instruction and corrective feedback (CF) in TBLT and ISLA research. With respect to the second theme, I will focus on how outcomes have been measured in TBLT (e.g., complexity, accuracy, fluency) and ISLA (e.g., accuracy, implicit/explicit knowledge). I will examine how these themes have been investigated in TBLT and ISLA and reflect on a few ways that research in each inform and enhance one other.

I added a third theme that I had not planned on addressing when I submitted my abstract a year ago — connections between theory, research, and pedagogy. As I read through the TBLT literature, it became evident that this has emerged as an important issue. Because this is a topic that is also of concern within ISLA and one that I have thought and written about, I decided to briefly address it as well.

Instruction

My research investigates the effects of instruction on L2 learning. More specifically, I have examined the effects of drawing learners' attention to language in meaning-based contexts — that is, in communicative language teaching (CLT) programs where the primary focus and organizing unit is topics and themes rather than linguistic units. Within these contexts, I have been interested in the different ways in which learners' attention can be drawn to language forms and whether there may be optimal times in the instructional sequence to do so. The central question motivating my research and that of many other ISLA researchers is whether and how these aspects of instruction affect L2 learning. Most of the research to investigate the effects of type of instruction on L2 learning have focused on explicit versus implicit approaches and this has resulted in several research syntheses and meta-analyses. The overall findings show that both types of instruction are beneficial but that there are stronger effects for explicit instruction (Ellis, 2000; Goo et al., 2015; Norris & Ortega, 2000; Spada, 1997; Spada & Tomita, 2010). These results are likely due to the fact that in most studies learners' progress is measured using controlled written grammar tests. There is also a bias in the research literature with a larger number of studies investigating explicit as opposed to implicit instruction (Doughty, 2003). In recent years, however, there has been an increase in research to investigate the effects of implicit instruction on L2 learning that include tests to measure learners' use of language in more natural, unrestricted, and communicative ways. Early findings indicate greater benefits for implicit compared with explicit instruction over the long term (Kang et al., 2018). These results clearly have relevance for TBLT with its focus on meaning-based communicative tasks to promote SLA.

Timing of instruction

Much more can be said about research that has examined the effects of type of instruction on L2 learning but I would like to turn my attention to the timing of instruction and specifically the question as to whether there are better times in the instructional sequence to draw learners' attention to language form. It is a question that I have investigated in my ISLA research and is one that I believe has direct applicability for TBLT. My own research on the timing of instruction has been guided by a distinction that Patsy Lightbown and I make between isolated and integrated form-focused instruction (FFI). We define isolated FFI as attention to language that is provided separately from communicative practice and integrated FFI as attention to language embedded within communicative practice. Both isolated and integrated FFI include attention to form and meaning. The only difference is when attention to form is provided in the instructional sequence, that is, before, after, or during communicative input and interaction activities. Both isolated and integrated FFI include instruction and CF, which can be explicit or implicit (Spada & Lightbown, 2008).

There are pedagogical arguments in support of both types of FFI. For example, some teachers and teacher educators argue that isolated FFI is best because learners, particularly those at low proficiency levels, are not able to pay attention to everything at once. Thus, it makes sense to separate attention to form and meaning. Isolated FFI is also thought to be more motivating for learners because they are not interrupted with CF or information about how language works when they are engaged in communicative interaction. Other L2 educators argue that integrated FFI is best because it is more efficient, that is, students can focus on form and meaning at the same time. Integrated FFI is also considered to be motivating for learners because they know that immediate help (e.g., CF) is available precisely when they need the correct forms to express their meanings. Interestingly, in research to investigate teachers' opinions about isolated and integrated FFI, even though they express a distinct preference for integrated FFI, they also emphasize the value of isolated FFI. Second and foreign language learners express similar views (Valeo & Spada, 2015).

A theory in cognitive psychology that is compatible with the view that both isolated and integrated FFI are beneficial for L2 learning is transfer-appropriate processing (TAP). It is based on the hypothesis that when we learn something our memories record not only the item learned but the cognitive and perceptual processes that were engaged during learning. For example, when we learn a new word, our memories encode information about the word and the context and processes engaged in when we learned it. Later, when we try to remember the word, the chances of retrieval are better if we are in a situation that is similar to the one in which it was originally learned (Blaxton, 1989; Morris et al., 1977). If we extend TAP to L2 learning, one could argue that L2 knowledge that derives from attention to language form in an isolated manner will be more easily retrieved in isolated grammar activities and L2 knowledge that derives from attention to form embedded in communicative interaction will be more easily retrieved in communicative interaction.

Viewing isolated and integrated FFI as complementary approaches, Patsy Lightbown and I hypothesized that their effects on L2 learning might differ depending on the type of language feature targeted. For example, isolated FFI may be more appropriate when it comes to learning less salient language features — ones that are not easily heard or noticed in the input (3rd person "s" in English) or with first language (L1) influenced features that are difficult to overcome. Integrated FFI, however, might work better with task-essential structures — ones that are highly likely to occur in communicative tasks (e.g., the use of the conditional in hypothetical situations). Integrated FFI might also be more beneficial for language features with complex rules that are difficult to teach in an isolated manner (e.g., articles in English) (Spada & Lightbown, 2008). To date, few studies in ISLA have investigated whether isolated and integrated FFI contribute to differences in L2 learning. I carried out one study with my research group at the University of Toronto (Spada et al., 2014) and there have been a handful of others (Barrot, 2014; Elgün-Gündüz et al., 2012; File & Adams, 2010). The results are mixed, showing equal benefits for both types of instruction as well as greater benefits for either integrated or isolated FFI in relation to different types of L2 knowledge and ability. Indeed, the diversity of findings almost matches the number of studies!

Reading through the TBLT literature, I was interested to discover that there is some recent research that has focused on the timing of FFI (Li et al., 2016). This is situated within TBLT work that calls for more attention to language form and is based on the assumption that meaningful interaction and implicit reactive feedback alone are not sufficient for L2 development. Indeed, the majority of instructed L2 learners do not have access to the vast amounts of input required to learn language in this way. Even L2 learners who have opportunities for considerable exposure do not acquire all aspects of language implicitly and continue to experience difficulties with specific aspects of language. This has been thoroughly documented in ISLA research investigating the L2 development of learners in content-based language teaching programs (Lightbown, 2014; Tedick & Lyster, 2020). Research in TBLT that has focused on questions about when to draw learners' attention to form is based on the view that there are benefits of explicit instruction and CF in L2 learning and that there is a role for a proactive approach to focusing on language. This necessarily involves a greater role for the teacher.

Looking at this strand of TBLT research from the prism of isolated and integrated FFI, it appears that most of it is consistent with integrated FFI. This is undoubtedly related to the fact that instruction has played a less prominent role in TBLT research. The focus has been on corrective CF and other interactional moves in communication, all of them by definition integrated FFI, and specifically on the type of CF (explicit or implicit). Indeed, many studies in TBLT and ISLA have been conducted to determine the utility and/or efficacy of different types of oral CF feedback in promoting L2 development. A beneficial role for CF is well established; several reviews and meta-analyses collectively indicate that CF facilitates L2 development and that both implicit and explicit CF are effective depending on a wide range of variables including learning context, linguistic targets, and learners' age and proficiency levels (e.g., Li, 2010; Lyster & Saito, 2010; Lyster et al., 2013; Mackey & Goo, 2007; Russell & Spada, 2006). As with ISLA research, few TBLT studies have investigated questions about whether the timing of CF makes a difference, but they are beginning to emerge.

Timing of CF

Questions about the timing of CF in TBLT have theoretical and pedagogical relevance. For example, the Interaction Hypothesis (Long, 1996) and Skill Acquisition Theory (SAT) (DeKeyser, 2007) argue for the benefits of providing immediate CF during communication (i.e., integrated FFI). This is thought to lead to implicit knowledge from the perspective of the Interaction Hypothesis and to proceduralized explicit knowledge within SAT. Another theory, Preparatory Attention and Memory (McDaniel et al., 1998), is based on the claim that learning is enhanced when complete attention is given to the task at hand rather than divided between multiple tasks. This is used to support delayed CF provided after communicative practice. It is thus consistent with isolated FFI.[1] Teachers are often

---

1. As pointed out by one of the reviewers, SAT also supports isolated FFI because it is based on the assumption that declarative knowledge can become procedural through communicative practice. See also Spada & Lightbown (2008).

advised to avoid correction when fluency practice is the objective (Hedge, 2000) and to provide immediate correction if accuracy is the objective (Scrivener, 2005). These recommendations are based to some extent on theory but primarily on the basis of pedagogical knowledge and experience. However, what is lacking in both these theoretical predictions and pedagogical recommendations is evidence. That is, what does research to examine these questions reveal about the timing of CF?

One of the earliest experimental studies to investigate the timing of CF was conducted by Paul Quinn, a former PhD student, and situated within the framework of isolated and integrated FFI (Quinn, 2014; Quinn & Nakata, 2017). A TBLT study that investigated the effects of delayed versus immediate CF on L2 learning was carried out by Shaofeng Li and colleagues (Li et al., 2016). Both studies focused on the passive voice and measured learners' knowledge of the target form in terms of implicit/procedural and declarative/explicit knowledge. Quinn's study revealed equal benefits for immediate and delayed CF on all language measures. The Li et al. (2016) study also indicated that both CF types were effective in improving learners' use of the passive, and that for the development of explicit/declarative knowledge. To my knowledge, there are no other carefully designed experimental studies that have manipulated timing of instruction and CF and measured their effects on L2 learning in either the ISLA or TBLT literature.

An early descriptive TBLT study that documented when in the pedagogical sequence a teacher focused on language in meaning-based instruction and interaction was conducted by Virginia Samuda (2001). What motivated her study was not the timing of instruction per se, but rather her observation that the teachers' role in TBLT was not getting sufficient attention despite the fact that the teacher is a crucial mediating factor in task-based language development. In her research, Samuda described in detail how the teacher can 'lead from behind' to help learners make important meaning-form connections by moving from a focus on meaning into a focus on form, back to meaning and then form again in implicit and explicit ways via instruction and CF. Her analyses highlighted the complementary roles of task and teacher — how tasks create opportunities for negotiation of meaning and how teachers guide learners in making form-meaning connections. From my perspective, this is an excellent example of integrated FFI.

There is a need for more research — observational and experimental — to explore the effects of differential timing of instruction and CF on L2 development. It seems to me that TBLT is an ideal context in which to investigate this question precisely because it is premised on the development and implementation of meaningful/communicative/purposeful tasks as the primary organizational unit of instruction. The use of tasks easily permits the manipulation of the integration or separation of attention to language and an examination of their effects on L2 learning.

Outcomes

Having considered the timing of instruction and CF I now turn to learner outcomes. Figure 1 illustrates that outcomes in TBLT research are most often measured in terms of complexity, accuracy, and fluency – referred to as the CAF triad. Definitions for these constructs vary. Some examples are: complexity refers to the learners' ability to use a range of sophisticated structures and vocabulary in the L2 (Bulté & Housen, 2012); accuracy refers to the extent to which an L2 learner's performance deviates from the norm (i.e., usually the native speaker) (Housen et al., 2012); fluency is intended to capture the rate and/or amount of production in a given time (Segalowitz, 2010) and can include speed fluency, breakdown fluency, and repair fluency (Skehan, 2009). While all three dimensions of L2 ability have been used in TBLT studies, according to a recent review of research on CAF in TBLT, the most frequently-used dimension is accuracy (Plonsky & Kim, 2016).

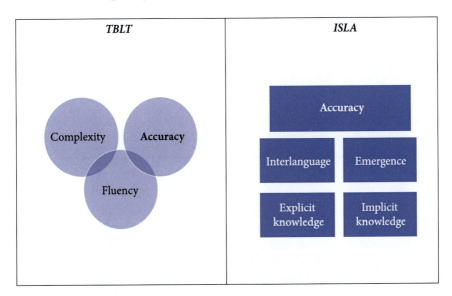

Figure 1. Measurement of outcomes in TBLT and ISLA

In ISLA research, outcomes have also been measured primarily in terms of accuracy and typically in pre/post-test designs. While there have been studies that have measured the effects of instruction on the learners' developing language using interlanguage (e.g., Doughty & Varela, 1998) and emergence criteria (Mackey, 1999; Spada & Lightbown, 1999), they are few in number. Most recently, efforts are underway to measure instructional effectiveness in terms of explicit (conscious, declarative) and implicit (unconscious, intuitive) knowledge (Akakura, 2012; Ellis et al., 2009).

Within the TBLT literature, several issues have been raised about CAF including differences in their definition and operationalization, concerns that CAF research is primarily performance based not developmental, and that CAF descriptors are not specific to particular domains of language (e.g., grammar, vocabulary, discourse) (Bygate, 2020). Other concerns point to a lack of clarity as to how CAF dimensions relate to functional dimensions of proficiency and communicative adequacy (Pallotti, 2009), and the need to investigate CAF as a dynamic and interrelated set of constantly changing subsystems (Norris & Ortega, 2009).

Recognizing the concerns with the CAF triad, I am nonetheless intrigued to explore how it might play a greater role in ISLA research — particularly fluency and complexity — given the predominance on accuracy as the focus of research. CAF analyses have the potential to provide a more multidimensional view of L2 development over time in instructional settings. Furthermore, given that the aim of L2 teaching is to develop the ability to communicate successfully, and that these three performance dimensions play important roles in L2 communicative success, this seems to be a worthwhile and important avenue to pursue.

Investigating the link between CAF measures in relation to the effects of instruction on L2 development has both theoretical and pedagogical significance. One could argue, for example, that isolated FFI leads to greater attention to accuracy and increased monitoring behavior on the part of learners. If one takes the perspective of L2 speech production models, this attention is likely to slow down speech formulation processes and lead to a decrease in fluency (Kormos, 2006). Thus, a potential pedagogical implication is that teachers should provide minimal CF during fluency work. On the other hand, attention to accuracy within communicative interaction (e.g., integrated FFI) could lead to greater fluency without a decrease in accuracy. Some models of task-based production predict a trade-off between accuracy and complexity (Skehan, 1998, 2015) or a simultaneous increase in both (Robinson, 2001). While these issues have been addressed in relation to learner performance under different task conditions, few studies have used CAF to measure instructional effects on L2 learning over time. Two exceptions include Alan Tonkyn (2012), who documented gains in CAF in L2 speaking skills after a 10-week English for Academic Purposes course, and Parvaneh Tavakoli and colleagues, who investigated the effects of a 4-week intervention of awareness-raising activities and fluency strategy training on learners' fluency development (Tavakoli et al., 2015).

No research, to my knowledge, has investigated the development of all three dimensions of the CAF triad in relation to different types of instruction. One explanation for this absence is that CAF measures are global in nature and not sufficiently sensitive to capture slight differences in performance after pedagogical interventions that typically focus on a specific linguistic feature. However, as pointed out by Marije Michel (2017), "with the development of more fine-grained measures (for example, the ones proposed by Lambert & Kormos, 2014, for syntactic and by Jarvis, 2013, for lexical complexity, respectively) and scores (for example, Foster & Wigglesworth, 2016, weighted accuracy score) future work will hopefully aim to capture instructional effects by means of CAF" (p. 63).

A focus of increased attention in ISLA is the development of measures for explicit and implicit L2 knowledge — especially implicit knowledge because it is more difficult to measure. Several efforts have been made to develop and validate different measures of implicit knowledge (Ellis et al., 2009; Jiang, 2007; Shiu et al., 2018; Spada et al., 2015; Suzuki & DeKeyser, 2015; Vafaee & Kachisnke, 2017; Zhang, 2015). This activity is motivated by a fundamental question in ISLA: Does instruction contribute to the development of both implicit and explicit knowledge? Some researchers argue that instruction contributes only to explicit knowledge (e.g. Krashen 1982; Schwartz, 1993). Others claim that instruction can lead to implicit knowledge via noticing (e.g., Schmidt, 1993), while others argue that instruction leads to implicit knowledge via practice (e.g., DeKeyser, 1998, 2005). This last argument is based on SAT, where the prediction is that through practice, explicit or declarative knowledge can become proceduralized and over time automatic, so that while it looks like implicit knowledge it is actually explicit proceduralized knowledge. This is most likely the case with the majority of instructed learners because we know that implicit learning requires vast amounts of exposure to the language and large quantities of time — two elements missing from the lives of most instructed L2ers.

As indicated in Figure 2, typical descriptors of implicit/proceduralized explicit knowledge are: fluent, effortless, skilled, and automatic. Fluency measures in CAF (e.g. breakdown, speed, and repair fluency) are designed to capture these dimensions of language use. It would be valuable if more ISLA research explored the ways in which these fluency measures can be used to investigate the effects of instruction on the development of implicit/proceduralized explicit knowledge. To be sure, the development of such measures is not easy, and they are often extremely time consuming to use. However, the growing availability of computerized tools to measure CAF dimensions both reliably and quickly (de Jong & Wempe, 2009; Leijten & Van Waes, 2013; MacWhinney, 2000) offers much promise for ISLA research to examine how complexity, accuracy, and fluency develop over time in relation to different types of instruction. Such research could also provide insights into the interactions between them and their relationships with other measures of proficiency (e.g., communicative adequacy) (Révész et al., 2016).

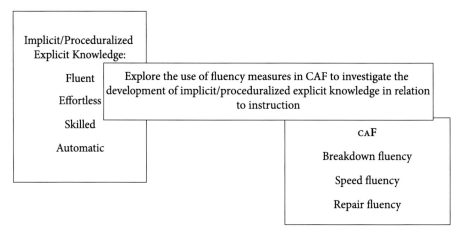

Figure 2. Fluency measures in CAF: Implicit/proceduralized explicit knowledge

Theory, research, and pedagogy

In the introduction to their edited volume *TBLT as researched pedagogy,* Virginia Samuda, Kris Van den Branden, and Martin Bygate state that "the application of research to classroom practice has always been at the heart of the TBLT project" (Samuda et al., 2018, p.6), but they express concerns that most of the research has focused on the psycholinguistic dimensions of tasks and that there is a need for more research to address the pedagogical dimensions. They are quick to point out that this does not mean that the psycholinguistically-oriented research on the design, sequencing, and implementation of tasks is not relevant to pedagogy. Their concern is that while a good deal of it is relevant to pedagogy, it is not focused on pedagogy. This is related to a distinction often made in education (and other professional disciplines) between top-down and bottom-up research. With the former, insights are derived from theoretically-motivated questions, the research often takes place in laboratory settings, and the emphasis is not on pedagogy or broader issues of L2 educational practices. Bottom-up research typically starts from pedagogically-motivated questions, and the research takes place in "real" classrooms. Similar issues are raised in the distinction that Kris Van den Branden (2015) makes between prescriptive and descriptive research in TBLT. In the former, pedagogical guidelines and recommendations are based on research that documents how people acquire the L2 in task-based interaction, and in the latter, the focus of research is on the pedagogical actions and decisions that are actually taken by teachers and students in authentic classrooms while they are working with tasks.

Some examples of descriptive research in TBLT include the long-term, large scale studies by Van den Branden and his colleagues researching all aspects of implementing TBLT language programs from curriculum development to the role of the teachers to assessment of learning outcomes and program evaluation (Van den Branden, 2006, 2009, 2015). Another example within TBLT is the collaborative research on teachers' implementation of tasks in German secondary schools (Müller-Hartmann & Schocker, 2011, 2018). There are also several descriptive case studies of teachers and learners engaged in TBLT activities in intact classrooms (Andon & Eckerth, 2009; McDonough & Chaikitmongkol, 2007; Oliver & Bogachenko, 2018).

One of the places where researchers and teachers come together is in teacher education and professional development courses. These contexts have enormous potential for both groups to share and build knowledge together. Martin East's work with novice teachers in the development, use, and interpretation of tasks is a good example of this (East, 2012, 2018), as well as the work of others in TBLT (Baralt, 2018; Nguyen et al., 2018). In ISLA, a good deal of the pedagogy-based research also comes from teacher professional development initiatives that have emerged in response to research findings. This includes investigations of how experienced teachers explore ways of focusing on language within content-based language teaching via professional development courses (Tedick & Zilmer, 2018); studies investigating teachers collaborating with researchers to develop and implement instructional materials focusing learners' attention on language in subject-matter French immersion classes (Lyster, 2019; Lyster et al., 2009); and investigations of the role of the teacher in creating opportunities for learners to co-construct knowledge of academic language in content and language integrated learning (CLIL) classrooms (Nikula, 2015; Van Gorp & Van den Branden, 2015).

Much has been written about the research-practice gap in ISLA and in applied linguistics generally (e.g., Borg, 2009; Bygate, 2005; Ellis, 2010; Ortega, 2012; Spada, 2015, 2022). Some of the explanations for it include the fact that laboratory studies outnumber classroom studies by 3 to 1, making the results less relevant/meaningful to teachers; research reports often appear in journals targeted at researchers and are written in technical language making them inaccessible to most language teachers; and teachers are skeptical of pedagogical recommendations from researchers who have little or no classroom experience. A top-down approach in which researchers are considered the "experts" and teachers the "recipients" of their knowledge fails to recognize that teachers and researchers have different types of knowledge. Some of that knowledge overlaps and some is specific to each group. What is important is that the knowledge be shared. There are a variety of ways to do this including writing for teachers, collaborative research, and professional development (Spada & Lightbown, 2019).

It appears that a good deal of the ISLA pedagogy-based research has taken place in content-based language teaching (CBLT) programs in the North American context as well as in CLIL programs in Europe and elsewhere. Clearly, TBLT, CBLT, and CLIL have much in common. They are all concerned with the simultaneous teaching of language and meaning/content. The focus in CBLT and CLIL is subject-matter instruction and in TBLT experiential and goal-oriented learning. While these programs differ in several respects (e.g., target populations, language learning contexts), in all three programs "teachers and students must interact and collaborate to do things with words in ways that maximize the learning of language while equally promoting the creation of 'meaning'" (Ortega, 2015, p.1).

The connections between TBLT, CBLT, and CLIL were recently brought to the forefront in a special issue of *System* entitled *The interface between task-based language teaching and content-based instruction* and edited by María del Pilar García Mayo (2015). Central questions within all three programs concern: whether, when, and how to integrate a focus on language within meaning/content/task-based instruction. These questions have theoretical and pedagogical relevance and are compatible with pedagogy-based and research-based studies allowing for explorations of questions of mutual interest from different perspectives. They also lend themselves to collaborative work between teachers and researchers and have the potential to merge empirical insights from top-down prescriptive approaches with those from bottom up/descriptive approaches.

Conclusion

To summarize and conclude, my goal in discussing the two primary themes of Instruction and Outcomes has been to offer some reflections on how research in ISLA and TBLT can further inform, build on, and enhance one another. With respect to Instruction, I see conceptual work and research on the timing of instruction in ISLA contributing to current and future work in TBLT (Figure 3). Specifically, more research to investigate isolated and integrated FFI would provide insights into whether and how the separation (before/after tasks) or integration (within tasks) contributes to different aspects of L2 learning. In terms of Outcomes, I view TBLT research on CAF as having the potential to expand the measurement of L2 learning in ISLA research by moving from almost exclusively accuracy-based descriptions of learning outcomes to exploring ways in which fluency and complexity measures can be used to characterize L2 development in relation to instruction.

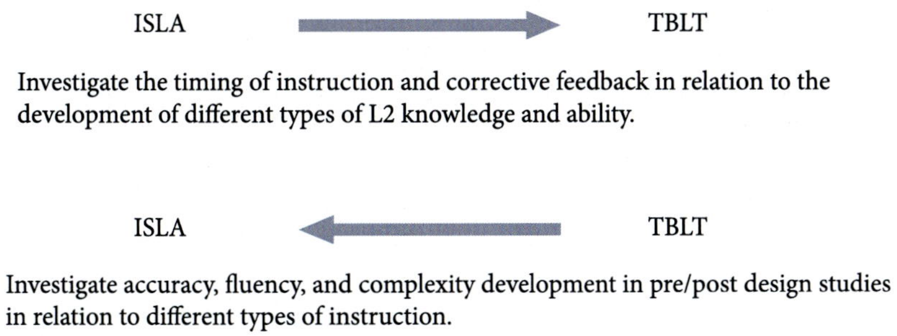

ISLA ⟶ TBLT

Investigate the timing of instruction and corrective feedback in relation to the development of different types of L2 knowledge and ability.

ISLA ⟵ TBLT

Investigate accuracy, fluency, and complexity development in pre/post design studies in relation to different types of instruction.

Figure 3. TBLT and ISLA influencing each other

With respect to the third theme, Theory, Research, and Pedagogy, my intent is to emphasize that both ISLA and TBLT have much to gain if there is more of a balance in terms of research carried out to investigate theoretical and pedagogical questions. It is equally important not to lose sight of the fact that the connections between theory, research, and pedagogy are not one-way. Just as theory and research can inform pedagogy, pedagogy can inform theory and research. Furthermore, given that ISLA and TBLT share the goal of improving L2 learning and teaching, a greater focus on research that is pedagogically motivated and situated will stimulate new questions, produce new knowledge, and provide insights into whether and to what extent the findings are compatible with those from theoretically-motivated research. This should help to create a better balance and synergy within both ISLA and TBLT.

References

Akakura, M. (2012). Evaluating the effectiveness of explicit instruction on implicit and explicit L2 knowledge. *Language Teaching Research, 16*(1), 9–37.

Andon, N., & Eckerth, J. (2009). Chacun à son gout? Task-based pedagogy from the teacher's point of view. *International Journal of Applied Linguistics, 19*(3), 286–310.

Baralt, M. (2018). Becoming a task-based teacher educator: A case study. In V. Samuda, K. Van den Branden, & M. Bygate (Eds.), *TBLT as a researched pedagogy* (pp. 23–50). John Benjamins.

Barrot, J. (2014). Combining isolated and integrated form-focused instruction: Effects on productive skills. *Language, Culture, and Curriculum, 27*(3), 278–293.

Blaxton, T.A. (1989). Investigating dissociations among memory measures: Support for a transfer-appropriate processing framework. *Journal of Experimental Psychology: Learning, Memory & Cognition, 15*(4), 657–668.

Borg, S. (2009). English language teachers' conceptions of research. *Applied Linguistics*, *30*(3), 358–88.

Bulté, B., & Housen, A. (2012). Defining and operationalizing L2 complexity. In A. Housen, F. Kuiken, & I. Vedder (Eds.), *Dimensions of L2 performance and proficiency: Complexity, accuracy and fluency in SLA* (pp. 21–46). John Benjamins.

Bygate, M. (2005). Applied linguistics: A pragmatic discipline, a generic discipline? *Applied Linguistics*, *26*(4), 568–581.

Bygate, M. (2020). Some directions for the possible survival of TBLT as a real-world project. *Language Teaching*, *53*(3), 275–288.

de Jong, N.H., & Wempe, T. (2009). Praat script to detect syllable nuclei and measure speech rate automatically. *Behavior Research Methods*, *41*, 385–390.

DeKeyser, R. (1998). Beyond focus on form: Cognitive perspectives on learning and practicing second language grammar. In C. Doughty & J. Williams (Eds.), *Focus on form in classroom second language acquisition* (pp. 42–63). Cambridge University Press.

DeKeyser, R. (2005). What makes learning second language grammar difficult? A review of issues. *Language Learning*, *55*(S1), 1–25.

DeKeyser, R. (2007). Skill acquisition theory. In B. Van Patten & J. Williams (Eds.), *Theories in second language acquisition* (pp. 97–114). Lawrence Erlbaum.

Doughty, C. (2003). Instructed SLA: Constraints, compensation, and enhancement. In C. Doughty, & M. Long (Eds.), *The handbook of second language acquisition* (pp. 256–310). Blackwell.

Doughty, C., & Varela, E. (1998). Communicative focus on form. In C. Doughty & J. Williams (Eds.), *Focus on form in classroom second language acquisition* (pp. 114–138). Cambridge University Press.

East, M. (2012). *Task-based language teaching from the teachers' perspective: Insights from New Zealand*. John Benjamins.

East, M. (2018). How do beginning teachers conceptualise and enact tasks in school foreign language classrooms? In V. Samuda, K. Van den Branden, & M. Bygate (Eds.), *TBLT as a researched pedagogy* (pp. 23–50). John Benjamins.

Elgün-Gündüz, Z., Akcan, S., & Bayyurt, Y. (2012). Isolated form-focused instruction and integrated form-focused instruction in primary school classrooms in Turkey. *Language, Culture and Curriculum*, *25*(2), 157–171.

Ellis, R. (2000). Task-based research and language pedagogy. *Language Teaching Research*, *4*(3), 193–220.

Ellis, R. (2010). Second language acquisition, teacher education and language pedagogy. *Language Teaching*, *43*(2), 182–201.

Ellis, R., Loewen, S., Elder, C., Erlam, R., Philp, J., & Reinders, H. (2009). *Implicit and explicit knowledge in second language learning: Testing and teaching*. Multilingual Matters.

File, K.A., & Adams, R. (2010). Should vocabulary instruction be integrated or isolated? *TESOL Quarterly*, *44*(2), 222–249.

Foster, P., & Wigglesworth, G. (2016). Capturing accuracy in second language performance: the case for a weighted clause ratio. *Annual Review of Applied Linguistics*, *36*, 98–116.

García Mayo, M.P. (2015). The interface between task-based language teaching and content-based instruction. *System*, *54*, 1–3.

Chapter 9. Reflecting on task-based language teaching from an Instructed SLA perspective 179

Goo, J., Granena, G., Yilmaz, Y., & Novella, M. (2015). Implicit and explicit instruction in L2 learning. In P. Rebuschat (Ed.), *Implicit and explicit learning of languages* (pp. 443–482). John Benjamins.

Hedge, T. (2000). *Teaching and learning in the language classroom.* Oxford University Press.

Housen, A., Kuiken, F., & Vedder, I. (2012). (Eds.). *Dimensions of L2 performance and proficiency: Complexity, accuracy and fluency in SLA.* John Benjamins.

Jarvis, S. (2013). Capturing the diversity in lexical diversity. *Language Learning, 63*(s1), 87–106.

Jiang, N. (2007). Selective integration of linguistic knowledge in adult second language learning. *Language Learning, 57*(1), 1–33.

Kang, E. Y., Sok, S., & Han, Z. H. (2018). Thirty-five years of ISLA on form-focused instruction: A methodological synthesis. *Language Teaching Research, 23*(4), 403–427.

Kormos, J. (2006). *Speech production and second language acquisition.* Lawrence Erlbaum Associates.

Krashen, S. D. (1982). *Principles and practice in second language acquisition.* Pergamon.

Lambert, C., & Kormos, J. (2014). Complexity, accuracy, and fluency in task-based l2 research: Toward more developmentally based measures of second language acquisition. *Applied Linguistics, 35*(5), 607–614.

Leijten, M., & Van Waes, L. (2013). Keystroke logging in writing research: Using Inputlog to analyze and visualize writing processes. *Written Communication, 30*, 358–392.

Li, S. (2010). The effectiveness of corrective feedback in SLA: A meta-analysis. *Language Learning, 60*(2), 309–365.

Li, S., Zhu, Y., & Ellis, R. (2016). The effects of the timing of corrective feedback on the acquisition of a new linguistic structure. *The Modern Language Journal, 100*(1), 276–295.

Lightbown, P. M. (2014). *Focus on content-based language teaching.* Oxford University Press.

Long, M. H. (1996). The role of the linguistic environment in second language acquisition. In W. Ritchie, & T. Bahtia (Eds.), *Handbook of second language acquisition* (pp. 413–468). Academic Press.

Lyster, R. (2019). Making research on instructed SLA relevant for teachers through professional development. *Language Teaching Research, 23*(4), 494–513.

Lyster, R., Collins, L., & Ballinger, S. (2009). Linking languages through a bilingual read-aloud project. *Language Awareness, 18*(3–4), 366–383.

Lyster, R., & Saito, K. (2010). Oral feedback in classroom SLA: A meta-analysis. *Studies in Second Language Acquisition, 32*(2), 265–302. https://www.jstor.org/stable/44488129.

Lyster, R., Saito, K., & Sato, M. (2013). Oral corrective feedback in second language classrooms. *Language Teaching, 46*(1), 1–40.

Mackey, A. (1999). Input, interaction and second language development: An empirical study of question formation in ESL. *Studies in Second Language Acquisition, 21*(4), 557–587. http://www.jstor.org/stable/44486830.

Mackey, A., & Goo, J. (2007). Interaction research in SLA: A meta-analysis and research synthesis. In A. Mackey (Ed.), *Conversational interaction and second language acquisition* (pp. 407–452). Oxford University Press.

MacWhinney, B. (2000). *The childes project: Tools for analyzing talk.* [Computer program].

McDaniel, M., Robinson, B., & Einstein, P. (1998). Prospective remembering: Perceptually driven or conceptually driven processes? *Memory & Cognition, 26*, 121–134.

McDonough, K., & Chaikitmongkol, W. (2007). Teachers' and learners' reactions to a task-based EFL course in Thailand. *TESOL Quarterly, 41*(1), 107–132.

Michel, M. (2017). Complexity, accuracy and fluency (CAF). In S. Loewen & M. Sato (Eds.), *The Routledge handbook of instructed second language acquisition* (pp. 50–68). Routledge.

Morris, D. D., Bransford, J. D., & Franks, J. J. (1977). Levels of processing versus transfer appropriate processing. *Journal of Verbal Learning and Verbal Behavior, 16*(5), 519–533.

Müller-Hartmann, A., & Schocker, M. (2011). *Teaching English. Task-supported language learning.* Schöningh.

Müller-Hartmann, A., & Schocker, M. (2018). The challenges of integrating focus on form within tasks: Findings from a classroom research project in secondary EFL classrooms. In V. Samuda, K. Van den Branden, & M. Bygate (Eds.), *TBLT as a researched pedagogy* (pp. 97–130). John Benjamins.

Nguyen, B. T., Newton, J., & Crabbe, D. (2018). Teacher transformation of textbook tasks in Vietnamese EFL high school classrooms. In V. Samuda, K. Van den Branden, & M. Bygate (Eds.), *TBLT as a researched pedagogy* (pp. 51–70). John Benjamins.

Nikula, T. (2015). Hands-on tasks in CLIL science classrooms as sites for subject-specific language use and learning. *System, 54*, 14–27.

Norris, J. M., & Ortega, L. (2000). Effectiveness of L2 instruction: A research synthesis and quantitative meta-analysis. *Language Learning, 50*(3), 417–528.

Norris, J. M., & Ortega, L. (2009). Towards an organic approach to investigating CAF in instructed SLA: The case of complexity. *Applied Linguistics, 30*(4), 555–578.

Oliver, R., & Bogachenko, T. (2018). Teacher perceptions and use of tasks in school ESL classrooms. In V. Samuda, K. Van den Branden, & M. Bygate (Eds.), *TBLT as a researched pedagogy* (pp. 71–96). John Benjamins.

Ortega, L. (2012). Language acquisition research for language teaching: Choosing between application and relevance. In Hinger, B., Unterrainer, E. M., & Newby, D. (Eds.), *Sprachen lernen: Kompetenzen entwickeln–Performanzen (über)prüfen* (pp. 24–38). Präsens Verlag.

Ortega, L. (2015). Researching CLIL and TBLT interfaces. *System, 54*, 103–109.

Pallotti, G. (2009). CAF: Defining, refining and differentiating constructs. *Applied Linguistics, 30*(4), 590–601.

Plonsky, L., & Kim, Y. (2016). Task-based learner production: A substantive and methodological review. *Annual Review of Applied Linguistics, 36*, 73–97.

Quinn, P. (2014). Delayed versus immediate corrective feedback on orally produced passive errors in English [Unpublished doctoral dissertation]. University of Toronto, Toronto.

Quinn, P., & Nakata, T. (2017). The timing of oral corrective feedback. In H. Nassaji & E. Kartchava (Eds.), *Corrective feedback in second language teaching and learning: Research, theory, applications, implications* (pp. 35–47). Routledge.

Révész, A., Ekiert, M., & Torgersen, E. N. (2016). The effects of complexity, accuracy, and fluency on communicative adequacy in oral task performance. *Applied Linguistics, 37*(6), 828–848.

Robinson, P. (2001). Task complexity, task difficulty, and task productions: Exploring interactions in a componential framework. *Applied Linguistics, 22*(1), 27–57.

Russell, J., & Spada, N. (2006). Corrective feedback makes a difference: A meta-analysis of the research. In J. Norris & L. Ortega (Eds.), *Synthesizing research on language learning and teaching* (pp. 134–164). John Benjamins.

Samuda, V. (2001). Guiding relationships between form and meaning during task performance: The role of the teacher. In M. Bygate, P. Skehan, & M. Swain (Eds.), *Researching pedagogic tasks: Second language learning, teaching and testing* (pp. 119–140). Pearson Education.

Samuda, V., Van den Branden, K., & Bygate, M. (2018). *TBLT as a researched pedagogy*. John Benjamins.

Schmidt, R. (1993). Awareness and second language acquisition. *Annual Review of Applied Linguistics, 13,* 206–226.

Schwartz, B. (1993). On explicit and-negative data effecting and affecting competence and linguistic behavior. *Studies in Second Language Acquisition, 15*(2), 147–163.

Scrivener, J. (2005). *Learning teaching: A guidebook for English language teachers*. Macmillan Education.

Segalowitz, N. (2010). *Cognitive bases of second language fluency*. Routledge.

Shiu, L. J., Yalçın, Ş., & Spada, N. (2018). Exploring second language learners' grammaticality judgment performance in relation to task design features. *System, 72,* 215–225.

Skehan, P. (1998). *A cognitive approach to language learning*. Oxford University Press.

Skehan, P. (2009). Modelling second language performance: Integrating complexity, accuracy, fluency, and lexis. *Applied Linguistics, 30*(4), 510–532.

Skehan, P. (2015). Limited attention capacity and cognition: Two hypotheses regarding second language performance on tasks. In Bygate, M. (Ed.), *Domains and directions in the development of TBLT: A decade of plenaries from the international conference* (pp. 123–156). John Benjamins.

Spada, N. (1997). Form-focused instruction and second language acquisition: A review of classroom and laboratory research. *Language Teaching, 30*(2),73–87.

Spada, N. (2015). SLA research and L2 pedagogy: Misapplications and questions of relevance. *Language Teaching, 48*(1), 69–81.

Spada, N. (2022). SLA research and language education: An uneasy relationship. In C. Bardel, C. Hedman, K. Rejman, & E. Zetterholm (Eds.), *Exploring language education. Global and local perspectives* (pp. 14–37). Stockholm University Press.

Spada, N., Jessop, L., Suzuki, W., Tomita, Y., & Valeo, A. (2014). Isolated and integrated form-focused instruction: Effects on different types of L2 knowledge. *Language Teaching Research, 18*(4), 453–473.

Spada, N., & Lightbown, P. M. (1999). Instruction, L1 influence and developmental "readiness" in second language acquisition. *The Modern Language Journal, 83*(1), 1–22.

Spada, N., & Lightbown, P. M. (2008). Form-focused instruction: Isolated or Integrated? *TESOL Quarterly, 42*(2), 181–207. http://www.jstor.org/stable/40264447.

Spada, N., & Lightbown, P. M. (2013). Instructed SLA. In Robinson, P. (Ed.), *The Routledge encyclopedia of second language acquisition* (pp. 319–327). Routledge.

Spada, N., & Lightbown, P. M. (2019). In it together: Teachers, researchers, and classroom SLA. Plenary presented at the American Association for Applied Linguistics, Atlanta, USA.

Spada, N., Shiu, L. J., & Tomita, Y. (2015). Validating an elicited imitation task as a measure of implicit knowledge: Comparisons with other validation studies. *Language Learning, 65*(3), 723–751.

Spada, N., & Tomita, Y. (2010). Interactions between type of instruction and type of language feature: A meta-analysis. *Language Learning, 60*(2), 263–308.

doi Suzuki, Y., & DeKeyser, R. (2015). The interface of explicit and implicit knowledge in a second language: Insights from individual differences in cognitive aptitudes. *Language Learning, 67*(4), 860–895.

doi Tavakoli, P., Campbell, C., & McCormack, J. (2015). Development of speech fluency over a short period of time: Effects of pedagogic intervention. *TESOL Quarterly, 50*(2), 1–25.

Tedick, D. J., & Lyster, R. (2020). *Scaffolding language development in immersion and dual language classrooms.* Routledge.

doi Tedick, D. J., & Zilmer, C. (2018). Teacher perceptions of immersion professional development experiences emphasizing language-focused content education. *Journal of Immersion and Content-Based Instruction, 6*(2), 269–294.

doi Tonkyn, A. (2012). Measuring and perceiving changes in oral complexity, accuracy and fluency. In A. Housen, F. Kuiken, & I. Vedder (Eds.), *Dimensions of L2 performance and proficiency* (pp. 221–245). John Benjamins.

doi Vafaee, P., & Kachisnke, I. (2017). Validating grammaticality judgment tests: Evidence from two new psycholinguistic measures. *Studies in Second Language Acquisition, 39*, 59–95. https://www.jstor.org/stable/26330952.

doi Valeo, A., & Spada, N. (2015). Is there a better time to focus on form? Teacher and learner views. *TESOL Quarterly, 50*(2), 314–339.

doi Van den Branden, K. (2006). *Task-based language education: From theory to practice.* Cambridge University Press.

doi Van den Branden, K. (2009). Mediating between predetermined order and complete chaos: The role of the teacher in task-based language education. *International Journal of Applied Linguistics, 19*(3), 264–285.

doi Van den Branden, K. (2015). Task-based language education: From theory to practice … and back again. In Bygate, M. (Ed.), *Domains and directions in the development of TBLT: A decade of plenaries from the international conference* (pp. 303–320). John Benjamins.

doi Van Gorp, K., & Van den Branden, K. (2015). Teachers, pupils and tasks: The genesis of dynamic learning opportunities. *System, 54*, 28–39.

doi Zhang, R. (2015). Measuring university-level L2 learners' implicit and explicit linguistic knowledge. *Studies in Second Language Acquisition, 37*, 457–486.

CHAPTER 10

How a processability perspective frames the potential of tasks in instructed second language acquisition[*]

Anke Lenzing
University of Innsbruck

Processability Theory (PT) focuses on the nature of second language (L2) learners' processing capacities to clarify the obstacles, achievements, and (some) systematic aspects of variation in L2 learning. In this chapter, I show that a processability perspective on tasks can contribute to our understanding of how both the universal and individual features of L2 development can be recognised in learners' speech. I investigate speech samples of different learners completing the same task at different points in their language development and explore: (1) their use of different linguistic structures reflecting their developmental stage; (2) the variation in their use of linguistic structures at the same developmental stage; and (3) the variability in the vocabulary of different semantic domains covered by the learners. I show that a PT perspective on tasks in second language acquisition can empower teachers to nuance the design of learning activities to take account of different learning needs.

Keywords: Processability Theory, tasks, linguistic structures, variation in L2 learning, developmental stages, learning needs; semantic domains, processing constraints, linguistic resources

Introduction

In this chapter, I apply a processability perspective to communicative tasks, and, in particular, how they are carried out by language learners, to examine in what ways they can contribute to our knowledge and understanding of instructed second language acquisition (ISLA). In particular, I focus on the development of sec-

---

[*] Revised version of a plenary given to the 9th International TBLT Conference, Innsbruck, Austria, 2022.

https://doi.org/10.1075/tblt.17.10len
© 2025 John Benjamins Publishing Company

ond language (L2) processing capacities and their implications for learners' oral speech production during task performance. In this context, processing refers to considering the different processes that are involved in the generation of L2 sentences as well as the constraints that L2 learners face at the different stages of their L2 development.

Van den Branden et al. (2009) spoke of the different purposes of tasks, one of which is to use them to elicit learner production. In my view, taking processing constraints into account when examining learner language produced in the context of tasks offers several advantages. On the one hand, this perspective has provided valuable insights into L2 learner development in the area of morphology and syntax. Numerous studies have demonstrated that tasks with a focus on oral speech production are valuable tools to diagnose learners' stages of development (e.g., Keßler, 2008; Lenzing, 2013, 2021; Pienemann, 1998; Roos, 2019). A further benefit of tasks is that the language that is produced by the learners in the context of task performance sheds light on the scope of structural variation in learner language at different stages of development (e.g., Lenzing, 2015). On the other hand, I argue that, in addition to the established insights into learner language, adopting a processability perspective on tasks also opens up opportunities to explore other aspects of language use in relation to learner development. In this chapter, I focus particularly on the field of semantic domains.

As I will explore in some detail later in this chapter, tasks have been shown to be valuable at every developmental stage and their benefits are not restricted to more advanced learners at higher stages of acquisition. In addition to using tasks in SLA research to diagnose learners' developmental stages and to gain insights into their actual language production at these stages, incorporating tasks into language teaching with a focus on structures that learners are ready to acquire has been shown to enhance the acquisition of these structures.

I begin my discussion on the benefits of a processability perspective on tasks by using learner development and variation in the areas of morphology and syntax as a starting point. I then extend this perspective to explore its potential in the domain of semantics. To support my argument, I present selected analyses of oral speech production by L2 learners of English in a school-based context. The analyses are based on data obtained by administering the same task to learners at different developmental stages and age groups. Before presenting the actual task, selected examples, and a more in-depth analysis of the data, I provide a brief introduction to the processability perspective that informs my approach.

Theoretical background: Processability Theory

PT explains L2 developmental stages

Research into developmental sequences related to particular aspects of the L2 language system dates back to the 1970s (for early studies, see, e.g., Clahsen 1980; Meisel et al., 1981; Ravem, 1968; Wode, 1976). Although the notion of developmental sequences has been a matter of controversy among some SLA scholars (see, e.g., Hulstijn et al., 2015), Ellis (1994) highlighted that there is a widespread recognition in the SLA community that "the acquisition of an L2 grammar ... occurs in stages" (p. 21), reflecting a relatively broad consensus in this regard (see, e.g., VanPatten et al., 2020, p. 10).

Processability Theory (PT) (e.g., Pienemann, 1998; Pienemann & Lenzing, 2020) provides an explanation for the observed developmental sequences in the acquisition of specific aspects of the L2 system. PT is a constraint-based theory of SLA, its core claim being that L2 learners' processing capacities are constrained by the architecture of the human language processor. The conceptualisation of the language processor is based on Levelt's (1989) model of language generation. According to PT, the L2 language processor is not fully developed at the beginning of L2 acquisition, thereby constraining the structural options that L2 learners can process. In the course of SLA, the processor develops in a step-wise fashion, as L2 learners acquire specific processing procedures crucial for language generation. These procedures enable them to access words in the mental lexicon, build noun phrases or verb phrases, and assemble sentences.

In language generation, the procedures are activated in a set order, as illustrated for the sentence "The cat eats the fish." In a first step, called *lemma access*, the lemma information for a word is accessed in the mental lexicon (e.g., "cat"). Second, the category procedure that assigns the lemma its syntactic category is activated (e.g., "noun" for "cat"). This activates the phrasal procedure to build the corresponding phrase — in this example, the noun phrase "the cat." In languages like English that have verb phrases, the verb phrase procedure then generates the verb phrase ("eats the fish"). Once the respective phrases are generated, the sentence procedure is activated and generates the whole sentence ("The cat eats the fish").

In L2 acquisition, the above procedures are acquired in the same sequence in which they are activated in the language generation process. They are hierarchically ordered and implicationally related, which means that each procedure builds upon the previous one. According to PT, these procedures are acquired, as previously stated, in a step-wise fashion, resulting in the observable staged development in the domain of morpho-syntax (Lenzing, 2013, 2021; Pienemann, 1998).

The core construct of PT is the processability hierarchy, a hierarchy of processing procedures that applies cross-linguistically. For L2 English, PT proposes six stages of acquisition, each characterised by specific morphological and syntactic structures.

The examples I present to illustrate which structures L2 learners can produce at the different stages of development are drawn from oral speech production data of L2 learners of English with German background elicited in the context of various communicative tasks that were specifically designed for the purpose of data elicitation (Lenzing, 2021).

At Stage 1 (lemma/word access), learners can only produce utterances that involve lexical processes. Typically, the utterances consist of single words or formulaic sequences — structures that are stored and retrieved as single units and occur invariantly in the learners' oral speech (see Lenzing, 2013, 2015). Examples of Stage 1 structures are provided in (1) and (2). The question form in (2) is considered a typical example of a formulaic sequence. The question is commonly introduced at an early stage in L2 learners' EFL textbooks, and it has been shown that L2 learners produce this form invariantly at the beginning of their L2 acquisition process (see Lenzing, 2013):

(1)   Yes. No. White.

(2)   What's your hobby?

The acquisition of the category procedure at Stage 2 enables learners to attach lexical morphemes to lexical items, such as the plural -s or the -ing morpheme, as in (3) and (4):

(3)   We eat stones.

(4)   I speaking English.

At this stage, learners are also capable of using simplified sentences that do not involve any unification of grammatical information. This is evidenced by the absence of morphological markers, such as the "3rd person -s" morpheme, or the absence of auxiliaries, as seen in Example (4). Consequently, these structures are not necessarily target-like.

At Stage 3, learners can produce restricted question forms. These are characterised by the fronting of a question word, such as "What" or "Do," while maintaining the canonical Subject Verb Object (SVO) word order. The question forms can be either target-like, as the "Do-Fronting" question form shown in (5), or non-target-like, as the Wh-SVO form in (6):

(5)   Do you have a house on Mars?

(6)   Which colour the bike has?

The acquisition of the Stage 4 processing mechanisms enables learners to produce more complex structures in terms of processing, such as the "Copula S (X)" form exemplified in Example (7):

(7) Are there three childs in the house?

Stage 5 is characterised by the production of question forms with the auxiliary in second position (Aux 2nd), as illustrated in (8). Furthermore, learners are able to exchange grammatical information between the subject and the verb, which is a prerequisite for the production of the "3rd person -s" morpheme (see 9):

(8) How was your life as a alien?

(9) She comes home.

Finally, the subordinate clause procedure at Stage 6 enables learners to generate subordinate clauses as exemplified in (10):

(10) He wonders where the platypus lives.

The developmental trajectory illustrated by the examples is constrained by the processing resources the learners have at their disposal at the different stages of L2 development, and the acquisition of additional processing procedures leads to the production of increasingly complex structures.

To reliably determine a learner's stage of acquisition, it is essential to analyse a sample of their spontaneous oral speech production. This sample has to meet specific criteria: First, it needs to include contexts for the morphological and syntactic structures indicative for a specific PT stage. For instance, in the case of English, the sample should include contexts for various types of question forms. Second, the sample needs to include sufficient contexts for the production of these structures to be able to make valid claims about their acquisition. Communicative tasks have been shown to be beneficial for this endeavour. This is particularly the case for those tasks that have explicitly been designed for the purpose of data elicitation, as they focus on specific morphological and syntactic structures without revealing the focus to the learners (Lenzing 2013, 2021; Pienemann & Mackey 1993; Roos, 2019).

The next step involves a distributional analysis of the data, examining the presence and/or absence of the structures under investigation in the sample. In a subsequent step, an acquisition criterion is applied to this analysis. Unlike accuracy criteria that were often applied in SLA research in the past (see, e.g., Dulay & Burt 1974; Ellis 1988), PT-based research employs the emergence criterion, which aims to capture the first productive use of a structure (for details see, e.g., Lenzing, 2021). The operationalisation of the emergence criterion in the study presented in this chapter is detailed in a subsequent section (Development and variation in the Martian task).

PT explains learner variation within developmental stages

It is important to note that the existence of L2 development does not imply complete uniformity in learners' acquisition processes. In fact, learner variability is a widely acknowledged phenomenon in SLA research across theoretical frameworks (e.g., Dyson, 2021; Verspoor et al., 2008). As regards variability in the domain of morpho-syntax, the existence of both universal developmental trajectories and individual learner variation is not mutually exclusive. PT addresses both aspects of L2 development by not only explaining the existence of developmental trajectories but also by accounting for variation in learner language at the level of morpho-syntax. This variation can be observed in the learners' spontaneous oral speech production in the context of communicative tasks.

According to PT, learner variation is constrained by the processing resources of the learner at the different stages of acquisition. The proposed interconnectedness between L2 development and variation is captured by the concept of Hypothesis Space depicted in Figure 1. As Pienemann (1998) notes, "[t]he key assumption underlying the concept of Hypothesis Space is that variation and development can be captured by one dynamic linguistic system" (p. 279). Hypothesis Space visually represents both the developmental progress of learners, depicted by the vertical lines in the diagram, and the extent of learner variation, illustrated by the horizontal lines (for details, see Pienemann, 1998, pp. 232ff).

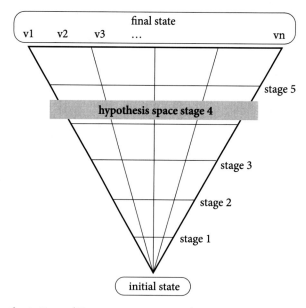

Figure 1. Hypothesis Space (Pienemann, 1998, p. 232)

As illustrated in Figure 1, a learner's L2 acquisition process starts at an initial state. Once learners progress to a new developmental stage, they acquire additional processing resources. These resources, in turn, facilitate the expansion of the learners' structural options, thus extending their linguistic repertoires in the course of acquisition. While the processing resources available at the different developmental stages constrain the structural choices of a learner, they also allow for a certain degree of flexibility. It is important to note that learner variation is not precisely predictable in that we cannot definitively determine the exact structural options a learner might choose to employ. However, this does not mean that they are entirely arbitrary. Instead, PT claims that all structural options are restricted by the processing constraints learners face at their respective developmental stage, and that they occur within the boundaries of Hypothesis Space.

As I will demonstrate below, the language produced by learners at the same stage of acquisition in the context of communicative tasks shows considerable variation in both syntactic and morphological structures. The following section addresses the issue of the variation in language produced by individual learners across different contexts, focusing particularly on whether the tasks they engage in influence their developmental stage.

The Steadiness Hypothesis

The concept of Hypothesis Space introduced above primarily addresses inter-learner variation, accounting for the scope of variation at different developmental stages as well as differences in learners' developmental trajectories. However, an equally important aspect in L2 acquisition is intra-learner variation, which refers to variation in language use observed within an individual learner. The following questions emerge: Do learners exhibit stable interlanguages, maintaining a consistent developmental stage across various tasks? Or is interlanguage inherently unstable, susceptible to change depending on the context of language production?

Research by Tarone (1985, 1988, 2000) indicates that learners' interlanguage exhibits variability depending on the task they are engaged in, and that it is sensitive to the social setting. Addressing the question of the stability of a learner's interlanguage, Bachman (1998) raises the question as to whether the actual elicitation context of a learner's oral speech production data has an influence on diagnosing their developmental stage. Indeed, tasks designed to target specific linguistic structures result in varying frequencies of those structures produced by learners. For instance, a task aimed at eliciting question forms typically yields more questions than one focusing on declarative sentences (see, e.g., Mackey, 1994). However, this observation does not necessarily imply instability in a learner's interlanguage; rather, it highlights the effect of focused tasks on the linguistic structures that learners produce.

Regarding the question as to whether learners' interlanguage is stable across different tasks in terms of their developmental stage, Pienemann (1998) proposed the Steadiness Hypothesis, which states that "[t]he basic nature of the grammatical system of an IL [interlanguage] does not change in different communicative tasks as long as those are based on the same skill type in language production" (p. 273). This implies that while the frequency and accuracy in the production of specific structures may vary between tasks, the learner's developmental stage remains consistent across tasks. The Steadiness Hypothesis has been supported by empirical research demonstrating that, despite variations in the production frequency and accuracy of different structures, the learner's developmental stage remains stable across different tasks (Pienemann, 1998; Pienemann & Mackey, 1993). The Steadiness Hypothesis aligns with the concept of Hypothesis Space, as learner variation is assumed to be constrained by a learner's developmental stage.

Tasks and developmental stages

In what ways can we relate our insights into learner language development to TBLT and the actual use of tasks in L2 learning/teaching? When considering the use of tasks at different developmental stages, Ellis (2009) argues:

> [o]ne of the aims of TBLT is, in fact, to create contexts in which learners can experience what it means to communicate at different stages of their development — using whatever resources at their disposal. Inevitably, with beginners, the interactions will be limited, but this does not mean that they are of no pedagogic value.
>
> (p. 230)

Ellis's (2009) argument implies that tasks are valuable at every developmental stage and that the benefits of tasks are not restricted to learners at higher stages of acquisition. Research findings indicate that tasks are not only valuable in order to experience language use but also because they can promote the acquisition process of specific structures if they include a so-called *developmentally moderated focus on form* (e.g., Di Biase, 2002; Keßler et al., 2011; Roos, 2016, 2019). This approach is based on the notion of *developmental readiness* (e.g., Di Biase, 2002, 2008) and the concept of *focus on form* as proposed by Long (e.g., 1991, 2000). Developmental readiness refers to the point in time when learners can, in principle, acquire a particular linguistic structure, as they have reached the respective developmental stage to process the structure. According to Long (1991), a focus on form approach "overtly draws students' attention to linguistic elements as they

Chapter 10. Processability perspective in instructed second language acquisition   **191**

arise incidentally in lessons whose overriding focus is on meaning or communication" (pp. 45–46). In a developmentally moderated focus on form approach, the learner's stage of acquisition is first diagnosed (for details, see Pienemann, 1998; Pienemann & Lenzing, 2025). In the next step, the task is adapted to suit the learner's developmental readiness. This involves tailoring the task to focus on grammatical structures from learners' current or next stage of acquisition, that is, structures they are considered developmentally ready to acquire. Studies such as those by Keßler et al. (2011) or Roos (2019) have demonstrated that tasks of this nature facilitate the acquisition process by enhancing both learners' rate of acquisition and their accuracy in the production of the targeted structures.

When examining tasks through a processability lens, particularly considering the concept of developmental readiness, a crucial question arises: do learners at different stages of acquisition necessarily have to engage in tasks that are tailored to their individual developmental stage? This question is particularly relevant in the context of language teaching in classroom settings, as L2 classrooms are often heterogeneous, including variations in learners' stages of acquisition (see, e.g., Keßler & Liebner, 2016; Lenzing, 2021). In what follows, I explore how learners at different stages of acquisition deal with the same task and what differences can be observed in their speech production. In particular, I address two different aspects:

1. Morphology and syntax: What kind of linguistic structures do learners at different stages produce?
2. Semantic domains: Which semantic domains do learners at different stages cover?

The Martian task

The task I chose for this endeavour is an open but focused task (García Mayo, 2018; Mackey, 2012). It is called "Martian task" (Lenzing, 2021) and involves a roleplay scenario where learners work in pairs. The task instructions are as follows:

> Imagine that one of you is a Martian and the other one is an Earthling. The Martian has just landed on earth in their spaceship. Now you meet each other for the first time and want to learn about life on Mars and life on Earth. Engage in a conversation and ask each other questions about life on Mars and life on Earth respectively. You can be creative.

Despite the extraterrestrial origin of the Martian, both characters surprisingly share a common language — the Martian can be likened to a universal "Babel fish"

— allowing the interlocutors to communicate. The time to complete the task is approximately five to seven minutes. The task prompts learners to exchange questions about life on Mars and life on Earth, creating diverse contexts for utilising various question forms. In addition, the task provides contexts for declarative sentences as well as other syntactic and morphological structures. The Martian task covers the core characteristics of a task as defined by Ellis (2009):

1. The primary focus should be on meaning (by which is meant that learners should be mainly concerned with processing the semantic and pragmatic meaning of utterances).
2. There should be some kind of gap (i.e., a need to convey information, to express an opinion, or to infer meaning).
3. Learners should largely have to rely on their own resources (linguistic and non-linguistic) in order to complete the activity.
4. There is a clearly defined outcome other than the use of language (i.e., the language serves as the means for achieving the outcome, not as an end in its own right). (p. 223)

A further characteristic of tasks that is widely adopted in the TBLT field relates to the notion of authenticity. Back in 1985, Long emphasised the importance of tasks having a real-world connection (see also Long & Crookes, 1992), arguing that authenticity is best achieved through real-world tasks. Similarly, East (2021) maintains that an essential characteristic of a task is "a relationship to real-world activities (a dimension of authenticity)" (p. 48). It might be argued that the Martian tasks does not meet this criterion, as its setting is fictional (and unlikely) and therefore the task lacks authenticity. However, the concept of authenticity can be extended beyond the so-called situational authenticity that may be replicated in real-world tasks. In line with Bachman's (1990) discussion of authenticity as "interactive language use" (p. 315), Skehan (2003), Ellis (2009), and East (2021), for example, highlight the importance of *interactional* authenticity, focusing on the learner's engagement with the task and the natural interaction that occurs, including negotiation for meaning (e.g., East, 2021, p. 58; Ellis, 2009, p. 227; see also Guariento & Morley, 2001). The Martian task arguably provides ample opportunities for interactional authenticity, engaging learners in meaningful interaction, even if it lacks situational authenticity due to its fictional setting.

Development and variation in the Martian task: Morphology & syntax

The first aspect of my exploration focuses on structural development and variation. To illustrate the range of structures that learners produce at different stages of acquisition when working on the Martian task, I present selected examples from a corpus of learner data I compiled for this purpose. The corpus consists of audio data of learner-learner interaction during the Martian task. It includes samples of L2 oral production data from 22 learners of L2 English with German background, collected in a school-based context in Germany. The learners completed the task in pairs, with the groups formed by the teacher. A researcher was present during the task performance, explaining the task to the learners and responding to questions that arose. Table 1 provides a summary of the learners' age range, stage of acquisition, and school grade.

Table 1. Overview of learner data — analysis development and variation

No of learners	Stage of acquisition	Age range	School grade	Instruction in English (years)
4	2	10–11	5	3.5
6	3	10–11	5	4
6	4	11–14	6 & 8	5 & 7
6	5	11–14	7 & 8	6 & 7

The data were collected at various secondary schools in Germany. Grade 5 corresponds to the first year of secondary school (age 11+). The learners' developmental stages were determined by analysing samples of their oral speech production. The data were elicited by using three different communicative tasks that provided numerous contexts for the morphological and syntactic structures under investigation (see Lenzing, 2021, for details). A distributional analysis of the data was carried out to identify the presence and/or absence of structures produced by the learners, and, in a next step, the emergence criterion was applied to the data. In this application, a distinction is made between morphological and syntactic structures. In the area of syntax, a minimum of three different instances of a particular structure needs to be present in the respective speech sample in order to distinguish between the formulaic and the productive use of structures. In morphology, a particular morpheme (e.g., the "past -ed") should occur with both lexical variation (the application of the morpheme to different lexical items, as in *play-ed, cook-ed*), and morphological variation (the application of different morphemes to one lexical item, as in *play-s, play-ed, play-ing*) (Lenzing et al., 2019; Pienemann 1998, pp. 145–148).

All learners received the same instructions for the Martian task. The instructions were provided in German to ensure that the Stage 2 learners could fully comprehend them. To create a supportive atmosphere, the learners were informed that they could ask the researcher if they encountered any unfamiliar words or had questions related to the task.

Development Stage 2 learners

Figure 2 displays an excerpt from a dialogue produced by Stage 2 learners. This excerpt illustrates the linguistic resources of the Stage 2 learners during their communicative interaction.

Participants:
Participant 1 (C1), age: 10, f, Stage 2 (Grade 5) (Martian)
Participant 1 (C2), age 10, f, Stage 2 (Grade 5) (Earthling)
Researcher (R)

C2	what's this?
C1	my antennas
	(...)
C1	what's this?
C2	{Wie sagt man Uhr auf englisch?} (How do you say 'watch' in English?)
R	watch
C2	ah watch I'm a watch
C1	what is a watch?
C2	{schwer zu erklären} (that's difficult to explain) a watch is I'm a numbers and time
C1	oh this and what's this?
C2	a pullover
C1	a pullover?
C2	no this
C1	oh what's this?
C2	this? {Ohrloch} (ear piercing) ear ear {nee was ist} (no what is)
R	ear hole
C2	ear
R	hole
C2	that's normal on the Mars

Figure 2. Example dialogue – Stage 2 learners

Figure 2 shows that the majority of structures the interactants produce are located at Stage 1 of acquisition, consisting of single words, as in "my antennas"

(C1) or "ear" (C2), and formulaic sequences, such as "What's this?" (C1 & C2). In addition to these fixed expressions, the data also contain formulaic patterns that consist of an unanalysed unit and an open slot X that can be filled with different lexical material. These patterns are not necessarily target-like and can be entirely idiosyncratic. An example of such a pattern is the structure "I'm a X" where the first part ("I'm a") constitutes the unanalysed unit, and "X" represents the open slot that is filled with different lexical items, as in "I'm a watch" or "I'm a numbers" (C2).

Furthermore, the complete data set contains other idiosyncratic structures that do not reflect sentence generation processes, such as question forms or sentences with missing subjects, as in "What eating?" (C02). In addition to the Stage 1 structures, the full dataset also contains SV(O) structures located at Stage 2, such as "I eating paper" (C1). These structures are characterised by the absence of auxiliaries and/or inflectional morphemes, as seen in "He sell paper" (C1) where the "3rd person -s" morpheme is missing.

While both learners are at Stage 2 of acquisition, the excerpt already demonstrates the variation in their use of formulaic sequences and idiosyncratic structures. It also shows that, despite these idiosyncratic utterances being non-target-like, the learners effectively convey their intended message.

Development Stage 3 learners

The utterances produced by Stage 3 learners display structures from Stages 1–3, as illustrated in the excerpt in Figure 3.

In the excerpt in Figure 3, Stage 1 structures are limited to single words. However, the full sample also contains some instances of formulaic patterns. In addition to Stage 1 structures, the learners produce various SV(O) structures (Stage 2), such as "I'm a teacher" (G05). In addition, they produce a number of "Do-Fronting" question forms located at Stage 3, such as "Do they eat people?" (G05). This instance nicely demonstrates that the task provides opportunities for negotiation for meaning, as learner G05 intended to ask whether people on earth eat (food). The example also shows that the learners at lower stages of acquisition frequently make recourse to their L1 German.

Participants:	
Participant 1 (G05), age: 10, f, Stage 3 (Grade 5) (Martian)	
Participant 2 (G06), age 11, f, Stage 3 (Grade 5) (Earthling)	
Researcher (R)	
G06	do you go work? to work?
G05	I don't know ((laughs))
G06	((laughs))
	....
G05	okay I'm a teacher
G05/G06	((laugh))
G06	uh oh that's great
G05	okay
G06	me too
G05	cool ((laughs))
G05	um um do they eat people?
G06	((laughs))
G05	{also esst ihr dort?} (so do you eat there?)
G06	{essen wir Menschen?} (do we eat humans?)
G05	{nein} ((laughing)) (no)
G06	{was denn?} (what else?)
G05	uhm the people do the people eats in the earth?
R	mhmm
G05	in the earth ((laughs))
G06	((laughs)) yes we do

Figure 3. Example dialogue — Stage 3 learners

Development Stage 5 learners

For reasons of scope, I will not discuss the structures used by Stage 4 learners here. Instead, I provide an example of communicative interaction between learners at Stage 5. (I will return to the Stage 4 learners in the section on learner variation.) Figure 4 presents an excerpt of learner-learner interaction during the Martian task, involving two Stage 5 learners.

Chapter 10. Processability perspective in instructed second language acquisition 197

Participants:
Participant 1 (P19) age: 13, m, Stage 5, (Grade 7), Martian
Participant 2 (P20) age: 11, m, Stage 5, (Grade 7), Earthling
Researcher (R)

P20   uhm we need a story first what I when do you come from the Mars with a (...)

R   spaceship

P20   (...) spaceship? and land here do you have questions or I?

R2   maybe both

P20   yes

P19   yes

P20   ok uhm ok I see you first then do you see me ok what's it?

P19   I am a Martian what are you? I never seen somebody like you

P20   what language do you have do you have my language?

P19   I'm an English Martian

P20   ok uhm ok I understand you uhm yes what's your question?

P19   uhm what are you doing on the Earth?

P20   ok I can do a lot I can play with you I can fight with you okay I can play I can drive with cars it's on the street like this

P19   ahh

     ...

P20   you uhm speak from food uhm what do you eat? what do you can eat at the Mars?

P19   oh we're eat we're drinking water and we're eating how I can pronounce it? we eat paper you know? paper?

P20   ok you have trees on the Mars?

P19   mmmh no it's metallic paper

P20   ok very special

Figure 4. Example dialogue — Stage 5 learners

It is evident from Figure 4 that the Stage 5 learners have extended their linguistic resources, as they produce more complex structures that require higher
processing skills. Naturally, the data sample includes structures from all stages
(1–5). In addition to single words (Stage 1), the data contain SV(O) sentences,
such as "We eat paper" (P19), as well as SV(O) question forms, such as "You have
trees on the Mars?" (P20). Figure 4 illustrates that the learners produce question
forms from various stages. These include Stage 3 "Do-Fronting" forms ("Do you
have my language?" P20) and Wh-SVO? questions ("How I can pronounce it?"

P19), the Stage 4 structure Wh Copula S, as in "What are you?" (P19) and Stage 5 structures, such as "What do you eat?" (P20). Once more, the structures produced by the learners not only shed light on their developmental stage, as determined by conducting a distributional analysis and applying the emergence criterion to the data, but also offer insights into inter-learner variability.

Learner variation: Stage 4 learners

At this stage it would be useful to explore the issue of inter-learner variability in more detail by analysing the structures present in the speech samples of the six Stage 4 learners in the data corpus. A distributional analysis of the structures produced by the six learners is presented in Table 2.

Table 2. Distributional analysis structures Stage 4 learners

Stage	Structures	SM09	SM10	G13	G14	SM13	SM14
5	Aux-2nd-?			1	1		
4	Copula S (x)		3	3	5	3	1
	Wh-copula S (x)	3	1	1	2		3
3	Wh-SV(O)-?	1					
	Aux SV(O)-?						1
	Do-SV(O)-?		4	2	1		
	Adverb-First						1
	Have-Fronting			2	1	1	
2	S neg V(O)	2					
	SVO	12	5	1	3	2	5
	-ing		*1*				
	Plural-s	*7*	*3*	*2*	*4*	*1*	
	Poss-s		*2*			*4*	
1	Formulaic sequences	[2]	[2]			[3]	
	Idiosyncratic structures					(1)	(2)

Table 2 is laid out as follows: Columns 1 and 2 provide information on the developmental stage and the corresponding structures. Columns 3–8 detail the information about the structures produced by the individual learners, including the frequency of occurrence of the respective structures in their speech samples. To illustrate the variability among learners at the same stage of acquisition, I will focus on selected features in Table 2:

1. Formulaic sequences (indicated in square brackets)
2. Idiosyncratic structures (indicated in round brackets)
3. Question forms (indicated in bold)
4. Morphological markers (indicated in italics).

As regards formulaic sequences and idiosyncratic structures located at Stage 1, Table 2 reveals that three learners (SM09, SM10 & SM13) use formulaic sequences, while two learners (SM13 & SM14) produce idiosyncratic utterances. As for the variability in the use of question forms, the data show that the six learners produce a variety of different question forms, ranging from Stage 3 structures to the single occurrence of Stage 5 question forms in the data sample of two learners (G13 & G14). Finally, the distributional analysis of morphological markers also sheds light on the variability between the six learners. Whereas some learners, such as SM10, produce a variety of inflectional markers, such as the "-ing" or the past "-ed" morpheme, Learner SM14 does not use any morphological markers at all in their speech production.

Thus far, I have aimed to demonstrate that the Martian task is a valuable tool for initiating learner-learner interaction at various stages of L2 development. The task offers ample opportunities for the production of a wide range of linguistic structures. On the one hand, these structures shed light on the individual learners' developmental stages. On the other hand, they provide insights into individual learner variation in the use of specific features within the scope of their linguistic resources constrained by their developmental stage.

Semantic domains addressed in the Martian task

The above presentation leaves a question about the second domain I mentioned at the start of this chapter — semantics. To explore the potential scope of the Martian task in this area, I focus on the following two questions that address semantic domains, that is, areas of meaning or "specific area[s] of cultural emphasis" (Ottenheimer, 2006, p.19) and the words used to address these areas:

1. What types of semantic domains do learners cover when working on the Martian task?
2. Is there a difference between learners at different stages of acquisition regarding the semantic domains addressed in the task?

The data

To investigate the above two questions, I analysed a second learner corpus compiled for this purpose. This consisted of the oral speech production data of 18 learners of L2 English at secondary school level. Similarly to the previous corpus, all learners had a German-speaking background. Table 3 summarises the details on the learners' stage of acquisition, their age range, school grade, and instruction in English.

Table 3. Overview of learner data — analysis semantic domains

No of learners	Stage of acquisition	Age range	School grade	Instruction in English (years)
4	2	10–11	5	4
5	3	10–14	5, 7 & 9	4, 6 & 8
5	4	11–14	6, 7 & 8	5, 6 & 7
4	5	11–15	6, 7 & 8	5, 6 & 7

The setting for this phase of data collection differs slightly from the previous one. The data I discussed earlier, focusing on learner development and variation, consisted of speech samples obtained during learner-learner interaction. In contrast, the data analysed in terms of semantic domains were collected in a learner-researcher setting. In this data set, all learners assumed the role of the earthling in the role play, while the researcher took on the role of the Martian. This was done to ensure the comparability of semantic domains in the data. The focus of analysis was on the questions the learners posed to the Martian (researcher) in their roles as earthlings. Similarly to the previous setting, instructions were given in German. The data were audio-recorded and analysed in terms of the semantic domains covered by the learners' questions.

Semantic domains in the Martian task: Overview of results

In total, I identified 21 different types of semantic domains in the data. The different types and the frequency of their occurrence in the data are presented in Table 4. The list is ordered based on the frequency of occurrence of the types of semantic domains in the samples. As can be seen from Table 4, the learners addressed a variety of semantic domains in the Martian task. These ranged from issues related to the individual, such as the Martian's living situation or family, to more general topics, such as technological aspects, the weather, or the political situation on Mars.

Table 4. Semantic domains in the Martian task

	Semantic domains	Occurrence in samples (types)
1	Living situation	8
2	General life	6
3	Activities	6
4	School	6
5	Pets	6
6	Food	6
7	Personal	5
8	Family	5
9	Features of planet	5
10	Technology	5
11	Weather	5
12	Politics	4
13	Hobbies	3
14	Occupation	3
15	Vegetation	2
16	Visit	2
17	Animals	2
18	Water	2
19	Population	2
20	Transportation	2
21	Clothing	2
22	Species	1
23	Friends	1

A more in-depth analysis of the data focused on examining the relationship between the learners' developmental stages and the number of semantic domain types they covered. The learners' stages of development were determined by conducting a PT-based analysis of their speech production data. The results of this analysis are presented in Table 5. The analysis indicates an increase in the number of semantic domains covered as learners progress in their developmental stages. This increase is observed in the total number of types of semantic domains, as well as in the mean and the range across the different speech samples.

Table 5. Semantic domains and stages of acquisition

Semantic fields domain (type)	Stage 2	Stage 3	Stage 4	Stage 5
total	10	14	19	19
mean	4	6	6,4	7
range	3–6	5–7	4–8	5–10

A Spearman's rank order correlation was run to assess the relationship between the learners' stages of acquisition and the types of semantic domains they addressed in their questions. The results show a strong positive correlation between the number of semantic domains addressed by learners and the learners' PT stages, r_s (18) = .544, p = .019 (two-tailed). However, this correlation must be interpreted with caution as the relationship between the two variables does not necessarily constitute a causal one. Thus, its exact nature requires further exploration: the correlation does not mean that learners at a particular stage necessarily cover specific semantic domains. It also does not mean that the learners' stage determines the scope of semantic domains covered. It shows nonetheless that increasing linguistic resources allow learners to broaden the range of topics they discuss.

In the following section, I present selected examples of the semantic domains covered by learners at different stages of acquisition. These examples illustrate the scope of topics the learners engage with during their interactions.

Semantic domains: Stage 2 learners

Figures 5 and 6 illustrate the semantic domains covered in the questions posed by two Stage 2 learners, P03 and P04. At the time of data collection, both learners were 11 years old and in Grade 5 at the same school.

A closer examination of the questions posed by the learners reveals some noticeable similarities between the two, such as their use of formulaic sequences. For instance, learner P03 uses the formulaic pattern "What's your favourite X" in her questions related to the field *Personal* ("What's your favourite subject?"). Learner P04 employs the same pattern but shows more variation in her question forms. In terms of semantic domains, learner P04 covers a wider range of topics (personal, activities, living situation, pets, visit, features of the planet). In contrast, learner P03 focuses more on questions related to the domain *Personal*.

Chapter 10. Processability perspective in instructed second language acquisition **203**

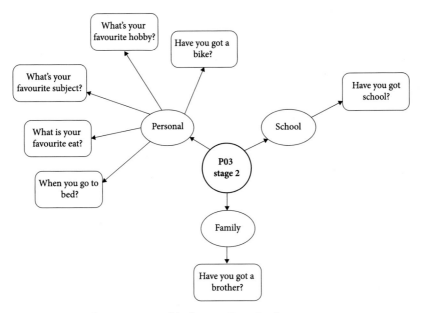

Figure 5. Semantic domains covered by learner P03, Grade 5, age 11

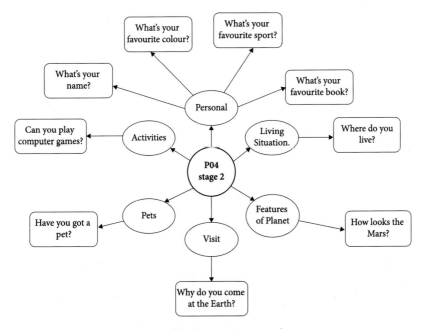

Figure 6. Semantic domains covered by learner P04, Grade 5, age 11

Semantic domains: Stage 3 learners

The two Stage 3 learners display heterogeneity in terms of their age and gender: Learner S08 is 14 years old and in Grade 7, whereas learner K09 is 15 years old and in Grade 9.

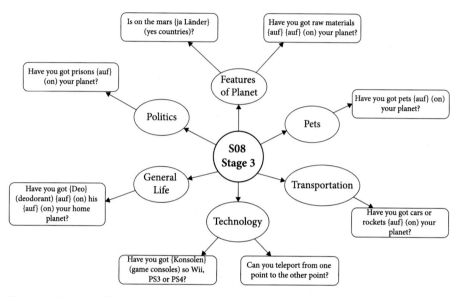

Figure 7. Semantic domains covered by learner S08, Grade 7, age 14

The learners also demonstrate diversity in their linguistic structures and in their coverage of semantic domains during the Martian task. This is illustrated in Figures 7 and 8, which depict the questions posed by learner S08 and learner K09, respectively. Regarding linguistic structures, learner S08 mainly employs "Have you got X?" question forms. In terms of semantic domains, we can observe that he focuses on technical aspects in his questions. The topics addressed include technology, as evidenced by questions like "Have you got {Konsolen} (game consoles) so Wii, PS3 or PS4?" transportation, as in "Can you teleport from one point to the other point?" or features of the planet ("Have you got raw materials {auf} {auf} (on) your planet?") (see Figure 7).

Learner K09, on the other hand, produces a wider variety of linguistic structures, as shown in Figure 8. The semantic domains he covers target more general issues, such as family ("Have you family?"), weather ("{Wie} (how) is the weather on the Mars?") or general life, as illustrated by the question "What are you doing {den ganzen Tag} (all day long)?"

Chapter 10. Processability perspective in instructed second language acquisition   205

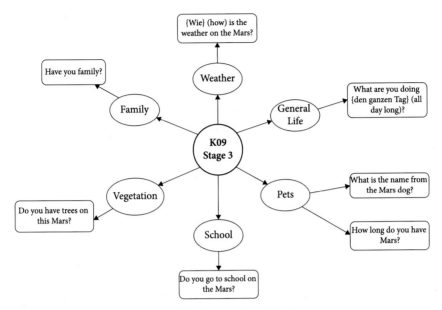

Figure 8. Semantic domains covered by learner K09, Grade 9, age 15

Semantic domains: Stage 4 learners

The two examples of Stage 4 learners displayed in Figures 9 and 10 nicely illustrate the variation within this stage. One learner, SM14, had just reached Stage 4 at the time of data collection, while the second learner, SM10, was a more advanced Stage 4 learner. This difference is mirrored in both the structures they produce and the range of semantic domains they cover.

As Figure 9 reveals, Learner SM14 mainly relies on formulaic question forms, as in "What are your X?" In contrast, Learner SM10 uses a more diverse range of question forms from Stages 3, 4 and 5. As demonstrated in Figure 10, SM10 also covers more semantic domains (7) than SM14 (4). These include topics like clothing, occupation, food, or pets. The questions posed by Learner SM14 address issues related to family, occupation, or hobbies.

206   Anke Lenzing

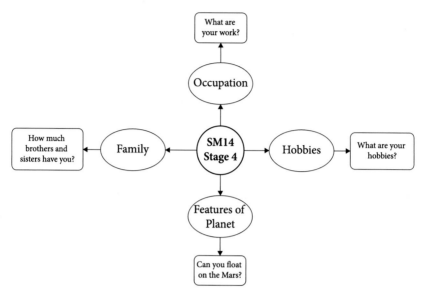

Figure 9. Semantic domains covered by learner SM14, Grade 6, age 12

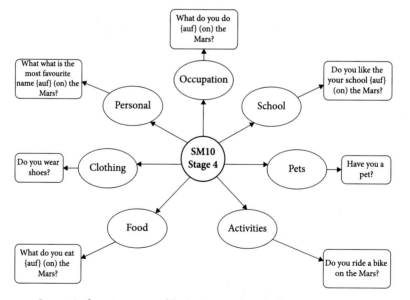

Figure 10. Semantic domains covered by learner SM10, Grade 6, age 11

Semantic domains: Stage 5 learners

The two examples of the Stage 5 learners in Figure 11 and Figure 12 illustrate the expansion of the learners' resources, as their production data display a wide variety of linguistic structures as well as a broad range of semantic domains.

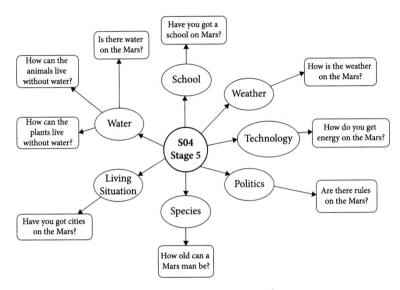

Figure 11. Semantic domains covered by learner S04, Grade 7, age 13

Learner S04 covers seven semantic domains, addressing issues such as technology ("How do you get energy on the Mars?"), politics, species ("How old can a Mars man be?"), or water ("How can the animals live without water?"). Learner G15 covers ten different domains, posing questions on topics such as transportation ("How can you fly to other planets?"), food ("What do you eat as a alien?"), or politics ("What {also} (so) do you have any {Feinde} (enemies)?").

To sum up the key results of the analysis of the data in terms of semantic domains, I have aimed to demonstrate that the Martian task offers opportunities to cover a broad range of topics, as reflected in different semantic domains covered. A gradual increase of semantic domains covered by the learners can be observed. Learners at a lower stage of acquisition mainly rely on domains that can be found in their textbooks, such as personal, family, school, or hobbies. Learners at higher stages (Stage 4 & 5) also ask technical and more specific questions, targeting, for instance, politics, technical issues related to the features of the planet, or transportation. However, the data also reveal a large amount of variation between learners at the same stage of acquisition. This variability applies to both the number as well as the type of semantic domains addressed by the learners.

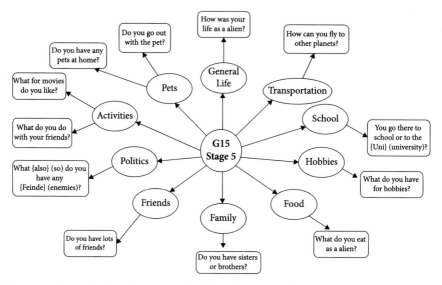

Figure 12. Semantic domains covered by learner G15, Grade 8, age 14

Conclusion

Overall, I conclude that exploring L2 learners at different stages of development working on the same task provides insights into what learners produce in relation to: (1) morphological and syntactic structures, both in terms of development and inter-learner variability; and (2) semantic domains covered by the learners in the context of the task. As for the latter, further investigation is required around whether there exists a causal relation with the PT stages or whether the increase in semantic domains with increasing proficiency hints at a rather general development as well as personal preferences in terms of the topics that are covered. Depending on the purpose, this kind of open task can be useful to challenge learners at different stages of development, as it provides space for a range of options in the different areas.

The above insights have implications for both SLA research and language teaching. They demonstrate how tasks like the Martian task can be employed to elicit learner language with a focus on particular syntactic structures, thereby aiding in diagnosing a learner's developmental stage. In addition, I argue that tasks with a focus on form – in this case different types of question forms – can also be beneficial in the language classroom. They provide opportunities to produce specific linguistic structures and, in this way, can promote the acquisition of these structures. A further advantage of this kind of task is its adaptability: the flexibility the task provides to address a wide range of semantic domains enables learners at different stages of development to talk about topics of their own choice. Thus, the

Chapter 10. Processability perspective in instructed second language acquisition **209**

task can be completed by learners at different stages of development and can be effectively integrated into heterogeneous classrooms.

Acknowledgements

I would like to thank Sam Cosper and Katharina Hagenfeld for their support in analysing the data in terms of semantic fields, Howard Nicholas and Brigitte Rath for their valuable comments on the plenary address, one reviewer for their helpful feedback on the paper, and the editor, Martin East, for his editorial support.

References

Bachman, L. F. (1990). *Fundamental considerations in language testing.* Oxford University Press.

Bachman, L. F. (1998). Language testing — SLA research interfaces: An update. In L. F. Bachman & A. D. Cohen (Eds.), *Interfaces between second language acquisition and language testing research* (pp. 193–209). Cambridge University Press.

Clahsen, H. (1980). Psycholinguistic aspects of L2 acquisition. In S. W. Felix (Ed.), *Second language development: Trends and issues* (pp. 57–79). Narr.

Di Biase, B. (2002). Focusing strategies in second language development: A classroom-based study of Italian L2 in primary school. In B. Di Biase (Ed.), *Developing a second language: Acquisition, processing and pedagogy of Arabic, Chinese, English, Italian, Japanese, Swedish* (pp. 95–120). Language Australia.

Di Biase, B. (2008). Focus-on-form and development in L2 learning. In J.-U. Keßler (Ed.), *Processability approaches to second language development and second language learning* (pp. 197–219). Cambridge Scholars.

Dulay, H., & Burt, M. (1974). Natural sequences in child second language acquisition. *Language Learning 24,* 37–53.

Dyson, B. (2021). *Dynamic variation in second language acquisition.* John Benjamins.

East, M. (2021). *Foundational principles in task-based language teaching.* Routledge.

Ellis, R. (1988). The effects of the linguistic environment on the second language acquisition of grammatical rules. *Applied Linguistics, 9*(3), 257–274.

Ellis, R. (1994). *The study of second language acquisition.* Oxford University Press.

Ellis, R. (2009). Task-based language teaching: Sorting out the misunderstandings. *International Journal of Applied Linguistics, 19*(3), 221–246.

García Mayo, M. P. (2018). Focused versus unfocused tasks. In J. I. Liontas (Ed.), *The TESOL encyclopedia of English language teaching* (pp. 1–5). Wiley.

Guariento, W., & Morley, J. (2001). Text and task authenticity in the EFL classroom. *English Language Teaching Journal, 55*(4), 347–353.

Hulstijn, J. H., Ellis, R., & Eskildsen, S. W. (2015). Orders and sequences in the acquisition of l2 morphosyntax, 40 years on: An introduction to the Special Issue. *Language Learning*, *65*(1), 1–5.

Keßler, J.-U. (2008). Communicative tasks and second language profiling: Linguistic and pedagogical implications. In J. Eckerth & S. Siepmann (Eds.), *Research on task-based language learning and teaching. Theoretical, methodological and pedagogical perspectives* (pp. 291–310). Peter Lang.

Keßler, J.-U., & Liebner, M. (2016). Diagnosing L2-English in the communicative EFL classroom: A task-based approach to individual and developmentally moderated focus on form in a meaning-focused setting. In J. Keßler, A. Lenzing, & M. Liebner (Eds.), *Developing, modelling and assessing second languages* (pp. 193–205). John Benjamins.

Keßler, J.-U., Liebner, M., & Mansouri, F. (2011). Teaching. In M. Pienemann & J.-U. Keßler (Eds.), *Studying processability theory* (pp. 148–155). John Benjamins.

Lenzing, A. (2013). *The development of the grammatical system in early second language acquisition. The multiple constraints hypothesis.* John Benjamins.

Lenzing, A. (2015). Exploring regularities and dynamic systems in L2 development. *Language Learning*, *65*(1), 89–122.

Lenzing, A., Nicholas, H., & Roos, J. (2019). Contextualising issues in processability theory. In A. Lenzing, H. Nicholas, & J. Roos (Eds.), *Widening contexts for processability theory: Theories and issues* (pp. 1–8). John Benjamins.

Lenzing, A. (2021). *The production-comprehension interface in second language acquisition: An integrated encoding-decoding model.* Bloomsbury Academic.

Levelt, W. J. M. (1989). *Speaking. From intention to articulation.* The MIT Press.

Long, M. H. (1991). Focus on form: A design feature in language teaching methodology. In K. de Bot, R. Ginsberg, & C. Kramsch (Eds.), *Foreign language research in cross-cultural perspective* (pp. 39–52). John Benjamins.

Long, M. H. (2000). Focus on form in task-based language teaching. In D. Richard, & E. Shohamy (Eds.), *Language policy and pedagogy. Essays in honour of A. Ronald Walton Lambert* (pp. 179–192). John Benjamins.

Long, M. H., & Crookes, G. (1992). Three approaches to task-based syllabus design. *TESOL Quarterly*, *26*(1), 27–56.

Mackey, A. (1994). Targeting morpho-syntax in children's ESL: An empirical study of the use of interactive goal-based tasks. *Working Papers in Educational Linguistics*, *10*(1), 67–91. https://wpel.gse.upenn.edu/archive/s1994

Mackey, A. (2012). *Input, interaction and corrective feedback in L2 learning.* Oxford University Press.

Meisel, J., Clahsen, H., & Pienemann, M. (1981). On determining developmental sequences in natural second language acquisition. *Studies in Second Language Acquisition*, *3*(2), 109–135.

Pienemann, M. (1998). *Language processing and second language development. Processability theory.* John Benjamins.

Pienemann, M., & Lenzing, A. (2020). Processability theory. In B. VanPatten, G. D. Keating, & S. Wulff (Eds.), *Theories in second language acquisition. An introduction* (pp. 162–191). Routledge.

Pienemann, M., & Lenzing, A. (2025). *Processability theory.* Cambridge University Press.

Pienemann, M., & Mackey, A. (1993). An empirical study of children's ESL development and Rapid Profile. In P. McKay (Ed.). *ESL development. Language and literacy in schools. Volume 2* (pp.115–259). Commonwealth of Australia and National Languages and Literacy Institute of Australia.

Ravem, R. (1968). Language acquisition in a second language environment. *International Review of Applied Linguistics, 6*(1), 165–185.

Roos, J. (2016). Acquisition as a gradual process: Second language development in the EFL classroom. In J.-U. Keßler, A. Lenzing, & M. Liebner (Eds.), *Developing, modelling and assessing second languages* (pp. 121–134) John Benjamins.

Roos, J. (2019). Exploiting the potential of tasks for targeted language learning in the EFL classroom. In A. Lenzing, H. Nicholas, & J. Roos (Eds.), *Widening contexts for processability theory: Theories and issues* (pp. 285–300). John Benjamins.

Skehan, P. (2003). Task-based instruction. *Language Teaching, 36*(1), 1–14.

Tarone, E. (1985). Variability in interlanguage use: A study of style-shifting in morphology and syntax. *Language Learning, 35*(3), 373–403.

Tarone, E. (1988). *Variation in interlanguage.* Edward Arnold.

Tarone, E. (2000). Still wrestling with 'context' in interlanguage theory. *Annual Review of Applied Linguistics, 20,* 182–198.

Van den Branden, K., Bygate, M., & Norris, J.M. (Eds.). (2009). *Task-based language teaching: A reader.* John Benjamins.

VanPatten, B., Williams, J., Keating, G.D., & Wulff, S. (2020). Introduction. The nature of theories. In B. VanPatten, G.D. Keating, & S. Wulff (Eds.), *Theories in second language acquisition. An introduction* (3rd ed., pp. 1–18). Routledge.

Verspoor, M., Lowie, W., & Van Dijk, M. (2008). Variability in second language development from a dynamic systems perspective. *The Modern Language Journal, 92*(2), 214–231.

Wode, H. (1976). Developmental sequences in naturalistic L2 acquisition. *Working Papers on Bilingualism, 11,* 1–13.

CHAPTER 11

Exploring task-based cognitive processes[*]
Methodological advances and challenges

Andrea Révész
University College London

This paper argues that TBLT researchers should dedicate more effort to investigating the cognitive processes in which L2 learners engage during task work to facilitate theory-construction and to inform pedagogical practices. To help achieve this, a review follows of various subjective (questionnaires, interviews, think-aloud/stimulated recall protocols) and objective (dual-task methodology, keystroke-logging, eye-tracking) methods that are available to TBLT researchers to examine cognitive processes underlying task-based performance. The paper concludes that, to obtain a more valid understanding of task-generated cognitive processes, it is best to combine various methods to overcome the limitations of each. Finally, some methodological recommendations are provided for future cognitively-oriented TBLT research.

Keywords: methodology, task, triangulation, eye-tracking, dual-task methodology, keystroke logging, verbal protocols

Introduction

The last three decades have seen an increased interest in exploring the usefulness of tasks in promoting second language use and development. Most of this research has been concerned with investigating task-based products, assessing the quality of task performance in terms of general linguistic outcome measures such as complexity, accuracy, and fluency (CAF) and gauging task-based development with pretest-posttest measures of specific linguistic constructions. So far, much less research has focused on the cognitive processes in which L2 learners engage

---

[*] Revised version of a plenary given to the 8th International TBLT Conference, Ottawa, Canada, 2019. First published as Révész, A. (2021). Exploring task-based cognitive processes: Methodological advances and challenges. *TASK, 1*(2), 266–288. Reproduced with permission from John Benjamins Publishing Company.

when they carry out tasks. Although some scholars had called for research into task-generated cognitive processes already in the 1990s (Mackey, 1999; Swain & Lapkin, 1995), research on task-based processes still remains sparse in the field of cognitively-oriented TBLT research. In this piece, I argue that, to facilitate TBLT theory-construction as well as pedagogical practices, it is crucial that researchers dedicate more attention to task-generated cognitive processes. Next, I review a variety of approaches, both more traditional and state-of-the art, to examining task-based processes, while highlighting the advantages and disadvantages of each method. Building on some recent work, I also describe and demonstrate how triangulating various methods can help us achieve fuller and more complete understanding of task-based processes and learning. Finally, I offer some recommendations for future TBLT research on cognitive processes.

Rationale for investigating task-based processes

The investigation of task-generated cognitive processes is important from both a theoretical and pedagogical perspective. On the theoretical front, examining task-based cognitive processes is essential to reach firm and valid conclusions about theoretical models of task-based performance and development. As Norris and Ortega (2003) point out and other validation frameworks (Kane, 2006; Messick, 1995) also highlight, to assess theoretical frameworks adequately, independent evidence needs to be provided for the validity of each and every construct included in them. This applies to any independent variables, causal processes, and dependent variables invoked by the models. Otherwise, it will not be possible to achieve valid and meaningful interpretations about them.

To give an example, the Limited Capacity Model (Skehan, 1998) and the Cognition Hypothesis (Robinson, 2001a), two widely studied task-based models of speech production and development, make several predictions about the effects of manipulating task complexity (independent variable) on CAF indices (dependent variable) as well as the cognitive processes mediating the presumed links between task complexity and CAF measures (causal processes). Therefore, if researchers would like to test the predictions of these frameworks, they need to provide specific and independent evidence for all the constructs entailed in them, starting with task complexity, continuing with the causal processes invoked, and ending with the CAF measures posited (Norris, 2010; Révész, 2014). In recent years, studies of task complexity increasingly include independent measures of cognitive load or mental effort into their design (e.g., Baralt, 2013; Lee, 2019; Malicka, 2020; Malicka & Levkina, 2012; Révész et al., 2014; Révész et al., 2016; Sasayama, 2016; Torres, 2018; Zalbidea, 2017; Xu et al., 2022), thereby providing validity evidence for the task complexity manipulations under scrutiny. A lot of progress has also been made to identify ways that may help increase validity when it comes to selecting CAF measures (Bulté & Housen, 2012; Housen & Kuiken, 2009; Housen, Kuiken & Vedder, 2012; Norris & Ortega, 2009). To date, however, relatively few studies have attempted to assess the causal cognitive processes, such as attentional allocation and speech production processes, postulated in the models. In the absence of such evidence, no valid conclusions can be reached about the predictions made by the Limited Capacity Model and the Cognition Hypothesis.

The same applies to other theoretical frameworks that TBLT researchers tend to draw on. For example, when task-based studies assess predictions made by Levelt's (1989) speech production model, direct evidence for processes such as conceptualisation, formulation, and monitoring should be provided. Similar, if researchers adopt Kellogg's (1996) model of writing as a theoretical basis when examining task effects on L2 writing, it is important to seek information about writing processes posited by Kellogg (e.g., planning, translation, and monitoring) to fully test any predictions made based on the model. In sum, to facilitate theory-building within TBLT, it is imperative that not only task-based outcomes, but also causal, task-generated cognitive processes are investigated.

In addition to advancing theory-building, information about task-based processes can also generate useful insights for second language instruction. For example, knowledge about links between observable task-based behaviours and associated cognitive processes may assist teachers in identifying sources of task difficulty, thus enabling them to fine-tune teaching to the specific needs of learners. For example, it is likely that a learner who is struggling primarily with planning what to say or write during task work will benefit from differential instruction than a learner who is struggling with linguistic encoding processes such as lexical and syntactic encoding. Research into task-based processes can also generate insights into the extent to which task-based work creates the type of learning opportunities that are assumed to promote L2 development.

Methods to investigate task-based processes

Having established the need to examine task-based processes, now we turn to a review of tools that TBLT researchers have available to look into cognitive processes generated during task-based work. There are two different types of methods that can be used to investigate cognitive processes: subjective approaches, which rely on learner self-reports of their thoughts and perceptions, and objective methods, which involve observations of learners' behaviours or brain activity during task performance. In what follows, I discuss various subjective and objective methods currently available to tap task-generated processes. In doing so, I will draw on my own and others' work to give representative examples how various methods can be employed to explore the cognitive processes involved in second language speaking, writing, reading, and listening task performance.

Questionnaires

Among the subjective techniques, the use of written self-report questionnaires has probably been the most widely used to examine task-based processes. Like in the larger field of second language acquisition (SLA) (Iwaniec, 2020), TBLT researchers have often elicited participants' perceptions about various aspects of their performance by the means of written questionnaires. The use of self-report questionnaires is based on the assumption that people can retrospectively report on the cognitive processes in which they have engaged during task performance.

Many task-based studies included closed-ended questionnaire items, which require respondents to select a response from a limited number of options (e.g., Baralt, 2013; Gilabert, 2007; Levkina & Gilabert, 2014; Michel, 2011; Robinson, 2001b). To illustrate, Révész (2011) used closed-ended items to obtain information about teachers' and students' perspectives on their subjective experience during simple and complex oral interactive tasks that students completed in a classroom environment. Among the questionnaire items, two concerned the attentional processes in which students engaged during task performance. In particular, both teachers and students were asked to assess on a 7-point scale which task version they found more effective in drawing the students' attention (1) to the quality of their output and (2) to the quality of their peers' production.

Fewer studies relied on open-ended questionnaire items to tap task-generated cognitive processes to get more detailed information about participants' experiences during task work. For example, Révész (2009) used open-ended questions to gain insight into participants' perspectives on task difficulty when performing tasks with or without visual support. In a more recent study, Sasayama and Norris (2019) also elicited open-ended responses, included in self-report measures, to assess participants' perceptions about task difficulty and mental effort during tasks which had been designed to generate differential cognitive demands. The participants were asked about what made the tasks they had performed easy/difficult and what made the tasks entail low/high mental effort (p. 100).

While questionnaire responses can yield interesting insights and have the advantage of being easy to administer, there are limitations associated with this method, especially if the researchers' aim is to elicit information about cognitive processes. A key issue is that participants, due to memory decay, might not have reliable memory of what they were thinking when they were completing the task. Also, questionnaire items often elicit short responses, which lack detail.

Subjective time estimation

Another subjective method that has been utilised in process-oriented TBLT research is subjective time estimation (e.g., Block et al., 2010, Zakay & Block, 1997). Subjective time estimation entails asking participants to estimate the amount of time they have spent carrying out a specific task without the use of an external timing device. According to a meta-analysis by Block et al. (2010) in the field of psychology, the interpretation of subjective time estimates depends on whether or not participants are made aware in advance that they will need to judge the duration of a task. If participants are asked to assess task duration retrospectively without being informed about the subsequent time estimation, a greater cognitive load is associated with an increase in the subjective-to-objective duration ratio, that is, the estimated time increases as a result of increasing processing demands. Simply put, when a person is working on a more cognitively demanding task, time is perceived to pass more slowly if they are asked to estimate time spent on task after task completion. On the other hand, if participants are made aware prior to task performance that they will need to estimate task duration, a greater cognitive load is related to a decrease in the subjective-to-objective duration ratio, that is, the estimated time elapsed will drop as cognitive demands increase.

This technique has been utilised in a number of studies in the field of TBLT (e.g., Baralt, 2013; Lee, 2019; Malicka & Levkina, 2012; Sasayama, 2016). Adopting the retrospective time estimation paradigm, Baralt (2013) asked her participants to provide a verbal estimation of how long a particular version of a task took after task completion. Malicka and Levkina (2012) also requested their participants to give retrospective time judgments. In addition, participants were asked to estimate which of the two task versions under investigation took them longer to complete. Sasayama (2016) opted for the use of prospective time estimation. Given that participants were asked to estimate time spent on task in the practice phase of the experiment, they were likely to expect that they would need to give time estimations during the actual experiment. The analytical procedures in these three studies, however, are not directly comparable to those employed in studies considered in Block et al.'s (2010) meta-analysis. As Lee (2019) pointed out, in cognitive psychology subjective-to-objective time ratios are typically computed, whereas these L2 studies compared raw difference scores calculated by subtracting the actual time from the guess time participants provided (guess time − actual time). Lee addressed this issue by using subjective-to-objective time ratios when studying native speaker task performance using the prospective time estimation approach.

Interviews

Interviews, another subjective technique, can also be employed to gain insights into learners' cognitive processes during task work. This technique has been used in some SLA and TBLT studies, but it has been less popular than verbal protocols such as the think-aloud and stimulated recall procedure (see below) to gain information about learners' cognitive processes. Among the various interview types, TBLT researchers have predominantly relied on semi-structured interviews when investigating task-generated cognitive processes. While addressing a prepared set of questions, this interview format enables the researcher to ask follow-up questions and thereby let the participant elaborate on issues of interest.

A study by Ortega (2005) provides a good example of how interviews can be used to gain in-depth information about participants' cognitive processes. Ortega employed semi-structured interviews to elicit information from L2 learners of Spanish about their strategic planning processes prior to task performance. As typical of semi-structured interviews, Ortega prepared a protocol to guide the interview process but also probed deeper into participants' thoughts by the means of follow-up questions. These probes were often inspired by the researchers' observations and field notes taken in the pre-task planning phase.

A more recent study by Pang and Skehan (2014) also illustrates well how interviews can be utilised to investigate participants' cognitive processes during pre-task planning. The researchers interviewed L2 learners of English about how they used a 10-minute planning period to prepare for their subsequent narrative performance. During the interviews, the participants were first prompted by some general questions about what they did while they planned. These were followed by more focused prompts, which aimed to tap what specific areas participants paid attention to during the planning stage, whether their emphasis was on words, grammar, ideas, structure of the story, rehearsal, or clarity of expression.

Both of these studies yielded detailed and in-depth insights into participants' thoughts during pre-task planning. Indeed, interviews are more prone to elicit elaborate and detailed responses than questionnaires. As compared to questionnaires, however, interviews have the disadvantage of being more time-consuming to set up, conduct, and analyse. In addition, the limitation remains that participants might not fully remember during the interview what they were thinking when they actually engaged in task work.

Think-aloud protocols

To decrease the risk of memory decay, a few TBLT researchers have relied on introspective methods such as the think-aloud procedure to shed light on task-based cognitive operations. Think-aloud protocols, as the name of the procedure suggests, involve participants in thinking aloud concurrently as they perform an activity; they are asked to verbalise whatever comes into their mind while they are carrying out the task (Bowles, 2010). This subjective technique has been used less often by TBLT researchers than researchers in the broader field of instructed SLA. This might be partly due to the fact that most TBLT research has so far focused on speaking tasks, and think-aloud protocols, as they themselves involve speaking, cannot be employed to investigate cognitive processes underlying listening and speaking task performances.

Nevertheless, some TBLT research has demonstrated that think-alouds can be successfully used to gain insights into participants' thought processes concurrently during task-based work. Sangarun (2005), another study on pre-task planning, was among the first to utilise the think-aloud procedure to investigate task effects. The aim of this study was to examine how strategic planning processes may differ as a function of planning instruction. The participants were Thai L2 English participants, who received one of three different instruction types to plan: to focus on meaning, focus on form, or focus on meaning and form. The experiment started with a 15-minute training session on how to think aloud. Then, participants had 15 minutes to plan each of their task performance, a monologic instruction and argumentative task. The think-aloud data allowed Sangarun to obtain detailed information about participants' planning processes under the various planning conditions.

A clear advantage of using think-alouds in this study was that there was no threat of memory loss. In general, during think-alouds there is little danger of inaccurate reporting due to memory decay given that participants are simultaneously reporting what they are thinking. One potential disadvantage of think-alouds, however, is that they may result in reactivity. This means that the act of thinking aloud may change the cognitive processes in which learners engage and thereby risk construct validity (see, however, Bowles, 2010; Leow et al., 2014). Another potential issue associated with think-aloud protocols is veridicality; verbal reports may not be able to capture all of the participant's thought processes.

Stimulated recall protocols

Like think-aloud protocols, the stimulated recall procedure is another introspective technique that can be used to investigate task-generated cognitive processes.

This method intends to elicit the thoughts that participants had while performing a task through *a posteriori* recall sessions (Gass & Mackey, 2017). Researchers use some reminder (e.g., video-recording of task performance) to prompt participants' recall.

Although L2 researchers have used this technique extensively in several areas of instructed SLA research to investigate topics such as attention/awareness/noticing, corrective feedback perception, and strategy use (see Gass & Mackey, 2017 for a review), few studies have utilized the stimulated recall technique to examine the effects of task-related variables (e.g., Révész, Kourtali et al., 2017; Torres, 2018). Among the few exceptions is Kim et al.'s (2015) study, which investigated how task complexity influences the cognitive processes in which L2 learners engage during oral task-based interaction. Learners' oral interactions were video-recorded during simple and complex tasks, and immediately after, they were invited to describe the thoughts they had during task performance. To stimulate recall, the researcher conducting the recall session replayed the video-recording of participants' performance and encouraged them to stop the recording whenever they wanted to comment on their behaviours. In addition, the researcher stopped the recording when the learners seem to have experienced difficulty or displayed an interesting behaviour when engaged in the original task performance.

Clearly, in Kim et al.'s research, the verbal protocol did not interfere with participants' task performance. As compared to think-alouds, the stimulated recall procedure carries less risk in terms of reactivity. Stimulated recalls, however, pose more substantial threat to veridicality. As a result of memory loss, participants are less likely to give entirely accurate and full reports of the cognitive processes in which they had previously engaged. Nevertheless, if the technique is carefully implemented, potential issues of veridicality can be considerably mitigated (Gass & Mackey, 2017).

Dual-task methodology

Given the limitations associated with subjective methods, more recently TBLT researchers have also begun to use objective methods to tap task-based processes. Dual-task methodology is one objective method that TBLT researchers started to employ to tap cognitive processes during task performance. Dual-task methodology entails performing a secondary task concurrently with the primary task. In the context of TBLT, primary tasks take the form of pedagogic tasks, and secondary tasks typically include simple activities that demand sustained attention, such as detecting simple auditory (Brünken et al., 2004) or visual (Cierniak et al., 2009) stimuli. The principle underlying the technique is that the amount of cognitive load generated by the primary task is mirrored in the accuracy and speed with which the secondary task is carried out. Slower or less accurate secondary task performance is taken to reflect greater cognitive demands posed by the primary task.

While dual-task methodology had been used by SLA researchers for other purposes in the past (e.g., Declerck & Kormos, 2012; DeKeyser, 1997), it was not until relatively recently that this technique began to be utilised in TBLT research. Studies by Révész et al. (2014), Révész et al. (2016), and Sasayama (2016) were among the first to employ dual-task methodology to investigate cognitive task demands during task performance. In Révész et al.'s (2014) work, the primary tasks asked participants to select one of two past events in a famous person's life and then produce a past counterfactual statement orally about the event. The events were displayed on the computer screen with the help of key phrases and pictures. Under the low-complexity condition, the choice between the two events was designed to be simple, requiring little reasoning. During the complex version of the task, however, the choice between the two events was intended to be more complex, posing greater reasoning demands. Révész et al. (2016) included low- and high-complexity versions of three types of primary tasks (a decision-making, a map, and a narrative task), with each being presented to the participants via computer. In both studies, during the secondary task the colour of the background screen randomly changed to green or red, and the participants were asked to respond as fast and accurately as possible when the colour changed to green while disregarding changes to red. In Sasayama's (2016) work, the primary tasks involved performing four computer-delivered narrative tasks based on picture stories. The tasks were constructed to involve differential cognitive demands through manipulating the number of elements included in the narratives. The secondary task asked participants to react as fast and accurately as possible when a change occurred in the colour of a capital letter (*A*), which appeared above the picture story on the participants' screen. Participants had to respond to changes from black to red but not to react to changes from red to black. In each study, it was expected that the task versions intended to be more cognitively demanding would lead to slower and less accurate secondary task performance.

All three studies, along with some more recent work (e.g., Lee, 2019; Xu et al., 2022), found that dual-task methodology, if operationalised and implemented carefully, can be useful for identifying differences between actual cognitive demands and intended mental effort or difficulty. Dual-task methodology is also regarded as a reliable and sensitive methodology in the area of cognitive psychology; it has the advantage of providing a concurrent and objective measure of processing load. One disadvantage of the technique, however, is that it is relatively obtrusive. Therefore, studies employing dual-task methodology need to include a baseline condition, which enables researchers to observe how participants would perform on the primary task in the absence of a secondary task.

Keystroke-logging

Keystroke-logging is another objective tool that TBLT researchers can rely on when studying L2 writing processes. Keystroke-logging programs register all the keystrokes and mouse movements that writers produce. The resulting log files then can be used for further analyses to obtain detailed information about concurrent writing behaviours, for example, by the means of fluency, pausing, and revision indices (Lindgren & Sullivan, 2019; Van Waes et al., 2016).

Keystroke logging was already used more than 20 years ago to study the impact of task-related variables on L2 writing behaviours. In a pioneering study, Spelman Miller (2000) employed keystroke-logging software to examine whether fluency and L2 pausing behaviours were different across evaluative and descriptive essay writing tasks. While the participants, L2 writers of English and L1 English writers, produced the two essays, their keystrokes were recorded. Then, the researcher analysed the log data for several fluency and pausing measures. Another seminal keystroke-logging study by Thorson (2000) examined how the revision behaviours of L2 writers vary by task genre. All the participants wrote a newspaper article as well as a letter in L1 English and L2 German, during which their keystrokes were captured. More recently, researchers have started to use keystroke-logging more widely to investigate L2 task effects. For example, Révész, Kourtali et al. (2017) have employed keystroke logging, in combination with stimulated recall, to explore the impact of a task complexity manipulation on the speed fluency, pausing, and revision behaviours of L2 writers. Keystroke-logging has also been utilised to look into how writing behaviours may vary across independent and integrated writing tasks, so far mostly focusing on testing tasks (Barkaoui, 2016; Michel et al., 2020). Another area where keystroke-logging is beginning to be used is the study of text-chat interactions. Charoenchaikorn's (2019) study provides a good example of how keystroke-logging can be utilised in this context. The researcher assessed participants' revision behaviours, speed fluency, and accuracy during task-based text-chat interactions based on logs obtained through keystroke-logging software.

It is not surprising that task-based researchers show an increased interest in using keystroke-logging to study writing processes. Being an unobtrusive data collection tool and generating real-time data, keystroke logging has several benefits in comparison to verbal protocols that have traditionally been used to investigate cognitive writing processes. Unlike verbal protocols, however, keystroke-logging data have the drawback of supplying no direct information about L2 writers' cognitive activities. Additionally, data gathered via keystroke logs cannot reveal insights about the reading processes in which L2 writers engage.

Eye-tracking

Eye-tracking constitutes another objective tool that can help us make inferences about task-generated cognitive processes, especially those that occur during tasks involving interaction with some type of visual input such as a reading text, picture prompt, or video (Conklin et al., 2018; Godfroid, 2019). Eye-tracking entails recording the participant's moment-to-moment movement of their gaze or eye fixations while they carry out a task. The principle underlying eye tracking is that where, in what order, and how long the participant fixates their eyes mirrors the attentional processes in which they engage when processing visual input (Reichle, 2006).

For the past decade, a growing number of TBLT studies have employed eye-tracking to investigate attentional allocation during task-based work, mirroring a trend in the larger field of instructed SLA. One area of task-related eye-tracking research focused on exploring the effects of task complexity manipulations on how learners distribute their attention during task performance. For example, Révész et al.'s (2014) previously discussed study employed eye-tracking, besides dual-task methodology, to investigate whether, as predicted, the complex version of the task would lead to quantitatively and/or qualitatively different eye-movements as compared to the simple version of the same task. The researchers employed two types of measures frequently used in eye-tracking: number of eye-fixations (i.e., how many times participants fixated at an area of interest) and duration of eye-fixations (i.e., how long the fixations were). It was hypothesised that, in the complex version, participants would spend more time looking at the area including the two alternative pictures (see above for a description of the task manipulation), given that a more complex decision had to be made.

In another, less controlled study of task complexity, Michel et al. (2014) examined how learners interacted with picture prompts during simple versus complex versions of three types of oral tasks, as part of the same project on which Révész et al.'s (2016) earlier described study was based. The researchers expected that, under the complex task conditions, participants would display longer and more eye-fixations, as they would need to work out more complex relationships (decision-making task), take into account more elements in more intricate arrangements (map task), or engage in more intentional reasoning (narrative task). Vasylets and Gilabert (2015), using data elicited by the same decision-making task as Michel et al. (2014) and Révész et al. (2016), conducted more sophisticated eye-tracking analyses to elucidate the potential effects of task complexity. Instead of relying on the whole picture prompt as an area of interest, the researchers defined their interest areas according to what factors were likely to differentiate participants' attentional processes during simple and complex task performance. To give an example, the decision-making task asked participants to explain what actions they would take in case of a fire in a building. Differences between the low- and high-complexity versions included whether people in the building were part of vulnerable groups (e.g., pregnant/elderly people) and how much equipment was available (e.g., fire engines, helicopters). Therefore, the interest areas comprised the people in the building, the fire engines, and helicopters; and the researchers compared fixation durations and counts for these areas under the simple and complex task conditions.

Focusing on oral task performance as well, McDonough et al. (2015) utilised eye tracking to explore another aspect of attentional allocation, whether joint attention achieved through eye gaze predicts L2 speakers' responses to corrective feedback during task-based interaction. The researchers coded for how long the feedback-provider gazed at the L2 speaker when giving feedback, and how long the L2 speaker gazed at the feedback-provider during their response to the feedback received. The analyses also involved coding for whether there was mutual eye gaze between the speaker and the interlocutor providing feedback. In the next step, researchers explored the relationship between these eye-movement measures and learners' responses to feedback, whether they provided no response or produced a target-like or a non-target-like reformulation. McDonough et al. (2020) replicated this research to address some limitations of the original study such as the relatively small sample size and issues with the experimental set-up (better placement of webcams).

A few studies have also used eye-tracking methodology to investigate features of task-based interaction in text-chat environments. Smith (2012) was the first to explore the potential of eye-tracking in examining the noticing of corrective feedback by L2 learners during text-chat interaction tasks. The researcher measured noticing in terms of stimulated recall comments and increased visual attention, which was operationalised as learners' total fixation time on recasts provided by a native speaker. Michel and Smith (2019) employed eye-tracking to study alignment, one's tendency to re-use their interlocutor's language patterns, during task-based text-chat interaction. The researchers first identified all examples of multi-word units (three- to ten-word *n-grams*) that both interlocutors produced. In case participants fixated on an overlapping n-gram at least on one occasion, this n-gram was identified as an area of interest. The eye-tracking analyses involved comparing participants' fixation times and counts for these interest areas with those for turns that their interlocutors had produced in the same text-chat interaction but resulted in no overlap. In a further text-chat study comparing alignment during tutor and peer task-based interaction, Michel and O'Rourke (2019) followed similar procedures in analysing the eye-tracking data collected. Notably, however, the authors in this study combined eye-tracking with cued interviews to gain fuller insights into attentional processes.

Another area within TBLT where researchers have begun to use eye-tracking is the study of task-generated L2 writing processes. Michel et al.'s (2020) previously mentioned study, for example, employed stimulated recall protocols and keystroke-logging together with eye-tracking to capture differences in composing processes across independent and integrated TOEFL iBT writing tasks. The researchers defined their area of interest as the whole writing window in the TOEFL iBT environment, as the spacing did not enable carrying out word-level eye-tracking analyses (see, however, Révész, Michel et al., 2017; Révész et al., 2019). Given the large interest area, the study has yielded relatively coarse-grained eye-tracking results. Nevertheless, the eye-movement data were helpful in obtaining some insights into differences in eye-movements during the two different task types.

Finally, it is worthwhile to highlight how eye-tracking may be exploited to explore attentional processes during multi-modal input-based tasks, where learners receive information through various channels such as audio, pictorial, and written input. In a recent study, Lee and Révész (2020) operationalised multimodal input-based tasks with the help of captions. The treatment task asked the participants to play the role of a newsroom editor, who was responsible for classifying news items. Participants had first watched a news clip, then their task was to evaluate whether a given category and title were appropriate for the news item. For one of the experimental groups, the target construction, the present perfect, was enhanced in the subtitles, whereas for the other experimental group there was no enhancement. To examine whether, as hypothesised, the enhanced constructions in the captions would attract greater amount of attention, the researchers calculated a variety of eye-tracking indices (number of visits, first pass reading time, second pass reading time, and skipping rate; see Conklin et al., 2018; Godfroid, 2019 for a review and definition of these eye-tracking measures).

In sum, eye-tracking appears to be a useful tool to investigate attentional processes in task-based work where visual stimuli play a key role. Advantages of this method include that it is an unobtrusive, concurrent, and online technique. An apparent limitation of eye-tracking methodology, however, is that it provides no direct insights into learners' cognitive processes. In other words, eye-gaze recordings can only give information about what learners are looking at and for how long, they cannot reveal why learners engage in the viewing behaviours observed. Another drawback to the use of eye-tracking is that sophisticated eye-tracking equipment is still not easily accessible for many.

Neuroimaging

Although neuroimaging has not yet been utilised in TBLT research, it is worth considering its potential to investigate task-generated neural processes based on research in other areas of L2 performance and learning. Functional magnetic resonance imaging or functional MRI (fMRI) appears to be one technique that might have the capacity to generate useful insights about the neural processes in which learners are involved during task-based work. fMRI scans detect increases in blood flow that accompany enhanced brain activity. When more blood is delivered to a part of the brain, this is reflected in scans captured by the fMRI machine.

Previously, L2 researchers have primarily used fMRI to examine L2 users' performance on highly controlled activities such as priming tasks (Pliatsikas et al., 2014). There are a few studies, however, which suggest that this method might also be suitable for assessing neural processes during task-based oral production. Jeong et al. (2016), for example, examined the neural processes involved in producing communicative versus descriptive utterances to identify brain areas relevant to communicative versus non-communicative speech production. Participants watched short videos, in which a person was handling an object or using a tool (e.g., playing the guitar). Under the communicative condition, participants were asked to casually talk to the actor in the video as if they were talking to him in daily life (e.g., asking "what kind of music are you playing"?). In the descriptive condition, on the other hand, they were instructed to describe the actor's situation (e.g., "he is playing the guitar"). The researchers also included a baseline condition in which the participants simply named the object in the video to control for articulatory motor processing. In the fMRI analyses, brain activation patterns were compared across the communicative and descriptive conditions. Building on Jeong et al.'s and others' work (e.g., Sassa et al., 2007), fMRI scans might also be utilised in TBLT research, for instance, to detect speech production processes such as conceptualisation and formulation. This is so because certain areas of the brain can be linked to intending to speak and planning a speech act (left posterior SMG), whereas other areas have been shown to be involved in linguistic processing (left middle frontal gyrus, dorsal part of the left inferior cortex, and opercular part of the left inferior frontal gyrus) (Jeong et al., 2016).

In light of this, it would seem that neuroimaging techniques might be useful for revealing task-induced brain activation patterns. The fMRI technique, in particular, has the benefit of yielding direct and objective insights into neural processes. The data obtained, however, fare low in terms of ecological validity; carrying out tasks in an fMRI scanner is quite different from completing tasks in classroom or real-life contexts. Also, for now, access to fMRI equipment is costly.

Triangulation of sources

Having reviewed some key methods to study task-generated cognitive processes, it is obvious that each and every one of them has advantages and disadvantages. To overcome the limitations associated with different techniques, TBLT researchers increasingly gather and triangulate various data sources, parallel with a generally growing trend to combine methods in instructed SLA research (King & Mackey, 2016; Gass & Mackey, 2017). To study the cognitive processes in which learners engage during task-based oral production, researchers have used together methods such as self-perception questionnaires, stimulated recall, dual-task methodology, and/or eye-tracking (e.g., Lee, 2019; Michel et al., 2014; Révész et al., 2014; Révész et al., 2016; Sasayama, 2016; Sasayama & Norris, 2019). Scholars working on text-chat task-based interaction have triangulated data gathered through interviews, the stimulated recall procedure, keystroke-logging, and/or eye-tracking (e.g., Charoenchaikorn, 2019; Michel & O'Rourke, 2019). Similar, studies investigating cognitive processes during task-based writing have combined insights from stimulated recall protocols, keystroke-logging, and eye-tracking (e.g., Michel et al., 2020; Révész, Kourtali et al., 2017; Révész, Michel et al., 2017; Révész et al., 2019; Stiefenhöfer & Michel, 2020). Bringing together multiple data-collection instruments, given the weaknesses inherent in each elicitation tool, helped produce, in each of these studies, a more comprehensive and valid picture of the cognitive processes underlying L2 task performance than the use of a single tool would have allowed for. Now a description and discussion follows of two pieces of TBLT research to illustrate how triangulation of sources can assist in achieving a more thorough account of task-based processes.

To date, probably the most comprehensive study in terms of triangulation has been the project presented in Michel et al.'s (2014) and Révész et al.'s (2016) previously mentioned work. The researchers triangulated data gathered by the means of four methods — dual-task methodology, eye-tracking, self-perception questionnaires, and stimulated recall — to assess the impact of task complexity manipulations on task-generated cognitive load and processes. The results from both objective and subjective measures included in the study, overall, converged on the finding that the versions of the tasks intended to be more cognitively demanding indeed required greater cognitive effort. On each of the three task types (decision-making, map, and narrative), the participants displayed lower accuracy on the secondary task while completing the high-complexity versions of the primary tasks, rated the high-complexity tasks as requiring more mental effort, and provided stimulated recall comments indicating greater effort at conceptualisation during the task versions designed to be more cognitively complex. The eye-tracking indices also found some evidence for greater attention to the visual prompts on the complex decision-making and map tasks. Importantly, however, for the narrative task, secondary reaction times, eye-tracking indices, and task difficulty self-ratings yielded no significant difference as a function of the task complexity manipulations. In sum, although evidence was accumulated for the validity of the task complexity manipulation for all three tasks, the project generated more convincing validity evidence for a difference between the high- and low- complexity versions of the decision-making and map tasks. From a methodological perspective, it is important to highlight that, if the researchers had only relied on eye-tracking or task difficulty self-ratings, they would have failed to capture some evidence for a difference between the simple and complex narratives and, as a result, would have arrived at the interpretation that the two task versions did not differ in terms of cognitive load. Vice versa, if only secondary accuracy rates, mental effort-ratings, and stimulated recall comments had been included in the design, the validity evidence for the narrative task-complexity manipulation would have emerged stronger than justified, in light of the overall picture that had emerged when all data sources had been considered.

A study by Révész et al. (2019) also demonstrates how triangulation of data elicitation techniques can be used to investigate task-generated cognitive processes. One aim of this research was to examine L2 writers' pausing behaviours and associated cognitive writing processes when completing an IELTS essay writing task. It was hypothesised that pauses between lower textual units (e.g., pauses within and between words) would be more often related to lower-level, linguistic encoding processes (e.g., lexical retrieval and morphological encoding), whereas pauses between higher textual units (e.g., between sentences) would more often correspond to higher-order writing processes (e.g., planning content and organisation). To test these predictions, the study employed three data elicitation tools: keystroke logging, eye-tracking, and stimulated recall protocols. By the means of the keystroke-logging data, the researchers were able to assess how long participants paused and where they paused, whether the pauses occurred within words, between words, or between sentences. Keystroke logging alone, however, would have supplied no information about the writers' viewing behaviours during pauses, resulting in relatively limited insights into writing processes, as rereading previously written text is a principal writing mechanism involved in idea generation and monitoring. The use of eye-tracking enabled the authors to deal with this possible limitation, allowing for an inspection of where participants were looking when they paused. Specifically, participants' eye movements were coded according to whether their eye gaze(s) stayed during the pause at the point of inscription (i.e., the leading edge of the text written so far) or visited the word/phrase, clause, sentence, or paragraph prior to the point of inscription. Finally, the stimulated recall comments, unlike keystroke-logging and eye tracking, had the capacity to offer a window into the conscious thought processes of the participating L2 writers. As part of the stimulated recall protocols, participants, among other things, were asked to share what they were thinking when they paused. As expected, the study found that, when writers paused between sentences, it was more probable that they engaged in planning content and looked back on longer texts. In contrast, during pauses within and between words, writers tended to engage in linguistic encoding processes and view shorter texts such as rereading a word or phrase. Unlike previous research, however, they confirmed these patterns from complimentary sources using a single dataset, which afforded more valid inferences about the cognitive processes associated with pausing behaviours than a single method would have made possible.

Recommendations for further research

Although some TBLT researchers have already used a variety of methods and combined these in innovative ways to examine cognitive processes during task work, it is worthwhile to consider how the methodological aspects of future research in this area could be further advanced.

First, TBLT research on cognitive processes would benefit from more sophisticated triangulation of data sources. In studies of task-based processes so far, researchers have usually obtained separate, group-level summaries from the various data collection methods and have triangulated the results at the group level. In the future, researchers could also attempt to triangulate data at the individual level to achieve more detailed insights about task-based processes, using a combination of subjective and objective measures to overcome the limitations of various techniques.

Second, future studies could also conduct more detailed, time-locked analyses of the process data rather than drawing conclusions based on summaries of process data. For example, researchers could calculate eye-tracking and keystroke-logging indices for every minute or even every second of the task as opposed for the whole duration of task performance. In this way, information could be obtained about task-based processing on a moment-to-moment basis to capture the dynamic nature of task performance (e.g., Bygate, 2013). A few TBLT researchers have already taken steps in this direction. For example, Baralt and Gurzynski-Weiss (2011), in a study of state anxiety during task-based interaction, measured learners' anxiety half-way and right after task-based interaction self-report state anxiety questionnaires. Similar, researchers in the area of L2 writing (e.g., Roca de Larios et al., 2008) often compare processes at different stages of the writing process by typically dividing it into 3–5 stages.

Third, like in other areas of instructed SLA research, more studies are needed to investigate longitudinal changes in task-generated cognitive processes. In the past two decades there has been an increasing number of studies examining task-based development, but the majority of these studies were still short-term, and only few have included process-based measures (e.g., Lee & Révész, 2020). To inform TBLT theory and guide task-based teaching, however, it is also important to conduct longer-term studies on task-generated cognitive processes. Without doubt, carrying out longitudinal studies is challenging due to various practical constraints.

Finally, to further TBLT research in general and on task-based processes in particular, it is crucial that TBLT researchers continue to share their instruments in open-science platforms (e.g., IRIS) to facilitate the transparency and replication of TBLT studies.

References

Baralt, M. (2013). The impact of cognitive complexity on feedback efficacy during online versus face-to-face interactive tasks. *Studies in Second Language Acquisition, 35*(4), 689–725.

Baralt, M., & Gurzynski-Weiss, L. (2011). Comparing learners' state anxiety during task-based interaction in computer-mediated and face-to-face communication. *Language Teaching Research, 15*(2), 201–229.

Barkaoui, K. (2016). What and when second-language learners revise when responding to timed writing tasks on the computer: The roles of task type, second language proficiency, and keyboarding skills. *The Modern Language Journal, 100*(1), 320–340.

Block, R.A., Hancock, P.A., & Zakay, D. (2010). How cognitive load affects duration judgments: A meta- analytic review. *Acta Psychologica, 134*(3), 330–343.

Bowles, M. (2010). *The think-aloud controversy in language acquisition research*. Routledge.

Brünken, R., Plass, J.L., & Leutner, D. (2004). Assessment of cognitive load in multimedia learning with dual-task methodology: Auditory load and modality effects. *Instructional Science, 32*, 115–132.

Bulté, B., & Housen, A. (2012). Defining and operationalising L2 complexity. In A. Housen, F. Kuiken, & I. Vedder (Eds.), Dimensions of L2 performance and proficiency: Complexity, accuracy and fluency in SLA (pp. 21–46). John Benjamins.

Bygate, M. (2013, October 3–5). *On fetters and goals, and the development of an empirical TBLT in terms of language, learning and teaching* [Plenary speech]. 5th Biennial International Conference on Task-based Language Teaching, Banff, AB, Canada.

Charoenchaikorn, V. (2019). L2 revision and post-task anticipation during text-based synchronous computer-mediated communication (SCMC) tasks [Unpublished doctoral dissertation]. Lancaster University.

Cierniak, G., Scheiter, K., & Gerjets, P. (2009). Explaining the split-attention effect: Is the reduction of extraneous cognitive load accompanied by an increase in germane cognitive load? *Computers in Human Behavior, 25*(2), 315–324.

doi Conklin, K., Pellicer-Sánchez, A., & Carrol, G. (2018). *Eye-tracking: A guide for applied linguistics research.* Cambridge University Press.

doi Declerck, M., & Kormos, J. (2012). The effect of dual task demands and proficiency on second language speech production. *Bilingualism: Language and Cognition, 15*(4), 782–796.

doi DeKeyser, R. (1997). Beyond explicit rule learning: Automatizing second language morphosyntax. *Studies in Second Language Acquisition, 19*(2), 195–221.

Gass, S.M., & Mackey, A. (2017). *Stimulated recall methodology in applied linguistics and L2 research.* Routledge.

doi Gilabert, R. (2007). Effects of manipulating task complexity on self-repairs during L2 oral production. *International Review of Applied Linguistics in Language Teaching, 45*(3), 215–240.

doi Godfroid, A. (2019). *Eye tracking in second language acquisition and bilingualism: A research synthesis and methodological guide.* Routledge.

doi Housen, A., & Kuiken, F. (2009). Complexity, accuracy and fluency in second language acquisition. *Applied Linguistics, 30*(4), 461–473.

doi Housen, A., Kuiken, F., & Vedder, I. (2012). Complexity, accuracy and fluency: Definitions, measurement and research. In A. Housen, F. Kuiken and I. Vedder (Eds.), *Dimensions of L2 performance and proficiency: Complexity, accuracy and fluency in SLA* (pp. 1–20). John Benjamins.

Iwaniec, J. (2020). Questionnaires: implications for effective implementation. In J. McKinley, & H. Rose (Eds.), *The Routledge handbook of research methods in applied linguistics* (pp. 324–335). Routledge.

doi Jeong, H., Sugiura, M., Suzuki, W., Sassa, Y., Hashizume, H., & Kawashima, R. (2016). Neural correlates of second-language communication and the effect of language anxiety. *Neuropsychologia, 84*, 2–12.

Kane, M. (2006). Validation. In R.L. Brennan (Ed.), *Educational measurement* (4th ed., pp. 17–64). American Council on Education.

Kellogg, R.T. (1996). A model of working memory in writing. In C.M. Levy, & S. Ransdell (Eds.), *The science of writing: Theories, methods, individual differences, and applications* (pp. 57–72). Lawrence Erlbaum Associates.

doi Kim, Y., Payant, C., & Pearson, P. (2015). The intersection of task-based interaction, task complexity, and working memory: L2 question development through recasts in a laboratory setting. *Studies in Second Language Acquisition, 37*(3), 549–581.

doi King, K., & Mackey, A. (2016). Research methodology in second language studies: Trends, concerns and new directions. *The Modern Language Journal, 100*(S1), 209–227.

doi Lee, J. (2019). Task complexity, cognitive load, and L1 speech. *Applied Linguistics, 40*(3), 506–539.

doi Lee, M., & Révész, A. (2020). Promoting grammatical development through captions and textual enhancement in multimodal input-based tasks. *Studies in Second Language Acquisition, 42*(3), 625–651.

doi Leow, R., Grey, S., Marijuan, S., & Moorman, C. (2014). Concurrent data elicitation procedures, processes, and the early stages of L2 learning: A critical overview. *Second Language Research, 30*(2), 111–127.

doi Levelt, W.J.M. (1989). *Speaking: From intention to articulation.* The MIT Press.

Levkina, M., & Gilabert, R. (2014). Task sequencing in the L2 development of spatial expressions. In M. Baralt, R. Gilabert, & P. Robinson (Eds.), *Task sequencing and instructed second language learning* (pp. 37–70). Bloomsbury.

Lindgren, E., & Sullivan, K. (Eds.). (2019). *Observing writing: Insights from keystroke logging and handwriting*. Brill.

Mackey, A. (1999). Input, interaction, and second language development: An empirical study of question formation in ESL. *Studies in Second Language Acquisition, 21*(4), 557–587.

Malicka, A. (2020). The role of task sequencing in fluency, accuracy, and complexity: Investigating the SSARC model of pedagogic task sequencing. *Language Teaching Research, 24*(5) 642–665.

Malicka, A. & Levkina, M. (2012). *Measuring task complexity: does L2 proficiency matter?* In A. Shehadeh, & C. Coombe (Eds.), *Task-based language teaching in foreign language contexts: Research and implementation (pp. 43–66).* John Benjamins.

McDonough, K., Crowther, D., Kielstra, P. & Trofimovich, P. (2015). Exploring the potential role of eye gaze in eliciting English L2 speakers' responses to recasts. *Second Language Research, 31*(4), 563–575.

McDonough, K., Trofimovich, P., Dao, P., & Abashidze, D. (2020). Eye gaze and L2 speakers' responses to recasts: A systematic replication study of McDonough, Crowther, Kielstra and Trofimovich (2015). *Language Teaching, 53*(1), 81–95.

Messick, S. (1995). Validity of psychological assessment: Validation of inferences from persons' responses and performances as scientific inquiry into score meaning. *American Psychologist, 50*(9), 741–749.

Michel, M. (2011). Effects of task complexity and interaction on L2 performance. In P. Robinson (Ed.), *Second language task complexity: Researching the Cognition Hypothesis of language learning and performance* (pp. 141–174). John Benjamins.

Michel, M., & O'Rourke, B. (2019). What drives alignment during text chat with a peer vs. a tutor? Insights from cued interviews and eye-tracking. *System, 83*, 50–63.

Michel, M., Révész, A., & Gilabert, R. (2014, August 10–15). *Eye movement prompts in stimulated recall: Tapping cognitive processes based on audio vs. visual stimuli.* [Conference presentation]. AILA, Brisbane, Australia.

Michel, M., Révész, A., Lu, X., Kourtali, N.-E., & Borges, L. (2020). Investigating L2 writing processes across independent and integrated tasks: A mixed-methods study. *Second Language Research, 36*(3), 243–255.

Michel, M., & Smith, B. (2019). Measuring lexical alignment during L2 chat interaction: An eye-tracking study. In S. Gass, P. Spinner, & J. Behney (2019) (Eds.), *Salience in second language acquisition* (pp. 244–268). Routledge.

Norris, J. M. (2010, September). *Understanding instructed SLA: Constructs, contexts, and consequences.* Plenary address delivered at the annual conference of the European Second Language Association (EUROSLA), Reggio Emilia, Italy.

Norris, J. M., & Ortega, L. (2003). Defining and measuring SLA. In C. J. Doughty & M. H. Long (Eds.), *The handbook of second language acquisition* (pp. 717–761). Blackwell.

Norris, J. M., & Ortega, L. (2009). Towards an organic approach to investigating CAF in instructed SLA: The case of complexity. *Applied Linguistics, 30*(4), 555–578.

Ortega, L. (2005). What do learners plan? Learner-driven attention to form during pre-task planning. In R. Ellis (Ed.), *Planning and task performance in a second language* (pp. 77–109). John Benjamins.

Pang, F., & Skehan, P. (2014). Self-reported planning behaviour and second language performance in narrative retelling. In Skehan, P. (Ed.), *Processing perspectives on task performance* (pp. 95–128). John Benjamins.

Pliatsikas, C., Johnstone, T., & Marinis, T. (2014). fMRI evidence for the involvement of the procedural memory system in morphological processing of a second language. *PLoS ONE, 9*(5), e97298.

Reichle, E. D. (2006). Theories of the "eye-mind" link: Computational models of eye-movement control during reading. *Cognitive Systems Research, 7*(1), 2–3.

Révész, A. (2009). Task complexity, focus on form, and second language development. *Studies in Second Language Acquisition, 31*(3), 437–470.

Révész, A. (2011). Task complexity, focus on L2 constructions, and individual differences: A classroom-based study. *The Modern Language Journal, 95*(S1), 162–181.

Révész, A. (2014). Towards a fuller assessment of cognitive models of task-based learning: Investigating task-generated cognitive demands and processes. *Applied Linguistics, 35*(1), 87–92.

Révész, A., Kourtali, N., & Mazgutova, D. (2017). Effects of task complexity on L2 writing behaviors and linguistic complexity. *Language Learning, 67*(1), 208–241.

Révész, A., Michel, M., & Gilabert, R. (2016). Measuring cognitive task demands using dual task methodology, subjective self-ratings, and expert judgments: A validation study. *Studies in Second Language Acquisition, 38*(4), 703–737.

Révész, A., Michel, M., & Lee, M. (2017). Investigating IELTS Academic Writing Task 2: Relationships between cognitive writing processes, text quality, and working memory. *IELTS Research Reports Online Series*, 2017/3.

Révész, A., Michel, M., & Lee, M. (2019). Exploring second language writers' pausing and revision behaviours: A mixed methods study. *Studies in Second Language Acquisition, 41*(S3), 605–631.

Révész, A., Sachs, R., & Hama, M. (2014). The effects of task complexity and input frequency on the acquisition of the past counterfactual construction through recasts. *Language Learning, 64*(3), 615–650.

Robinson, P. (2001a). Task complexity, cognitive resources, and syllabus design: A triadic framework for investigating task influences on SLA. In P. Robinson (Ed.), Cognition and second language instruction (pp. 287–318). Cambridge University Press.

Robinson, P. (2001b). Task complexity, task difficulty, and task production: Exploring interactions in a componential framework. *Applied Linguistics, 22*(1), 27–57.

Roca de Larios, J., Manchón, R. M., Murphy, L., & Marín, J. (2008). The foreign language writer's strategic behaviour in the allocation of time to writing processes. *Journal of Second Language Writing, 17*(1), 30–47.

Sangarun, J. (2005). The effects of focusing on meaning and form in strategic planning. In R. Ellis (Ed.), *Planning and task performance in a second language* (pp. 111–141). John Benjamins.

Sasayama, S. (2016). Is a 'complex' task really complex? Validating the assumption of cognitive task complexity. *The Modern Language Journal, 100*(1), 231–254.

Sasayama, S., & Norris, J. M. (2019). Unravelling cognitive task complexity: Learning from learners' perspectives on task characteristics and second language performance. In Z. Wen & M. J. Ahmadian (Eds.), *Researching L2 task performance and pedagogy: In honour of Peter Skehan* (pp. 95–132). John Benjamins.

Sassa, Y., Sugiura, M., Jeong, H., Horie, K., Sato, S., & Kawashima, R. (2007). Cortical mechanism of communicative speech production. *NeuroImage, 37*(3), 985–992.

Skehan, P. (1998). *A cognitive approach to language learning.* Oxford University Press.

Smith, B. (2012). Eye tracking as a measure of noticing: A study of explicit recasts in SCMC. *Language Learning & Technology, 16*(3), 53–81.

Spelman Miller, K. (2000). Academic writers on-line: Investigating pausing in the production of text. *Language Teaching Research, 4*(2), 123–148.

Stiefenhöfer, L., & Michel, M. (2020). Investigating the relationship between peer interaction and writing processes in computer-supported collaborative L2 writing: A mixed-methods study. In R. M. Manchón (Ed.), *Writing and language learning: Advancing research agendas (pp. 255–280).* John Benjamins.

Swain, M. & Lapkin, S. (1995). Problems in output and the cognitive processes they generate: A step towards second language learning. *Applied Linguistics, 16*(3), 371–391.

Thorson, H. (2000). Using the computer to compare foreign- and native-language writing processes: A statistical and case study approach. *The Modern Language Journal, 84*(2), 55–70.

Torres, J. (2018). The effects of task complexity on heritage and L2 Spanish development. *Canadian Modern Language Review, 74*(1), 128–152.

Van Waes, L., Leijten, M., Lindgren, E., & Wengelin, A. (2016). Keystroke logging in writing research: Analyzing online writing processes. In C. A. MacArthur, S. Graham, & J. Fitzgerald (Eds.), *Handbook of writing research* (pp. 410–426). The Guilford Press.

Vasylets, L., & Gilabert, R. (2015, September 16–18). *Exploring the visual-dynamic and linguistic conceptualisation traces in task-based performance* [Conference presentation]. 6th Biennial International Conference on Task-based Language Teaching, Leuven, Belgium.

Xu, T. S., Zhang, L. J., & Gaffney, J. S. (2022). Examining the relative effectiveness of task complexity and cognitive demands on students' writing in a second language. *Studies in Second Language Acquisition, 44*(2), 483–506.

Zakay, D., & Block, R. A. (1997). Temporal cognition. *Current Directions in Psychological Science, 16*(1), 12–16.

Zalbidea, J. (2017). One task fits all? The roles of task complexity, modality, and working memory capacity in L2 performance. *The Modern Language Journal, 101*(2), 335–352.

SECTION 6

Ethnographic studies into TBLT as researched pedagogy

CHAPTER 12

Tasks for diverse learners in diverse contexts[*]

A case study of Australian Aboriginal vocational students

Rhonda Oliver
Curtin University

In this chapter, based on my plenary given at the 9th International Conference on Task-Based Language Teaching in Innsbruck, Austria, in 2022, I describe how authentic tasks can support vocational skill learning whilst promoting second language learning. I focus on Aboriginal, high school students who come from remote locations in Western Australia and who have English as their second, third, or even fourth language or dialect. The research setting for this study is a vocational boarding school that is located a considerable distance from the students' homes. By 2025 I will have spent 15 years researching and working alongside the staff and students at this school. In this chapter I report on the Needs Analysis (NA) research I undertook there using an ethnographic approach and classroom observations supplemented with interviews and written resources (e.g., trade manuals). This NA provided the evidence necessary to develop and select suitable tasks — ones that are contextually relevant, culturally appropriate, and serve the learners' long-term needs. I also describe how this was translated into the ongoing implementation of a TBLT approach at this school.

Keywords: authentic tasks, vocational skill learning, second language learning, high school students, First Nation students, Australian Aboriginal students, ethnographic approach, observations, interviews

---

[*] Revised version of a plenary given to the 9th International TBLT Conference, Innsbruck, Austria, 2022.

https://doi.org/10.1075/tblt.17.12oli
© 2025 John Benjamins Publishing Company

Introduction

As this is a chapter about Australian Aboriginal students, I would like to begin by acknowledging the world's First Nations people and, in particular, those living in the various traditional nations of Western Australia. I recognise their long history of subjugation, but also their personal and cultural resilience and efforts to maintain and revitalise their traditional languages. I would also like to pay my respects to their elders — past, present, and emerging. As is culturally appropriate when working with Australian Aboriginal people, I will start by describing my positionality, who I am, or, in Aboriginal English terms, answering the questions "where you from, who's your mob?" (Ober et al., 2024).

I am a non-Aboriginal person born in Australia and on my father's side I go back to at least the beginning of colonisation. I was a TESOL teacher who worked mainly with newly arrived migrant and refugee children and did so using what I now know to be a task-based approach to promote interaction within my classroom. I have been fortunate to have task pioneers as part of my research career — my PhD supervisor was Mike Long, and Rod Ellis and Mike Breen have been my esteemed colleagues. As a lecturer I have taught TBLT as part of Masters of Applied Linguistics/TESOL courses, and I have undertaken a number of research projects using tasks either as the primary source of data collection and/or as a way to examine those factors that impact task-based interaction.

This chapter describes some of my task-based research work at an Aboriginal vocational boarding school, namely Kutja School, located in the great southern region of Western Australia, a nine-hour drive from Perth — the capital city where I live and work. The name *Kutja* was a pseudonym selected by the school's elder because in the local language it means learning to speak. The school was originally set up mid last century as a religious mission to support young Aboriginal men to be trained for employment, but it is now an independent and co-educational school governed by a board made up almost entirely of Aboriginal people. Most of the students who attend the school come from very remote parts of the country and have Standard Australian English (SAE) as their second, third, or even fourth language or dialect. Understanding that communicative competence in English is one of the key factors for students' successful transition to life beyond school and especially into the workplace, the development of the students' English proficiency has become a primary focus at the school.

Initially I visited the school to pilot a study designed to test theory — namely to examine whether oral corrective feedback worked as well with second dialect speakers as it did with younger second language learners. Whilst the pilot test was successful, it was clear to me that it was not what was needed at that time for those students. And so began my accidental journey into Indigenous Education.[1]

I have now spent 15 years visiting and working collaboratively with staff and students at this research site. Together we have undertaken numerous studies, including more recently having the students work as co-researchers with my research team. However, in this chapter I will focus on undertaking a Needs Analysis (NA) and the subsequent implementation of a TBLT approach which I introduced to teachers at the school with the aim of addressing the diverse needs of learners in this context.

Background

Australian Aboriginal people

Noongar Elder Professor Uncle Simon Forrest describes how Aboriginal people have been in Australia for at least 60,000 years. As he puts it, they are "the first of the first nations" people of the world. Like many first nations peoples they have been dispossessed and continue to experience disadvantage — often as a direct consequence of colonisation. However, Aboriginal people in Australia are diverse — in their history, where they live, their employment status, employment opportunities, and, importantly, in their language and culture.

Before colonisation, approximately 250 languages were spoken by First Nations people in Australia. Today only about 12 traditional languages are learnt as a first language, although in recent times considerable effort is being expended for language maintenance and revitalisation. Within the state of Western Australia there are about 60 language groups or, more appropriately, language nations. For those people living on their traditional lands, their language use varies considerably (see Oliver & Forrest, 2021). Some speak traditional Aboriginal languages (e.g., Gooniyandi, Kija, Jaru, Walmarjarri) to various degrees — from the occasional use of lexical items right through to full fluency. Others speak Kriol — a type of creole found across the north of the nation. Aboriginal English — a specific dialect of English — is used as a lingua franca between Aboriginal people and with non-Aboriginal people. They may also speak SAE, with various degrees of proficiency, but generally with less proficiency in more remote locations. For work, family, and cultural reasons, Aboriginal people travel considerable distances across the nation, and this impacts their language use and which codes they have access to and subsequently use.

---

1. One of my students, Carly Steele, later completed the original study as part of her Masters' programme (see Steele & Oliver, 2019).

Regardless of whether they speak their traditional language or not, many Australian Aboriginal people have a close connection to their culture and to their homelands, and this is particularly the case in the communities of the students at Kutja School. For Aboriginal people their culture is reflected in their language and in their ways of knowing, being, and doing (Bessarab, 2015; Martin & Mirraboopa, 2003). This has important implications for education, particularly with respect to what needs to be learnt and how this might be done and, therefore, how pedagogy is designed and undertaken. These key concerns were the impetus for my research after my initial visit to the school.

The students at Kutja School

As noted, the students at Kutja School come from some of the most remote locations in Australia, and their employment prospects can be limited. This situation is made even more difficult because of their low SAE proficiency. The consequences are significant: young people who do not successfully make the transition from education to work are at risk of long-term disadvantage. Without appropriate skills they will experience continuing inequality and poor quality of life (e.g., low socio-economic status; high levels of unemployment, ill-health, and rates of death) (Australian Bureau of Statistics [ABS], 2016a, b).

The enrolment at the school ranges from 60–70 students. The students are aged from approximately 15 to 19 years. As noted, they come from mostly remote home communities where culture and oral traditions remain strong. They speak a range of traditional languages, Kriol, Aboriginal English, and SAE, but with regards to the last of these, with least proficiency. The literacy level of most of the students, compared to other students in the nation of similar age, is generally quite low.

The staff at Kutja School

There are approximately 20 staff connected to the school and boarding house. Over half of the staff are trained teachers; and the rest have trade qualifications or are unqualified support staff, including returning ex-students who fulfil a variety of roles (e.g., teaching support, ground staff). The school is governed by the board, but the leadership group within the school consists of a principal, a deputy principal, and also heads of areas (i.e., English, Maths, Vocational Education and Training [VET], and boarding house). During my time at Kutja there have been two principals. The first held the role for 10 years, and the second has just completed his fourth year. This type of stability is quite unusual and unlike the situation in many remote Aboriginal schools where there is a high turnover of staff.

A number of the teachers have been at Kutja School long term (over 15 years). Although the majority of staff members have Anglo-Australian backgrounds, during most of my years visiting the school there have been up to seven Aboriginal staff members (including an Aboriginal elder), and there are also staff from other countries working at the school.

Needs analysis

As noted, I first visited the school to undertake a study about corrective feedback. However, based on my initial observations I very quickly changed direction. My observations pointed to a need much greater than my own (of testing theory). Despite the students being Australian born, I found myself in a context where English was like a foreign language. I heard and saw students with very low SAE proficiency. They had enormous difficulty understanding me and other unfamiliar non-Aboriginal people. I also noticed that, despite interacting with them often, they also had some level of difficulty communicating with their non-Aboriginal teachers and also their co-workers and "bosses" in their Structured Workplace Learning program (SWPL). SWPL is an important part of the vocational program at the school — it is where the students are placed out in community so that they gain experience in "real" workplaces. I noticed that, when out in these workplaces, the students were unfamiliar and uncomfortable with non-Aboriginal cultural workplace discourse practices. Communication break-down often occurred, leaving all those involved (the students, their co-workers, and the bosses) uncomfortable and embarrassed. It often induced what in Aboriginal English is described as "shame." This is a feeling beyond embarrassment, an emotion that can be overwhelming and disempowering (Leitner & Malcolm, 2007), negatively impacting education and workplace engagement (Oliver & Exell, 2019).

It was clear from my early visits that, with its vocational mandate, the school was understandably very skill focused. The VET teachers' instruction was concerned with teaching students how to do or make things, and how to use tools appropriately and safely. At that time the English language needed for the workplace was a peripheral part of the curriculum. Concurrently, the English, Maths, and Science courses that were being taught were very 'mainstream' in approach, with the school following the Australian national curriculum. For instance, the English classes were text based with the lessons often based on a book the class was reading together. Speaking and listening skill development did not appear to be a focus at the school and Aboriginal English was often used by the students, but also by the staff in their interactions, including in the classroom.

Although after graduation many of the students return to their home communities where SAE is not the predominant language, SAE is needed if they engage in further education (such as Technical and Further Education [TAFE] trade certificates), and when they need to access services (e.g., banking, medical, police, social security, etc.). Importantly, they need SAE for their future employability and for their success and safety in the workplace. What language they would need in the future and what the school should focus on became the foci of my research. With the encouragement and collaboration of the school leadership team we were successful in applying for funding from the Australian Research Council and embarked on an ambitious plan to determine the language needs of the students, and not just within the school grounds, but in situ in workplaces and during exchanges with service providers. Our aim was to collect information from all the stakeholders — staff, students, community members and elders, future employers, and training organisations. That is, the research to be undertaken was a NA.

What is a Needs Analysis?

A NA is a systematic research process that aims to identify the language tasks that can be used to develop an appropriate and "defensible" curriculum (Long, 2005). It involves the identification of the language needed in order to make meaning as part of undertaking real-world tasks (Long, 2015). This also requires the identification of the specific language tasks that learners are expected to and/or may engage in as part of their life — in this case when they graduate from high school. Finally, by identifying the language that is needed, it is possible to develop TBLT activities and assessments (Grote & Oliver, 2022).

Why a Needs Analysis at this school?

An advantage of employing a NA approach in this context is that it aligned strongly with the primary goal of Kutja School, namely: *to prepare the students for a successful transition to life beyond the classroom.*

The NA approach also aligned with the school's motto which was (and still is) "training for life." It also closely matched the specific aims, which were: *to help students to gain a wide range of employability skills* (i.e., the NA would enable the school to enhance the students' skill development); *to help students with planning a career* (i.e., understanding students' language needs through a NA would help them to better plan for their career development, specifically helping them to identify and understand what language they would need for their future careers); and *to increase self-esteem and confidence in the students* (i.e., the NA would enable identification of language skills that would support self-esteem and, therefore, confidence in using English).

Later, and as a direct result of our research, an additional aim was developed and added by the school leadership team, namely: *to help students develop communication skills with people outside the school* (and the NAs explicitly addressed this aim).

With the above aims in mind and alongside the vocational skill focus of the school, the purpose of the NA was to not only make language teaching an integral part of the school, but also to provide clear direction about the type and form of the language that needed to be taught. That is, as well as helping students have the skills for the workplace, they would develop the language needed for work. Beyond the workplace, the NA would also provide information about the language needed for interacting with service providers and for achieving everyday goals. For example, as part of helping the students to learn to drive, the school would give attention to the language needed for getting a license. Overall, therefore, this meant that the objective of the NA was to determine which aspects of SAE needed to be learnt by the students so that they could communicate effectively and independently as they transitioned from school to life beyond school. This would be ascertained from actual data (Long, 2005) and not by relying on the intuition of teachers, course designers, or even textbook writers. Furthermore, by using a NA countenance could be given to all involved, thereby helping 'buy-in' from stakeholders and, in this case, particularly from the teachers. In addition, we recognised that the students themselves had an important contribution to make to the NA because they also brought to the research an understanding about their own needs.

Data collection and analysis

Following Long (2015) we used multiple sources and a variety of ethnographic methods to collect and then triangulate data to ensure the quality of the results. My team and I used:

- non-participant observation of workplaces, interactions with service providers (e.g., whilst students were shopping, at the bank, engaging with police and medical staff);
- informal unstructured interviews with the SWPL learning program staff, future employers, teachers at Kutja, and also those working in registered training organisations in the students' home communities, as well as the students, community members, and elders;

- photographic records of real-world tasks being undertaken by others — ones that the students might engage in either at or outside of work in their life beyond school;
- copies of relevant documents (e.g., training manuals, safety guidelines, etc.).

We collected all the above information to identify target tasks and their sub-tasks which involved recognising the "differentiated process domain experts have to carry out ... which is divided into steps, each of which must have an outcome, and not be dependent on or part of other tasks" (Gilabert, 2005, p.184). These could then be used to inform the design of pedagogic tasks for use at the school (Lambert, 2010; Long, 2005, 2015; Nunan, 2004).

The "trustworthiness" of the data

We were able to collect abundant, reliable, and authentic data mostly because staff at the school granted us access to all the sources we needed. This occurred because the school leadership understood the importance and the implications of the NA for the teachers at the school and their teaching practices. If the data were not available at the school, the school staff were able to provide us with introductions to those people from whom we could collect suitable data. Because of this we were able to visit a range of various workplaces and also the communities where the students lived (i.e., we were able to look beyond the classroom). We were also able to undertake interviews with Aboriginal participants and did so in culturally appropriate ways, namely by using *yarning* (i.e., telling a yarn or storytelling) as the method of data collection (Ober, 2017). Additionally, for the student interviews we employed a culturally aware young person with whom they were very familiar and whom they respected.

Beyond this, we were able to collect "trustworthy" data (Williams & Morrow, 2009), particularly from members of the school community, because of the relationships we had developed over time. Strong relationships are an important component for most qualitative research approaches, but especially so in Indigenous contexts (see Exell & Gower, 2021). To develop these relationships, built on trust, we made multiple visits to the school. Beyond this, we got involved with many aspects of the school, including involving family members. For example, my son provided basketball coaching to the students, I would umpire and score at school basketball games, and our family provided support for school members during their visits to Perth — including having individual students come to stay with us. It became, and still is, a two-way relationship.

Findings

Based on our data, we were able to determine that students needed a syllabus to help them learn SAE related to:

- vocational terms (e.g., knowing the English words for tool names and workplace procedures, including both formal and more colloquial expressions, e.g., "Get me a 2 *by* 4!");
- safety (e.g., understanding equipment and product warnings such as recommendations about the need for protective gear);
- workplace duties (e.g., being able to indicate they understood instructions or being able to ask for clarification if they were unsure);
- socialising at work (e.g., using appropriate greetings, sharing personal information, and engaging with workplace humour);
- their functional needs in their life beyond the classroom (e.g., doing banking, filling in forms, communicating with health care professionals);
- their personal needs (e.g., engaging in positive and proactive ways with people, especially those in authority — e.g., workers who manage their communities; support workers; police);
- general interaction in SAE (e.g., with bosses, fellow non-Aboriginal workers, and clients — a need emphasised particularly by Aboriginal community members).

Whilst addressing the above identified needs might seem relatively straightforward, it is complicated by considerable language differences between the students' linguistic repertoires and how they use and understand language, and how this is different from what occurs in non-Aboriginal settings. Furthermore, in their home communities the students have little exposure to the type of language and behaviours considered everyday communicative events in urban and regional areas where SAE is the dominant language. This can lead to the type of miscommunication that results in "shame" as described earlier. During our data collection, we heard many examples from various sources where such miscommunication had considerable and negative impacts on the students, with respect to their workplace training success, future employment prospects, and comfort and willingness to engage in everyday interactions. For instance, one of the differences between Aboriginal languages and SAE leading to miscommunication relates to the use of gestures (e.g., pointing) and body language, with the former involving non-verbal communication to a much greater extent than the latter. When greeting each other in an SAE context, non-Aboriginal people will say things such as "Good morning, how are you?" For Aboriginal people from remote areas, especially the north of WA, they often use a hand gesture that translates to the expression in Aboriginal English said as: "Wot [What] now?"

However, those without the cultural awareness and understanding of this gesture may judge such a way of interacting as rude or disrespectful, especially in the workplace. Similar miscommunication can occur when Aboriginal language speakers ask for or give directions — all of which can be provided simply by using gestures — the lift of an eyebrow and pointing using lips. These non-verbal behaviours, appropriate and acceptable within Aboriginal discourse, can not only lead to serious miscommunication, but also lead to negative attributions in the workplace. In this way, our findings pointed to the need for instruction that could help to overcome these potential problems. For example, within the classroom teachers could help students to understand the need for verbal communication in SAE, especially in the workplace.

Another clear finding emerging from the data was the need for students to develop confidence when interacting with non-Aboriginal people. In their interviews the students explained that they wanted explicit instruction on how to talk with confidence to "whitefellows." Similarly, a teacher noted, "we can teach them the skills they need for the job, we can't teach them to be confident to talk to us." The students suggested they needed more opportunities to interact with non-Aboriginal people, not just in the workplace, but also socially — both at school and away from school. As one student indicated, "most of them [students who get shame] don't know any ... white kids" (or adults) and need to "be around more [non-Aboriginal] people they don't know." When presented to them, this finding was a revelation to the staff — they thought keeping the students together and "feeling safe" would be what the students wanted — they were surprised that the students wanted the opportunity to step outside their comfort zone.

Related to the above was a further need, namely helping the students to develop skills so they could engage in small talk in social situations and at work. In relation to this, one SWPL "boss" identified the need to help students learn how to exchange personal information and stories about themselves, and also how and when to use humour appropriately (e.g., being "willing to take the mickey"). Another described how much they liked having a particular student do workplace experience at their business, not because he had great trade skills, but because he joined in the chat at morning tea and could "joke around." This person described how this was important because it made everyone feel comfortable (noting here that even in rural areas of Australia, non-Aboriginal people may not have interacted a great deal with Aboriginal people and lacked confidence in doing so).

One key issue to emerge from the data was the need to help students to overcome their feelings of shame when interacting with non-Aboriginal people, especially in the workplace and also when seeking support from different services.

The school nurse, for instance, described how some students failed to seek medical support because they did not have the English words to describe their condition. Their level of shame, which was as much related to their poor English proficiency as to the illness, was such that they preferred to remain unwell rather than to expose themselves to this feeling of overwhelming embarrassment. Within the workplace, shame would be felt because they were often "the only blackfella in that [work] environment" and, therefore, noticed. What was especially shame inducing in these contexts was communicating with non-Aboriginal people — as one student said, "[that] is the hardest." Another student described how speaking on the telephone to an unfamiliar non-Aboriginal person was actually "frightening." Providing opportunities to practise and then to experience such interactions was a necessary step for the school to undertake with the students — and something the students recognised as a need to be addressed. Presenting this information to the staff members prompted some to immediately reflect upon and then change their common behaviours. For example, the Deputy at the time (and now Principal) described how he would do all the talking when taking individual students to set up bank accounts. He said taking the information about providing spaces for interaction on board led him to step back and give the students an opportunity to negotiate such interactions themselves.

A final key identified language need was developing the students' ability to use language that demonstrated they had a "strong work ethic." For example, learning to say loudly and clearly something like "yes, sure" when asked to perform a task at work, rather than using an almost indiscernible nod of the head or a quiet "OK." According to some of the SWPL staff and potential employers, the students also needed to learn to express pleasure at achieving well as it conveyed the level of pride that is expected in the workplace. However, making such positive claims about oneself is not something that is normally culturally acceptable and, therefore, the students needed explicit instruction about why this is important.

With the NA complete, I had fulfilled my obligations in terms of the funding I had received to undertake the project. However, it was clear to me and to the leadership at the school that there was a further need to be addressed, specifically helping the staff to translate the NA into practice. In particular, there was a need to shift the teaching at the school from being predominantly skills-based and based on the use of mainstream approaches to one that integrated these with second language pedagogy. Using TBLT was the logical way forward.

From NA to TBLT

Part of the rationale for selecting a TBLT approach to address the students' needs was because of the centrality of tasks. According to Long (2015), *task* is a non-technical, commonplace, and everyday term, making it understandable by most people regardless of age, experience, and professional background — an ideal choice for a VET school and for the staff who worked there. In fact, tasks were already very strongly aligned with the vocational focus of the school. However, there was a need to shift the idea of tasks from just things to be done to include a much more explicit focus on language. Here again the functional goal of tasks within TBLT — where there is an authentic as well as a linguistic (meaning) focus — was appropriate for this context. Furthermore, as tasks can be dynamic as well as flexible, they suited the diverse workplace environments the students would be engaged with as well as the range of language backgrounds and experiences the students brought to the situation. As East (2017) notes, tasks inherently have the type of relevance that can support a diversity of learners from a range of backgrounds. A final utility of tasks is that they can be selected and/or designed in ways that are culturally appropriate — something that is essential for the pedagogy at this school.

The school leadership understood and embraced the need for change. They also recognised the need to implement a number of strategies to support the staff — teachers and support workers — to enable this shift in the teaching practices. As a first step to achieving this, together we agreed that we should raise the staff members' awareness of the students' language learning needs, about the students' low SAE proficiency, and the consequences of this. We also needed to increase staff members' understanding about language learning more generally. Providing the staff with information about the findings of the NA helped to kick start their professional learning. Some were shocked by the findings — especially the student data. Others expressed gratitude for the research because they had intuitively determined that what they had been doing was not addressing the real needs of their students. Many were ready to embrace change but were uncertain about what needed to be done. There were a few who remained skeptical — particularly the VET teachers. As former trades people, they felt their focus should remain on the skills they needed to teach, not on language issues — with at least one expressing the sentiment that it was the role of the English teachers to improve the students' English communication abilities, not something they should have to do. However, the leadership was firm on the need for a whole-school approach.

Armed with this manifesto and based on ongoing communication with the school leadership team, I began working with the staff to implement a TBLT approach. Because a high proportion of the staff had worked at the school long term, they were "used to" interacting with the students, often using Aboriginal English themselves as an effective communication tool. However, by providing teachers with some information regarding the core components of second language acquisition (i.e., opportunities for language learners to receive comprehensible input, to produce comprehensible output, to engage in interaction with a focus on form, and getting feedback on their communicative attempts), I was able to help them to understand what was needed. Although some were reticent to move in new directions with a language focus, the qualitative data we outlined proved persuasive. Those VET staff who were also involved in the SWPL, although the most reluctant to begin with, became the greatest advocates for change because they heard directly from those in "outside" workplaces the need for good language skills, particularly for the sake of the future employability of the students.

We also needed to help the school to develop the skills necessary to design and include appropriate pedagogic tasks — those genuinely relevant to their students' real-life communicative needs (e.g., those relating to their future occupations — see Oliver, 2020). These tasks needed to be designed to be purposeful and authentic, but with a focus on language. I was able to do this during a series of formal and less formal professional development sessions with the teachers. These were conducted in an iterative process of development, rather than as "one-shot" learning experiences. To further support the ongoing development, the school also appointed a TESOL specialist to the school (one of my previous post-graduate students). Hence, the teachers began their journeys of implementing TBLT tasks.

I continued visiting the school and providing ongoing professional development, but also working with the leadership to determine the "where to next?" for the school. During these visits I observed increasing evidence of the inclusion of language and literacy skills, particularly in the VET classes. For example, with respect to the need to develop vocational-related vocabulary (e.g., names of tools, safety signs, written information related to following procedures), I saw an increasing use of written labels for most items in the workshops. I heard staff using SAE more often, such as for the names of equipment, and doing this as part of their daily practice. I also saw the uptake of more written assessments related to vocational practices. Overall, interactions were being undertaken more often in SAE, including in the VET classes, between the hostel staff and the students, and in preparation for and during work-experience. Importantly, over time I saw an increasing uptake of tasks being used in VET classrooms, but also in the English, Maths, and Science lessons. I described some of the tasks that had been developed in two different book chapters (Oliver, 2020, 2022). For illustrative purposes I outline these again below:

Changing a spark plug

A task I observed in the mechanic VET class was a one-way task involving changing a spark plug. The teacher selected a more experienced student (A) to provide directions to a newer student (B) about how to change a spark plug for an excavator. The first step required them to identify the key information from the specifications on a label located on the machine. They then identified the right equipment and the correct spark plug to use, as outlined in the workshop manual. Together the pair then found the appropriate page in the manual and worked through the pages until the correct specifications were found. Student A pointed to the key pieces of information in the text when Student B was uncertain. In the final stages, Student B worked to replace the spark plug and Student A stepped back and took a less hands-on approach — simply giving oral directions for Student B to follow as required.

Giving fencing directions

A second task occurred in the Stock and Station VET class (a class with the lowest SAE proficiency). As part of the pre-task stage of the lesson, the teacher revised the hand signals needed for fencing. He then selected a student (F) who stood some distance away from the rest of the class (a group of about six students). Student F judged the position of the new post by eye and then conveyed directions to the group using the hand signals. Following these, the rest of the group moved the post in such a way that it aligned with other posts they had previously put in. Although Student F was not involved in interacting with the group verbally, the directions he gave created opportunities for the rest of the group to interact with each other, working together to ascertain his meaning in a purposeful way. It should be noted that, in this context, the teacher engaged as a member of the group and was therefore able to model language that other members used. SAE expressions that were modelled and then used included "move it up a bit," "move it to the left/right/sideways," and so on. This language was used purposefully, and deliberations were undertaken within the group when they were unsure. A particular advantage of this task was the alignment between the students' home language — which is very gestural — and the provision of directions using hand signals. In this way, the task was both functionally and culturally relevant to the learners.

TBLT implementation

One of the advantages of a long-term relationship with a school is that it is possible to ascertain if long-term change — in this case the implementation of TBLT — has occurred. After a decade I was able to see whether (or not) tasks were still being used and if the NA and the professional development we had provided at the school had an ongoing impact. I was able to do this by observing what was happening at the school and also by undertaking a case study of a teacher who had arrived at the school six years after we had undertaken the NAs. His arrival was also after we had completed our formal professional development with the teachers. In this way he served as a "litmus test" regarding the ongoing uptake of a TBLT approach within the school. If it was sufficiently embedded within the whole school, then it would be expected that a new staff member would also follow this approach.

Jamie was the participant in the case study I undertook for this purpose. When I began this research, he was relatively new to teaching but had a wealth of "outside" school experience: he had been a butcher for thirty years, then a youth worker and school chaplain, before retraining to become a teacher at the age of fifty. He reported his own learning style as "to see and do," and from my observation his English and Maths classes were very much based on a TBLT approach. Furthermore, he was able to do this in culturally appropriate ways (as noted above), a core part of the professional development I had provided to the staff before his arrival at the school.

Cultural appropriacy is especially important within task-based interactions because these can be complicated and even compromised in Aboriginal contexts. This is because of various cultural constraints. For example, genders tend to interact separately, and some individuals, even of the same age, have seniority because of their position in the family ("I'm his uncle/father") or because they have been through traditional "law" (something akin to tribal initiation in other cultures). At the school there is also an ever-changing student enrolment, with new students arriving and others leaving to return home for cultural business being undertaken in their communities (e.g., attending funerals) or departing permanently for various reasons. As a consequence of these constant changes, the class dynamics are also in a state of flux. Jamie addressed these issues by using motivating tasks that related to the real-life needs of his students and by granting agency to the students in terms of who they interacted with during the group work tasks.

Budgeting and managing money

As part of his own informal NA, Jamie identified considerable personal issues related to money management. On that basis, he designed tasks aimed at increasing students' mathematical skills and also their familiarity with financial terms and decision making related to personal finances. The task was based on a process of "paying" each of the students a set salary each week. To make it interesting, but also as a way to provide extrinsic motivation, amounts were deducted or bonuses given according to poor or good behaviour and achievement in class. The amounts were added to a virtual bank balance and monthly interest was paid. The students were then formed into "shared house" groups according to the people they decided they would like to share a house with (i.e., who would be in their group). In this way Jamie was able to overcome some of the issues about who could work with whom in class. Next, each group had to decide on their household budget — how they would spend their money for bills, food, etc. As a next step they had to decide who would buy the different items of furniture for their home and then how to manage their weekly budget. Their spending was deducted from their individual accounts, with the students always needing to have enough in their account to make their purchases.

Responsibilities of having a driver's licence

A disproportionate number of young Aboriginal people, particularly in remote communities, are injured or lose their lives in road accidents. To draw attention to the impact of road accidents and the consequence, not only to those involved but also on their family and friends, of such things as not wearing seat belts (or helmets on motor bikes), driving after drinking, or doing drugs, Jamie developed open-ended group discussion tasks, using selected newspaper articles as a stimulus.

Jamie assigned roles to different members of the group, including leader, secretary, and person who reports to the class, etc. In the different groups students shared their personal experiences, recorded their responses in a table, and then as a group determined ways to counter some of the issues. Based on their responses, the students then developed road safety posters and wrote poems or personal reflections in their journals. Finally, these outputs were shared with other members of the class.

Case study findings

I found Jamie effectively designed and used tasks to meet the functional and language needs of his students. The needs he sought to address aligned with those we had identified in our NA, but he had extended this based on his visits to the students' communities, his discussions with the students, and his observations of their behaviours. The tasks Jamie used in his class had a meaning focus and a "gap." They were also authentic, aimed at developing the students' understanding and/or helping them resolve real-life problems. They were designed to be undertaken collaboratively and interactively in groups and pairs. Finally, they required the students to use their own language resources. In this way, the tasks that Jamie implemented in his class involved the four conditions as described by Ellis (e.g., 2018). It also appeared that TBLT was continuing to be implemented at the school, with the needs of the students central to what was being done. Thus, it seemed that this part of my research at the school was complete. I add the following postscript.

Postscript

My ongoing interactions with the leadership team have led me to further research and the development of more resources for this school and for other schools and people living in remote communities — see, for example, Shay et al. (2022) and Shay et al. (2023). With this, my accidental journey in Indigenous education continues.

References

Australian Bureau of Statistics (2016a). *National Aboriginal and Torres Strait Islander social survey*. Retrieved from www.abs.gov.au

Australian Bureau of Statistics. (2016b). *Schools, Australia*. Retrieved from www.abs.gov.au

Bessarab, D. (2015). Changing how and what we do: The significance of embedding Aboriginal and Torres Strait Islander ways of knowing, being, and doing in social work education and practice, *Australian Social Work, 68*(1), 1–4.

East, M. (2017). Research into practice: The task-based approach to instructed second language acquisition. *Language Teaching, 50*(3), 412–424.

Exell, M., & Gower, G. (2021). Developing strong relationships with Aboriginal students, families, and communities. In M. Shay & R. Oliver (Eds.). *Learning and teaching for deadly futures: Aboriginal and Torres Strait Islander students in Australian classrooms* (pp. 86–96). Routledge.

Chapter 12. Tasks for diverse learners in diverse contexts **253**

Gilabert, R. (2005). Evaluating the use of multiple sources and methods in needs analysis: A case study of journalists in the Autonomous Community of Catalonia (Spain). In M.H. Long (Ed.), *Second language needs analysis* (pp. 182–199). Cambridge University Press.

Grote, E., & Oliver, R. (2022). A task-based needs analysis framework for TBLT: Theory, purpose, and application. In A.G. Benati & J.W. Schwieter (Eds), *Second language theory: The legacy of Professor Michael H. Long* (pp. 235–255). John Benjamins.

Lambert, C. (2010). A task-based needs analysis: Putting principles into practice. *Language Teaching Research, 14*(1), 99–112.

Leitner, G., & Malcolm, I.G. (2007). *The habitat of Australia's aboriginal languages: Past, present, and future.* De Gruyter.

Long, M.H. (2015). *Second language acquisition and task-based language teaching.* Wiley-Blackwell.

Long, M.H. (2005). *Second language needs analysis.* Cambridge University Press.

Martin, K., & Mirraboopa, B. (2003). Ways of knowing, being and doing: A theoretical framework and methods for indigenous and indigenist re-search, *Journal of Australian Studies, 27*(76), 203–214.

Nunan, D. (2004). *Task-based language teaching.* Cambridge University Press.

Ober, R. (2017). Kapati time: Storytelling as a data collection method in Indigenous research. *International Journal of Learning in Social Contexts, 22*, 8–15.

Ober, R., Dovchin, S., & Oliver, R. (2024). "Where you from, who's your mob?": Ethical considerations when undertaking Australian Aboriginal and Torres Strait Islander applied linguistic research. In P. DeCosta, A. Rabie-Ahmed, & C. Cinaglia (Eds.), *Ethical issues in applied linguistics scholarship* (pp. 193–210). John Benjamins.

Oliver, R. (2022). Developing a task-based approach: A case study of Australian Aboriginal VET students. In M.J. Ahmadian & M.H. Long (Eds.), *The Cambridge handbook of task-based language teaching* (pp. 99–108). Cambridge University Press.

Oliver, R. (2020). Developing authentic tasks for the workplace using Needs Analysis: A case study of Australian Aboriginal Vocational students. In C. Lambert & R. Oliver (Eds.), *Using tasks in diverse contexts* (pp. 146–161). Multilingual Matters.

Oliver, R., & Exell, M. (2019). Promoting positive self-identity in Aboriginal students: Case studies of Clontarf Academy youth living in a rural community. *Australian and International Journal of Rural Education, 29*(1), 30–44.

Oliver, R., & Forrest, S. (2021). Supporting the diverse language background of Aboriginal and Islander children. In M. Shay & R. Oliver (Eds.), *Learning and teaching for deadly futures: Aboriginal and Torres Strait Islander students in Australian classrooms* (pp. 97–11). Routledge.

Shay, M., Oliver, R., Bogachenko, T., & McCarthy, H. (2023). "From the bottom to the top": Learning through stories of transitioning from an Aboriginal boarding school to the workplace and life beyond school. *Australian and International Journal of Rural Education, 33*(3), 30–46.

Shay, M., Oliver, R., Bogachenko, T., McCarthy, H., & Pryor, B. (2022). Developing culturally relevant and collaborative research approaches: A case study of working with remote and regional Aboriginal students to prepare them for life beyond school. *The Australian Educational Researcher, 49*(4), 1–18.

Steele, C., & Oliver, R. (2019). Can print literacy impact upon learning to speak Standard Australian English? In H. Nicholas, A. Lenzing, & J. Roos (Eds.). *Widening contexts for processability theory: Theories and issues* (pp. 349–370). Johns Benjamins.

Williams, E. N., & Morrow, S. L. (2009). Achieving trustworthiness in qualitative research: A pan-paradigmatic perspective. *Psychotherapy Research*, *19*(4–5), 576–582.

CHAPTER 13

The teacher variable in TBLT[*]

Broadening the horizon through teacher education and support

Martin East
The University of Auckland

Over the last 40 years, TBLT has received growing attention from a wide range of stakeholders in the language teaching and learning endeavour. Among these stakeholders, teachers have increasingly shown great interest in TBLT, whether motivated by what they hear about TBLT in different contexts or responding to task-based initiatives in their own locations. However, it is evident from studies into the impact of TBLT from the perspective of teachers working in a variety of contexts across the world that TBLT in practice continues to face obstacles. Research into the teachers' perspective has demonstrated that teachers show variable understandings of and commitment to TBLT ideas, leading to a range of practices and outcomes in classrooms. This makes teachers a crucial variable in the success (or otherwise) of TBLT and teacher education an important mediator of change. This chapter presents an account of how my own work as a teacher educator has been shaped and influenced by my own lived experiences as a language learner and language teacher. It also outlines what I have learned about effective TBLT-oriented teacher education in the course of ten years of working with pre-service teachers of languages in schools.

Keywords: TBLT, teachers and teaching, teacher variable, teacher perspectives, teacher education

---

[*] Revised version of a plenary given to the 9th International TBLT Conference, Innsbruck, Austria, 2022.

https://doi.org/10.1075/tblt.17.13eas
© 2025 John Benjamins Publishing Company

Introduction

It was a great privilege to attend the 9th International Conference on Task-Based Language Teaching in Innsbruck, Austria, in 2022. I appreciated the kind invitation from the Conference Chair, Barbara Hinger, for me to give a plenary address where I could share something of what I have learned about the *practice* side of TBLT over the years that I have worked, predominantly as a language teacher educator. I also looked forward to the opportunity for me to reconnect with my knowledge and use of German as an additional language (L2), a language I rarely get to use now that I live over 17,000 kilometres away from the heart of Europe, but one that I have loved for many, many years. A plenary address provides a valuable opportunity to step back somewhat from presenting the research work that is directly connected to the presenter and to give a more personal standpoint on who the presenter is. My plenary therefore turned the spotlight onto me. This chapter expands on and advances the personal story I told, touching, for illustrative purposes, on those occasions when German as L2 has been an important component of my own journey.

By way of framing the narrative that I present in this chapter, I begin with a caveat: a good deal of research in the TBLT space is carried out through empirical studies into tasks and how they work to enhance second language acquisition, and this is important, indeed critical for our developing understanding of task efficacy. However, I am not essentially an "empirical" researcher — at least not in the sense of undertaking controlled studies that manipulate variables and investigate outcomes. I have carried out and published that kind of work before, but what principally drives me as a TBLT researcher is to understand better the practitioner perspective on TBLT. I believe that TBLT must be demonstrated to be effective, not just in empirical studies, but, more importantly, in real classrooms with real teachers and learners. I am interested in particular in how *teachers themselves* understand and enact task-based principles and the difference that *teacher education* can make to their understanding and practices.

Stating the problem: The teacher variable in TBLT

From a research/theory perspective, TBLT is commended as a learner-centred and experiential alternative to more traditional teacher-led models of language pedagogy (see my introductory chapter, this volume). From a practice perspective, teachers are a foundational variable in the effective realisation of TBLT (Van den Branden, 2016). Put bluntly: without teachers, TBLT is simply not going to happen. Over the last 40 years, teachers have increasingly demonstrated considerable interest in TBLT, whether motivated by what they hear about the approach in different contexts or responding to task-based initiatives in their own locations. That said, it is evident that TBLT in practice continues to face obstacles. This is apparent in the research that has looked at the impact of TBLT from the viewpoint of teachers working in diverse contexts across the world (see, e.g., Andon & Eckerth, 2009; Zheng & Borg, 2014). Bygate (2020) explained the contemporary reality:

> TBLT is yet to fulfil its promise as a free-standing approach to second language education, endorsed not only by researchers but also by teachers and other stakeholders. ... it is apparent that there is a fundamental challenge in translating the TBLT project from research and theory to the widespread practice that its proponents claim for it. (p. 276)

The fundamental challenge, it seems, is that TBLT appears to clash with established wisdom about the most effective ways to teach. An approach where the teacher is viewed as the expert who imparts knowledge to learners has become very deeply rooted into teachers' thinking and practices and is arguably still often seen as *the* way to ensure successful teaching and learning in classrooms (see, e.g., Griffiths, 2023). This leads to the persistent reality that teachers are, figuratively or actually, "still standing in front of a group of students with a piece of chalk in their hand" (Van den Branden, 2009, p. 659).

However, as Griffiths (2023) made clear, the structuralist or behaviourist principles underpinning the teacher-led approach have been challenged in education circles. From the social/experiential or constructivist viewpoint, the teacher is encouraged to move into the role of a facilitator who guides learners as they seek to develop their knowledge and understanding for themselves. Group work and collaborative learning may be central components. This leads to a tension — teacher-led and expository (what teachers are often used to) versus learner-centred and experiential (what teachers may perceive as innovative). TBLT presents particular challenges precisely because it is built on the constructivist philosophy. As Norris (2009) expressed it, TBLT "comes with a price. It counters our traditions of practice, requires rethinking the outcomes of our programs, and implies an overhaul of the teaching and testing that is going on in many language classrooms" (p. 591).

The price Norris (2009) referred to is illustrated in how things played out in the 1960s and 1970s with the advent of Communicative Language Teaching (CLT), the foundation on which TBLT is built. Seen against the backdrop of the constructivist theorising emerging at that time, Medgyes (1986), for example, spoke somewhat scornfully of the CLT initiative. In his view, the push towards learner-centredness in CLT necessitated "a teacher of extraordinary abilities: a multi-dimensional, high-tech, Wizard-of-Oz-like superperson." He perceived learner-centredness as "the great gimmick of today," with those advocating for it within CLT "brandishing this magic compound with particular vehemence and dedication" (p.107). Rose's (2019) commentary on Medgyes' (1986) standpoint concluded that teacher uptake of CLT ideas was rather slow. This seemed to be because the attempts at innovation signalled by CLT were being imposed in a top-down way as a consequence of what *researchers* were asserting about what was effective pedagogically, without engaging *teachers* in that discussion.

What is apparent today is that, when it comes to CLT in practice, stronger (highly learner-centred) versions, as exemplified, for example, by Terrell's Natural Approach (1977, 1982), did not really take root in classrooms. Rather, a *teacher-led* version, which became known as the "weak" model, typified many teachers' practices. It still persists today, for example in the very familiar classroom sequence of Presentation – Practice – Production or PPP: first teach the rule, then practise the rule, then produce the rule in some kind of communicative scenario.

The emergence of TBLT in the early 1980s was an attempt to nudge teachers' practices back towards learner-centredness, in particular as a response to the teacher-dominated practices of weak CLT or PPP. However, it seems that the theoretical justifications for TBLT, and also often the findings of empirical research into the effectiveness of tasks, do not necessarily find their way into teachers' thinking and classroom procedures. The conclusion that Rose (2019) expressed with regard to CLT would seem apposite to TBLT. Teachers need to be invited into the dialogue about effective pedagogy. This raises the crucial question of the effect that teacher education can have in moving teachers' practices forward, since, as Hattie (2012) reminded us, teachers represent the major source of *controllable* variance in education systems.

My story

The emergence of CLT and the challenges for practice that ensued were influential in shaping the experiences I have gone through – as a language learner, as a language teacher, and ultimately as a language teacher educator. These experiences have contributed to developing my perspective on what is effective in language teaching and my motivation to promote TBLT as a viable option in language classrooms. They have also affected my understanding and appreciation of just how complex and challenging the task-based endeavour can be.

The findings of my longitudinal TBLT-oriented research on teachers and the mediating effect of teacher education have been published extensively. In East (2022a), I interwove a summative overview of key findings with what I presented as a self-study into teacher education practices or S-STEP — a kind of autoethnographic reflection on my own positioning and work as a teacher educator. My plenary address was framed from that perspective. This chapter dovetails in with, and also adds a complementary angle to, my S-STEP journey as presented in East (2022a). In this chapter, I set the findings aside (at least initially) in order to provide some insight into who I am and the influences that have shaped me over many years.

An important question to ask is why my personal journey should have broader relevance for others involved with the TBLT project. In this regard, Peercy et al. (2019) acknowledged, "we currently know relatively little about teacher educators as *learners* and as *reflective scholars* open to examining *their own practice and research*" (p.2, my emphases). The narrative presented in this chapter is important as a way to address "an overarching need for teacher educators to pay attention to *their own* pedagogical reasoning" (Loughran, 2005, p.9, my emphasis) and what influences it. This is not, however, just an egoistic exercise in self-introspection. Self-study is predicated on a clear responsibility to utilise reflection to "seek to improve the learning situation not only for the self but [also] for the other" (Bullough & Pinnegar, 2001, p.17). We as teacher educators do things for particular reasons. We need to ask ourselves *why* we do what we do, and we need to look critically at our actions and the reasons for them so that we can *improve* our practices for the sake of those we work with. This *self-other* improvement factor has led to self-study research being acknowledged as a uniquely significant development that has potential to transform teacher education practice (Tidwell et al., 2009; Zeichner, 1999). In what follows, I present those aspects of my own experiences that have particularly influenced my thinking and practices.

The 1970s: Martin the language learner

My passion for language learning developed at school in the UK in the 1970s. As was the tradition at that time (a tradition that persists into the present in many cases), I started learning French from Year 7 (11+ years of age). Having demonstrated a sufficient level of proficiency, I picked up German the following year. This was very much the beginning of the time of transition for language teaching and learning when more behaviourist-informed and teacher-led approaches exemplified by grammar-translation and audio-lingualism were starting to defer to more learner-centred communicatively-oriented programmes (Benson & Voller, 1997).

The resource that was drawn on when I started learning German as L2 effectively illustrates the background debates and tensions that were apparent in the field at the time, of which I was blissfully unaware as a young language learner. My initial learning was textbook-driven. The textbook my teachers chose was *Sprich mal Deutsch!* (Rowlinson, 1967). The book's title ("just speak German!") suggests a very early attempt to place an emphasis on the primary development of oral skills in contrast to the reading and writing emphases of grammar-translation.

A review published a few years after *Sprich mal Deutsch!* had appeared described the textbook as "challenging, interesting, informative, up-to-date, and ingenious in its method" (Thornton, 1971, p.57). Each chapter, or lesson, was designed to begin with spoken language. Indeed, the textbook author (a prolific writer of a range of textbooks and reference works) demonstrated his own commitment to the emerging communicative agenda in a more theoretical work published somewhat later (Rowlinson, 1985). That said, the textbook itself, being published in the very early stages of transition away from more structural approaches when constructivism really had not taken root, was still very much a product of its time (originally published almost 60 years ago). Alongside an ostensibly primary focus on oral language, there was a strong behaviourist-informed emphasis on repetition and memorisation, as well as strong prominence attached to explaining and practising grammatical rules. Nevertheless, Thornton's review at the time hailed this dual reality as a distinct advantage — the textbook "combines the best of the oral approach with a careful and thorough foundation in grammar" such that students using the book "really can speak German, right from the beginning; and at the same time they learn what they need of grammar, without being burdened" (p.57).

Tasks were definitely not part of the agenda for *Sprich mal Deutsch!* However, its two-fold emphasis on oral skills and grammatical competence foreshadowed elements that would become crucial to TBLT in practice. I must admit that I, personally, enjoyed the intellectual challenges of grappling with the nuances and complexities of German grammar as presented in the book (for example, elements of German's complex case system were introduced in the very first lessons). A tongue-in-cheek acknowledgment of the potential limitations of the book may perhaps be found in the humorous transliteration of its title as "speak bad German!" There is, however, no doubt that, despite its behaviourist-informed grammar orientation, this text was an influential initial step in instilling in me an appreciation of the central importance of communication, in helping me to develop a high level of genuinely communicative competence in the language, and in motivating me towards more advanced study.

The 1980s and 1990s: Martin the language teacher

After completing my first degree in German (and Philosophy) at the University of London, I stumbled into secondary school teaching, less as a chosen and more as a default career option. My entry into the teaching profession in the early 1980s coincided with the beginnings of a Europe-wide project to research effective curricula and methodology for L2 teaching and learning. This project culminated in a report (Council of Europe, 1988) that reflected "a consensus in Europe on the importance of *international communication* as a basic aim of modern language teaching" (Dobson, 2018, p.74, my emphasis). This work was influential in shaping the first iteration of the UK's National Curriculum (Department for Education and Science/The Welsh Office, 1991; UK Statutory Instruments, 1991). As Dobson explained, the emphases of the National Curriculum for languages included: a communicative approach underpinned by a Programme of Study (PoS); predominant use of the target language aligned with helping students to develop competence in dealing with unpredictable elements and maintaining spontaneous interaction; and outcomes measured in accordance with a framework of Attainment Targets (ATs).

By the mid-1990s, when I had become Head of Modern Foreign Languages (MFL) in a medium-sized boys' comprehensive school on the outskirts of London, the communicative agenda had become very embedded into language teachers' thinking, due largely to the requirements of the mandatory National Curriculum. This was reflected in my choice of resources for teaching German. I selected *Gute Reise!* (Hermann et al., 1992), primarily because this course (which was more than just a textbook) reflected published curricular aims as outlined in the PoS and ATs. This meant that a lot of the curriculum mapping work had already been done by the course's authors.

Dobson (2018) noted that the PoS evolved over a series of National Curriculum revisions (1995, 1999, 2007), although "certain strands of continuity" (p.75) could be seen, such as ensuring central use of the target language and ongoing reference to dealing with unpredictable elements of language. A new edition of *Gute Reise!* (Hermann et al., 2000) was published to reflect not only changes to the PoS but also two significant changes — one in German (*die neue Rechtschreibung* or new spelling rules, initiated from 1996 and coming into force from 1998) and the other in Germany (the introduction of the *euro* as currency in place of the *Deutsche Mark*, adopted in principle from 1 January 1999 and fully implemented from 1 January 2002). However, the new edition retained the central hallmarks of the original (1992) edition. The course continued to be "designed for communicative language teaching," with its main published aim being "to enable pupils to express ideas which are important to them at their particular age" (p.11), and with "German as the medium of instruction from the very start" (p.14).

A tacit nod towards a task-oriented approach was found, for example, in paired information-gap speaking and listening activities (*Partnerarbeit; Hör zu*), as well as in facilitating learners' own creative use of German through a dedicated "personal dossier" section. This section was designed to offer students opportunities to present information about themselves, family, friends, and immediate environment. It was acknowledged that this might require vocabulary that had not been encountered more directly in the context of the course, and students were "encouraged to use their creative abilities to produce lively and varying pieces of work relevant to themselves" (Hermann et al., 2000, p. 12).

The approach adopted in *Gute Reise!* helped to solidify my perspective that authentic and spontaneous communication lay at the centre of the language teaching and learning endeavour. Importantly, *Gute Reise!* represented a significant conceptual and communicative step forward from *Sprich mal Deutsch!* — and a step forward that I embraced in my search for an effective approach to language pedagogy. However, neither TBLT nor task were specifically mentioned, and adherence to a prescriptive PoS and ATs meant that the approach would largely replicate aspects of a weak CLT model. As I observed in East (2024), it was essentially "down to us, as the teachers, to interpret issues such as authenticity, spontaneity and real communication in our own contexts, and we often did this intuitively and without any introduction to the task-based literature" (p. 417).

The 2000s and beyond: Martin the language teacher educator

When I left the UK for New Zealand at the turn of the century, I quickly embarked on a significantly new path which included undertaking a PhD in Language Teaching and Learning at the University of Auckland. My PhD gave me the opportunity, at the academic level, to wrestle with aspects of what it meant, in both theory and practice, to embed L2 pedagogy within a communicative paradigm.

The change of direction precipitated by my academic studies, as well as my considerable experience as a language teacher, led to my appointment as a language teacher educator at the University of Auckland, responsible for preparing new teachers who would go on to teach a language other than English at secondary school level in New Zealand. For ten years, between 2008 and 2017, I worked as a member of the team responsible for the one-year initial teacher education programme, the Graduate Diploma in Teaching (Secondary). Those who wanted to become teachers of languages took a year-long course, *Teaching Languages*, which was taught by me. Additionally, they enrolled in at least one year-long language specialist course (e.g., *Teaching Chinese; Teaching French*). These were mainly taught by external tutors who were usually currently teaching in local schools and who could apply a language-specific dimension to the ideas explored in *Teaching Languages*.

When I first began my initial teacher education work, language teaching in New Zealand's schools was supported by quite detailed language-specific curriculum documents (similar to the UK PoS) that reflected a traditional and hierarchical model of language acquisition, with achievement objectives alongside suggested topics, vocabulary, and grammar foci. Unlike in the UK, the prescriptions were not mandatory but were provided for guidance and planning purposes. These documents made overt and detailed reference to CLT. For example, the German document defined CLT as "teaching that encourages learners to engage in meaningful communication in the target language — communication that has a function over and above that of language learning itself" (Ministry of Education, 2002, p.16). In practice, teachers relied heavily on the documents, leading to a predominant teacher-led weak CLT approach. Teacher education focused largely on helping teachers to use the documents to plan communicatively-oriented classroom experiences for their students, something for which my own experiences as a language learner and language teacher had more than adequately prepared me.

However, a revised national curriculum for New Zealand's schools, published in 2007 and mandated from 2010 (Ministry of Education, 2007), emphasised, across all curriculum areas, a more constructivist philosophy whereby learners were to be seen as active and collaborative participators in their own learning. The mandate was accompanied by the withdrawal of the language-specific documents as guides to language pedagogy and a far more open-ended approach for which the construct of task became relevant.

Rod Ellis, a university colleague at that time, had earlier published a significant work on TBLT (Ellis, 2003), and, in anticipation of the imminent publication of the revised learner-centred curriculum, had been commissioned by New Zealand's Ministry of Education to put together a literature-informed set of principles that could guide teachers' choices about language pedagogy (Ellis, 2005). The task construct in the broader context of the ten principles he proposed began to influence thinking and practice in the New Zealand school sector, and indeed continues to do so (Ministry of Education, 2021).

Contemplating the implications of Ellis (2003, 2005), I came to view TBLT as a possible resolution to what I, as a language teacher, had been aiming to achieve for my students, in particular as a Head of Department during the 1990s, but with limited understanding and zero exposure to the task-based literature. I began to grapple with the idea that TBLT could adequately meet the expectations of New Zealand's revised curriculum. For me as someone who had already become established as a researcher in the field of language pedagogy, the conceptual leap from CLT to TBLT was not that huge. I perceived TBLT as a natural progression to the CLT agenda that I was already very familiar with and committed to, and "an ideal operationalisation of CLT" (East, 2018, p.25). That said, TBLT also represented a significant departure from previous teacher-led practices guided by specific curriculum documents and, for many teachers of languages up and down the country, was potentially a massive jump. My recognition of this reality ignited my research interest in the *teacher variable* as a component of the success of TBLT and precipitated a significant, interview-based research project which began my research along this path (East, 2012).

The publication of East (2012) was accompanied by an overhaul of the *Teaching Languages* course to reflect both revised curriculum aims and TBLT. The challenge became to support course participants as they transitioned into this new approach to L2 pedagogy. I began to introduce TBLT and tasks to my novice teacher students. I devoted a lot of time on campus to presenting and interrogating the new ideas as students moved into and out of working in schools during two seven-week practicum placements, providing pivotal opportunities for us to discuss how their in-school work was going in light of the theory. Being open to questioning and debate was a large part of my approach. East (2012) became the required text due to its focus on teachers' perspectives on TBLT in the context of New Zealand's curriculum reform.

Coursework assignments were crucial to the course's theory-practice interface. One of these was a year-long reading log assignment. As the year progressed, participants were required to read a chapter or chapters from East (2012), and to engage in critical reflection on the content and what it might mean for practice. As students gained more experience of working in schools and trying out task-based ideas, the readings supported a developing theory-practice interface.

Does teacher education make a difference?

Over the years that I worked in initial teacher education I collected a broad range of data on teachers' reception and uptake of TBLT principles, including my students' reading logs as a significant source of evidence. Below I outline the key issues that have emerged and relate these back to my own experiences as learner, teacher, and teacher educator.

When I first began the TBLT emphasis with my students back in 2012, I came into that work with a high degree of optimism that those just starting out in the teaching profession would grasp the importance of innovation in the face of published curricular reform and would become change agents in their own classrooms and schools. In a sense, I had "discovered" TBLT as a potentially optimum realisation of the communicative agenda that had influenced so much of my earlier encounters with language pedagogy — implicitly as a language learner, but certainly more explicitly as a language teacher charged with managing a department and overseeing the implementation of a National Curriculum. As a teacher educator, I attempted to pass on this discovery to my own students.

On the positive side, it did seem that an emphasis on TBLT in theory and practice in this one-year initial teacher education programme could make positive differences to beliefs and practices. It seemed from the data that prior beliefs based on students' own learning experiences can be confronted successfully and innovative practices can be welcomed *and* maintained by beginning teachers. That is, teachers perceived benefit in using communicative tasks, and this perception of benefit was often sustained even after students had graduated from the programme. This would suggest that teachers can be nudged away from current or more mainstream practices and towards more innovative practices by placing emphasis on the innovation. All this is reassuring for those of us involved in TBLT-oriented teacher education.

That said, as I reflected on the emerging evidence, I became aware that there was often a clash between the theoretical perspectives I was delving into with my students and the situations these students were encountering in real classrooms and reporting back to me. My students' reception of TBLT ideas was often ambivalent and sometimes resistant. Initially, this took me by surprise. However, Van den Branden (2022) advises that any attempt at innovation that "tends to take the shape of a revolution that turns the familiar world of the language classroom upside down … is *not* how successful innovations in education are usually realized" (pp. 641–642, my emphasis). It seemed that a more softly-softly approach was needed, and challenges in practice needed to be owned and explored.

It was evident that teachers do not accept and implement innovative practices without careful thought and consideration. Instead, they make choices. These may include the deliberate inclusion of various more traditional components. Some choices may arise as a result of responses to the realities of the local classroom context — such as lack of time and resources or how the *learners* are receiving the innovation. Other choices may be influenced by external contextual factors such as other colleagues' attitudes and practices or established assessment systems. Contextual constraints can have a huge impact on innovating practices as presented through teacher education. A clear emerging challenge was what I labelled the "experienced teacher" variable. My students were new to teaching and, in a sense, in a position of acquiescence to more experienced or senior colleagues. Perhaps most crucially, there was still the battle with cultural mores and conventional wisdom — or "we've always done it like this."

As I considered all the evidence before me, I reached the following conclusion: it is valuable and important to focus on TBLT *in theory* in initial teacher education, but there is a likelihood that TBLT *in practice* will become one of a range of options. The resultant "eclecticism in practice" (East, 2022a, p. 54) does not have to mean that the drive towards innovation has been ineffective. That said, there is a theory-practice tension that needs to be owned.

Particularly when the focus is on innovations, teacher eclecticism and teacher ambivalence are recognised in the broader education literature. As Borg (2015) put it, what teachers end up doing in classrooms is influenced by a range of "complex, practically-oriented, personalized, and context-sensitive networks of knowledge, thoughts and beliefs" (p.321). For beginning teachers in particular, these networks inevitably include older or more experienced colleagues. In a process that Brouwer and Korthagen (2005) described as "more one of survival than of learning from experiences," beginning teachers may "come to view colleagues in their schools as 'realistic' role models, as the people who 'do know' how one should go about teaching" (p.155) — even when these colleagues may themselves be holding onto more traditional or entrenched practices.

Furthermore, it is important to recognise that a perceptual binary often exists between teacher-led (behaviourist-influenced) and learner-centred (constructivist-influenced) teaching practices that places the two in opposition to (and therefore mutually exclusive of) each other (Buttler, 2020). This perception can operate as "a polarising force that attempts to push practitioners into one or the other camp" (East, 2022a, p.53) — either it is all about the teacher, or it is all about the learners. The reality of contemporary classrooms demonstrates that it is a question of *both-and*.

At the *micro-level* of the classroom, teachers will always make their own independent choices about accepting or rejecting aspects of innovation. The balance between teacher-led and learner-centred is subject to change — between teachers, between classes, and even at different points in the same lesson — as teachers respond to the context-specific realities of what is happening in their classrooms. After all, teachers are "individuals with their own ... individual differences, beliefs, and characteristics" (Griffiths, 2012, p.475) who will make individual choices based on "what seem to *them* to be appropriate contingent actions" (Mitchell et al., 2019, p.406, my emphasis).

At the *macro-level*, what teachers choose to do is influenced by a range of factors which will include "dominant discourses, power and hierarchies, conflicts, tensions and dilemmas" (Kayi-Aydar et al., 2019, p.1). The dominant discourse in a teacher education programme may well be different to the dominant discourse in schools — we as the teacher educators may be the ones touting the innovation, but colleagues in schools may be the ones holding onto tradition. This may well lead to tension and conflict. Beginning teachers are potentially put between a rock and a hard place.

Where does this leave teacher education?

I began this chapter with the premise that the teacher variable is crucial to the mediation of TBLT in practice, and that *teacher education* can play a role in moving teachers' practices forward. The position I have presented in this chapter might leave the impression that, despite Hattie's (2012) claim that the teacher variable is controllable, the teacher education endeavour will result in limited success. The reality that teacher education does not guarantee complete success when it comes to TBLT implementation has certainly been acknowledged by others (e.g., Bryfonski, 2022; Jackson, 2022).

Seen from a constructivist perspective, it is important for teacher education programmes to give teachers "opportunities to engage with contrasting theoretical arguments, to come to their own positions, and to take ownership for their own decisions" (East, 2022b, p. 457). There is a risk inherent in this positioning. The ultimate risk is that innovative ideas may be completely rejected. Nonetheless, the risk must be taken if we are to truly honour and respect teacher agency.

It is also critical to take seriously what *teachers* tell us about how innovation is going in practice. Sato (2023) noted that teachers are "the ones who have direct and concrete experience with L2 learning challenges that students face and L2 teaching challenges that hinder effective teaching" (p. 9). Bygate (2016) argued, "engaging our theories with the realities of real world practice is the one thing that can genuinely inform — and enable us to refine, change or indeed if necessary abandon — our theories" (p. 12). According to Rose (2019), advances in theory related to teaching practices should actively include teachers, ideally being shaped by their experiences. Rose advocated for more research that is informed by teaching practices, thereby challenging the one-way flow of knowledge from researchers to teachers. He emphasised the importance of fostering greater collaboration between teachers, teacher educators, and researchers to enhance our understanding of language teaching. Such an approach, he contended, would address more effectively the real-world consequences of changes in theoretical perspectives.

My own work as a teacher educator has been shaped and influenced both by my own experiences as learner and teacher and by a recognition of the importance of the teachers' voice when it comes to implementing TBLT. The position I have reached so far is that there is benefit in the balanced viewpoints that the teachers I worked with ended up holding. Indeed, as I reflect back on my own early experiences as a young language learner, the behaviourist-informed and grammar-oriented elements of textbook-based learning, albeit using a textbook that had been described as "ingenious in its method" and capitalising on "the best of the oral approach" (Thornton, 1971, p. 57), certainly did me no harm.[1]

Despite an acknowledgment of eclecticism in practice, I would not wish to conclude this chapter with the impression that our teacher education efforts may be futile. It is important to recognise and accept the data-supported claim (as outlined above) that "a critically reflective focus on TBLT as innovation *can* successfully challenge and change existing beliefs, and *can* bring about successful changes to practice" (East, 2022b, p. 459, my emphases). Widdowson (1992) early declared that "taking local conditions into account ... is not the same as conceding to them as determinants of what can be done. There must always be the possibility of change" (p. 271). Furthermore, my commitment to reflecting on my own beliefs and practices means that it is important for me to remain open to shifts in perspective as new research findings emerge. Reflection is, after all, "an *ongoing* cycle of learning about one's teaching ... [that] does not necessarily resolve issues, but perhaps generates even more questions and problems" (Brandenberg & Jones, 2017, my emphasis).

Where does this leave TBLT?

Many advocates of TBLT may point to empirical research findings as providing the evidence that TBLT is the solution to the dilemma of effective language pedagogy today. Their stance may potentially portray TBLT as "the long-awaited elixir of language teaching" (Richards & Rodgers, 2014, p. 177). In this chapter, I have outlined several challenges and questions about the TBLT project from the teachers' perspective. This may seem somewhat unsettling and disruptive for those committed to the project, especially given my earlier assertion that, without teachers, TBLT is simply not going to happen.

Nevertheless, we need to own the reality that the potential clash between teacher-led and learner-centred in both theory and practice creates a highly complex situation for teachers when they try to put approaches like TBLT into practice. This is especially so as they grapple with the important message that TBLT *is* essentially learner-centred and experiential. As Ellis (2018) expressed it, TBLT (at least in its most experiential guises) "can conflict with teachers' and learners' beliefs about language, leading at best to doubts and at worst to rejection of TBLT" (p. 274). The effect of this is that defining or prescribing exactly what TBLT *should* be in practice, especially at the individual classroom level, can be highly

---

1. This assertion begs the question of language aptitude as a variable in my own language acquisition. It is possible that I acquired language *in spite of* rather than *because of* how I was taught. This issue is, however, beyond the scope of this chapter.

problematic. Carless (2012) noted the consequential reality that "there are many variations and choices for teachers to select from when they are carrying out TBLT." This, he suggested, is "part of the beauty of TBLT," but it is also "part of its complexity" (p. 4).

In East (2023), I outlined ten guiding principles that might support the implementation of effective TBLT-oriented teacher education. Central to what I presented there is a focus on the task construct itself. I argue for this focus on the basis that getting the task right in the sense that we have a degree of confidence in how the task fits against theoretical definitions (i.e., it is a genuine task and not just a grammar practice activity) means that we are "at least half way towards putting a communicative approach into practice that is 'task-based'" (East, 2021, p. 88). After all, this was very much the missing component of my own experiences as both learner and teacher.

As for those elements that surround the task in the various phases of a task-based lesson — that is, situating the task or tasks within wider pedagogical considerations — we need to subject TBLT to "on-going reflection to continually evaluate its success, and its theoretical claims, in light of evidence emerging from practice" (East, 2022b, p. 459). That is, we need to continue to look seriously at those teaching practices that will enhance rather than hinder task performance and language acquisition, whether teacher-led or learner-centred. Again, my own early experiences suggest that teacher-led elements can have beneficial roles to play.

Conclusion

Norris's (2009) proposal that a price is to be paid with the introduction of TBLT has led me to pose several crucial reflective questions which have no doubt been influenced by what I have encountered as learner, teacher, and teacher educator:

> If a price is to be paid, how high should that price be? Or what negotiations are required to reduce the price? Put another way, when is innovation to be embraced wholeheartedly, when is it to be eschewed and when is it to be moderated?
>
> (East, 2014, p. 273)

I suggested that the above questions are not easy to answer, but they necessitate ongoing research into TBLT in both experimental and real-world contexts. Indeed, Long (2015) referred to TBLT as "a journey along a road as yet unbuilt," where "[t]he rationale and the objectives are clear, but the route is uncertain" (pp. 20–21). Elsewhere, Long (2016) conceded that, although many of the criticisms lodged against TBLT can be dismissed, several criticisms flag up important concerns. He reflected, "[n]o approach to LT [language teaching] has proven 'correct' to date, and there should be no illusion as to TBLT's chances of breaking the tradition. Real issues remain" (p. 28). He went on to assert:

> Advances in theory and research, coupled with further field trials, will assuredly refine current models, and quite probably identify needed changes. The goal is for researchers and practitioners to move forward *together* systematically in what must be a *collaborative* endeavor. (pp. 28–29, my emphases)

We know where we would ultimately like to get to but, for the time being, we will continue to encounter bumps and hazards along the road, perhaps even a few false turns here and there. As we continue the journey together and take account of the viewpoints of *all* those who have a stake in the TBLT project, I share Long's confidence that the way ahead will become clearer as we get closer to our destination.

References

Andon, N., & Eckerth, J. (2009). Chacun à son goût? Task-based L2 pedagogy from the teacher's point of view. *International Journal of Applied Linguistics, 19*(3), 286–310.

Benson, P., & Voller, P. (Eds.). (1997). *Autonomy and independence in language learning.* Longman.

Borg, S. (2015). *Teacher cognition and language education: Research and practice.* Bloomsbury Academic.

Brandenberg, R., & Jones, M. (2017). Toward transformative reflective practice in teacher education. In R. Brandenberg, K. Glasswell, M. Jones, & J. Ryan (Eds.), *Reflective theory and practice in teacher education* (pp. 259–273). Springer.

Brouwer, N., & Korthagen, F. (2005). Can teacher education make a difference? *American Educational Research Journal, 42*(1), 153–224.

Bryfonski, L. (2022). Connecting teacher training to task-based language teaching implementation. In M. J. Ahmadian & M. H. Long (Eds.), *The Cambridge handbook of task-based language teaching* (pp. 463–477). Cambridge University Press.

Bullough, R. V., & Pinnegar, S. (2001). Guidelines for quality in autobiographical forms of self-study research. *Educational Researcher, 30*(3), 13–21.

Buttler, T. (2020). Disrupting my teaching practices: A teacher educator living as a contradiction. *Studying Teacher Education, 16*(2), 222–239.

Bygate, M. (2016). TBLT through the lens of applied linguistics: Engaging with the real world of the classroom. *ITL International Journal of Applied Linguistics, 167*(1), 3–15.

Bygate, M. (2020). Some directions for the possible survival of TBLT as a real world project. *Language Teaching, 53*(3), 275–288.

Carless, D. (2012). Task-based language teaching in Confucian-heritage settings: Prospects and challenges. *On Task, 2*(1), 4–8. Retrieved from https://www.tblsig.org/publications

Council of Europe. (1988). *Learning and teaching modern languages for communication: Final report of the Project Group (Activities 1982–87).* Council of Europe.

Department for Education and Science/The Welsh Office. (1991). *Modern foreign languages in the National Curriculum.* Her Majesty's Stationery Office.

Dobson, A. (2018). Towards 'MFL for all' in England: A historical perspective. *The Language Learning Journal, 46*(1), 71–85.

East, M. (2012). *Task-based language teaching from the teachers' perspective: Insights from New Zealand.* John Benjamins.

East, M. (2014). Encouraging innovation in a modern foreign language initial teacher education programme: What do beginning teachers make of task-based language teaching? *The Language Learning Journal, 42*(3), 261–274.

East, M. (2018). How do beginning teachers conceptualise and enact tasks in school foreign language classrooms? In V. Samuda, M. Bygate, & K. Van den Branden (Eds.), *TBLT as a researched pedagogy* (pp. 23–50). John Benjamins.

East, M. (2021). *Foundational principles of task-based language teaching.* Routledge.

East, M. (2022a). *Mediating innovation through language teacher education.* Cambridge University Press.

East, M. (2022b). Teacher preparation and support for task-based language teaching. In M. J. Ahmadian & M. H. Long (Eds.), *The Cambridge handbook of task-based language teaching* (pp. 447–462). Cambridge University Press.

East, M. (2023). Supporting TBLT through teacher education: A critical perspective. *TASK, 3*(1), 5–27.

East, M. (2024). Martin East's essential bookshelf: Task-based language teaching. *Language Teaching, 57*(3), 408–418.

Ellis, R. (2003). *Task-based language teaching and learning.* Oxford University Press.

Ellis, R. (2005). *Instructed second language acquisition: A literature review.* Ministry of Education. https://www.educationcounts.govt.nz/publications/schooling/5163

Ellis, R. (2018). *Reflections on task-based language teaching.* Multilingual Matters.

Griffiths, C. (2012). Focus on the teacher. *ELT Journal, 66*(4), 468–476.

Griffiths, C. (2023). What about the teacher? *Language Teaching, 56*(2), 210–222.

Hattie, J. (2012). *Visible learning for teachers: Maximizing impact on learning.* Routledge.

Hermann, C., Hill, J., & Pomfrett, G. (1992). *Gute Reise!* Mary Glasgow Publications.

Hermann, C., Hill, J., & Pomfrett, G. (2000). *Gute Reise! neu — Teacher's book.* Mary Glasgow Publications.

Jackson, D. (2022). *Task-based language teaching.* Cambridge University Press.

Kayi-Aydar, H., Gao, X., Miller, E. R., Varghese, M., & Vitanova, G. (Eds.). (2019). *Theorizing and analyzing language teacher agency.* Multilingual Matters.

Long, M. H. (2015). TBLT: Building the road as we travel. In M. Bygate (Ed.), *Domains and directions in the development of TBLT: A decade of plenaries from the international conference* (pp. 1–26). John Benjamins.

Long, M. H. (2016). In defense of tasks and TBLT: Nonissues and real issues. *Annual Review of Applied Linguistics, 36*, 5–33.

Loughran, J. (2005). Researching teaching about teaching: Self-study of teacher education practices. *Studying Teacher Education, 1*(1), 5–16.

Medgyes, P. (1986). Queries from a communicative teacher. *ELT Journal, 40*(2), 107–112.

Ministry of Education. (2002). *German in the New Zealand curriculum.* Learning Media.

Ministry of Education. (2007). *The New Zealand Curriculum.* Learning Media.

Ministry of Education. (2021). *Principles and actions that underpin effective teaching in languages.* http://seniorsecondary.tki.org.nz/Learning-languages/Pedagogy/Principles-and-actions

Mitchell, R., Myles, F., & Marsden, E. (2019). *Second language learning theories* (4th ed.). Routledge.

Norris, J.M. (2009). Task-based teaching and testing. In M. Long & C. Doughty (Eds.), *The handbook of language teaching* (pp. 578–594). Wiley Blackwell.

Peercy, M.M., Sharkey, J., Baecher, L., Motha, S., & Varghese, M. (2019). Exploring TESOL teacher educators as learners and reflective scholars: A shared narrative inquiry. *TESOL Journal, 10*(4), 1–16.

Richards, J.C., & Rodgers, T.S. (2014). *Approaches and methods in language teaching* (3rd ed.). Cambridge University Press.

Rose, H. (2019). Dismantling the ivory tower in TESOL: A renewed call for teaching-informed research. *TESOL Quarterly, 53*(3), 895–905.

Rowlinson, W. (1967). *Sprich mal Deutsch!* (1st ed.). Oxford University Press.

Rowlinson, W. (1985). *Personally speaking: Teaching languages for use.* Oxford University Press.

Sato, M. (2023). Navigating the research-practice relationship: Professional goals and constraints. *Language Teaching,* 1–16.

Terrell, T.D. (1977). A natural approach to second language acquisition and learning. *The Modern Language Journal, 61*(7), 325–336.

Terrell, T.D. (1982). The natural approach to language teaching: An update. *The Modern Language Journal, 66*(2), 121–132.

Thornton, G. (1971). Looking for a better text? *Canadian Modern Language Review, 27*(3), 57–63.

Tidwell, D., Heston, M., & Fitzgerald, L. (2009). Introduction. In D. Tidwell, M. Heston, & L. Fitzgerald (Eds.), *Research methods for the self-study of practice* (pp. xiii–xxii). Springer.

UK Statutory Instruments. (1991). *The Education (National Curriculum) (Modern Foreign Languages) Order 1991.* https://www.legislation.gov.uk/uksi/1991/2567/made

Van den Branden, K. (2009). Diffusion and implementation of innovations. In M. Long & C. Doughty (Eds.), *The handbook of language teaching* (pp. 659–672). Wiley Blackwell.

Van den Branden, K. (2016). The role of teachers in task-based language education. *Annual Review of Applied Linguistics, 36*, 164–181.

Van den Branden, K. (2022). Task-based language teaching as an innovation: A task for teachers. In M.J. Ahmadian & M.H. Long (Eds.), *The Cambridge handbook of task-based language teaching* (pp. 628–648). Cambridge University Press.

Widdowson, H.G. (1992). Innovation in teacher development. *Annual Review of Applied Linguistics, 13*, 260–275.

Zeichner, K.M. (1999). The new scholarship in teacher education. *Educational Researcher, 28*(9), 4–15.

Zheng, X., & Borg, S. (2014). Task-based learning and teaching in China: Secondary school teachers' beliefs and practices. *Language Teaching Research, 18*(2), 205–221.

List of contributors

Volume editor

Martin East is Professor of Language Education in the School of Cultures, Languages, and Linguistics, the University of Auckland, New Zealand. Prior to this, he was a language teacher educator in the University's Faculty of Education and Social Work. He is the author of numerous publications in the field of language pedagogy and assessment. Drawing on his years of experience as a language teacher and teacher educator, his book *Foundational Principles of Task-Based Language Teaching* (2021, Routledge, Open Access) outlines, in an accessible and reader-friendly way, the core theories that inform and central practices that make up TBLT. He is a past president of the International Association for Task-based Language Teaching. (ORCID ID: 0000-0003-3681-5028)

Authors of chapters

María del Pilar García Mayo (https://laslab.org/staff/pilar) is Full Professor of English Language and Linguistics at the University of the Basque Country. She has published widely on the L2/L3 acquisition of English morphosyntax and the study of conversational interaction in EFL. She has been an invited speaker to universities in Europe, Asia, and North-Central America, and is an Honorary Consultant for the Shanghai Center for Research in English Language Education. Professor Garcia Mayo is the director of the research group *Language and Speech* and the MA program *Language Acquisition in Multilingual Settings* as well as co-editor of *Language Teaching Research*. She was a member of AILA Executive Board-International Committee and the international relations representative of the Spanish Society for Applied Linguistics, and currently belongs to the Steering Committee of the Spanish State Research Agency. (ORCID ID: 0000-0002-1987-4889)

Roger Gilabert is a researcher and lecturer at the University of Barcelona. He is a member of the Language Acquisition Research Group (GRAL). He has published extensively in the areas of needs analysis, task and syllabus design, task complexity and task sequencing, and the role of genre in multimodal input. His most recent projects have included the development of reading skills through game-based learning, and he is currently leading a project on the automation of task design. Both projects have revolved around the central concern of transfer of SLA and TBLT theoretical principles and findings to second language instruction. (ORCID ID: 0000-0001-6464-4161)

YouJin Kim is Professor and the Director of Graduate Studies in the Department of Applied Linguistics and ESL, where she mentors undergraduate and graduate students and conducts research on topics related to additional language acquisition. In particular, Dr. Kim specialises in task-based language learning, second language acquisition in diverse instructional contexts such as classrooms, study abroad programs, and mobile applications, as well as research methods in Applied Linguistics. She is passionate about connecting research and practice and offering evidence-based suggestions on how additional languages are learned effectively through her research. She is currently co-editor of the *Journal of Second Language Writing*. (ORCID ID: 0000-0002-5741-9369)

Folkert Kuiken is Professor Emeritus of Dutch as a Second Language and Multilingualism at the University of Amsterdam. He co-edited *Dimensions of L2 Performance and Proficiency* (Housen, Kuiken, & Vedder, 2012), as well as various special issues on complexity related topics for *Applied Linguistics* (Housen & Kuiken, 2009), *Second Language Research* (Housen, De Clercq, Kuiken, & Vedder, 2019), *Instructed Second Language Acquisition* (Kuiken, Michel, & Vedder, 2019) and *International Journal of Applied Linguistics* (Kuiken, Vedder, De Clercq, & Housen, 2019). In 2024 he received a Distinguished Scholar Award from EurosLA for his work on complexity, accuracy, fluency, and functional adequacy in L2 writing. (ORCID ID: 0000-0002-1667-2501)

Anke Lenzing is Professor of English Language Education at Innsbruck University. Her research interests encompass psycholinguistic aspects of (instructed) second language acquisition. She has published on topics such as language processing in beginning second language learners, the role of formulaic sequences in instructed SLA, relationships between L2 production and comprehension, and the internal dynamics of L2 acquisition. She is the author of the books *The Development of the Grammatical System in Early Second Language Acquisition: The Multiple Constraints Hypothesis* (2013, John Benjamins) and *The Production-Comprehension Interface in Second Language Acquisition: An Integrated Encoding-Decoding Model* (2021, Bloomsbury). Her current research engages with psycholinguistic perspectives on L2 turn-taking. (ORCID ID: 0000-0002-2684-7774)

Jonathan Newton is Associate Professor and Programme Director for the Master of TESOL/Applied Linguistics programmes at Victoria University of Wellington, New Zealand. As a language teacher educator, he has worked alongside teachers from around the world to better understand classroom language teaching and learning, especially in relation to task-based language teaching, teaching listening and speaking, teaching vocabulary, and teaching for intercultural capabilities. He has published widely — his recent books include: *Teaching ESL/EFL Listening and Speaking* (Routledge, 2021), *Using Tasks in Language Teaching* (RELC, 2021), *and Teaching English to Second Language Learners in Academic Contexts* (Routledge, 2018). See: https://people.wgtn.ac.nz/jonathan.newton. (ORCID ID: 0000-0001-7264-6829)

Rhonda Oliver is Professor of Education at Curtin University, Australia. She has researched extensively and is widely published in the areas of second language and dialect acquisition, age differences, and task-based language learning. Over the years many of the participants in her research have been children and adolescents learning a second language or dialect, a heritage language, and in CLIL and TBLT contexts. Her more recent work includes studies within Australian Aboriginal education settings. Her extensive publication record includes her award-winning textbook *Indigenous Education in Australia: Learning and Teaching for Deadly Futures* (Routledge, 2021). (ORCID ID: 0000-0001-6233-8750)

Andrea Révész is a Professor of Second Language Acquisition at the IOE, University College London. Her research interests lie in second language acquisition, instruction, and assessment, with a particular focus on tasks, input, individual differences, and the neurocognitive processes underlying second language speaking and writing. She is a winner of the 2017 TBLT Best Research Article Award and a recipient of the 2018 TESOL Award for Distinguished Research. She serves as editor of the *Annual Review of Applied Linguistics* and co-editor of the *John Benjamins Task-based Language Teaching* series. She is Immediate Past President of the International Association for Task-based Language Teaching. (ORCID ID: 0000-0003-1093-4336)

Nina Spada is Professor Emerita in the Language and Literacy Education Program at OISE University of Toronto. Dr. Spada's research is concerned with the role of instruction in second language acquisition. Her classroom-based research investigates the contributions of the type and timing of attention to language form within meaning-based/communicative instruction and their effects on different aspects of L2 knowledge and ability. Included in Dr. Spada's publications are over 100 articles in journals and collected editions and five books/edited volumes. She is a co-author of *How Languages are Learned*, currently in its fifth edition and published by Oxford University Press. Dr. Spada authored the second edition of *The COLT Observation Scheme: Digital Versions and Updated Research Applications,* published in 2024 by John Benjamins.

Kris Van den Branden is a Full Professor of Linguistics at the Faculty of Arts at Leuven University (Belgium) and the current Head of the Teacher Education Department at the same faculty. At the same university, he is the academic promoter of the Centre for Language and Education which supports schools in improving their (second) language education. He is one of the chief editors of the journal *Task — Journal for Task-Based Language Teaching and Learning.* His research interests are with the implementation of TBLT, the role of the teacher, and interaction in the second language classroom. He was the Founding President of the International Association for Task-based Language Teaching. (ORCID ID: 0000-0001-8348-7034)

Ineke Vedder is Research Associate at the Amsterdam Center for Language and Communication, University of Amsterdam. Her research focuses on development of complexity and assessment of functional adequacy in L2. She co-edited *Dimensions of L2 Performance and Proficiency* (Housen, Kuiken, & Vedder, 2012), and several special issues on L2 complexity, *Second Language Research* (Housen, De Clercq, Kuiken, & Vedder, 2019), *Instructed Second Language Acquisition* (Kuiken, Michel, & Vedder, 2019) and *International Journal of Applied Linguistics* (Kuiken, Vedder, De Clercq, & Housen, 2019). In 2024 she received the Distinguished Scholar Award from EuroSLA for her work on complexity, accuracy, fluency, and functional adequacy in L2 writing and her contribution to SLA, particularly Italian. (ORCID ID: 0000-0002-2677-0228)

Paula Winke is the inaugural "Arts and Letters Professor" at Michigan State University, where she teaches in the Applied Linguistics Program within the Department of Linguistics, Languages, and Cultures. She researches language testing and assessment methods, individual differences in SLA, and task-based language teaching and assessment methods. She is a former editor of the journal *Language Testing,* and recently won the NFMLTA/MLJ Paul Pimsleur Award for Research in World Language Education. Paula is currently a visiting scholar at the Universität Innsbruck, Institut für Fachdidaktik, and within the Language Testing Research Group Innsbruck (LTRGI). (ORCID ID: 0000-0002-8169-650X)

Index

Entries in *italics* refer to figures; entries in **bold** refer to tables.

A

Aboriginal English 237–240, 245, 248
Aboriginal languages 238, 244–245
Aboriginal people 238–239
    cultural constraints 250
    interacting with non-Aboriginal people 240, 244–246
Aboriginal students 15, 236–239
    collecting data from 242–243
    language needs 240–242, 244–246
    pedagogical tasks for 248–249
    and TBLT implementation 250–252
ACTFL Proficiency Guidelines 133–136, 141–143
action research cycles 73
agency: and Can-do statements 128, 144
    of teachers 267
alignment 223–224
anaphoric devices 150, 152, 155
applied linguistics 8
    and coursebooks 64
    research-practice gap 175
artificial intelligence (AI) 33, 37
ATs (Attainment Targets) 261–262
attentional allocation 214, 222–223
attentional processes 87, 215, 222–224
attentional resources 87, 89
attention to form: and FFI 167–169
    and TR 87–89, 94

attention to language 89, 166–167, 170
audio-lingualism 5, 74, 259
authentic contexts 6–7, 49, 55, 111
authenticity 4, 13
    layers of 41, 47–58
    and Martian task 192
    and spontaneous communication 262
    in the task-based classroom 44–47
    in TBLA 149
    in TBLT 42–43
    and textbooks 57–58
autonomy 52–53, 109

B

Bava Harji, and Jia 3, 6, 8
behaviourist principles 257, 260, 266
beliefs, changing 75
Blanquerna Department of Communication Studies 24
bottom-up approach 174
    to task design 22, 31, 36
BPA (Border Patrol Academy) 49–50
Breen, Mike 237
Business English 107–108
Bygate, Martin 9–11, 15–16, 174

C

CAF (complexity, accuracy, and fluency) 14, 166
    definitions for 171–172
    and FA 147–149, 153–156
    fluency measures in *174*
    and ISLA 172–173
    and task-based processes 212–214
    TBLT research on 176–177
    and TR 87–88
Can-do statements 14, 124–125, 127–130, 142–144

customizing 140–141, **141**
describing curricular goals 132–133
item bank **135**
and language frameworks 133–140, *135–136*, *139*
and proficiency gains 141–142
and self-assessment 126–127
teacher use of 130–132
causal processes 213
CBLT (content-based language teaching) 169, 175–176
CEFR (Common European Framework of Reference) 134, 142
    and Can-do statements 127–128, *136*, *137–138*, *139*
    and FA rating 150–152, 155
ChatGPT 37
Chiang Mai University 109
China: EFL coursebooks in 63–64, 67, 69–70, 74
    TBLT in 13, 23
clarification requests 49, 85, 87, 155
classroom learning loop 133
classroom tasks 13
class size 74, 110
CLB (Canadian Language Benchmarks) 134
CLIL (content and language integrated learning) 13, 82, 84–86, 89, 94, 175–176
closed-ended questionnaire items 215
CLT (communicative language teaching) 4–6, 91, 166, 257–258, 261, 263
Cognition Hypothesis 25, 31, 213–214
cognitive complexity 27
cognitive-interactionism 5, 13, 35, 84, 86

cognitive load 27
  task-generated 213, 215–216, 220, 226
cognitive processes 15
  task-generated (see task-based processes)
cognitive psychology 168, 216, 220
cognitive research agenda 25–26
coherence & cohesion 150, 152, 154–156, 160
collaboration models 107–109, 111–112, 114
collaborative learning 91, 257
collaborative patterns 82, 88, 90, 94
collaborative research 175–176
communicative adequacy 172, 174
communicative approach 5, 261, 269
communicative competence 46, 85
communicative interaction 8
  and FA 154
  and FFI 167–168, 172
communicative outcomes 67, 70
communicative proficiency, measuring 14
communicative skills 8, 69, 76, 142
communicative tasks: Can-do statements as 133, 143
  competence to perform 42–43, 124–125
  in coursebooks 73
  design of 32
  identifying developmental stage 186–187, 189
  in teacher education 265
community of teachers 34, 62, 77
comprehensibility, in FA rating scale 150, 154–155
comprehension checks 85, 87
conditional clauses 45
confidence, self-evaluated 129
confirmation checks 85, 88
constructivism 5, 26, 257, 260, 263, 266–267
content, in FA rating scale 150
content-related authenticity 45, 48, 51–52, 56–57

contextual authenticity 44, 48–52, 55
conversational adjustments 85–86, 94
conversations: authentic 55–56
  informal 48–49, 56
corrective feedback (CF) 15, 172
  and FFI 167, 169
  oral 237
  perception of 219, 223
  timing of 164, 166, 169–171
  written (see SWCF; WCF)
coursebooks 13, 60–61, 75–76
  case against 64–68
  case for 68–71
  PhD research on 61–62
  task-informed design 77
  teacher agency and mentoring 71–75
Crookes, Graham 24
CSE (China's Standards of English) 134
C-tests 144, 153
cultural appropriacy 250
curricular goals 47, 124, 132–133
curriculum design teams 103–104, 114

D

data elicitation 186–187
decision-making, and research findings 22–23, 32
decision-making tasks 151, 220, 222–223, 226–227
declarative knowledge See explicit knowledge
descriptive research 174–175
design variables 25
developmental readiness 190–191
developmental trajectories 72, 187–189
dictogloss 92
difficulty, level of 65, 240
distributional analysis 187, 193, 198–199, **198**
domain experts 27–28, 36, 243
dual-task methodology 212, 219–221, 226
duration ratios, subjective-to-objective 216–217
Dynamic Systems Theories 26

E

EAL (English as an Additional Language) 6–7, 12
East, Martin 175
  personal story of 259–264
eclecticism in practice 265–266, 268
EFL (English as Foreign Language) 7
  for children 13, 82–83, 85–95
  coursebooks in 61, 64
  in Flanders 46
  in Korea 108
Ellis, Rod 237, 263
ELLRA (Early Language Learning Research Association) 84
ELT (English Language Teaching), and coursebooks 63, 68
e-mail writing 28–29, 53
  tasks for 28, **29**
emergence criterion 171, 187, 193, 198
emojis 132
English language, in-class use of 7
ESL (English as Second Language) 6–7, 86, 94
ETR (exact task repetition) 89–90
European Union 24, 137
Eurydice Report 83
expert judgements 134
explicit instruction 166–167, 169, 245–246
explicit knowledge 169–173, *174*
eye tracking 212, 222–224, 226–228

F

FA (functional adequacy) 14, 147–149
  in classroom practice 154
  and components of CAF 153–154
  in interactional tasks 154–155
FA (functional adequacy) rating scale 150, 154–156
  for interactional adequacy 161

reliability and validity
152–153, 155
in research 151
for writing 159–160
Flanders 43–44, 46–49, 51–54
Florida International University
(FIU) 35, 110–112
fluency, measures of 148, 171,
173, *174*
fMRI scans 225
focus on form 6, 13
and authentic tasks 46, 49
in child EFL 82
developmentally
moderated 190, 208
and meaning 58, 167, 170
and NLP 33
and task design 31, 36
and task repetition 87
foreign language (FL) 7, 23
children learning 83–84
and TBLT 35 *See also* EFL
foreign language (FL) contexts
83, 94
formative assessment 130
form-focused exercises 47–48,
67
form-focused instruction (FFI)
15, 66, 85, 94
isolated and integrated
167–170, 172, 176
timing of 164, 168
form-meaning connections 170
formulaic sequences 186, 195,
198–199, 202
Forrest, Uncle Simon 238

G
gaming 94
García Mayo, María del Pilar 176
Gass, Susan 24
general interest topics 57
Georgetown Startalk program
117
German language: learning and
teaching 259–263
and Martian task 193–195,
200
gestures, Aboriginal students
and 244–245
goal-related authenticity 45, 52,
56

grammar-based syllabi 64–65
grammar explanation, explicit
67
grammar instruction, and
authenticity 45–46
grammar-translation model
4–5, 67, 74, 259–260
grammatical information,
unification of 186–187

H
Hindi language 130, 138, **141**
Hinger, Barbara 256
Hong Kong 71, 106
human-machine interaction
design 22, 31, 33–34
Hypothesis Space 188–190, *188*

I
IATBLT (International
Association for Task-Based
Language Teaching) 11, 84,
108
ICTBLT (International
Consortium on Task-Based
Language Teaching) 9
idiosyncratic structures 195,
198–199
ILR (Interagency Language
Roundtable) 134
immersion settings 6–7, 83, 175
implementation variables 82,
85–86, 90, 102
implicit instruction 166–167
implicit knowledge 164,
169–170, 172–173, *174*
indigenous education 238, 252
See also Aboriginal students
indigenous languages 7–9, 12
See also Aboriginal languages
information distribution and
flow 25, 31
information gap tasks 5, 49, 155,
261
innovation 22, 31, 36
and curriculum
development 115
diffusion of 62, 77
input hypothesis 5
instructed second language
acquisition *See* ISLA
instruction 166–167

and implicit and explicit
knowledge 173
timing of 167–170
interactional adequacy 161
interactional authenticity 45, 48,
50–52, 56, 192
interactional tasks, and FA 147,
154–156
interaction design 33–34, 36–37
interaction hypothesis 5, 25, 31,
169
interactive activities 66, 71
interactive research agenda 25
intercultural dimensions 31, 55
interlanguage 90, 171, 189–190
International Conferences on
Task-Based Language
Teaching 2–3
interviews, and task-based
processes 217, 226
ISLA (instructed second
language acquisition) 14–15,
164–165
and FFI 168–169
mutual influence with
TBLT 176, *177*
outcomes measurement
171, 172–173
and processability 183
research-practice gap
175–176
and task-based processes
218, 222, 226
and TBLT 165–166

J
joint attention 223
journalists, L2 use by 27

K
keystroke logging 212, 221–222,
224, 226–228
Korean language 112–113
Kriol 238–239
Kutja School 237, 239–242,
247–248

L
L1 (first language): EFL children's
use of 85–87
metacognitive use of 89
as scaffolding 8

L1 (first language) speakers, as teachers 111

L2 (target language):
effectiveness and appropriacy of use 14
effects of instruction on learning 167
features of development 15
learning grammar of 45
as object 65
performance evaluation in 147–149, 151, 153, 155
processing capacities in 184
registers and varieties of 53
in TBLT curricular research 104, *105*
use outside classroom 7, 46
See also SLA

L2 (target language) interaction 90

L2 (target language) tasks 6–7, 13
in authentic conditions 41–43, 55
design 23, 32
pedagogical tasks approximating 47–50, 64

language abilities, communicative 134, 137–138

language acquisition: and learning 4 *See also* SLA

language and task-based depth 144

language aptitude 268N1

language assessment 10, 124–125

language-awareness strategies 84

language competences, for "real life," 42–43

language development, stages in 15

language education, effectiveness of 53

language frameworks 124, 127
explaining 136–140
reflecting 133–136

language generation, Levelt's model of 185

language learning 4
implicit 46

language learning motivation 52

Language Learning Task Bank 75, 117, 153, 156

language performance 143
linguistic and functional dimensions 147–149, 151

language proficiency scales 128, 133–143, *135–136*, *140*

languages other than English 7–8, 14

language teaching: explicit and implicit 57–58
historical transitions in 256, 258–264
TBLT and 268

languaging 92

learner attention 6

learner-centredness 4, 76, 256–258, 266, 268

learner development stages 183, 208–209
and Can-do statements 143
and Martian task 191–199
and Processability Theory 185–189
and semantic domains 199–207, **202**
and tasks 190–191
tools to diagnose 184

learner engagement 74

learner-learner interaction 6, 85, 193, 196, 199–200

learner setup 82, 85, 90–91

learner variation 188–190, 196, 198–199

learning design 22, 31, 33–34, 36–37

Learning Designer software 34–36

learning outcomes 128, 148, 175–176

lemma access 185–186

less commonly taught languages 12

lesson planning, collaborative 72–73

lexico-grammatical exercises 73

Li, Shaofeng 170

Lightbown, Patsy 167–168

Likert-scales 128, 131–132, 139, 150

Limited Capacity Model 31, 213–214

linguistic authenticity 45, 48, 50–52, 56–57

linguistic encoding processes 214, 227–228

linguistic repertoires 46, 189, 244

linguistic resources 8, 91

lived experiences 129, 255

Long, Mike 16, 24, 237

longitudinal research design 86

LREs (language-related episodes) 88–94

M

McDonough, Kim 108

map tasks 220, 222, 226–227

Martian task 191–192, 207–208
development and variation in 192–199, **193**
example dialogue *194*, *196–197*
semantic domains in 199–207, **200–201**, *203–208*

materials evaluation 63–64

meaning, negotiation of 8, 85–87, 113, 170

meaning and form 57–58, 85, 218

meaning-based instruction 170, 176

memory decay 215, 218–219

mentoring, and coursebooks 62, 68, 71–77

mentor-trainee model 52

metacognitive instruction 94

metalinguistic explanations 94

Michel, Marije 173

model texts 92–94

monitoring behaviour 172

morphological markers 186, 199

morphological structures 186–187, 193, 208

morphosyntax 185, 188

motivation, and Can-do statements 128

motivational power 47, 55

multi-modal input-based tasks 224

N

narrative tasks 89, 220, 222, 227

Natural Approach 258

needs analysis (NA) 13, 15, 22–24, 241

for Aboriginal students
236, 238, 240–243,
246–247, 251–252
and coursebooks 64
and curriculum
development 105–106,
108
and link with reality 42–45,
50
and task design 27–30, 28,
32, 34, 36
neuroimaging 225
New Zealand 83, 134
teacher education in
262–263
Nicaragua 63
NLP (Natural Language
Processing) 33, 36
Norris, John 9, 11
NZALT (New Zealand
Association of Language
Teachers) 11

O

open-ended questionnaire items
215
opinion gap tasks 5
oral approach 260, 268
oral interactions 85, 88, 219
oral production: cognitive
processes in 225–226
and processability
perspective 184, 186–189,
193, 200
and TR 87, 89, 92
Output Hypothesis 25, 31, 91

P

pair dynamics 87–88
pair formation method 90
participatory action research 73
passive-parallel patterns 88
pedagogical interventions 94,
173
pedagogic decisions, informed
72
pedagogic tasks 6–7, 13
in Aboriginal schools 243,
248
authenticity of 41–42,
47–49
and coursebooks 69
in dual-task methodology
219

sequencing and grading 28,
64
pedagogy: effective 5, 258
researched 3, 13, 15
peer feedback 154, 156
performance standards 27–28,
143
personalisation 36, 63, 72
pictures, describing 48–49
planning time 26, 32
plenary addresses 12–15
policy makers 35, 109–110,
115–117
PoS (Programme of Study)
261–263
PPP (Presentation — Practice —
Production) 63, 65–68, 71, 258
practice-based research 113, 118
pragmatics, task-based 26
Preparatory Attention and
Memory 169
prescriptive research 174
pre-task planning 52, 94,
217–218
primary sources 57, 237
prior knowledge 26, 32, 54
proceduralized knowledge 173,
174
procedural repetition 113
processability hierarchy 186
processability perspective
183–184, 191
processability theory See PT
processing capacities 183–185
processing procedures 185–187
processing resources 187–189
professional development 10
in Aboriginal schools 248,
250
and coursebooks 62
and ISLA 175–176
task-based 23
and TBLT ambassadors 118
proficiency development 130,
132–133, 135
proficiency levels: and Can-do
statements 124
proficiency scales 133–136,
138–139
program evaluation 105, 109–111,
115–116, 118, 175
prototypical standardised tasks
153, 156
psycholinguistics 174

PT (processability theory) 15,
183, 185–189
PTR (procedural task
repetition) 89–90

Q

Qingdao University 110–112
question forms 208
in Martian task 192, 195,
197, 199, 202, 204–205
in Processability Theory
186–187
questionnaires, and task-based
processes 215–216, 226, 228

R

Ranjan, Rajiv 130, 132–134,
138–139
reactivity 218–219
"real life," 41–42, 58
gradually approximating
49–51
language learning in 53–56
use of term 43 See also
authenticity
reasoning demands 26–27, 220
reasoning gap tasks 5
reflective questions 269
repair fluency 171, 173
research agendas 10, 12, 16,
25–26
researcher-teacher collaboration
85, 94, 101, 107, 117
revision behaviours 221
Rubin, Vera 125, 126, 144

S

SAE (Standard Australian
English) 237
Aboriginal proficiency in
238–242
in Aboriginal schools 248
Aboriginal students' needs
for 244–245
Samuda, Virginia 170, 174
scaffolding 52
and authenticity 49, 52
L1 use as 8
teacher development 34
scaling research 115–116
school administrators, and
curriculum development
106–107

SCRELE (Shanghai Center for Research in English Language Education) 70
self-assessments: and Can-do statements 126–127, 130–132, 137–141, *139–140*, 143
and FA 154, 156
self-esteem 241–242
self-reflection 132
self-report measures 214–215
self-study research 259
semantic domains 183–184, 191, 199–208, **200–202**, *203–208*
semi-structured interviews 217
sequencing: in coursebooks 65
criteria used for 28, **29**
shame, in Aboriginal English 240, 244–246
Situational Approach 65
situational authenticity 44, 48–49, 52, 56–57, 192
skill acquisition theory (SAT) 169
SLA (second language acquisition) 5–6, 84–85
adapting theories of 126
child-instructed 84–85
and coursebooks 64, 76
Processability Theory on 185–186, 189
questionnaires in 215
research methods 101
task-based research 117
and task design 32, 36
sociocultural-interactionism 5, 13
sociocultural theory 5–6, 84, 91
South Korea, coursebooks in 63
Spain, EFL in 84–85, 87, 90–93
Spanish language: in rural US 111–112
in TBLT curricula 104
and US Border Patrol 49–50
speech production, oral *See* oral production
speech production models 87, 172, 214
speech samples 15
speed fluency 171, 221
spot-the-difference task 85–87, 89

S-STEP 259
standardized tests 85, 126, 142–143
Stanza NLP package 33
state anxiety 228
Steadiness Hypothesis 189–190
stimulated recall protocols 218–219, 221, 223–224, 226–228
strong CLT 4–5
structuralist principles 5, 257
subordination ratio 153
SWCF (synchronous written corrective feedback) 113
SWPL (Structured Workplace Learning program) 240, 242, 245–246, 248
syntactic structures 186–187, 193, 208
synthetic syllabi 60, 64–66, 68, 71, 75
systematization 115, 118–119

T
task and syllabus design 13, 22–23, 35–37
in 21st century 30–35
overview 24–30
task-based assessment 22, 101–102, 111, 143
task-based classrooms 41–47, 58
task-based courses 13, 41, 50
task-based curriculum *See* TBLT curriculum
task-based interaction 174
and task-based processes 223–224, 226, 228
task-based learning 74, 108
task-based lessons 73, 269
task-based performance 130, 212–213
task-based principles 68, 256
task-based processes 212–213
further research directions 228–229
objective methods to investigate 219–225
rationale for investigating 213–214
subjective methods to investigate 214–219
triangulating sources 226–228

task-based programmes 23–24, 35
task-based syllabi 43–44, 105
task characteristics 102
task complexity 26, 102
and authenticity 51
changing 49, 213
and cognitive load 213–214, 219
and sequencing 113
task complexity manipulations 26, 214, 221–222, 226–227
task design 101–102
in 21st century 31–33
and child FL learning 84
and coursebooks 73
features to be considered during 32 *See also* task and syllabus design
task difficulty self-ratings 227
task-essential structures 168
taskGen 32–36
task goals 30, 143
task modality 82, 85, 90–91
and curriculum design 113
task performance: and authenticity 43, 49–50
information flow during 31
language processing during 33
research agendas on 25–26, 28
support during 52
task planning 102
task requirements, in FA rating scale 150, 152, 154–155
tasks: core characteristics of 192
use of term 247
task sequencing 30, 102, 108, 113
task structures 28, 30
task types 26, 113
in FA 150, 152–154, 156
representative 5
and task-based processing 224, 226
Tavakoli, Parvaneh 172
TBLA (task-based language assessment) 14, 128
and Can-do statements 130
and FA 147, 149, 153
TBLT (Task-based Language Teaching): actualizers 112

ambassadors 110–112, 116–120
and CBLT and CLIL 176
conferences 9–12
and coursebooks 60–64, 67–77
criticisms of 269–270
and developmental stages 190
emergence and development of 4–9
essential drivers for 6
experts, and curriculum development 107–115, 117–119
implementation in Aboriginal schools 247, 250–251
link with reality in 41–42
literature review 24–27
mentoring in 72
mutual influence with ISLA 176, *177*
outcomes measurement *171*
policy implementer for 109–110
prescriptive and descriptive research in 174–175
proliferation of 35
research in 101–102
student focus of 127, 129
teacher's role in 170
teacher variable in 256–258, 263–269
TBLT (Task-based Language Teaching) curricula 13–14, 42, 101–102, 110, 124
Can-Do statements in 124
collaborative models for 107–114
development 103–107, *106*

and needs analysis 42
pedagogic tasks in 64
research on *104*
sustainability of 115–120, *116*, *119*
teacher agency 71–76
teacher-centredness 66, 71, 113
teacher education 10
in-service 101
task-based 23–24, 31, 34–35
TBLT in 66, 72, 75, 255–256, 258–259, 262–269
teacher-led approach 5, 63, 256–259, 263, 266, 268
teamwork 50, 116–117
technology 8, 11
and authenticity 53
and task design 26–28, 36
TESOL teachers 237, 248
Thailand, TBLT in 13, 23, 66
theory-building 212, 214
theory-practice tensions 265–266
think-aloud protocols 218–219
three-stage task framework 73
time estimation, subjective 216–217
time-locked analyses 228
TOEFL iBT environment 224
Tonkyn, Alan 172
top-down approaches 13, 174–175
and task design 22–24, 27, 36
TR (task repetition) 26, 82, 85, 94, 102
as implementation variable 86–90
trade-off effects 88
Trade-off Hypothesis 25–26

transfer-appropriate processing 168
transfer problem 42, 52, 58
translanguaging 8–9, 12
triangulation of sources 212–213, 226–228, 242
trustworthy data 243
TSLT (task-supported language teaching) 64, 103

U
University of Auckland 10, 35, 262
University of Hawaii 107
University of Toronto 168
utility value 52, 55, 58

V
Van den Branden, Kris 9, 11, 52, 174–175, 265
VET (Vocational Education and Training) 239–240, 247–249
Vietnam, EFL coursebooks in 60, 64–67, 69–73, 76

W
WCF (written corrective feedback) 92, 113
weak CLT 5–6, 10, 258, 262
Western Australia 15, 236–238
WIDA (World-Class Instructional Design and Assessment) 133
work ethic, demonstrating 246
writing: collaborative 89–94, 113
Kellogg's model of 214
writing processes, task-generated 224, 227–228

Y
yarning 243